6-30-07

To the Alan & Alice Ben

Much happiness & success
to you all

Always

Gil Hodges

STEPS TOWARD FREEDOM

SEQUEL TO THE AUTHOR'S ROADS TRILOGY SAGA ABOUT THE SETTLEMENT AND DEFENSE OF NEW YORK'S MOHAWK VALLEY DURING THE 1700's AS IT EXPLORES THE TRIALS AND TRIBULATIONS OF AMERICA'S FIRST CIVIL WAR BETWEEN ITS AMERICAN TORIES AND PATRIOTS

By

GIL HERKIMER

1663 LIBERTY DRIVE, SUITE 200
BLOOMINGTON, INDIANA 47403
(800) 839-8640
WWW.AUTHORHOUSE.COM

This book is a work of non-fiction. Unless otherwise noted, the author and the publisher make no explicit guarantees as to the accuracy of the information contained in this book and in some cases, names of people and places have been altered to protect their privacy.

© 2005 GIL HERKIMER. All Rights Reserved.

No part of this book may be reproduced, stored in a retrieval system, or transmitted by any means without the written permission of the author.

First published by AuthorHouse 04/18/05

ISBN: 1-4208-1031-6 (sc)

Printed in the United States of America
Bloomington, Indiana

This book is printed on acid-free paper.

We cannot intermeddle in this dispute
between two brothers. The quarrle seems
unnatural. If the great king of England
apply to us for aid, we shall deny him;
if the Colonies apply, we shall refuse.

> Oneida delegation to govenor
> of Connecticut, 1775

The Mohawks have on all occasions shown their
zeal and loyalty to the Great King; yet they have
been very badly treated by his people. Indeed it
is very hard, when we have let the King's subjects
have so much of our lands for so little value. We are
tired out in making complaints and getting no redress.

> Thayendanegea (Joseph Brant)
> Mohawk, 1776

Love one another and do not strive for another's undoing.
Even as you desire good treatment, so render it.

Ganeodiyo, the Iroquois prophet, also known as
(Handsome Lake) Seneca name for Lake Ontario.

Mr. [William] Strahan,   Philada. July 5, 1775
You are a Member of Parliament, and one of that Majority which
has doomed my Country to Destruction. You have begun to burn
our Towns, and murder our People. Look upon your Hands!
They are stained with the Blood of your Relations! You and I
were long Friends: You are now my Enemy, and I am, Yours.

Benjamin Franklin to William Strahn, Member of Parliament July 5, 1775

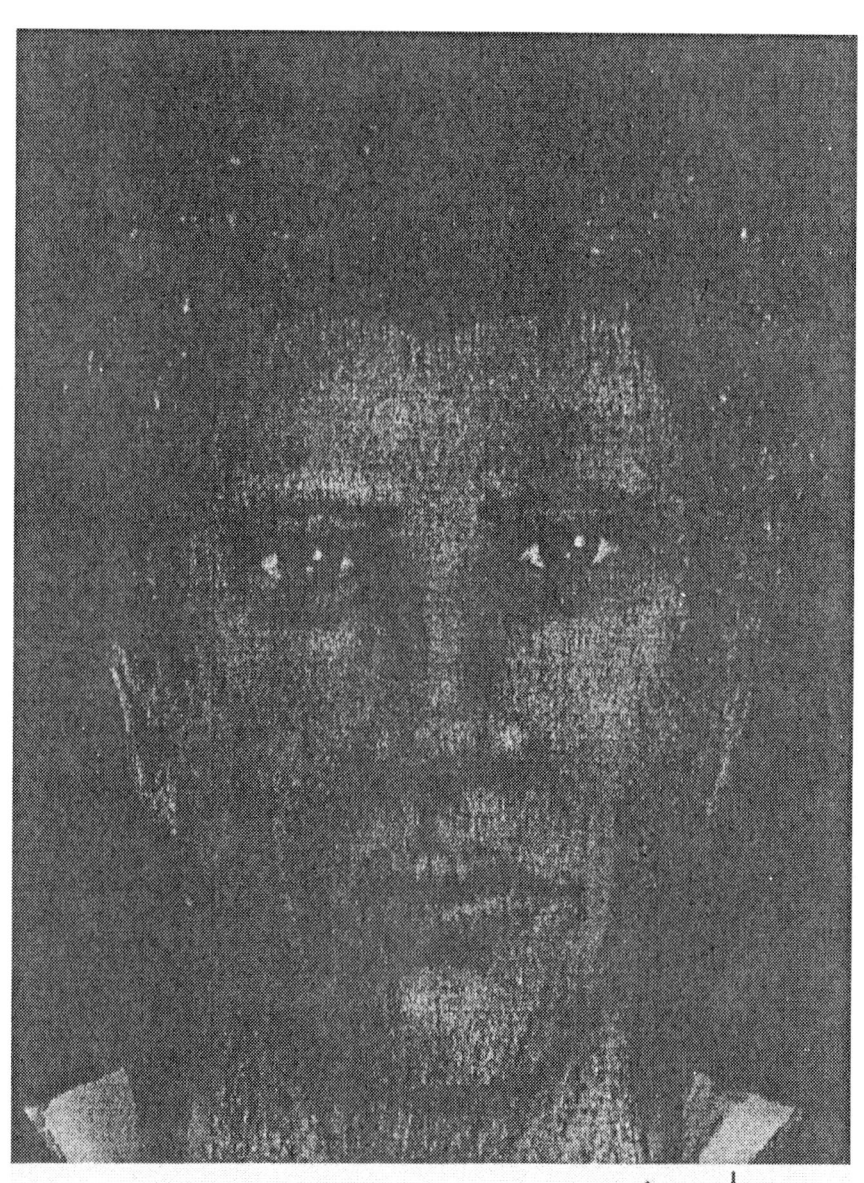

ACKNOWLEDGEMENTS

I never imagined my original book, *Roads to Oriskany,* which dealt with the German Palatines' early 1700 emmigration to the New York colony as the British endentured servants, and ending with the Battle of Oriskany, would evolve into a trilogy. As I researched the subject, I discovered more and more stones which needed to be uncovered and explored. This resulted in the second book, *Roads to Saratoga,* overlaps the period just after the Battle of Oriskany and continues through the time when the British general, Gentleman Johnny Burgoyne, surrenders to the American general, Horatio Gates at Saratoga. As in the Oriskany book, the author interweaves the lives and activities of the fictious Palatine Hendrick family and their firends who live in New Palatine, a fictious settlement located in the Mohawk Valley's western frontier just west of Fort Dayton and Fort Herkimer.

My first acknowledgement is to my ancestors who emigrated from Germany's Palatine area during the very early 1700's, worked as British indentured servants in their futile effort to manufacture naval supplies, especially pine tar and masts, for the British growing naval armada. Following this disasterous venture, these newcomers settled in New York's Mohawk Valley, surviving its inclement weather and other adversities associated with life in the New York colony's western most frontier with it's primative forests.

One individual to whom I am greatly indebted is Walter Rose, a longtime friend who helped me comb through numerous books and libraries for factual information about the Palatines, General John Burgoyne, General Philip Schuyler, Joseph Brant, their associates, and accompanying me on some of my hikes through the Mohawk Valley.

A special acknowledgement to my friend and mentor, Dr. Seymour Eiseman, in whose memory Chapter 2/4 (page 185) is written and reference to Psalm 121, and to John Rhodehamel, editor of the American Revolution, published 2001 By Literary Classics of the United States, Inc. New York, N.Y.

A very special thanks to the Board of Trustees of Utica Public Library, Utica, New York, for its permission to reprint *Battle of Oriskany: "I Will Face the Enemy,"* by Frederick Yohn.

I am also indebted to my AuthorHouse Account Manager Trina Lee, her patience and cooperation have been excellent.

Unfortunatly, I think I've found another stone about the era which needs to be uncovered and explored, but that will take me to Canada, and Benedict Arnold.

G.H
Corpus Christi, Texas
March 31, 2005

TABLE OF CONTENTS

Acknowledgements xi
Introduction Facts or Fiction? xv
Maps xxv
Family Charts xxix
Prologue to America's First Civil War xxxi

BOOK ONE CIVIL WAR 1
   ONE Like Women Breasts, Bare and Open 3
   TWO End Justifies the Means 12
   THREE Steins and Blue Holland Punch Bowls 21
   FOUR Behind the Scenes 31
   FIVE New Command 41
   SIX Around the Cracker Barrel 48
   SEVEN End Justifies the Means 61
   EIGHT You're My Brother! 70
   NINE Stranger Within the Ranks 89
   TEN The Risk is not Taking One 98
   ELEVEN Stand By the King 110
   TWELVE A Journeyman's Tale 115
   THIRTEEN This is a Fraticidal War! 122
   FOURTEEN Subject or Citizen? 135

BOOK TWO FREEDOM! 145
   ONE The Beginning of the End 147
   TWO Concerns 160
   THREE He Merits Unrestrained Confidence 167

FOUR A New World's a Coming! 177
FIVE Civil War Within the Iroquois 189
SIX Along the Mohawk Trail..199
SEVEN Canada, A Neighborly Border? 209
EIGHT Here's Your Marching Orders!.....................................221
NINE Freedom in Canada...235
TEN Search and Recover...247
ELEVEN Move Up the Hill! 266
TWELVE Dreams of the Future 272
THIRTEEN The Lady Doth Volunteer! 281
FOURTEEN Reunion and Freedom 294
FIFTEEN To Each Their Own!...312
SIXTEEN Seeds of Freedom 326
SEVEVTEEN Rehabilitation and More 334
EIGHTEEN Freedom! What Does It Mean? 341
Epilogue 352
Sources and References 367

INTRODUCTION
Facts or Fiction?

Steps Toward Freedom is based upon historical individuals and events. The author has taken the *freedom* to introduce fictional characters and events in the persons of the Palatine family of Karl and Rebecca Heindrick, their friends, neighbors, and acquaintances. Through these characters' fictional activities and experiences, the author has interwoven historical characters and events to give the reader a realistic and meaningful account of the Palatines' experiences, who were living along New York State's Mohawk Valley during the middle 1700's after the Palatines were relatively well settled, to the later 1700's after the Americans under the command of Generals John Sullivan and James Clinton conducted their devastating sweep through the Iroquois country under the orders of General George Washington, who stated that the Americans intended to settle *"where they damn well pleased——-even clear to the Mississippi River."*

The author believes that the interweaving of the fictional characters' beliefs and activities with those of the historical figures result in a more interesting approach to study America's history, while preserving the authenticity of events and characters.

The following notes are the author's attempt to distinguish the fictional from the historical facts and personalities.

BOOK ONE CIVIL WAR!

ONE   **Like Women Breasts, Bare and Open**

The first name mentioned in this chapter is King Hendrick, who was a forceful chief with the Indian name of Thayanoge, and the French called him Tete Blanche after his silver hair. He was one of the visiting Indian notables who caused such excitement at Queen Anne's court. This great chief, who was more of a politician than a scholar like his brother Abraham, looked upon the whites with mixed emotions. Governor Clinton of New York had been known to inquire solicitously "how poor old Hendrick does, but a Pennsylvania official called him "that vile Indian Henry," and very likely did not care how he did. Other historical figures mentioned in this chapter include Major General William Johnson, who served the British royalty as Superintendent of Indian Affairs. On July 9, 1755, British General Edward Braddock, whose forces were surprised and attacked by over 600 Iroquois braves, with about 150 French Canadian militia led by 72 French officers and regulars killing Braddock and his troops "broke and ran like sheep pursued by dogs" (so George Washington recorded). Other historical individuals mentioned in this chapter include Missionary Samuel Kirkland, Molly Brant, Sir John Johnson (Sir William's son), and Sir William's son-in-law, Daniel Claus.

The only fictional character in this chapter is Martha Butler, who is the tavern owner in the fictional town of New Palatine.

On November 12, 1757 was one of the bloodiest days of the Palatines' years in the Mohawk Valley when French and Indian supporters swept through German Flats, incinerating homes, blockhouses and carried away over 150 residents as captives.

TWO   **End Justifies the Means**

This attempts to accurately report the happenings as the result of Sir William Johnson's death, and the activities reported about another of Sir William "son-in-laws, Guy Johnson is well recorded, as well as those of George Klock. The borders established by the shocking 1768 Fort Stanwix Treaty with the Americans should have forewarned the Indians of things they could expect from the white settlers.

THREE   **Steins and Blue Holland Punch Bowls**

The chapter introduces many of the fictional characters in New Palatine, as well as Martha Butler, the proprietor of the Heidelberg Tavern, her handy man Harry Hunter, her disappeared husband Jerome Butler, Karl Heindrick, Cal Swartz. George Raab Harvey Perry, as well as, the settlement's innocuous mayor Rudolph Helm, and Attorney Christopher Yates, a guest from Albany, New York.

FOUR   **Behind the Scenes**

All the activities and historical characters mentioned have been well researched for accuracy.

FIVE   **New Command**

History of Fort Niagara accurately researched.

SIX   **Around the Cracker Barrel**

Wilhelm Kerchner, his wife Sarah, and daughter Helena are fictional characters who reside in the fictional Palatine settlement of New Palatine located west of Albany, New York in the Mohawk Valley. Other fictional character who reside in New Palatine include, George Raab, Harvey Perry, Karl Heindrick and family, Cal Swartz, and Martha Butler, proprietor of New Palatine's only tavern, The Heidleburg Tarvern. Nicholas Herkimer, Brigadier General of the Tryon County militia is the only historical character mentioned in this chapter. The story Raab tells of the Barnet Davenport and Malley is reported as true. The story as related by Karl Heindrick to his son, Walter represents factual activities concerning the Palatine emigrants to New York and to Livingston Manor, and the British experiment in manufacturing naval supplies. The story Karl tells about his black "blood brother," George Jefferson and his mother Georgia Franklin are fictional, but they represent what may have actually occurred during those days along the Mohawk Valley. The story of the "Spanish Negroes" is an historical fact.

SEVEN   **End Justifies the End**

This chapter accurately relates the events which occurred slightly before and after Sir William Johnson's death. Sir John Johnson, Sir William's "only admitted" son, did inherit the family's Johnson Hall and the large surrounding estate. Six months after his wife Catherine's death, and true to form, Sir William courted Chief

Joseph Brant's sister, Molly Brant, and she gave birth to a son, Peter. Mentioned in this chapter is George Klock, a well-to-do farmer, appears and is involved in future rather shady deals.

EIGHT   **You're My Brother**

The two middle aged brothers, Nicholas and Johan Jost Jr. (Herkimer) are factual individuals. They talk about their Palatine refugee father, Johan Jost Herkimer. Although their verbal exchange is not verbatim, their expressed thoughts convey their individual beliefs as display by their future actions.

The valley's circuit riding preacher, Reverend Johan Stouffer, hi Oneida princess, Red Bird, and Martha Butler proprietor of New Palatine's one and only tavern are fictional characters. In their discussion, Stouffer and Butler identify Jonathan Mayhew who is an actual historical individual, and identified as "the father of civil religious liberty in Massachusetts and America." All the other individuals and their activities are historically factual.

NINE   **Strange With the Ranks**

Samuel Shoemaker's tavern or home is an actual historical building, but most of the activities and discussion which are presented in this chapter are the product of the author's imagination and based upon future occurrences. The fictional characters mentioned in this chapter are Wilhem Kerchner, his wife Sarah, Harvey Perry and George Raab, and Alexander "Sandy" McKnight.

TEN   **The Risk is Not Taking One**

Johan Jost Jr., his wife Maria, and General Nicholas, his wife Maria are historical individuals; their discussions are based upon historical facts and the results of their actions. The stories about Colonel John Butler, his wife Catherine, their son Captain Walter, Gorge Klock, Guy Johnson, Daniel Claus and the Reverends John Stuart and Samuel Kirkland are all historical individuals, as are their individual thoughts based upon their future actions.

ELEVEN   **Stand By the King**

Again, Johan Jost Jr. and his wife Maria enter the story, and meet a fictional character Alexander "Sandy" McKnight, who together with an historical individual William Caldwell successfully assist Johan Jost Jr. in escaping from a Albany, New York jail, and eventually to Fort Niagara.

TWELVE   **A Journeyman's Tale**

The fictional character, Sandy McKnight, continues along with Johan Jost Jr. and William Caldwell. Collectively their conversation about New York City accurately reflect the circumstances at the time. The story about New York frontiersman, Jeptha Simms tells about George Washington is recorded as researched, as is the story about the North Carolina slave, Thomas Peters and the Black Pioneers.

THIRTEEN   **This Is a Fratricidal War!**

The episode about Walter Butler, wife and family is accurate as researched, as well as their observations. The story about Wilhelm Kerchner, his wife Sara and daughter Helena is fictional as the author envisioned what might have happened to Loyalists under their particular circumstances. The episode about Chief Joseph Brant, his sister Molly Brant, General Sir William Howe, General Barry St.Leger, General John Burgoyne and his frequent distraction Fanny Loescher, the commissary officer's wife. A couple other interesting factual characters 13 year old Jan Van Eps from Schenectady, and Hon Jost who, under the orders of General Benedict Arnold, scares the Indians and Loyalists into retreating from their positions near Fort Stanwix.

FOURTEEN   **Subject or Citizen?**

Harvey Perry and George Raab are fictional characters as are all of their fellow residents of New Palatine. Together with their tales, they accurately reflect the Rebel opinions and circumstances they face in the Mohawk Valley. The episode about the Indians' *Dark Eagle*, General Benedict Arnold and his trick he used to frighten the Indians, the Loyalists and their British generals is factual.

BOOK TWO FREEDOM!

ONE   **The Beginning of the End**

The conversations between Benjamin Franklin and King Louis XVI's talented foreign minister and Franklin's good friend, Comte de Vergennes, and the minister's Master Josiah Qunicy accurately reflects the circumstances at the time. Their conversations are based upon their researched opinions and future actions.

TWO   **Concerns**

Franklin and Vergennes continue their conversation, and try to project what Britain's Prime Minister Lord Frederick North might react to Burgoyne's defeat at Saratoga. The account of the exchange between Burgoyne and Arnold was thoroughly researched.

THREE   **He Merits Unrestrained Confidence**

The diary entries of Albigence Waldo and John Laurens are recorded as researched, as is General Washington's reasoning to withdraw and winter at nearby Valley Forge.

FOUR   **A World's A Coming!**

Again the fictional New Palatine residents including Rev. Johan Stouffer, his wife Red Bird, Martha Butler, George Jefferson, Karl and Rebecca Heindrick and their many friends enter relating some of their fictional incidents, as well as describing factual occupance which they either participated in or were heard about. Ambrose Serle's journal entries are recorded as researched.

FIVE   **Civil War Within the Iroquois**

Colonel John Butler adventures with the three principal Iroquois chiefs to Governor Sir Guy Carleton's headquarters were thoroughly researched and reported as such, as are the incidents between the Iroquois.

SIX   **Along the Mohawk Tail**

The story about Colonel Peter Bellinger and his Rangers is factual, as are the other related events about Captain William Caldwell, Chief Joseph Brant, and Captain Walter Butler, which led to the Iroquois and Loyalist assault on Cherry Valley. As result, truly Captain Walter Butler never ventured on another expedition.

SEVEN   **Canada, A Neighborly Border?**

The episode involving Governor General Haldimand, Colonel Bolten, Colonel John Butler are recorded as researched, as was the fact that General Washington was seriously considering various proposals of staging an American invasion against Canada. As a result an expedition commanded by General Robert Montgomery and Benedict Arnold, and assisted by Colonel Daniel Morgan and some of his Virginia riflemen did stage a siege against Quebec. The story of the siege is recorded as researched.

The letter written by Joseph Warren to Samuel Adams is recorded verbatim, as is Washington's response to his friend Henry Laurens, who was serving as the president of the Continental Congress.

EIGHT   **Here's Your Marching Orders!**

Washington letter to his friend Henry Laurens identifies his concerns of the deplorable condition of the war. Washington used this letter as an introduction in a meeting of a select group of generals including a relatively new comer Major General John Sullivan. His plan was to discuss the pros and cons of planning an expedition into the Iroquois country.

The balance of this chapter accurately related how General Haldimand and the Iroquois prepared for the anticipated invasion. Although the battle of Minisink is factual, the episode involving Thunder Cloud, Red Squirrel, George and Benjamin Jefferson, Walter Heindrick is the product of the author's imagination, but the events concerning Chief Joseph Brant and other factual individual are accurately reported.

NINE   **Freedom in Canada**

The involvement of Johan Jost Jr. and his family in the Loyalist force and Canada is accurately recorded, while the activities of his fictional friend Sandy McKnight are the product of the author's imagination.

TEN   **Search and Recover**

The story of John House and his excursions with Brant's Indians and American General James Clinton are factual, except that the episode which involves George Jefferson is fictional based upon the known circumstances and results of the adventure. The events involving Benjamin Jefferson, Walter Heindrick, Samuel Montgomery and his sister Maria are fictional. In this event the author was trying to dramatis the capture and escape of an Indian captive. General Clinton's campaign against Chief Brant warriors reasonably reports what may have occurred based upon research. However, Brant's prediction, "We shall begin to know what is to befall us, the People of the Long House" is accurately quoted, as her could see the hand-writing upon the wall.

ELEVEN   **Move Up the Hill!**

In this chapter the factual Captain Johan Jost Jr. and fictional adjutant and best friend Sandy McKnight return to Butler's Rangers and Chief Brant's warriors to continue their conflict with the Rebels as accurately reported as researched.

TWELVE   **Dreams of the Future**

This chapter attempts to portray the process the fictional former slaves, Samuel and Marie Montgomery, of master slave owner Gunther Haas of Minisink procured their freedom with the assistance of the historical General Philip Schuyler and New York State's Governor George Clinton. All the other characters in this chapter are fictional.

THIRTEEN   **The Lady Doeth Volunteer!**

Most of the characters in this chapter are fictional. What the author hopes to convey are mechanics within a military hospital of the time. The story Burgoyne ordering his troops to burn down General Philip Schuyler's home is factual, as are the incidents reporting General John Burgoyne visiting his nemesis General Benedict Arnold while hospitalized. Dr. Benjamin Rush is a factual physician, but Dr. Blake McDuff and Mrs Riedesel, Director of Volunteers are fictional characters.

FOURTEEN   **Reunion and Freedom**

In this chapter the principal fictional residents of New Palatine and the surrounding area gather together with the Jefferson family in their home in Albany, New York, and discuss various exploits. Although Oriska is a factual Oneida settlement, the white woman who has been living with the Indians since captivity at very early age is fictional, as is White Tail as his relation to Chief Brant,

FIFTEEN   **To Each Their Own!**

The fictional characters reminisce about the years past, the good times and the threatening times as they perceive the trials and tribulations of America's first civil war. The Seneca leader whose given name is Segoyewatha, and who earned the familiar name of Red Jacket because of color of the coat he wore. The quotation to the

Protestant missionaries inscribed in this chapter is attributed to Red Jacket. Red Jacket's hard-line approach was significantly different than his principle rival, the Seneca leader and bold and talented warrior named Cornplanter.

SIXTEEN   **Seeds of Freedom!**

The episode involving Red Bird, her husband Rev. Johan Stouffer and Cornplanter is a product of the author's imagination to add intrigue to the story. However, the story of General James Clinton and John Sullivan starting their expedition to carry out Washington's orders, "not merely be overrun, but destroy the Indian Country." The story about Chief Black Fish, as told by Cornplanter, is factual. Black Fish's warriors did, in fact, capture Daniel Boone, eventually adopting Boone into their tribe.

SEVENTEEN   **Rehabilitation and More**

In this chapter, the author attempts to portray the role of both white and black volunteer members in a military hospital of the times.

EIGHTEEN   **Freedom! What Does it Mean?**

Red Jacket's quotation as presented in this chapter is well researched and accurate, as is Washington's May 31, 1779 quotation and his other presented quotations. The story of Santa Claus and his raccoon is an incident which the author actually experienced himself.

MAPS

CANADA AND THE NORTHERN CAMPAIGN

NORTHERN CAMPAIGN ENLARGEMENT

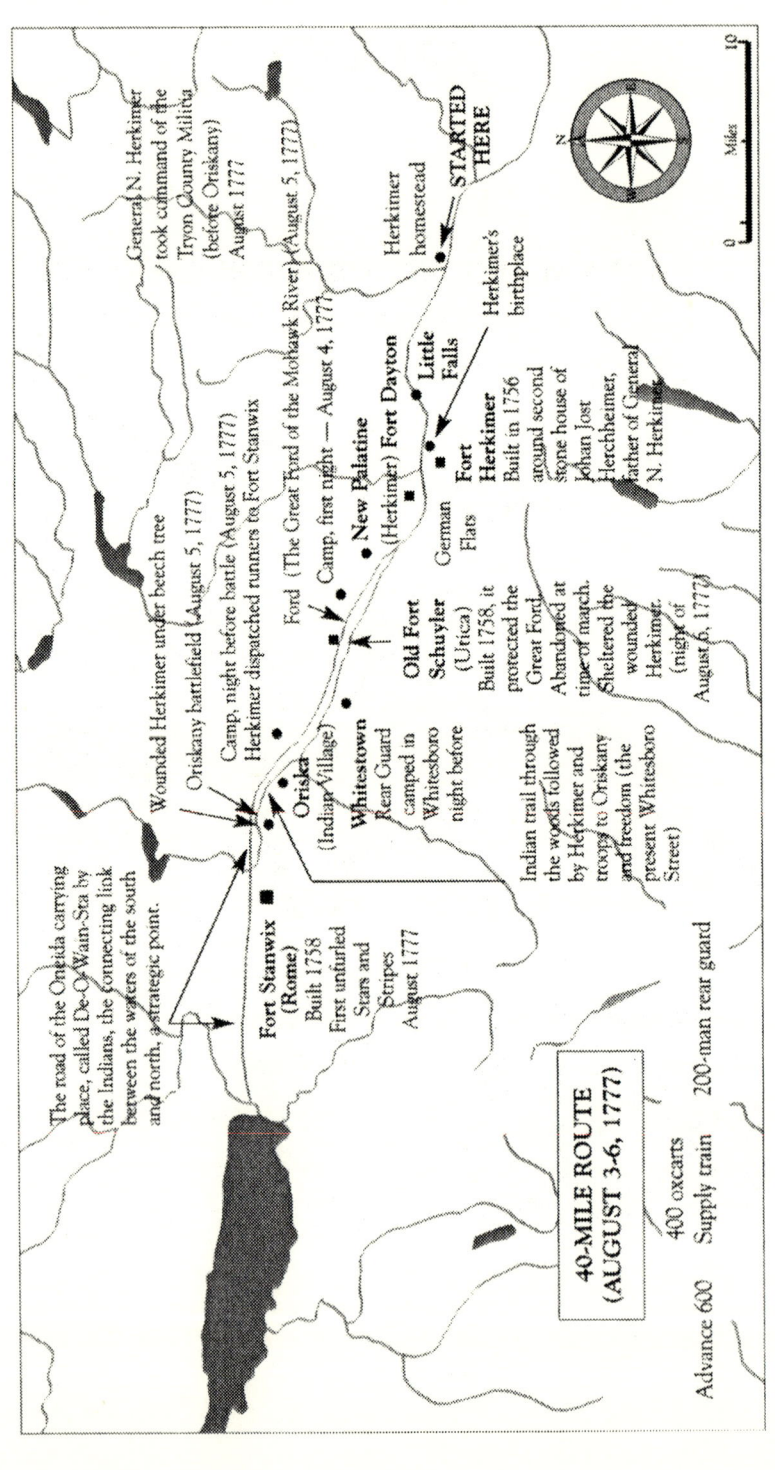

THE BATTLE OF FREEMAN'S FARM
SEPTEMBER 19TH, 1777

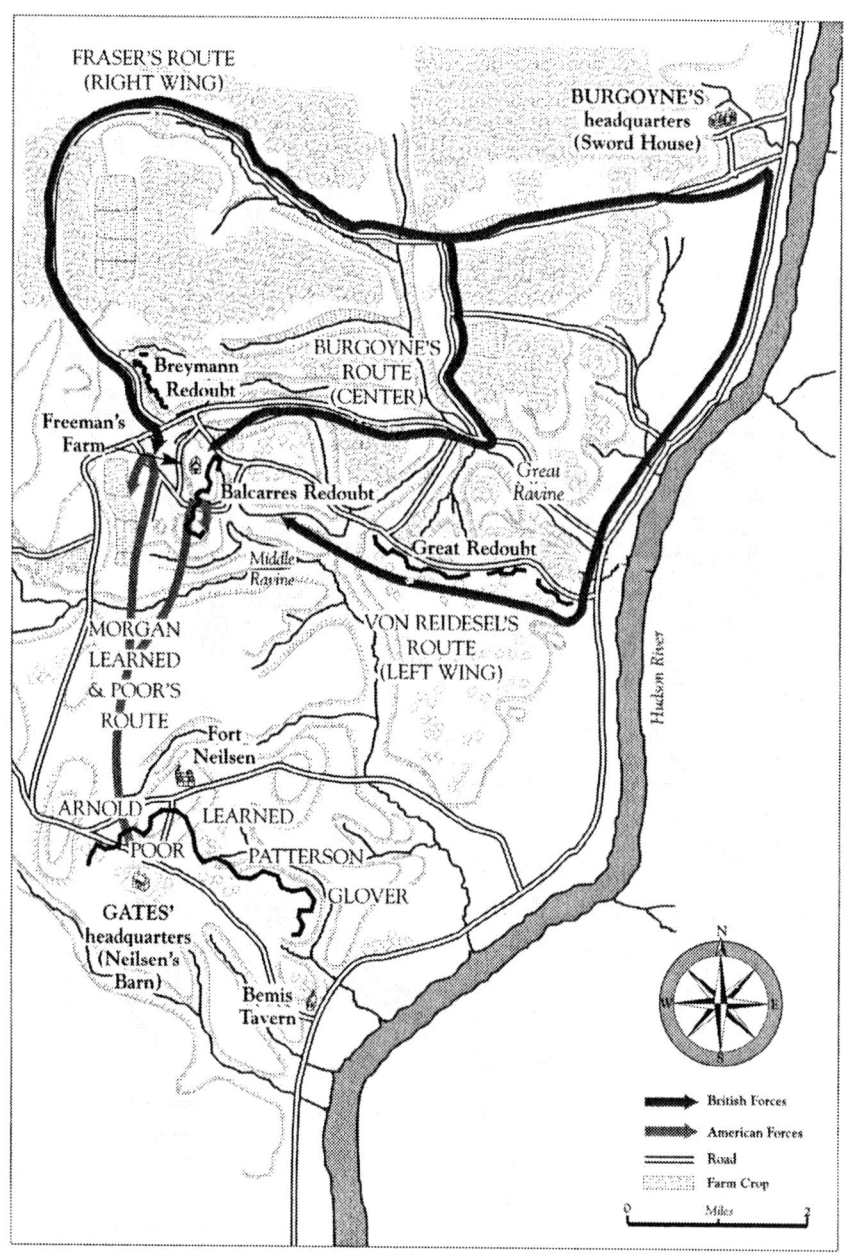

THE BATTLE OF BEMIS HEIGHTS
OCTOBER 7TH, 1777

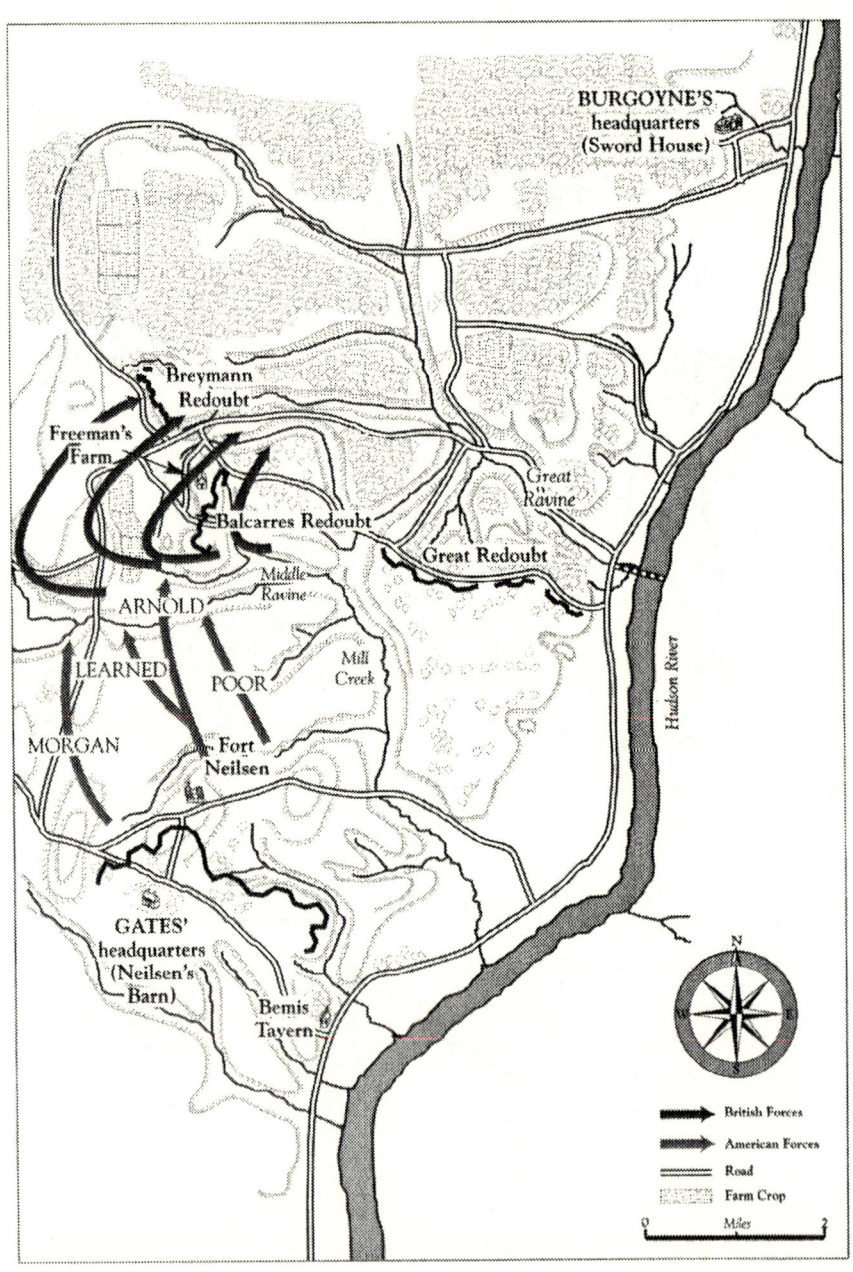

FAMILY CHARTS

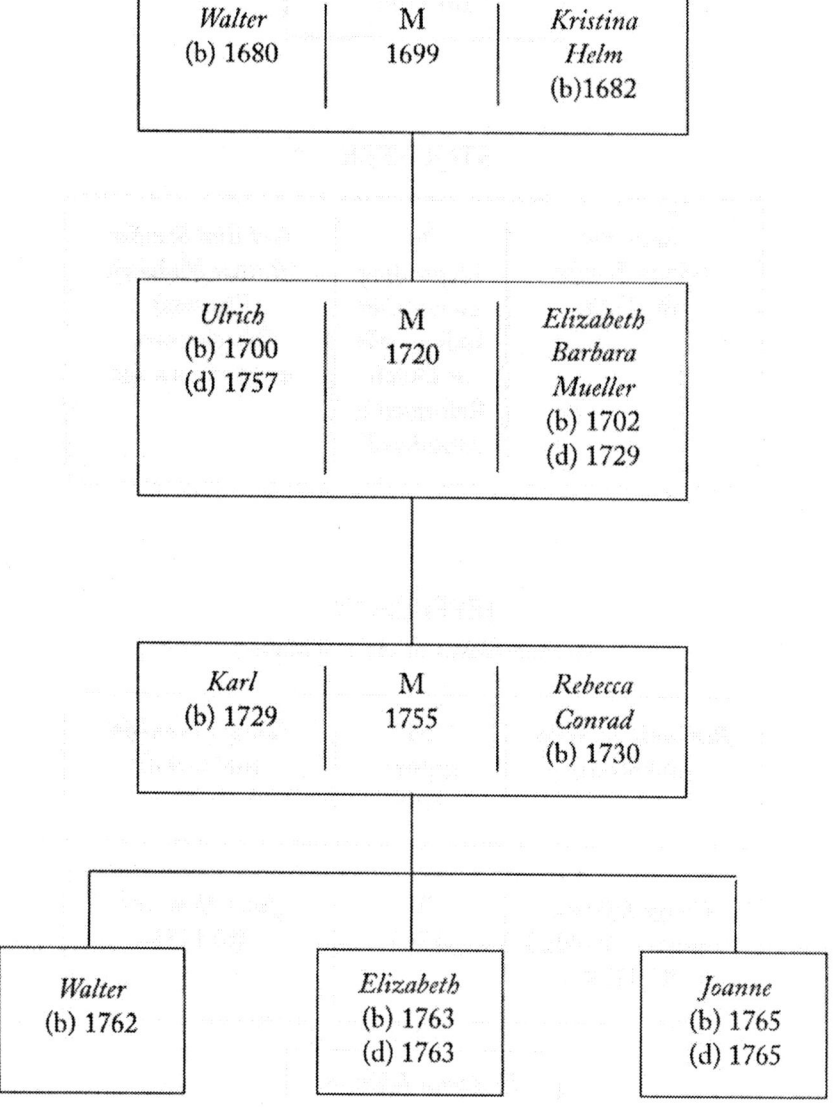

KERCHNER

| Willhelm Kerchner (b) 1758 | M 1756 | Sarah Mueller (b) 1731 |

Helena Kerchner (b) 1764

STOUFFER

| Reverend Johnan Stouffer (b) 1739 | M (depending on whether Indian style or Dutch Reformed is considered) | Red Bird Stouffer (former Mohawk Princess) (b) unknown, many moons ago |

JEFFERSON
(former Slaves of Herr Schuyler)

| Benjamin Jefferson (unknown) | M approx. 1739 | Georgia Franklin (unknown) |

| George Jefferson (formerly Franklin) (b) 1729 | M 1753 | Julia Hamilton (b) 1731 |

Benjamin Jefferson (b) 1760

Prologue to America's First Civil War

Just a short time ago in 1712, almost the entire New York state we presently know was covered entirely with hardwood and evergreen forests except for three white settlements located: the village of Schenectady, the fur-trading capital of Fort Orange (Albany), and the Manhattan Island seaport called New Amsterdam (New York). Living in New York's Mohawk Valley's forests which skirted Lakes Ontario and Erie were the noble Iroquois League of Six Nations comprised of the Mohawk, Oneida, Onondaga, Cayuga and Seneca living in fortified villages. Eventually, the Tuscaroras were admitted to complete the confederacy of Six Nations. Although they moved from time to time, and used fire to clear land for crops and to keep the forests open, a practice that encouraged the growth of bushy browse for deer and other animals; they had earned the reputation of being some of the fiercest warriors in North America.

During the late 1600's and early 1700's, an explosively volatile fuel had been introduced into the commerce among the Indians and whites. In 1708, New York's governor Daniel D. Tompkins stated, "Some times we have a vessel or two to go to the Coast of Guinea, & bring Negroes from thence, but they seldom come to this place [New York state], but rather go to Virginia or Maryland, where they find a much better market for their Negroes than they can do here." On the tip of Manhattan, transplanted Atlantic Creoles rubbed elbows with sailors of various nationalities and Native Americans with diverse tribal allegiances. African slaves were becoming an intricate segment of the colonial Dutch, English, and French economy while Spanish merchant ships all carried on an extensive trade in Indian, as well as African slaves; this sort of slavery where West Indian natives worked alongside of Africans, had long been common among Southeastern tribes. Setting tribe against tribe not only produced slaves for the market, but it also reduced the threat that Indians would unite in large numbers against the whites. In fact, slavery existed in New York as early as 1628. There was a slave market at the foot of Wall Street in 1709 when the city's population was slightly over 5,000. In 1723, when the city's population was estimated to be about 7,000, it became apparent that the slaves constituted a considerable proportion of its inhabitants. Slavery, by no means confined to African Negroes, was becoming more and more important in the New York colony. On various occasions people would "sell" themselves for a term of years during which time they were practically slaves. Men and women frequently "sold" themselves, knowingly or innocently, for a term of years in order to secure passage to America. For example, the Palatines unwittingly committed themselves and their families to the British under the pretense they would be transported to America, understanding that they would be rewarded a certain amount of forested land for their labor in the British naval and tar supply venture located just north of New York City.

The Dutch West India Company housed most of its slaves in barracks and worked them under an overseer. But before long some of the company's slaves secured the right to live out, and work on their own in return for a stipulated amount of labor and an annual tribute. Free to reside independently and frequently to work on their own, they mastered the Dutch language, many took Dutch surnames, attached themselves to the Dutch Reformed Church, and most importantly, established families. During the first generation,, some twenty-six black couples took their vows in the Dutch Reformed Church in New Amsterdam, where they also baptized their children As early as 1644, the Dutch West India Company emancipated a group of slave men, probably the first male arrivals, their wives and children, so they could continue "to support their wives and children, as they have been accustomed to do."

Slaves in New York City usually did remarkably well, informally enjoying many of the privileges of an earlier era during the early eighteenth century. Surprisingly, many slaves had the right to hold property of their own, which greatly enhanced their ability to expand their independent economic activities. As a regular practice, numerous slave owners conceded the right of slaves to select their owners, so that slaves might live near kin or change an unsatisfactory situation. Elsewhere in the northern New York colony, black people tired to replicate the experiences of those in New Amsterdam. As early as 1737, the black population of Albany County, including all of the Mohawk Valley exceeded fifteen percent of the county's total population, of this portion ninety-five percent were slaves. The year 1763 not only marked the transient of France's sovereignty of Canada over to Great Britain, but it also cleared way for England's development of its New York Colony with its strategically located bountiful and beautiful Mohawk Valley.

By 1771, nine to ten percent of the total 40,000 population of Albany County was black. What is interesting to note is that shortly before the *revolution,* slave ownership in the area remained largely confined to the old Dutch and German families. By the last half of the 18th century, slave ownership in New York and the New England states was on a decline, partly due to economics and to the growing abolitionist movement. In a more direct and immediate move, New York state enacted legislation called *manumission,* which served as an incentive for blacks to join the state's militia.

During the early 18th century, the Mohawk valley's sparsely populated topography was similar and reminiscent of the western European landscape, which had served as the battle ground of Europe's Seven Year War pitting France, Austria, Sweden, and a few small German states against Great Britain and Prussia. Meanwhile, colonial America's French and Indian War had served as the battleground for the American segment of Europe's Seven Year War. To Europe's war weary inhabitants were tired of years of war, famine, excessive taxes, and tyrannical rule, New York's Mohawk valley offered a beacon and a safety harbor in life's storm. As a result, the Mohawk valley was fast becoming an inviting haven of opportunity to escape these wartime woes, and to gain freedom to *white* Europeans such as the German-Palatine, Dutch, Irish, and Scotch-Irish settlers.

Interestingly, during 1775 and early 1776, the New York legislature was reluctant to sign the proclaimed Declaration of Independence. Finally, New York became the last of the original thirteen states to agree to sign the declaration. One reason for this fact is that the *Empire State*, as New York had became known, bordered directly on Canada's boundaries, and was strongly influenced by the Loyalists' interests there. Especially, when its commercial interests made the English empire's powerful protection most desirable. As a result, it is not surprising to learn that New York was a vast haven for those settlers loyal to King George III. It is not surprising, either, to learn about a man in Weathersfield, Connecticut who wrote, "The eyes of America are on New York, winning its title of *Empire State* because of its huge area, its variety of peoples and its imperial resources." Before the Declaration of Independence was approved, it was estimated that approximately ninety-five percent of the state's inhabitants acknowledged loyalty (Tories) to the King, to the Empire, and to the British constitution. The remaining five percent were those ardent republicans (Whigs) who advocated outright independence from the English crown. The ratification of the Declaration of Independence made a dramatic impact upon all those living in New York, because it forced its residents to proclaim their loyalty to either the British King or to the new republic's Continental Congress. Not to be an exception, New York slowly, but more slowly, began adopting the similar characteristics of its neighboring New England states, as well as the republic's southern states. As result two distinct political parties, the Tories and the Whigs, evolved.

The Tories or Loyalists were those who maintained their loyalty to Great Britain and its monarchy. As one resident of the day defined a Tory: "A Tory is a thing whose head is in England

and its body in America and its neck ought to be stretched." A Tory New York newspaper offered its own thoughts about what the local Tories thought of the Whigs in both England and America, and the Continental Congress:

> ….. the instigators of the Revolution were regarded as unprincipled and a disappointed faction in the mother country and an infernal, dark-designing group of men in America, audaciously styling themselves a Congress….. Obscure, pettifogging, attorneys, bankrupt shop-keepers, outlawed smugglers, wretched banditti, the refuse and dregs of mankind."

As a result of numerous raiding activities conducted against each others' estates and rich country sides, each of these political groups had acquired additional identification labels. The Whigs or those of the rebel ranks became also known as "skinners," because they often "skinned" right off the badly needed clothing right off their victim's corpse. The fact that most of their victim's clothing was more substantial was an added attraction to their victim's clothing. Not to be slighted, the British and Tory raiders became known as "cowboys," because their main objective was to steal the local cattle, which they desperately needed as food for the British army.

Add to this rebellious mixture of whites, the often misguided and misled eager members of each Indian tribe were anxious to protect their own territory. Meanwhile, the valley's "white folks" were just as eager to retain and obtain control of the entire New York colony. The Seneca Chief Sagoyewatha, sometimes referred to as Red Jacket, while addressing a group of Protestant missionaries about the growing resentment and division between the whites and Indians, made the following statements:

> Your forefathers crossed the great water and landed on this island. Their numbers were small. We took pity on them, and they sat down among us. We gave them corn and meat. They gave us poison (alcohol) in return.

You have now become a great people, and we have scarcely a place left to spread our blankets. You have got our country now, but you are not satisfied. You want to force your religion upon us.

We are told that you have been preaching to the white people in this place. These people are our neighbors. We will wait a little while, and see what effect your preaching has upon them. If we find it does them good, makes them honest and less disposed to cheat Indians, we will consider again what you have said.

Illustrating the growing animosity between the peoples of the young nation, Jonathan Boucher of Maryland, a high-minded and well respected Tory preacher born in England, came to Virginia when he was only twenty-one. Since there was not an Anglican bishop in America, he returned to England; he was ordained by the Bishop of London. Thereafter, this colorful and combative preacher returned to America and lived on the western shore of Maryland; strongly advocated the cause of King Charles III. In fear of reprisals from the numerous Whigs who lived in his area, Boucher preached regularly for six months with two loaded pistols lying beside him on the pulpit cushion, and explained that if he had to use them, he believed the Lord would approve such self-defense. He believed that the idea of an armed revolt was foreign to his old-fashioned belief on the divine right of the king and government. To another minister, Boucher wrote, "The people who now bid defiance to this great and glorious nation are, in every point of view, worthless in the extreme."

Regardless, Boucher was held in relatively good standing with George Washington. He once told of a meeting with Washington as he was going to Massachusetts to take charge of the new Continental army. "There had been a great meeting of people, and great doing, in Alexandra (Virginia) on the occasion and everybody seemed to be on fire, either with rum or patriotism or both." The two talked briefly and Boucher warned Washington that "there would certainly be a *civil war,* and that the Americans would soon declare for independency." Boucher blamed not only the leaders of the war, but some American institutions as well. He believed that "the cruel abettors of violence are young men of good parts but spoiled by a strange, imperfect, desultory find of Education which has crept into fashion all over America. Some of these Northern academies, which in my wrath I can scarcely forbear calling Seminars of Sedition, lead the way, and like other Plagues, it soon spreads.... It is plainly and truly a war against the Constitution, a Catalinian Combination of individual Scoundrels."

The important word in Boucher's dialogue with the soon to be Commander-in-Chief of the American Army was that he stated "there would certainly be a *civil* war."

Boucher was fiery in the denunciation of the patriot ministers as well as the leaders of the colonial cause. These patriot ministers were equally combative, and from their pulpits they defended their positions and activities, quoting especially John Lock's principle that "it was the people's right to choose their rulers and fix the bounds of their authority." And so the *civil* war was fought from the colonial pulpits as well as on the open battle fields. The Congregationalists, Presbyterians, Baptists, Lutherans, the Reformed Church and the Roman Catholics all mainly supported the independence movement. The comparatively small number of Jews in America were nearly all supported the patriots' movement. Obviously, the Anglicans supported the king and his ministers, while the Quakers, Mennonites, Moravians, and Amish refused to fight because they believed that war was wrong, and as a consequence these pacifist groups were distrusted and harassed by both sides. Nine of the colonies had established churches. In Massachusetts, Connecticut and New Hampshire, there was the Congregational Church, established by law and supported by taxation. In six of the colonies including all the colonies south of Pennsylvania and New York, the established church was the Anglican, as well as, in only New York City and the three adjourning counties.

In May 1774, a resident of New York City, with its population now well over 22,000, wrote to a friend in London as evidence of the stayed support and loyalty of the city's churches to the crown. He also expressed his opinion of the New England clergy as "their most wicked, malicious, and inflammatory harangues...... spiriting their godly hearers to the most violent opposition to Government; persuading them that the intention of the Government was to rule them with a rod of iron and to make them all slaves." In contrast to this sweeping indictment, Governor Thomas Hutchinson expressed his belief that the Congregationalists had been most extreme in their push for independence from the crown, and he also expressed concern about the neutrality position the Baptists, Quakers, Presbyterians, and Methodists had adopted.

Regardless of the ups and downs of the undeclared *civil war* and its leaders, most of the leaders of the evangelical churches feared that Parliament would appoint bishops in America and thereby hurt their own organizations. One of the primary reasons why many immigrants came to America was to escape the Anglican bishop and to seek religious freedom and self expression. John Adams boldly stated that the religious situation was one of the major contributing factors in arousing the patriots to question the authority of Parliament over the colonies. In fact, Adams' doctrine prompted the Congregational and Episcopal churches to openly support the crown, and oppose the New England evangelical churches. But it did not stop here! The Presbyterians and the Baptists, who were constantly receiving harsh treatment from the Anglicans in Ireland, believed that by relocating in America they would receive the religious freedom they were always seeking in Ireland. Such experiences caused resentment toward establishing the Church of England as the official church in America. One of the most impassioned leaders against such an occurrence was Jonathan Mayhew, pastor of the West Church in Boston. His friend Robert Treat Paine called Mayhew "the father of civil and religious liberty in Massachusetts and America." Mayhew's approach to religion was from an intellectual side, and soon he established the first church in New England to avow itself as "Unitarian." He fervently believed that the Church of England with its sedate hierarchy was foreign to the new American nation and would, if established in America, eventually would ruin America's culture with its "flood of Episcopacy."

Before the battle of Lexington, a number of ministers called upon the patriots (Whigs) of their congregations "to be stout of heart and good courage and to be ready to wield the sword of the Lord." One New England minister is quoted as saying in a public prayer, "O Lord, bind up all the Tories on this and the other side of the water, into one bundle and cast them into the bottomless pit, and let the smoke of their torment ascend forever and ever." Evidently, both groups of clergy had quite unlearned the Gospel and substituted Politics instead. An acid tongued Tory minister stated that he knew one of the Whig preachers "with the reputation of learning, preaching upon the Eleventh Commandment to his parish, declared to them that *it was no sin to kill Tories."*

And so, America's first *civil war* was incinerated from most of the pulpits of the colonial churches, as well politicians and just ordinary plain citizens representing both sides, vigorously added fuel to differences of opinion and expression which had germinated in the young republic. Evidently, many were not heeding Benjamin Franklin's warnings: "a republic, if you can keep it," and "we must all hang together, or assuredly we shall all hang separately."

England undertook to defend her colonies in time of war with fleets and armies, for which Parliament usually repaid a good part of the colonies' war expenditures. But it did not attempt to tax them directly until 1765, when the Stamp Act started to trouble the colonists, eventually leading to what is commonly called the *American Revolution*. However, this author chooses to reclassify this so called "American Revolution" as "America's First Civil War," which had started long before the Stamp Act, and "the shot that was heard around the world."

One of the instruments which the Whigs used to ferret out Tories was the formation of the local Committees of Safety. The primary purpose of these committees and their members was to identify any person believed to be a *Loyalist* to the king, and endanger the colonies in their quest toward freedom. Once identified most of these individuals were arrested and sent away; occasionally, being subjected to a public taring and feathering in the community's common. According to Beverly Robinson, a well-to-do estate owner of the day, who was having a difficult time to decide with which side he was going to aline himself stated, "I believe that the committees through their severity have made a great many Tories, for it is natural when a man is hurt, to kick." The committee gave him several weeks to make up his mind. Eventually, Robinson decided to join the Tories, and was awarded the commission of a Tory colonel.

Women were not immune to the committee's maltreatment. According to this same Mr. Robinson, "the vindictive Legislature of New York, in order to get possession of these estates, took a step that no civilized nation ever before took, they attained the women.... for adhering to the enemies of the State, that is to say, in eating, drinking, living and sleeping with their husbands, an injunction commanded by the decrees of the Almighty."

The reader may ask why the author prefers to identify the commonly known American Revolution as America's First Civil War. For this response, the author has researched Webster's New World Dictionary, which defines a "civil war" as:

a war between geographical sections or
political factions of the same nation.

To draw an elementary analogy of the author's hypothesis that the American Revolution was, in fact, this nation's first *civil war*. Let's pretend that a group of children gathered on a sand-lot and decided that most of them wanted to have a game of baseball, which would require two teams composed of those who wanted to play baseball These would-be "ball players" some way or other, divided themselves into two baseball teams, as well as selecting their respective "captain." Further, let's assume that the first group of players decide that their team was to be named the "Whigs." Meanwhile, the second group of players have, too, selected their "captain," and has decided to call themselves the "Tories." However, there were a few of the participants who decided, for one reason or another, that they'd rather watch from the sidelines than play ball.

After examining the members of the Whigs ball team, we find that some of its members were Roman Catholic, Reformed Dutch Church, a few Jews and Indians, most coming from the evangelical churches in the Mohawk Valley and New England area. In contrast, the players who chose to be on the Tories ball team were primarily composed of Anglicans, plus a few Indians. Those who chose not to play baseball were identified as Mennonites, Amish, Quakers, and Moravians, plus even a few Indians.

So now, there are two distinct teams, and after some heated debate two *objective and impartial* individuals are identified to serve as the game's designated umpires announce, who at an agreed upon time shout, "Let's play ball!" Or should we say let's start a *war*?

We've forgotten that two or three of the team sponsors were required to pay for the bats, balls, gloves and other needed equipment to assure the game is properly played. So three individuals from the group of non-players volunteer to serve as *sponsors*. For the purpose of this analogy, we'll call them England, Canada and France

Now we have two teams that for some reason or other want to play (fight) a game of baseball. Now they can play the game (war)! A *civilized* war between two groups of players, which matches Webster's definition of a civil war: "a war between two geographical sections or political factions of the same nation."

Again, we've identified the teams, the players, the sponsors, and the spectators. So! Let's play ball!

"Go Tories, Beat the Whigs!" "Rah, Whigs, Crush the Tories!" Shout the spectators, and the players. Meanwhile, the sponsors are silently praying that they will not be asked to pay any more money to their respective team.

While the spectators watch and cheer for specific team or the other, each team member is praying that their batter is going to hit the ball and make a run. In addition, in this game of "civil baseball (war)" many of the players had placed "side bets" staking all of their wealth, earthly possessions and reputations that their selected team would eventually win the "game."

Both teams of this civil war clung to their respective visions of liberties and the protection of their earthly possessions. It was to be a fight to the bitter end, with only one victor. The Tories clung to the security of England's crown and Parliament. The Whigs, on the other hand, believed that their freedom and independence depended upon owning their own property; without their property they would become "slaves," and unable to reap the rewards of their labor.

Alan Taylor and his editor, Eric Foner, in their interesting and well-documented book, "American Colonies," published by Viking Penguin in 2001 state that:

>............Until the American Revolutionary War began in 1775, few colonists aspired to national independence, for they felt great pride in the empire, derived great economic benefits from trading within its network, and dreaded the death and destruction of a civil war.
>
>..........When the civil war within the empire erupted in 1775, the less populous and more marginal colonies to the north-Nova Scotia, Newfoundland, Quebec- remained loyal, for they depended upon British protection and markets. Similarly, to the south, the West Indian planters felt too inhibited by their slave majority and too reliant upon the British market for sugar to consider rebellion.
>
>……...The Atlantic seaboard colonists felt a new confidence in their own power as they noted their growing population………from 1.5 million in 1754 to 2.5 million in 1775……their swelling population, the colonial (Whig) leaders detected an importance and maturity that deserved greater respect from Parliament. When denied that respect. many (but not all) mainland colonists felt a new capacity to reject British rule.
>
>…….John Adams warned that the British risked provoking a colonial rebellion. "They (the British)

will find it a more obstinate War, than the Conquest of Canada and Louisiana."

.......Triumphant (in the "civil war"), the new United States embraced the continental expansion that had unleashed only to regret. Learning from the abject failure of the British to slow frontier settlement, the American leaders shrewdly dedicated their nation to creating new farms by the thousands to accommodate the proliferating population...... completing the Whigs' belief that property ownership alone made men truly independent and free.

But at a price!

.......that vision of white liberty depended upon the systematic dispossession of native peoples and, until the Civil War of the 1860's, upon the perpetuation of black slavery. Thomas Jefferson aptly described the United States as an "empire of liberty," by and for the white citizenry. The new American empire liberated their enterprise as it provided military assistance to subdue Indians and Hispanics across the continent to the Pacific.

* * *

The purpose of this book is to acquaint the reader with each sides' Steps Toward Freedom during America's first *civil war* through the eyes, actions, and beliefs of factual historic individuals along with activities and sayings of the fictional characters introduced in my *Roads* trilogy, *Roads to Oriskany, Roads to Saratoga,* and *Roads to Niagara*.

The battles of and for Oriskany, Saratoga and Niagara staged along New York's Mohawk River valley were some of the most stubbornly fought battles during the war, and they were second to none other in relation to their consequences. During these engagements, sons, fathers, brothers, brothers-in-law and nephews were fighting and killing each other. In fact, General Nicholas Herkimer was leading the Rebels' (Whig) militia relief force toward Fort Stanwix against one of his brothers who was a Tory captain with Sir John Johnson; while one of his brothers-in-law was a leading Tory in the valley. The successful culmination of the Battle of Oriskany was directly responsible for neutralizing the British and the Tory forces in the valley, thus preventing a Tory uprising, and facilitating the Whigs' victory at Saratoga. These successful campaigns were promptly followed by Generals Sullivan and Clinton's decisive campaign on their roads to Niagara.

The traditional historians seldom explore or publicize the degree of importance of "upstate" New York's Mohawk Valley played in this war of factions. It has been stated that "the 1777 victory over the British and the Loyalists at Saratoga is considered the turning point of the Revolutionary War." General George Washington's Continental Army depended upon the valley's bountiful harvest from its lush and fertile fields of grain, fruits, vegetables and live stock to feed his army. Likewise, the British also needed these harvests to feed their ever-growing military forces' requirements. The Indians, too, had historically depended upon the bountiful offerings of the valley's rich river valley and its deep forests. It took one brilliant British general, Gentleman Johnny Burgoyne, to recognize the strategic position and worth the valley offered to whatever party controlled the river. The author's *Roads* trilogy explores the valley's settlement and defense, as well as the intrigue of these three major campaigns which occurred during the early years of the conflict, and eventually leading to France's entrance into "America's first civil war."

In each war or game, there is usually a winner and a loser, unless the conflict is determined a "draw." In America's civil war, there was definitely a winner and a loser. This book is divided into two parts:

Book One- Civil War!- explores some of the highlights and symptoms of this nation's first civil war with special emphasis upon the happenings in New York States's Mohawk Valley, and occasionally referring to the author's *Roads* trilogy.

Book Two- Freedom! concentrates upon exploring what happened to the "losers," including the Indians, as well as the Loyalists or Tories, many of whom immigrated into Canada.

The author has endeavored to report a "balanced" account of the civil strife and conflict between the Whigs and the Tories. If there appears to be an "imbalance," this is purely unintentional.

Gil Herkimer
Corpus Christi
March 31, 2005

BOOK ONE

CIVIL WAR!

ONE

LIKE WOMEN BREASTS, BARE AND OPEN

The Mohawk Valley
during the middle 1700's

New York's Mohawk Valley was seriously becoming a divided area as far as its political sentiment was concerned. Nowhere in the thirteen colonies was the passion between the Whigs and Tories as deeply divided. New York City and its surrounding area was predominately *strong for the Crown,* as was the far western part of the state in and about Fort Niagara. The Mohawk River and its valley, referred to by the Indians as Te-non-an-at-che, *"the river flowing through the mountains,"* was fast becoming America's incubator for the nation's first *civil war.* France, even with some assistance from the Iroquois, had failed in its efforts to capture and dominate the Mohawk valley. Next, it was England's turn to desperately cling to the valley and its vibrant river with its numerous tributaries and their fertile and bounteous land. The river's eastern junction, just about a mile below the falls at Cohoes, together with the great Hudson River presented an open water route to the Atlantic Ocean. Toward the west, the Mohawk ended at a *carrying place* on Wood Creek near the Fort Stanwix where settlers and traders ferried their trade goods to and with the Indians far into the Lake country, and serving the young nation's only waterway into the open west lands between Georgia and the St. Lawrence Valley into the Genesee country, through the Great Lakes country, and into the great beyond with its apparent limitless boundaries. New York State was truly the colonies' *Empire State*. The Mohawk River and its valley was the colonies' main east-west transportation artery, but it also served as the major breadbasket for the Continental Army, as well as to the British troops and their Indian allies.. The struggle for control of this artery was rapidly pitting neighbor against neighbor, brother against brother, and *American* families against each other…..America's first *civil war!*

Interestingly, it took a Mohawk sachem, King Hendrick, to awaken the English to the *treasure* they had in the Mohawk, and that most advantageous method to attack the river and its valley was from it's western frontier. At the Albany congress of 1754, King Hendrick delivered a speech which must have awakened the sleepy eyed members of Parliament. "Look about your country," the sachem said to the gathering of governors and generals, "and see; you have no fortifications about you…..no, not even to this city. 'Tis but one step from Canada hither, and the French may come and easily turn you out of doors. Brethren, you were desirous we should open our hearts and minds to you; look at the French, they are men….. they are fortifying everywhere; but you without fortifications. We are ashamed to say it, but you are like women with open and bare breasts."

As a result of this warning, the conference charged Governor William Shirley of Massachusetts to lead an army against Fort Niagara by way of the Mohawk valley and Oswego. In addition, Major General William Johnson, superintendent of Indian Affairs, at the head of a mixed army of militia and Indians, was to dispatched to take Forts Ticonderoga and Crown Point, so as to remove the routine and irritating French attacks into New York State.

It is said that one learns through making mistakes. None could have been a more bitter pill for the British as General Edward Braddock marched his brightly clad Redcoats into a French ambush. It might not have happened if the bull-headed general had not been so aloof ignoring the advise of a much younger Indian fighter named George Washington and King Hendrick and his Indians, who had been ordered by Indian Agent William Johnson to act as guides and scouts. Unlike Braddock, Johnson was a very shrewd and savvy man blessed with a gifted tongue and great personal charm. Adopted by the Indians and called Warraghiyagey, or "He who does much business" or "A man who undertakes great things," Johnson routinely visited the Indian villages, fluently spoke their language, slept and ate in and around their huts, caressed their girls, wore their clothes, and joined in their dances and feasts He relished eating their special cooked meal, boiled dog and soup enriched with lice without turning a hair.

It took only a few days of Major General Edward Braddock's parade-posturing to suggest that his army would have been safer if they quietly slipped back into the deep, dark forest; and from there retreat back to jolly ole England. On July 9, 1755, as the commander-in-chief of the British forces, Major General Edward Braddock, was killed and the British troops suffered a disastrous and humiliating defeat in the wilds of western Pennsylvania at the hands of a force of French and allied Indians not half the size of his own army. The news of Braddock's defeat spread like wildfire taking the courage out of Governor Shirley's men as they returned to Schenectady and Albany. William Johnson, on the other hand, returned to Lac St. Sacrement late in August with no more than three hundred of the eleven hundred Iroquois, who had just drunk to the king's health with him by the Mohawk, at Mt. Johnson. A few days later, William Johnson arrived at the lake named for Father Jogues's Lac St. Sacrement to Lake George, *not only,* he wrote, *in honor of his majesty, but to ascertain his undoubted dominion here."* Johnson's pack of farmers and part-time soldiers allowed the French to escape from their overwhelming defeat, and played it *safe,* and never attempting to capture Crown Point. Instead, the victorious Johnson and his band of misfits, scattered in November, after applying their carpentry skills to construct Fort William Henry.

Believing that the Mohawk Valley and its western border, as well as the colony's capital, Albany were safe for a while, Johnson troops were rewarded with leaves. Johnson, too, was rewarded for the campaign's success, returning to his stockade and fine mansion as a "baronet." Afterwards, Johnson sported the title of Sir William, and was also five thousand pounds richer thanks to the appreciative British Crown and its Parliament. Unable to cope with their victory, the British foolishly transferred two *textbook* generals, Abercrombie and Loudon, the caliber of General Braddock. These arrogant misfits scoffed at the colonial levies, and converted Albany and New York City into brawling military settlements. They were too busy planning campaigns based upon their European military training, which did not include how to fight war *Indian style.* They ignored Johnson's appeals to construct forts and garrison his stockaded farmhouse already in the valley. As a result, the French acquired Oswego and Wood Creek by default. The Iroquois, all except the Mohawks, Oneidas, and Tuscaroras, were sufficiently repulsed by the way England was managing the war. These tribes sent a peace delegation to Canada stating that they were through fighting for any of the white men; "let them fight their own white man wars."

On November 12, 1757, all of the rising tensions between the valley residents, the Indians, the French and the British, came to a head. The French, along with some of their *Indian* supporters, swept through German Flats and New Palatine, scalping or burning at least forty Palatines, and incinerating sixty homes, five blockhouses, and one hundred and fifty horrified valley residents hauled north to captivity. This was the very day when Karl and Rebecca Heindrick returned from their shopping trip in the hamlet of New Palatine to their farm about five miles west along the King's Highway, and found Karl's father Ulrich Heindrick's body lying as a prisoner in the lane in front of their burning home with a spear pierced through his chest into the frozen ground in front of their burning home.

Again, Sir William came to the valley's rescue from a much worse disaster by preventing the ignorant General Loudon from marching against the Iroquois, who he blamed for the attack. Loudon did not know that white men could and would masquerade as Indians. As a result of this massacre, the valley's western frontier was pushed further east toward Albany.

In their quest, the French were determined to forge a chain from Quebec to Louisiana, cutting off the English colonies. The British were equally resolute to drive the French from North America. By the end of 1759, Fort Niagara had fallen to General William Johnson, and General Jeffrey Amherst, and the British had driven the French back to the St. Lawrence River from Ticonderoga and Crown Point. These two generals had conceived a squeeze play. Amherst assembled the greatest army the Mohawk valley had ever witnessed composed of six thousand colonials and four thousand British regulars. Their joint plan called for one British army to march against Montreal from Quebec, and the other to push north from Crown Point. The two armies were to meet before the city of Montreal. The squeeze plan came off without a hitch, and the French were cut off from any possibility of a retreat. Something unforeseen, however, did happen! General Johnson's Indians, except his Mohawks, all returned to their homes, thoroughly disgusted that the generals did not allow them to massacre the French garrison of Abbe' Picquet's little mission school of Oswegatchie, which fell to Amherst as his army moved down the St. Lawrence. According to Captain Jelles Fonda, it was all over in September 1760. Even though Captain Fonda's spelling needed improvement, he records the event as: *Septr 8th in the morning, as we laid before Moreial ye French Sent a flag of Truse to Jenral amhost that theay would Capetelate and give up all the Country to ous. agreed open and the graneders Marched in Montereial this Day and placed centrys Round the Cetty.* The English had prevailed and peace was secured during the 1763 Treaty of Paris ending the Seven Years' War, and its American counterpart, The French and Indian War.

After almost a century of backwoods butchery, in a sense peace had arrived in the Mohawk valley, a skull cap would be worn for life by many a Mohawk farmer, his wife and their children who had managed to survive the Indians' and the *White Indians'* scalping knife. When Johannes Roof put up his squatter's house and barns at the carrying place near Wood Creek and Fort Stanwix the year after the war ended, he opened the *white* settlers' western frontier approximately one hundred miles further west of Albany to the very end of the navigable Mohawk River. Agreeing with King Hendrick's quotation, Johannes Roof believed that New York's western frontier was like women breasts, bare and open, without any fortifications.

With the valley's white settlers' frontier open, all they had to do was to burn, to blast out tree stumps, to plow, to plant, to grow, and to reap the harvest of their efforts. Thus, allowing Sir William, who had it right down to the simple exercise of giving the Indians wampum belts to guarantee the promises of the colonial governors to keep the white invaders off their land, as they threatened to take their hatchets against the white *poachers* who were trespassing on their hunting grounds. Regardless of the number of handshakes, promises, or written documents, there was no boundary the Tories or the Whigs would not traverse. If the Indians did not like the circumstances, the Redcoats would be called in to lay out the facts to the Indians.

Between the random skirmishes with the Indians and other trespassers, the valley settlers did find time to stage local Fairs to exhibit Sir William's pure blood horses, his first sheep to be introduced into the valley. Besides exhibiting one's livestock during these Fairs, there were sack races, greased pig chases, and see-who-can-make-the-worse-face contests, and on the best straightways of the narrow, wooded King's Highway, the settlers would place wagers on the fastest horses in the valley, which was moved from the *highway* onto the frozen Mohawk river during the winter.

Sir William was beginning to worry about his neighbors, the *Mohawk Dutch (Palatine)*, and their mulish resistance to change. These stubborn and tireless farmers believed in *Equality* as one of the "universal trinity" of which *Liberty* and *Fraternity* were the other parts. They acknowledged that they accepted change only when the distinction between Tory and Whig was less confusing. They particularly did not approve when the likes of Sir John Johnson, Sir William's oldest son, started to push them around, and when Sheriff White would dare someone to shoot one of the local *Sons of Liberty.* To these industrious Palatine farmers, however, peace also included among others, celebrating the joyous holidays of Christmas and New Year in the manner in which these holidays were celebrated in their homeland. To a great surprise to one of the valley's prominent missionary, Samuel Kirkland, who preferred the New England manner of holiday celebration. Kirkland described the Mohawk holidays as: "very affect'g and strik'g. They generally assemble for read'g prayers or Divine service..... but after that, they eat, drink, and make merry. They allow of no work or servile labour on ye day, and ye following... their servants are free... but drinking, swearing, fighting, frolic'g are not only allowed, but seem to be essential for ye joy of ye day." Whitsunday was a sort of slaves holiday, when the valley Negroes would dress up in their best and, with bunches of "pinkster-bloomies" in their hands, go calling on their friends. The fiddlers came down from the walls, and between dances they'd gossip about Sir William and his favorite Molly Brant, or about Sir John and Colonel Daniel Claus, even talked about the latest rumors about the latest Indian raid, and about who was the latest *turncoat* from Tory to Whig or vicea- versa.

In the Iroquois country, peace took a different turn. West of their Confederacy in the Great Lake country, bitterness and resentment was becoming fervent. "Englishmen!" stormed a Chippewa chief to an English trader at Michilimackinac. "Although you have conquered the French, you have not yet conquered us!..... We are not your slaves! These lakes, these woods, these mountains.... we will part from them to no one." The Indians' vexation became like a contagious disease spreading from Schonowe, the *gate* at Schenectady through the Iroquois Long House, westward along the Seneca's *Forbidden Path*, to Niagara, onto the plains of the Illinois, pitching north to the Great Lakes and south along the river channels of the Ohio and the Tennessee and the Mississippi rivers. The Indians were convinced that the British forts were to be used in a war of extermination against them. As usual, the Indians vehemently protested because they were constantly being cheated by the *unlicensed* traders who had rushed into the newly opened wilderness, which the Indians presumably believed they still owned. Even Sir William Johnson could not totally pacify the Indians, yet he towered head and shoulders over all the crown's officers and the colonial assemblymen. He almost single-handed endeavored for the rest of his life to save the lands for his Indian *brothers.* Even though he had obtained his land for little more than a *song,* he knew that when the *rum-bottle* speculator ever started to negotiate with them, the Indians were sitting ducks. These speculators applied their magic formula, "Get a few Indians drunk, then unknown to their tribe, have them sign a deed for a *little farm,* pay them off with trade junk and trinkets along with a small amount of cash. Then, if you're a *Yorker,* you'd hurry back to New York City, pay the governor's fee, arrange for a crooked survey, and emerge from the deal with a crown patent for a *little farm* of one thousand acres."

All went well during the ensuing years until the night of July 11, 1774 at Johnson Hall, when Sir William Johnson, his Majesty's superintendent of the Northern Indians, died. Less than two years later, the Hall was looted by men who had been his neighbors; American officers who, with their soldiers, marched up the old King's Highway in an attempt to capture Sir John, Sir William's son, then the Mohawk valley's most menacing Tory.

Settlers' loyalties shifted the least stable boundary lines overnight. *Lady Washington* and the *Long Nine Pounder,* two cannons from the old fort in Schenectady, were set up in the dorp's streets to guard the main stockade gates leading into the open country. Rumors were flying about like maples leaves during the Fall of the year about how Johnny Johnson, together with hundreds of his fanatically loyal Roman Catholics and club-swinging Scotch tenants who were fanatically loyal to Sir John, who had inherited his father's barony and the king's authority, would soon be headed down the valley, burning and shooting. The tavern regulars and their friends hurriedly cleaned their guns ready to shoot the first *varmint* who looked cross-eyed toward them.

For the two years after Sir William's death, the *civil war* in the Mohawk valley was largely a war of correspondence. Unlike an angry dog with its hackles on its neck and back ready to fight for the slightest reason, the fuming Tories and Whigs used feathered quills to express their displeasure with each other. But, the patrons and their beer steins together with the blue Holland punch bowls at Martha Butler's Heidelberg Tavern in New Palatine had different ideas as they watched the head on their beers disappear into the warm, amber liquid in their steins.

Thus, some of the seeds of America's first *civil war* were planted!

TWO

END JUSTIFIES THE MEANS

Late 1774 along the Mohawk Valley

At eight o'clock in the evening of July 11, 1774, the unexpected death of Sir William Johnson had sent just as powerful reverberations throughout the Loyalists' communities as the proverbial *shots heard around the world* from the scrimmages at Lexington and Concord. The main difference being was that Sir William's death sent even greater anxiety and uneasiness throughout the Iroquois Confederacy, than it did in the Whig and Tory communities.

At the time of Sir William's death, he was one of the Mohawk valley's largest land holders, as well as one of Britain's Loyalist land holders. After July 14, 1774, of course, his only admitted son, Sir John Johnson, inherited Johnson Hall and the surrounding estate around Onondaga Lake., as well as most of his father's personal property. At the time, Sir John was only thirty-two years of age, and a comparative stranger to the valley. Having lived much of his life within Albany or New York City before and after his marriage to Miss Watts, an heiress and lady of fashion. During these years, two-thirds of New York City was owned by Loyalists, consisting of wealthy more numerous than elsewhere.

Sir John's sisters, one of whom had married her cousin Guy Johnson of Guy Park, the other sister married Colonel Daniel Claus, each receiving 14,000 acres of valley property. Sir William's second wife, Miss Molly, whom he supposedly married Indian style, was liberally provided for, as well as their admitted children. Also, Sir William bequeathed 1,500 to Miss Molly's brother, Joseph Brant. In fact, there was an enormous quantity of land which he had parceled out to a few of his active followers.

Sir William was a completely different person than his son, Sir John. He started his life as a frontiersman and trader along the Mohawk river. During the French and Indian War, he abandoned this profession to accept the position to manage Indian affairs for the British. His opinions concerning the Indians seemed to be guided by a single-minded philosophy, *we enjoy the most security when they (the Indians) are divided amongst themselves.* His feelings toward the Indians ran the spectrum from a friendly opinion to sheer pity. Generally, Sir William was considered a *white politician* who treated the Indians well and fairly with his decisions and trinkets, and often fighting their battles with government officials or between tribal disputes. Even though his primary loyalty was to his first love of "land speculating." However, no one ever questioned his loyalty to the king of England. This favorite baronet, who was constantly working on *official duty on behalf of the Indians and on the authority of the king,* also conducted a rather secret personal life. Even though he never had a legal wife, he fathered three children with a rather quiet and undemanding young German servant girl named Catherine Weissenberg. It had been rumored that Sir William married her in April, 1759 as she lay on her death bed dying of tuberculosis.

After Catherine's death, Sir William did not waste much time before he met in Canajoharie, New York Joseph Brant's twenty-three or twenty-four year old attractive and very intelligent sister, Molly, who was endowed with other attractions for this crude politician and land speculator. Molly's step-father, Brant, was a sachem of the lordly Turtle clan and leader of the Mohawks, who possessed rich holdings of land along the Mohawk river and vast hunting grounds to the north. It took Sir William little time to recognize that he needed to cast his net over this jewel of an Indian maid who could accept his remoteness, and his occasional crude manner of living. Knowing that he needed not only a housekeeper, he also was firmly aware that in his political position he required an attractive hostess who could makeup for his lack of social graces. In Molly Brant, Sir William Johnson believed that he had literally struck a gold mine which would increase not only his value to himself, but also to King George III and his Indian allies by opening new roads to political influence and personal wealth. Not surprisingly, very soon Molly became pregnant and their son, Peter, was born in September, 1759. On December 22, 1760, Sir William, the Mohawks' *Affectionate Brother and Friend,* and Molly were invited to visit the Mohawks at Canajoharie. Shortly after they arrived, the Mohawks completed a land deed as their *wedding* present to Sir William and Molly, his legal wife as the Mohawks envisioned the Johnson's relationship. Their gift represented nearly eighty thousand acres, which was nearly all the land that the Canajoharie Mohawks had left and that bordered the Mohawk river. The Mohawks assured Johnson that they wanted to grant him the land *Whilst it is in our power to give you this proof of our friendship, which we fear, will not be long, as our White Brethren are getting all our lands from us.*

From there on Sir William Johnson, his Miss Molly, and her brother Joseph Brant would exercise authority and influence over the Mohawk valley, especially over the Indians, on behalf of Sir William and King George III. After conducting his last Indian Council on the blindly hot and humid July 11, 1774, Sir William, who had been ill, managed to complete his speech to the assembled Indians and their followers. Shortly thereafter, he was assisted to his bedroom in Johnson Hall. Sir William's sudden death, according to his son-in-law and British Indian agent, Daniel Claus, served as the *eve* of what might have been called a *civil war, the Iroquois scattered like a flock of helpless sheep.*

In the Indians' minds, they had lost their one and only *white* friend.

STEPS TOWARD FREEDOM

* * *

Earlier in 1774, the supervisor of Tryon County had flatly refused to take sides in any disputes between the Loyalists and the Whigs, who were being to referred to as Tories and Rebels respectively. The county supervisor declared that their opinions "did not appear to tend to be the violation of their religious rights, but merely regarded a single article of commerce which no person was compelled to purchase, and which persons or real virtue and resolution might easily have avoided or dispensed with." Continuing, the supervisor said, "They do therefore resolve to bear faithful and true allegiance to their lawful sovereign King George III, and that in the true and plain sense of the words."

After Sir William's death, his nephew and younger son-in-law, assumed his father-in-law's business, as recommended by Sir William Johnson after his son, Sir John had declined the position. With the assumption of his father-in-law's responsibilities for Sir William's vast financial affairs and properties, as well as his related patronage obligations, Guy Johnson, with the Indians' hearty support and enthusiasm, was able to persuade the Iroquois to *keep the peace.* In so doing, Guy sent a message throughout the Iroquois nation vowing that the *fire still burns, and the road is open to this place (Johnson Hall).* The Indians took Guy Johnson at his word, and scheduled a Council Meeting on September 12-18, 1775 where approximately 235 sachems, chiefs, and their entourage assembled about the great mansion which they thought to be the noblest building had ever seen. Sir William had built his home some nine miles from Fort Johnson of great white clapboards arranged like blocks of stone on a handsome Palladian platform, which helped to symbolize as in the legendary days of the Greeks the safety and security Johnson Hall. During this Council Meeting the Indians gave Guy a new name, Urghquadirha, or "Rays of the Sun Enlightening the Earth." New name or not, Guy Johnson had been well schooled by Sir William, and he had adopted Sir William's Indian policy: "to make friends with the Indians when you can, to redress their grievances when possible (and practicable), and to give them presents in public and in private." Indeed, the Indians had become accustomed to being "on the dole" for years. But mostly, Guy Johnson adopted Sir William's first and fast rule of conduct: *to divide and rule.*

Following his mentor's practice, after this Council Meeting Guy detained six of the most *principal men* and gave each a *handsome gift.* Joseph Brant, Sir William's adopted son, was just beginning to gain not only Guy Johnson's attention and resentment, which had been festering ever since a certain George Klock, a well-to-do-farmer of German extraction moved into their neighborhood. Klock had *purchased* out many of the claims of the Livingston Manor heirs. The Indians were always, usually justifiably, suspicious whenever white people and land were concerned. They would grow uneasy and frightened, expecting the worse to happen to them. George Klock confirmed all their fears about white men and land. He was a person with little formal education, but he made up for this deficiency being a formative man and willing (and usually able) to stand his ground to any individual he was facing, including the newly appointed Superintendent of Indian Affairs.

There is a story which was widely circulated about that Klock had told Sir William to "go and hang yourself." Thus, confirming the fact that there was no love lost between these two diametrically opposed principled men.

Indeed the Indians, especially the Mohawks, had something to worry about. In a moment of weakness, the Fort Hunter Indians, in varying degrees of drunkenness, had deeded their homesite where their village stood to the Corporation of Albany, which was controlled by George Klock. In some fashion of other, a royal governor had later burned the deed, and had taken a similar deed to the king. The Corporation of Albany made no immediate claims, believing that the *Indians would die out,* but the *local whites* would periodically bring up the matter. This is where George Klock entered the picture! He was threatening to evict the white tenants from the land of the Upper Mohawks, who had been renting the land to the white tenants. Thus, Klock had endangered a seemingly peaceful arrangement for both the whites and the Indians.

Up to his usual roguery, Klock still kept the Canajoharie community in turmoil. Besides serving them with *writs of ejection* on the white tenants, who had regularly and faithfully paid their rents to the Indians, he had managed to divide the Indians themselves into quarreling factions by plying a few with drink and getting them to sign a deed in his favor for the disputed land. Sir William, the Indians' ever guardian and healer, was informed by the court that a *land patent* was a valid title no matter how obtained. Even with the evidence of fraud, it was not even admissible at common law. In addition, there were technical reasons why the suit could not be tried in the chancery. The Indians' only hope lay in an appeal to the king of England. King George III, through his ministers and encouraged by Sir William, wanted to know the seriousness of settling their land disputes with the whites.

To prove their security, the Six Nations delegated one sachem, each one could neither read nor wrote English, to the Council Meeting held on November 5, 1768 at Fort Stanwix. Each sachem made his *mark* on the document, subsequently referred to as the Fort Stanwix Treaty. Without a question none of the sachems was aware of the seriousness of their commitment and folly, nor of what they had actually signed over to the greedy and sanctimonious whites, who according to tradition had filled the sachem's bellies and numbed their brains with hardy, English rum. With their marks, the trusting sachems of the Six Nations had deeded over an incredible amount of land to the avaricious and unconscionable British brigands. This unimaginable amount of land included large parts of present-day Tennessee, Kentucky, West Virginia, Pennsylvania and New York states. The boundary began on the Ohio River at the mouth of the Tennessee River, flowing along the Ohio River up to Fort Pitt (formally Fort Duquesne and present day site of the city of Pittsburgh). From Fort Pitt the treaty's the boundary proceeded up the Allegheny River to Kittanning, then directly overland to the west branch of the Susquehanna River, continuing down that river and thence by two smaller streams to the east branch of the Susquehanna and up to Owegy and the east to the upper Delaware River. From there the circumference went on up the Delaware and back again to the Susquehanna at the Iroquois Castle at Unadilla, in the state of New York, and continuing up the Unadilla River to its source, and eventually to a point on Wood Creek near Fort Stanwix. Simply stated, all the land south and east of these perimeters, except for the immediate land the Mohawks still dwelled on and *owned,* would be known as *white man's country* thanks to the *generosity* and conniving of Sir William and his able associates! For all of this land, the Indians received stacks of blankets, kettles, knives, brooches, and other colorful trinkets, which were laid hither and yon on the common square in front of the fort, along with a few piles of currency neatly stacked on a table, all of which were to be divided amongst the six sachems.

The total price tag?

Perhaps about the equivalent of present day fifty thousand dollars!

The Indians, in their trusting state of drunken oblivion, had totally ignored one of their long-standing negotiating principles: *never trust a white land trader!*

Joseph Brant, along with the six sachems, returned to their respective homes believing that the Ohio River could be considered a gift of the *white traders*, but it was perhaps too far away for them to consider.

As the years passed by, there was a growing fear by the various claimants of the clandestine negotiated Canajoharie patent, believing that was very real danger that the Mohawks and even the entire Iroquois Nation might go on the warpath. Another Council Meeting was called to settle these disputes. Everybody who had signed this release of the patent the Indians actually occupied, except the *epitome of unctuous,* in the shadowy person of George Klock. This rather slippery, scheming and affected person was, on one occasion, brought before the then New York State governor, Sir Henry Moore. On another occasion and before another governor, Joseph Brant attempted to settle the Klock controversy by warning the governor, "Now, Brother, we rely on your justice for relief, and hope we may obtain it, so as to continue to live peaceably, as we have hitherto done. We are sensible that we are at present but a small number, but nevertheless our connections are powerful, and our alliances many & should any of these perceive that we who have been so remarkable for our fidelity and attachment to you, are ill used and defrauded, it may alarm them, and be productive of dangerous consequences." Brant's speech angered Governor William Tryon, but the governor promised to try to obtain some degree of justice for the Indians, all the while knowing that his power did not extend sufficiently far enough to assist the Indians.

The truth was the Indians had placed their entire faith in the royal crown and in Sir William Johnson. The only thing even Sir William could do was to sooth the Indians emotions. The king's ministers, too, did wish to give justice to the Indians, but there was little they could do. In reality, the Indians were victims of the squatters, landgrabbers, dishonest traders, and the malicious purveyors of gossip and even the murdered of Indians. The Indians were literally trapped between the swelling assortment of charlatans from all ides, including those representing the king, who was relatively ignorant of the trickery, chicanery and deliberate deceit foisted upon the Indians. Nor did it seem likely that the self-centered colonial legislatures would be able to, or even care to exercise greater authority to assist the Indians.

What it all boiled down to the *whites* (Tories and Whigs) consciously or unconsciously were planning to acquire (one way or another) all the land possessed by the Indians. The Tories and Whigs exercising the principle: *the end justifies the means.* During the French and Indian War, the whites had recognized the potential value of the virgin land in western New York, Pennsylvania and other areas to the south and west. Washington believed that it was imperative that the Rebels conquer as much of the Indian territory as possible before the pending "civil war" ended, it the inevitable, new free nation was to ever amount to more than a narrow strip of coastal land. In Washington's orders to General John Sullivan prior to the general's invasion into the Indian territory, he called for "the total destruction and devastation of the Indian settlements and the capture of as many prisoners of every sex and age as possible." Continuing Washington ordered Sullivan that "it will be essential to ruin their crops in the ground and prevent their planting more."

* * *

In 1777, Governor Tryon visited the Mohawk Valley and wrote rapturously of the evident prosperity and contentment of the people, who were not seemingly pleased with the presence of the governor, than he with them. He reviewed the militia an reported that it exceeded 1,400 men under arms.

Either by happenstance or by design, both the British and the American communities had successfully followed Sir William's principle of *divide and conquer.* Through a series of maneuvers the one great Iroquois Confederacy of Six Nations had split its loyalty between the American Tories and the British on one side, and the American Whigs and Rebel patriots of the other side. Plainly the differences in America's public and private opinions and beliefs had involved into a controversy between two political factions of the same nation, which would eventually tear itself asunder, and erupt into open warfare between the two American political groups. America's first civil war was in its infancy stage!

THREE

STEINS AND BLUE HOLLAND PUNCH BOWLS

April 1775 at Martha Butler's
Heidelberg Tavern in New Palatine

It was nine-thirty in the evening, Martha Butler, the Heidelberg Tavern's proprietor, and her handy man, Harry Hunter, were preparing for a very special meeting scheduled to begin in just about one-half an hour. After Martha had cut off the sale of all beverages, including black coffee, she finished securing the bar's liquor supply for the next day, and was busying herself with something she loved to do. Count money! With the money all stored in a safe place, she gathered a host of clean steins on top of the taverns' bar, along with an adequate supply of beer. In addition, she stirred up a small batch of non-alcoholic punch made with the hard cider from the apple trees behind the tavern. She remembered her grandparents telling her of the two reasons why the British had brought her Palatine ancestors to New York. First, the Palatines had earned a good reputation for their industrious nature, which could aptly applied as excellent harvesters and manufactures of naval supplies. Second, they would serve as effective buffers against the French and the Indians on New York's western frontier. What more could the British have wanted from their Palatine indentured servants?

About a generation before the Palatines emigrated to America, an astute Philip Livingston, with the assistance a moonlight night and plenty liquor, persuaded a few Iroquois tribesmen, to sign a deed in his favor for a tract of land east of their village. Shortly thereafter, the Indians claimed that this tract of land had been secretly surveyed by moonlight, instead of in their pretence as was proper, and that the land boundaries had been extended westward until it actually included their own little cabins and planting grounds. Soon after the Palatines arrival to the Mohawk valley and in the present-day area referred as the Catskill Mountains, this very same *noble white buyer* had learned many years before that while negotiating with the Indians, it was always to his advantage to cut a few corners, never minding the consequences to the Indians. Experience had also taught him that it was much easier and cheaper to influence a few Indians to his way of thinking with a few bottles of cheap liquor served in a comfortable setting; while the Indians' minds were vulnerable Livingston, as well as most of the *white land grabbers,* would be almost assured that the Indians would consent to most of their desires. To the Palatines, Livingston promised each Palatine would receive a daily ration of one-third of a loaf of black, crusted bread, and one quart of "ship's beer;" not surprisingly a very low grade of beer.

Meanwhile, Harry had completed sweeping the broad, maple-planked floor, and was preparing the sitting arrangement to accommodate approximately twenty people with a head table facing the bar. Harry was not sure what kind of meeting Miss Martha was preparing for, but when Miss Martha told him to do something for her, he never asked any questions,. He, however, had an immense dislike, and distrust for Miss Martha's husband, Jerome. To Harry, Jerome Butler was an *arrogant bastard.* He always went around thinking that *his dung didn't stink,* just about like Sir Johnny Johnson and his buddy Captain John Butler, as well as John's little brat of a son, Walter. *"Those Butlers, they're are all alike,"* Harry would tell his closest drinking buddies. Harry would tell them, *never trust a guy who never looks you straight in the eyes.* What puzzled Harry the most was that he could never understand why Miss Martha had married Jerome Butler. As near as he could figure it, what had attracted Martha to Jerome, was their shared interest in local politics, especially after he was elected New Palatine's second mayor. Soon after the Butlers were married, Harry started to see a change in their behavior. Martha always had an open ear to all of her clients Whigs and Tories alike, but she seemed to have a special ear for her Palatine cousins and friends, while Jerome seemed to hang around with his cousin, John Butler and his cronies. While both of them tried to give the appearance of a happily married couple, it was obvious to Harry that all was not well behind their closed doors.

Harry had just finished stoking the fireplace with a fresh supply of logs. What a beautiful sight, he thought, as his eyes glanced from the roaring fire toward his voluptuous boss. Oh, how he'd love to snuggle up to her log, he thought. His attention was quickly changed as he recognized a group of New Palatine residents enter the tavern's solid oak, front door. There were Karl Heindrick the local cheese maker and his assistant Cal Swartz, George Raab the local smithy, and Harvey Perry assistant manager of Kerchner's General Store. As other people entered and all were graciously greeted by Martha Butler, Harry noticed that most of them were Palatines, some of whom he knew traveled every Sunday down to German Flats to attend the area's lone Dutch Reformed Church. He noticed, however, they were not just Palatines as he saw one of his old Irish drinking buddies, Larry O'Brien, enter with some farmers from west of Johnson Hall on the river's flat land where they spent most of their time. These people, Harry thought, certainly were not regular customers, so Miss Martha must be expecting a very special kind of meeting. At exactly ten minutes after ten o'clock, the tavern's front door opened and the settlement's mayor, Rudolph Helm, entered followed by a gentlemen Harry didn't recognize.

"Mrs. Butler," Mayor Helm said as he shook her hands, "I'd like to introduce you to Mr. Christopher Yates. He's the gentlemen I've been telling you so much about."

"Mr. Yates," said the gracious hostess and proprietor of the Heidelberg Tavern, "our mayor has been telling me many good things about you."

"Mrs. Butler," responded the mayor's guest admiringly, "I am pleased to make your acquaintance."

"Oh, please, Mr. Yates, just call me plain Martha," she requested. "At this stage of the valley's politics, I am not very proud to be associated with the Butler clan," as she led the two gentlemen to the head table, which Harry Hunter had so efficiently arranged.

Martha opened the meeting by suggesting that everyone refill their beer steins or their punch mugs from the Holland Blue bowls, "Then we'll settle down to the order of the day." After everyone was comfortably seated either in the rough, straight-back chairs available, or on the split log benches, Martha returned to her hostess role by introducing their good friend and mayor of New Palatine.

"Rudolph Helm has graciously urged his friend and our guest to join us here tonight to discuss with us the disheartening change of events which are occurring throughout our state, especially as they may effect the Mohawk Valley. Most of us are familiar with some of the activities happening here in New Palatine, but our guest will inform us of what is happening in Albany and there about. Mr. Mayor, it's your floor," said the pensive tavern proprietor as she courteously bowed in his direction, and took her seat next to their guest.

"Good evening, gentlemen, friends, neighbors and our lady," said the mayor respectfully nodded his head toward Martha Butler, "We are fortunate to have our guest here with us tonight. He has been traveling the valley and conducting meetings such as this one to inform us all of the politics in the valley, and especially what is happening in our state's legislature in Albany. It is, indeed, my pleasure to introduce my good friend and lawyer, Christopher Yates from Schenectady."

The tall, lean man in his middle forties was dressed in a dark, wool tweed suit, and knee-high leather boots still with some partially melted snow hiding between their soles and heels. "Thank you, Rudolph, and thank you all for being here on such a cold, snowy and blustery evening. It is truly, a night not fit for man or beast, but I will try to make my presentation as short as possible, however, I will allow you all plenty of time you need to ask me questions. I'm certain you're not going to enjoy all of my responses, but we'll deal with those inquiries when we get to them. That is, if our hostess, has provided sleeping quarters for those of us who'll need them."

There was a muffled snicker from the back, and everyone turned to identify the culprit. It was Harry Hunter, before arranging the chairs in the tavern, he had taken fresh straw up to the tavern's loft, and as he was spreading the straw throughout the loft's low ceiling, yet spacious open floor, when he stumbled across a couple coupling. Harry thought to himself, that's a pretty good idea for a bar song, *as I was spreading hay in the attic, I saw a couple coupling and making hay,* after he heard that Mr. Yates was expecting to spend the evening in hamlet's one and only sleeping tavern. Harry just took another drink from his stein, and said, "Sorry, continue Mr. Yates, I'm anxious to hear what you have to say."

Somewhat disturbed, Attorney Yates acknowledged Harry's apology, and proceeded, "As Mayor Helm has said, there are many things with which we all must be familiar. One of the most important issues is a document consisting of a series of resolutions developed by some knowledgeable individuals in Albany. The first resolution views with alarm the recent acts of the British Parliament, which abridges the privileges of all the American Colonies, as well as blocks the Port of Boston. The document solemnly acknowledges that George III was the *rightful* monarch and ruler of the Mohawk Valley, entitled to *true faith and allegiance,* giving him our lives and fortunes to maintain and support him."

Immediately, there were a considerable amount of whispering and murmuring throughout the audience. "To put your minds at ease," Yates continued as he removed his tongue from his cheeks, and started to clarify his last statement, "….. the resolution states, we think it is our undeniable privilege to be taxed only with our own consent." The resolution continues, "we will join and unite with our brethren of the rest of the country in anything tending to support and defend our rights and liberties."

"What can we do about all of this stuff," declared one of the flatland farmers who seldom ventured into hamlet of New Palatine, "I have to spend all my days plowing, planting, harvesting and feeding my milch cows. In between times, I only have to milk my cows two times a day, everyday. The cows wont even let me and my wife take Sundays off," he concluded with a jovial laugh.

This time there were no single snicker, rather there was a considerable amount of heads nodding agreement with the concerned farmer, as well as verbal acknowledgments. To quell their concern, Yates raised his arm, and stated, "What I'd like to receive from you people here tonight, is the name of two of New Palatine's constituents who will to agree to travel with me to Albany, and as New Palatine's delegates to a general Continental Congress to join with the eastern delegates in establishing a Committee of Correspondence for the whole Tryon County.

"We have to remember," Yates continued, "that we've had a considerable amount of excitement here in the valley which demands our presence to protect our farms and homes. But, if we don't speak up and defend ourselves, the king and his henchmen will be taxing us out of our businesses, farms and our homes. We must remember, gentlemen and lady, that the Crown's men still carry a vast amount of authority, property and money. We must not forget that Sir Johnny Johnson still resides not far from here at Johnson Hall, while his brother-in-law, Guy Johnson, lives at Guy's Park, carrying the title and influence as the Crown's superintendent for Indian Affairs. And," Attorney Yates hesitated sufficiently long enough for himself to collect his thoughts, and continued, "And, there is no one here, or anywhere who would dare to predict what the Six Nations will do."

Throughout the meeting, Yates' oratorical talents and his knowledgeable responses to his concerned audience's inquiries impressed him. By the time the meeting was ready for adjournment, all of Martha's supply of hard, apple cider punch was exhausted, and the beer steins were empty. Some of the residents of New Palatine, including Karl Heindrick and his associate Cal Swartz, chose to sleep over in the tavern rather than risk the long five mile distance traveling through the snow to their homes. However, George Raab and Harvey Perry decided to escape the tavern's smell of stale beer, and to tramp through the snow to their homes near the center of the hamlet. As expected, Martha Butler offered the mayor and Attorney Yates, as well as Karl and Cal, mugs of hot buttered rum before they adjourned for the evening.

* * *

It was not until the 18th of May, 1775 when an organized *civil war* movement made its first public appearance in Tryon county. Earlier, a Whig committee had been formed at Cherry Valley, but its members were reluctant to speak up, because evidently they were self-conscious, believing that they represented an uninfluential and insignificant local minority. But on May 18th, thanks to Christopher Yates and a number of individuals like him, a group of influential and stalwart county residents congregated in Albany to register their complaints to Albany's Committee of Safety "that this county has for a series of years been ruled primarily by one family, the Johnsons, several branches of which are still strenuously trying to dissuade the people from discussing and debating the Congressional measures. Last week, they went to numerous meetings throughout the Mohawk and Tryon district, appeared with all their dependents; armed to oppose the people considering their grievances. Their numbers being so great, that the harried and unorganized people were struck with terror into most of their hearts. They were so intimidated, they quickly and quietly dispersed keeping thoughts to themselves."

Afterwards, Colonel Guy Johnson scornfully described this meeting as having been called by an *itinerant New England leather-dresser, and conducted by others, if possible more contemptible.* "I had, therefore," Guy Johnson continued, "little inclination to revisit such men, or attend to their absurdities."

Guy Johnson's remarks did little to quell any of the settlers discontent. In fact, Colonel Guy had stoked the fire, which Sir William had started with his latest project for improving his estates and peopling the county, which was being vigorously carried out by his son, Sir John, and sons-in-law, Guy Johnson and Daniel Claus. For the most part, those who had attended the May 18th meeting were descendants of sturdy Palatine recusants, refusing to obey the established authority of the Church of England. In their minds, they had suffered the extremity of ill for conscience sake, and to them the very name of Papist was abominable. For once, not only Guy Johnson, but the entire Johnson clan, failed to fathom the intensity of the Palatine settlers' religious prejudice. Accordingly, Sir John Johnson chose to fortify his Hall and surround himself with a body of Highland Roman Catholics for its defense. To the Palatines, Sir John could not have made a better choice, because they had already learned to dislike the Highlanders, and they detested their religion. Apparently, the Johnsons chose to adopt a defensive stance, and constrain their differences with the Palatines through temperate negotiations. Accordingly, throughout the Colonies the Tories, though numerous, were hesitating and timid, while a certain segment of the Whigs were becoming daring and aggressive.

* * *

By the ravages of pestilence and almost incessant warfare, the once mighty Six Nations of the Iroquois population had dwindled in numbers to less than ten thousand, of whom about one-fifth were warriors. Consequently, they wisely adopted a *stop-and-look* position of the *white man's* civil war.

The Mohawks were considered to be the bravest and most influential of all the Six Nations. Interestingly, they were populated by the fewest numbers, numbering only approximately five hundred warriors, occupying only three small villages or castles as the Mohawks called their settlements. Two of these castles were located on the Mohawk River and one in the Schoharie valley. All three of these villages were almost totally surrounded by white settlements. Nearly all of the Mohawks, even though they were considered some of the fiercest and bravest of the tribes, professed Christianity under the instruction of Reverend John Stuart of the Church of England. Traveling west just beyond the Mohawks' boundary near Oneida Lake, lived the Oneidas in two villages, named *old* and *new* Oneida.

The most the Oneidas could roster out was about two hundred and fifty warriors. About six miles beyond the Oneidas was a Tuscarora village inhabited by about one-hundred men competent enough to bear arms. The Onondagas living on the lake, which currently bares their name, could only gather only approximately one-hundred and fifty warriors. These three tribes, the Oneidas, Onondagas, and Tuscaroras, were closely related by inter-marriages, and had been converted by the Presbyterian missionaries from New England.

The Cayugas, who lived in one relatively large village on a lake, which is currently named Cayuga Lake, could muster only about two hundred fighting men. Just west of the Cayugas' settlement, the Senecas had established a string of their villages which extended from within fifty miles of Cayuga lake to the upper waters of the Ohio River. It was estimated that the Senecas could be counted on for at least one thousand warriors. In addition to these Six Nations, there were the remnants of four allied or vassal tribes from the southward which had settled not long before on lands allotted to them by the Six Nations on the eastern branch of the Susquehanna River. There were with the above mentioned Indian tribes, the Delawares (600) inhabiting the Susquehanna and the Muskingum, the Shawanese (300) on the Scioto, and the Hurons (200) in the Sandusky united *in close alliance* with the earlier mentioned tribes, and were regarded as their *elder brothers.* As a whole the Six Nations and their allied Indians had made considerable advances in civilization, considering where they had originated. At times, one had to wonder who was in a better position to evaluate whether the Indians or the *white men* were the most civilized. According to a Mrs. Grant of Laggan in writing from personal experiences, she asks the question: "Were they savages?" Mrs. Grant repeats her question, "Were they the Indians savages who had fixed habitations; who cultivated rich fields; who built castles (for so they called their not incommodious wooden houses, surrounded with palisades); who planted maize and beans, and showed considerable ingenuity in constructing and adorning their canoes, arms, and clothing? They who had wise though unwritten laws and conducted their wars, treaties, and alliances with deep and sound policy; they whose eloquence was bold and nervous and animated; whose language was sonorous, musical, and expressive; who possessed generous and elevated sentiments, heroic fortitude and unstained probity?"

The Mohawks, whose principle castle was located very near to Johnson Hall, had lived for years in close association with their white neighbors. They even followed Sir William Johnson, who had been received into their tribe, into battle along with Butler, Hare, and Lottridge and other provincial officers. Many of the Mohawks had white blood flowing in their veins, and had gradually adopted the dress and many customs of the whites, and had taken on at least a thin veneer of European civilization. The Mohawks regarded Sir John Johnson, as well as his father Sir William, as one of *their own blood.*

Governor Tryon of New York, too, was very complimentary about the Mohawks; "Nothing less than manifest injury, in my opinion, will drive the Mohawks from their steady attachment to His Majesty's interest. They appear to be actuated as a community by principles which would do honor to the most civilized nations. Indeed, they are in a civilized state, and many of them good farmers."

On the other hand, the Senecas and Cayugas, who lived farthest west and far beyond the white settlements, still rigidly adhered to their ancient rites and customs.

The Native Americans, regardless to which tribe they belonged, made TWO big mistakes .... they believed the *white man* and they drank too much of his liquor!

FOUR

BEHIND THE SCENES

Mohawk Valley
July, 1775

The Whigs along the Mohawk Valley were energized by the news of Bunker Hill. Actually, the Continental Army composed of homespun militia, which included a few good engineers, had the British hemmed in on every land side except Charlestown, and their fortifying of Breed's (not Bunker's) Hill on the evening of June 16-17, 1775 brought on the Battle of Bunker Hill. This was the first stand-up engagement between the rag-tag New England volunteers and the British regulars. Although the Redcoats captured the hill, they paid dearly for their *victory*. The British experienced 1,054 killed and wounded out of the 2,200 engaged had engaged in the battle, as compared to the American losses of 441 out of 3,200 engaged. After the battle, the British General Sir Henry Clinton wrote: "A dearly bought victory, another such battle would have ruined us." British General Thomas Gage wrote ruefully "Those people shew a spirit and conduct against us, they never shewed against the French."

Although the Battle of Bunker Hill was a tactical victory for the British, it was a strategic and moral victory for the Americans, especially for the proud and loyal Whigs, who proved to themselves that they were not simply clerks with quills and ink, or farmers who planted, dug potatoes and milked cows. They had stood up to some of the best troops the British had to offer. The battle aroused a spirit of exultation and confidence throughout the colonies. The Continental Congress requested King George III to interpose his authority to stop the war, repeal the Coercive Acts, and bring about "a happy and permanent reconciliation." This petition, signed by John Hancock and almost every subsequent signer of the Declaration of Independence, was sent to the king in duplicate by two colonial agents, who tried without success to persuade Lord Dartmouth to present the document to the king. They were informed that the king would receive no petition from a Rebel body. The king's reaction was no surprise in that the British government had already heard of Congress's launching Benedict Arnold's expedition against Quebec, which looked like a wanton act of aggression against a loyal and peaceful colony. On August 23, 1775, George III proclaimed that a general rebellion existed, and that "utmost endeavors" should be made "to suppress such a rebellion, and to bring the traitors to justice."

Meanwhile behind the scenes, the pendulum of military activity was being drawn away from the New England coastal areas to upstate New York to where the brilliant British general John Burgoyne, fondly referred to as "Gentleman Johnny," was developing a strategic plan for the British to defeat the Rebels and divide the northern from the southern colonies. The cagey Burgoyne formally entitled his plan "Thoughts for Conducting the War from the Side of Canada." His "Thoughts," as he fondly referred to the plan was ready to be presented to his monarch and friend, King George III, and the king's Council of ministers. Burgoyne had no doubts about the soundness of the plan. Burgoyne's main concern was that his friend and Prime Minister, Lord George Germain, fancied himself a general and military strategist. He could just envision Germain or even the king himself specifying the exact number of troops to be dispatched in his expedition, as well as the number to be retained in Canada.

Burgoyne's main objective was to separate the New England states from the balance of the other American colonies by capturing New York's Mohawk Valley. He recognized that this fertile valley served not only as the gateway to the great western lake country, but also to the territory of the Iroquois Indians. The Mohawk Valley, thanks to its sparsely populated area settled and farmed by Palatines (Germans), Dutch, Irish, and Scotch-Irish, served as the Continental Army's breadbasket; which Burgoyne and the British coveted. For the Rebels, the valley, however, was in a precarious position. Almost the entire region was generally considered as a Tory stronghold. As one historian estimated, "the Loyalists in that (Mohawk) valley were probably more numerous than in almost any other section of the northern states."

The critical obstacle in Burgoyne's strategy for the ultimate capture of the Mohawk valley was to be Fort Stanwix. This *Little Fort in the Wilderness*, as Fort Stanwix was affectionately referred to by the locals, was initially constructed in 1758 as a strong fortifications with bastions believed to be artillery-proof, a covered way and a well-picketed ditch. By the middle 1770's, the fort had deteriorated into almost total decay. General Peter Gansevoort, a competent twenty-eight year old Continental officer, was assigned the command post of the fort, and charged to repair and ready it for any possible attack. Along with his assistant, Lieutenant Colonel Marinus Willet, and a patriot garrison they soon had the fort respectfully restored to a defensible condition. Any force coming from Oswego toward Albany would have to seize the *Little Fort in the Wilderness*.

It was May when Colonel Gansevoort had arrived at Fort Stanwix. Except for having taken part in the Yankee invasion of Canada, Gansevoort's military experience consisted of parading of his militia up and down Albany's main street. However, he came from a dauntless family, a family of courage and iron will. When the young commander frantically plead for troops, ammunition and supplies, and receiving very little in response, Gansevoort made do with what he had. What he had was trees, sod and fish. Day and night, the colonel dispatched his few men out to labor. They choked off Wood Creek with logs, shored up the dilapidated fort with sod, and everybody ate fish. To alleviate his fiancee's worries back in Albany, he wrote to her that he was having a good time fishing. Later on August 6, 1777, this stouthearted, young Fort Stanwix commander ordered the unfurling of the colonies' first "stars and strips" flag in combat, sewed from material from an soldier's wife's red petticoat and an officer's blue cloak.

Most of Burgoyne's associates, including King George III and Lord Germain and others, believed that the plan was brilliantly conceived. Its success all depended upon how well the plan was executed, and what time of the year it would be conducted. The plan called for one expedition to leave from Montreal and travel down through Lake Champlain and Lake George, toward Albany, New York. A second expedition would start from the south in New York City and travel the Hudson River north toward Albany. A third expedition would start at Montreal, sail down the St. Lawrence River, land at Oswego, march eastward, capture Fort Stanwix, and sweep through the valley toward Albany. At Albany, the three expeditions would converge and engage the American forces into a pincers maneuver.

Armed with his confidence and his documented "Thoughts," Gentleman Johnny presented his plan to King George III for his ultimate endorsement in March 1777. Thanks to Germain's early campaigning on Burgoyne's behalf, the ministers were receptive, and the king readily gave his hearty approval. It remained to Lord Germain, in the absence of any general staff, to draft the necessary instructions.

* * *

While General Burgoyne was working diligently upon developing, documenting and promoting his *Thoughts,* Colonel Guy Johnson, Colonel John Butler, and his son Walter Butler had left their homes and held a council with their Indian friends on the shore of Lake Ontario at Oswego. During this meeting, the Troy leaders, along with some of the Indian chiefs, made their way to Montreal and had another conference with Sir Guy Carleton, the British commander in

Canada. The Rebel General, Philip Schuyler, the person for whom the original name (Fort Schuyler) of Fort Stanwix was named in honor of, learned of this meeting. Fearing that some menacing plans against the Mohawk valley were being developed, Schuyler called out the Tryon County Militia under the command of General Nicholas Herkimer. Under Schuyler's orders, Herkimer and the militia marched to Johnson Hall, and met with Sir William Johnson who promised not to engage in hostilities against the Americans. As soon as Herkimer and the militia's back was turned, Sir William reneged on his agreement. Within four months, Johnson, his tenants and other Tories made their way to Canada. In Montreal, strategies were developed with the British against the rebellious Rebels to their South. Sir John Johnson was commissioned a colonel and was charged to raise a Tory regiment to be called the Royal Greens, from the distinctive color of the regiment's uniforms. Colonel John Butler, whose knowledge of several Indian languages, frequently worked in most of the Indians councils up to Sir William's death, as an Indian interpreter, was dispatched to raise a similarly Royal Green clad corps of Tory Rangers who were dispatched to bring terror to the beautiful and strategically located Mohawk Valley. Prior to these instructions, Colonel Butler, who was next in rank to Guy Johnson and Daniel Claus in the department, had been named by Johnson as his deputy during his absence while Sir John and Claus sailed to England in November, much to Carleton's chagrin. At this time, Carleton's instructions was "to preserve the good will of the Indians and retain them in an attitude of absolute neutrality." This alone proved to be a task of supreme difficulty, because the Indian country was extremely overrun with Rebel spies of shapes and sizes. Some were emissaries in the service of the Continental Congress, of whom the missionaries Crosby and Kirkland, their interpreter Deane, were the most zealous and influential. It was reported that these individuals even plotted to capture Fort Niagara where there was a substantial quantity of military stores to tempt an attack. The Indians's confidence was greatly shaken by the *successful* invasion of Canada, which was constantly boasted about to them by these men.

To counteract these overtures, Butler assembled Indian councils after Indian councils with varying degrees of success. He liberally distributed presents and trinkets, and reminded the Indians of "their pledges and their ancient friendship and alliance with the great white king across the big water." There is conclusive evidence that Colonel John Butler obeyed Governor's Carleton's instructions: "speak to them of nothing but peace," until March, 1776, when he received a message requesting him to send down a body of warriors to assist in the recapture of the province. In this campaign, Butler proved himself quite efficient and daringly successful. Together with one hundred Senecas and Cayugas, Butler readily consented to go to Montreal to open a passage for traders and to "make a path," for Colonel Johnson, whom they expected to return shortly from England. Butler's forces were joined with an equal number of Mississaugas, assembled from the north shore of Lake Ontario, and a small contingent of the 8th regiment under Captain Forester.

A small detachment of Americans under the command of General Benedict Arnold, after failing to capture Quebec, fought a series of stubborn retiring actions against Butler's troops from the St. Lawrence to Lake Champlain that consumed most of the summer of 1776. Butler admittedly agreed that Governor Sir Guy Carleton was a capable military officer, but Arnold's energy and foresight in building a small naval fleet on Lake Champlain, and his skill in handling the fleet in the Battle of Valcour Island (opposite Burlington, Vermont) in October 11, 1776, and sending scouting ships scurrying around the island to warn the Americans of the first on-slaught of the British invasion delaying the British long enough to keep them off of Washington's back during the critical summer of 1776. The war in Canada had settled down to duel of wits and munitions between two extremely competent generals, Sir Guy Carleton and Benedict Arnold. Even though Carleton's successor, "Gentleman Johnny" Burgoyne, was much dramatic, it was Carleton's brilliance which defended and held Quebec, chased the Americans out of Canada, and came closer than any other British general to splitting the colonies in half and squelching the "civil war." Some historians believe that Carleton was prepared to smash through the American forces at Crown Point and Ticonderoga, and was better equipped and his strategy was better planned than Burgoyne's. There was only one man standing between Carleton and victory —— Benedict Arnold. In fact, there was no American officer feared more, nor respected by the British command than Benedict Arnold. He had the reputation for persistence, for surprise, and the ability to recover from almost certain jaws of defeat, then inspiring his troops to an unbelievably high energy level to assure an overwhelming victory or to an organized retreat.

Meanwhile, Gentleman Johnny Burgoyne was still promoting his *Thoughts* to the British ministry and the king.

Due to this unexpected diversion, Colonel John Butler believed, as many reasonably thought, that no small share of the campaign's success was due to himself as the organizer of the expedition. Somewhat alienated, Butler began to urge the Six Nations, as a body, to declare that they would not participate any further in the war. In fact, he contrived to strengthen his own influence among the Indians. He knew, without a doubt, that every council meeting he convened was attended by a number of spies hired by the Continental Congress. Some of these spies were white men, but usually they were either Oneida or Delaware Indians, whom it was difficult to discover and exclude. His next task, to identify and to deal with any known Rebel emissaries, was not an easy. Butler quietly organized his own spy network in the major Indian villages in order to collect and to "preserve the good will of the Indians" as Carleton had instructed. One of the ablest of Butler's emissaries was William Caldwell, a young adventurer belonging to a good Tory family in Philadelphia, who had assisted a number of British officers to escape prison and safely guided them through the intervening wilderness to Niagara. Butler was able to enlist as his efficient and trustworthy assistants such men as Barnet Frey, brother of Colonel Hendrick Frey of Tryon county, John Johnson, an Oneida trader of much experience, and William and Peter, half-blood sons of Sir William Johnson. A steady, yet lean, stream of Tory sympathizers, most of whom were able to speak at least one or more of the Indian languages, from New York and Pennsylvania, were settling in with Butler at Niagara.

***

Recognizing Butler as a major threat to the success of the Rebels' cause, General Philip Schuyler approved a $1,000 reward for Colonel John Butler's scalp or person. To add to Schuyler's concern was intelligence reports of the capture of New York City by General Sir William Howe. Howe's subsequent success produced an incredible attitude and confidence among the Indians, that excited some tribes to rise up and immediately attack the Rebel's frontiers. It was at about this time Joseph Brant, who had witnessed Howe's victories and was thoroughly convinced of the power of England, appeared among the Senecas, accompanied by Captain Gilbert Tice, Brant, too, constantly believed in his dream of a great Indian confederacy extending from Detroit to Montreal, independent of, but united in close alliance with England. By the time, Brant had arrived in Niagara with Captain Tice, he had already succeeded in obtaining many assurance of active support, due to his fiery eloquence and sheer determination. Brant, however did not fit into Butler's plans. Reluctantly, the colonel decided to obey Carleton's original instructions, and he received Brant rather coolly. Shortly after the two met, Brant resumed his campaign by traveling from Indian village to Indian village throughout the length and breadth of the Iroquois territory, including the Oneidas, among whom he possessed some personal influence through marriage, urging all he talked with to prepare for hostilities in the spring.

After Brant's village-to-village campaign was completed, he spent most of the winter at Fort Niagara, where on a friendlier footing, he and Seneca Chief Sayengaraghta planned the next campaign. While Sayengaraghta had his eyes on the Wyoming (Pennsylvania) settlements whose leaders had been making some threats against the Indians and who held several of their chiefs in prison, Brant was interested in reclaiming his own Mohawk valley; each equally shared the responsibility in mapping out their strategy.

Meanwhile, a terrific under-current had developed, almost to the point of hatred, between Daniel Claus and John Butler. Claus a prolific memoir writer, scarcely wrote a line that was not meant to discredit John Butler. In his consuming hatred for the man who had usurped his own rightful place (as he believed), Claus counseled with Joseph Brant and his sister Molly, as well as anyone else he believed could help to make Butler look insignificant and inefficient. According to Claus, Butler was an nonentity, an ignoramus, a slothful incompetent. The only thing Butler was good at was spending huge sums of money for which the British and the Tories received nothing in return.

In the spite of Claus's frustration and jealousy of Butler, Governor Carleton still liked Butler and trusted him, stating that he would always give him a good character reference to his successor. Through his serenely appearance, Colonel John Butler had more to be concerned about than Claus's machinations. Butler's wife and children were still virtual prisoners on the Mohawk and his eldest son, Walter, was actually held in irons at Albany. Walter had been captured after the Battle of Oriskany while he was on a secret mission to some of his faithful Loyalists friends in German Flats. Without the invention of some of these friends, he would have had to pay with his life for his activities. Walter did not think so much about his blessings, rather he chose to brood upon the *wrongs* thrust upon him. Completely influenced by Claus, Joseph Brant presented ominous implications for both Colonel John and Walter Butler. Through Claus, Brant was able to obtain necessities for himself and his men from merchants at Niagara. He, therefore, was beholden to either of the Butlers.

In mid-December the British convened another great council at Niagara with their Indian allies. In spite of the meeting being called during the winter, there were nearly three thousand chiefs. sachems and warriors there. During the council meeting, Colonel Mason Bolton, the new commander of Fort Niagara, and John Butler made sure that the Indians received all they could eat, and promised them all that they could drink would be delivered to their villages. Meanwhile, consoling the bereaved Senecas, covering the grave of each fallen warrior with scalps and wampum, and making light of Burgoyne's *small disappointment* (his defeat at Saratoga). Regardless, Bolton and Butler declared that the king had stated that "we have just begun to fight, and he will show the

Rebels no mercy." Presents where exchanged, amounting to more than thirty-four thousand pounds. "We are determined to make the War our own," declared the gratified Sayengaraghta. Captain Bolton complimented Joseph Brant saying: "Joseph….. has been of great service & deserves every favour I can shew him."

FIVE

NEW COMMAND

Fort Niagara, July 26, 1775

On the warm July 26, 1775 afternoon, Major John Butler escorted one hundred Mohawk warriors to Fort Niagara's wharf bringing the colonies' first civil war between the Whigs and Tories, who were gradually becoming known as Rebels and Loyalists respectively, to Fort Niagara. As the prize-winning historian, Samuel Eliot Morison, states in *The Oxford History of the American People:*
> The War of American Independence was a true "civil war.") [author's quotation marks].
>
> In America itself a strong minority who called themselves Loyalists, and by their enemies were called Tories, supported the mother country; and there was much fighting between Loyalists and Patriot partisan (guerrilla) bands. In England itself there was no fighting, apart from the exploits of John Paul Jones in coastal waters; yet sympathy with

the American cause was widespread. Vice Admiral Augustus Keppel and General Sir Jeffery Amherst refused to serve against America; General Harry Conway refused to "draw his sword in that cause;" the Earl of Effingham, colonel of a regiment ordered to America, turned in his commission because "the duties of a soldier and a citizen" had become "inconsistent." Even Gentleman Johnny Burgoyne's friend, Charles James Fox, the one he had made a bet with on Christmas Day, 1776 in London's ultra-fashionable Brook's Club, adopted blue and buff for the colors of the Whig opposition because they were those of General Washington's uniform.

………The number of the Loyalists varied from colony to colony. They were strongest in New York, [especially] New York City, partly because the city was occupied by the British after the Battle of Long Island and held by them throughout the war; party because New York had an aristocratic social structure. They [Loyalists] were weakest in Connecticut, Massachusetts, and Virginia, where the radical leaders were talented, respectable men and good organizers.

……estimates of as high as 50 percent of the total population have been made for New York and as low as 8 percent for Connecticut.

…..a guess is that not more than 10 percent of the white population of the United States was actively Loyalist; that about 40 percent was actively Patriot, and about 50 percent indifferent or neutral.

......the significant fact is that nowhere, except Georgia and in occupied seaports, were the British able to organize a Loyalist civil government.

Few historical sites in America had experienced as much military occupation as Fort Niagara's slightly elevated peninsula commanding the confluence of the four Great Lakes that then flows south and east into the Lake Erie. On the eastern shore of Lake Erie, the waters amass from the interior of the continent and flows into the Niagara River racing and tumbling down a series of rapids and takes fearful plunges 327 feet from Lake Erie's high level down to the level of Lake Ontario and over the renown Niagara Falls, the third largest waterfall on earth and creating a great gorge and whirlpool rapid in its wake commonly referred to as "the Throatway," occasionally referred to as "Thundergate." Once free of the cataracts and the Niagara gorge, the waters quietly enter Lake Ontario, the last of the Great Lakes, and ultimately flow along the St Lawrence River into the Atlantic Ocean.

The earliest fort discovered so far on the Throatway portage, was built c.160 A.D. by the Moundbuilders of the Ohio-Indiana. A legend tells of a virgin being sent over the falls in a canoe each spring as a sacrifice to Hawenio, the Majestic Voice, symbolizing the battles for control of the portage that occurred between 160 and 1600 A.D. The early importance of the location of Fort Niagara was due almost entirely to its portage position around the huge falls. During this point, the Great Lakes receded to almost their present shorelines. Scores of palisaded villages overlooked bottom-land fields of maize, pole beans, pumpkins, squash, and herbs, while fruit trees, jungles of berry bushes, and acres of grapevines decked the forest edge, One tribal alliance of invaders to this "country of plenty" called themselves the Hurons. These raiders came through the Throatway, and conquered the Ontario-St. Lawrence paddleway. Some of the conquered Huron refugees fled south through the Adirondacks toward the Mohawk and Hudson idyllic valleys.

Amazingly, five regional tribes of similar beliefs, mores, and social philosophy evolved into a Five Nations confederacy and gained control of the Throatway portage, as well as the Mohawk River. Throughout the mid-seventeenth century, the Senecas, who were *guardians of the west,* did not populate the Niagara area heavily, thus inviting their warlike Huron neighbors to challenge the Senecas' territorial rights. These Huron invasions called for Seneca counterstrikes, which resulted in the ruthless destruction of Huron communities beginning in earnest during the 1640's. These ferocities caused the Hurons to name the confederacy the collective hate-name, *Iroquois,* meaning *Vipers who Strike without Warning.* However, the Dutch and British chose to use the formal *The Five Nations* in their documents and at council orations. By 1660, the Five Nations controlled the upper St. Lawrence valley, the Ontario basin, the Niagara portage, and the Lake Erie shores. The name, Niagara, is attributed to the Senecas, who named the falls and its thirty-mile channel *Oughniagara* meaning *The Throat*, controlled the portage trail around the Niagara Falls thus forcing the French and their Indian allies to use the deadly Ottawa River-Georgian Bay route to the Michigan and Wisconsin fur lands.

In 1666, a twenty-three year-old French, Robert Cavelier de La Salle, arrived in Montreal with the intention to establish the providence of New France to enable the French to control Lake Ontario and the Niagara portage, and to confine the British to their settlements along the Atlantic Ocean's coastline. Within a year, La Salle had established a hamlet near the Niagara rapids, convinced a few families to settle there. Surprisingly, he had also successfully persuaded a group of Seneca hunters to spend the winter there. As time passed, it was reported that more than one million dollars worth of beaver, mink, elk, bear, bison, deer, and otter pelts were shipped on the St. Lawrence River with most coming from the Seneca, Cayuga and Onondaga. Consequently, La Salle and his fort angered the Mohawks, Oneidas and the Hudson valley traders, as well as the Montreal merchants who depended upon the Ottawa-Georgian trade. Tensions became so acute that throughout the Mohawk castles there was constant plotting to raid the fort and hatchet La Salle, while some residents of Montreal were threatening to poison the *young upstart.* Taking heed of the situation, La Salle resigned his post and returned to France in 1677.

Early in the 1700's, one of La Salle's replacements, Louis-Thomas Chabert de Joncaire, proposed that the Confederacy construct a *trading post* on the Niagara River to alleviate the Five Nations' suspicions. Chabert justified his decision by promising to construct a place for trade, calling it a *House of Peace,* where the Iroquois could barter for furs and meet representatives of the French king. Finally in 1725, the Iroquois agreed to permit the French to begin Chabert's plan. Next came the most formidable portion of the Frenchman's scheme to construct the "House of Peace," which would be sufficiently strong enough to resist any military attack, yet not give the appearance of a true fortification. The French decided the solution was to build a large stone house surrounded by a simple wooden stockade, which they referred as a "machicolated house," referring to the overhanging dormers of the second floor that allowed defenders to fire down upon attackers.

In the 1740's the rivalry between the French and British continued. The neutrality of the Iroquois prevented a British attack, and also prevented the French from using their "House of Peace" as a launching pad for attacks upon the British controlled western frontiers in the New York Colony. The surrounding prairie, forest and navigable waterways west of Niagara resurrected La Salle's dream of a New France which would dwarf France itself. To accomplish La Salle's dream, the French believed that the first essential step was to control Lake Ontario, but the Iroquois controlled the Niagara portage. Unfortunately, for the Iroquois, the plague and their abuse of alcohol continued to be far more effective weapons for the British, as well as the French in their efforts to influence the Five Nations.

By the spring of 1756, the House of Peace was greatly enlarged with earthwork defenses, and filled with new buildings, including barracks, storerooms, powder magazine, and even a church constructed of wood and stone. During the following two years, the House of Peace (Fort Niagara) garrison busily supported their Iroquois allies in raids against the Pennsylvania and Virginia frontiers. During these years, the Iroquois, which now included the

Tuscaroras as their sixth nation, remained relatively neutral. Their neutrality all came to crushing end late in 1758 when Sir William Johnson, the British Indian-Superintendent, persuaded the new Six Nation Confederacy to join with the British in attacking Fort Niagara. With 2,000 British regulars and 1,500 Iroquois warriors, Sir William himself led the attack and landed four miles east of the fort and laid siege to La Salle's dream of a New France. For more than two weeks the 600 garrisoned Frenchmen courageously defended their fort against constant pounding from the heavy British batteries. Meanwhile, the British were busily digging trenches toward the fortress's walls. By July 24, 1758, the trenches were only eighty-yards from the fort's bulwarks, and the stockade and its garrison were on the verge of collapse. The fort's garrison and its commanding officer, Captain Pierre Pouchot, desperately held their posts believing that reinforcements from Detroit and the Ohio Valley would shortly arrive. Indeed on July 23rd, 1,500 Frenchmen and Indians started down the Niagara River from Lake Erie intent on fighting their way through the British lines to the beleaguered fortress. The cagey British leader, Sir William Johnson, expecting reinforcements despatched a detachment of Redcoats to block the road at a place one mile up the river known as *La Belle Famille*. The next morning the French charged against the Redcoats, who gallantly stood their ground while firing well disciplined volleys into the French ranks. Within twenty minutes the decisive battle was over; the French and Indian survivors together with their decimated relief force were sent fleeing toward Lake Erie. After hearing of the rout, Captain Pouchot asked for terms of surrender. On July 25, 1759, the French surrendered Fort Niagara to the British.

After the victory, the energetic and bawdy Irishman, Sir William Johnson, who was accepted by most the valley residents as a true *White Indian* (a white man with an Indian wife, later sometimes referred as "squaw man"), was awarded a knighthood, plus 100,000 acres of land accumulating more wealth than the Van Rensselaers and the Schuylers combined. It is legendary that Johnson's wife, Molly Brant, and sister of Mohawk Chief Joseph Brant, held reign over her lord's household and until his last days. Some allege that

Sir William sired more than 700 half-breeds, and scores of Mohawk Dutch. As could be expected from such an energetic opportunist, Sir William practiced the tired-and-true principles, which included the lure of rum or applejack, half breeds, and the contemptible dependence on white-man goods, practiced by most of the White Indian traders, which had become the British policy after the conquest of New Netherlands, in 1664 and its reorganization as His Majesty's Colony of New York. The Royal Governors of New York discovered military engagements against the Iroquois were largely things of the past, because the British, especially Sir William who manipulated the Iroquois with the above mentioned tried-and-true principles supplemented with the Indians' growing dependence upon the new iron-and-gunpowder economy. Smuggling and its lore of new wealth was another White Indian scheme the British used to tie their knot tighter around the Iroquois.

After defeating the French at Fort Niagara, Sir William left 500 militiamen at the fort to repair and protect it from French raids from either the Upper (Great) Lakes or Louisiana, unfortunately, the frontier's two old dependables, disease and interracial relations created major problems for the fort's command. Some of the fort's boisterous garrison were attracted to and courted Seneca maidens. As a result. there were accusations of rape, counter-accusations of the *pox*. Most of the fort's garrison had been reared in small hamlets and villages where their parents had *very carefully* taught them that "the only good Indian was a dead one." This *White Supremacy* doctrine, which was supplemented with rampant scandalous chatter about the Six Nations' tortures, cannibalism, and "very sexy wenches," infected the newly arrived Scot, Irish, and German immigrants adding to the newly commissioned Colonel John Butler's troubles as he was escorted by one hundred Mohawk warriors to the fort's warf to assume the command of Fort Niagara on July 26, 1775, thus beginning America's first "civil war" between America's Tories and its Whigs.

SIX

AROUND THE CRACKER BARREL

August 27, 1775 in Kerchner's General Store Located on Main Street in the Hamlet of New Palatine along the Mohawk Valley

It was nearly seven o'clock in the evening, Wilhelm Kerchner, owner of New Palatine's only general store, was anxious to lock up, because he had a very important eight o'clock meeting at the home of a Mr. Shoemaker some two or three miles east. To Wilhelm Kerchner, Shoemaker was a very important person having been a justice of peace under the commission of King George III, and was a man of prominence in Tory circles. Late in the afternoon, Kerchner had sent wife, Sarah, and daughter Helena home informing them that he was about to close, and that it would not arrive at home until about ten o'clock, because he wanted to take an inventory of the store's stock so as to make a list of purchases he needed in order to restock the store. When he told Sarah the reason he was going to be

STEPS TOWARD FREEDOM

late, she had looked rather questionably toward him. In the Kerchner family, no one questioned Wilhelm's word or authority. His *women* left the store without making an utterance, but thinking *what is he up to?*

"Now," Wilhelm said to himself, "they're gone, and now I've got to get rid of this stupid smithy, George Raab and my assistant Harvey Perry who are always sitting around the iron, pot-belly stove, occasionally, sampling soda crackers from an open barrel with a transparent cover.

"Say, Wilhelm," said the stout, burly smithy with his shirt unbuttoned down to his navel and exposing his silver-colored hairy chest, "did you hear about someone named Barnet Davenport from Connecticut in the American forces who killed a Tory named Malley, his wife, and two children in Litchfield County?"

"No, I didn't hear about anybody in Connecticut, I've been too busy satisfying the needs of the residents here in New Palatine to be interested with those New England rabble rousers," snarled Wilhelm in his broken English which he was trying to improve. "How would you or anybody else know about what's going on in Connecticut?" he said as he tried to give signs of closing to his fellow Palatines. They, too, were wondering what was getting under Kerchner's felt hat, because he was usually anxious to talk about religion, farming, and especially politics with them. In fact, it was their usual Friday night gab session around this very stove and cracker barrel where they would usually congregate. Many times they were joined by Karl Heindrick, Cal Swartz. Even Nicholas Herkimer, who had recently been appointed brigadier general and had been busy lately drilling the Tryon County Militia, would occasionally drop in for a *taste* of liquid malt or whatever.. On such occasions, the general would make arrangement with Martha Butler for sleeping quarters in her Heidelberg Tavern, he didn't particularly enjoy the long ride to his home near a place called the *little falls* in the Mohawk River.

"Well, this morning," started the muscular smithy twisting the hair on his chest, "this man rode up to my shop. Said he'd been riding all the way from Litchfield County, and his horse was going lame if he didn't get a new set of shoes on him. To nail four shoes on a horse, as you know takes quite a long time. The Yankee seemed to want to talk," informed Raab as he lifted the brim of his leather cap, and scratched his forehead, "so I let him talk."

"What did he tell you?" quizzed Kerchner's jovial assistant manager, Harvey Perry, as he gained interest in his buddy's story. Everybody in New Palatine used to joke about these two men, whose families along with Heindricks had crossed the Atlantic Ocean, for weeks suffering together in the crowded in the *Lyon* the ship entered New York Harbor on June 13, 1710. Almost every time one of the men would be seen, the other one would soon be there, except during normal working hours which were from 6 o'clock in the morning to 6 or 7 o'clock at night. But on Sundays, holidays and other special days not only were the men together, but their wives completed the faithful God-fearing foursome. About one Sunday a month, their families would travel the twenty miles it took to travel to German Flats and back to attend the area's only Dutch Reformed Church.

The smithy continued, "Well, as his story goes, a Connecticut soldier of the American forces; someone with the name of Barnet Davenport was hunting Tories. He found a Tory named Malley and killed him. Then he went into Malley's house, and killed Malley's wife and his two children. After all of that," the smithy took a deep breath and continued, "he plundered their home. In order to conceal his crime, Davenport burned the Malley's home along with the corpses. Shortly thereafter, some of the locals discovered Davenport was wearing some of the Malley family's clothes. They captured Davenport and arrested, and quickly tried him. During his trial, he yelled *you damn Rebels don't know what you're doing, that's one less Tory family we have to deal with.* In the trial's attendance were some of Colonel Daniel Morgan's frisky riflemen on their way from Virginia to Massachusetts to join the main army. These men had been amusing themselves as they traveled along by *chasin' Tories.*"

Wilhelm cringed when he heard Raab's last remark, fighting to keep his emotions hidden, especially, after the smithy had completed the sentence with a slight snicker.

"It seems that Morgan's men were fascinated with a brand new discipline they had learned about while they were coming up from the south. As I recall they called it *tarred and feathered*. Somehow or other they convinced the court to tar and feather Davenport."

"We all know what the Bible tells us to do," declared Harvey, as his two friends directed their attention toward him. Perry knew that he would have to be careful on what he said, not to offend his authoritarian employer. "The Bible says," he repeated, "An eye for an eye, and a tooth for a tooth, so I guess they had every right to hang him," cautiously concluded Wilhelm's assistant manager.

"But what makes this story different than any other one I've ever heard," continued the smithy, "before they strung Davenport up, they gave him two live geese, and made him stand in the settlement's common picking the feathers off the geese, and placing the feathers in a burlap bag. With the geese squawking, Davenport trying to hold the geese and pick them at the same time. This comical sight attracted a large crowd, and the crowd was laughing and making fun of the poor bugger. After Davenport had fulled bag with feathers, the Tory leader told him to let the geese go free, and to strip himself of all his clothes, and paint himself with the tar. After he had completely covered himself with tar, he was told to empty the bag of feathers on the ground, and then roll around in the feathers. Finally, after all the feathers were stuck to Davenport's body, a group of men began chasing him around the common, while all the men, women and children laughed and yelled for the chasers to catch him. Finally, they caught the poor devil right under the hanging tree, there some persons had pulled up a stubborn old jackass. They hoisted Davenport astride the jackass, tied a hangman's knot around his neck, and gave a few jabs to the jackass's rear-end with a pitchfork. The jackass kicked up his hind feet, and threw Davenport up in the air. He was left swinging in the breeze, while the jackass headed for the tall timbers, and the townspeople laughed hysterically. From what my customer told me," continued the smithy, "all the people in the huge crowd declared a holiday, and celebrated the rest of the day at the local tavern."

"Killing a whole family and burning their home, that bloodthirsty murderer and thief deserved what they gave him," snarled Kerchner as he bounced up from the barrel he was sitting on. "I've got to get the hell out here. You, Harvey," he stared toward his assistant manager, "when you and Raab get through sitting around here and shooting the bull-shit, lock up the store, because I've got an important meeting which I must attend."

"Bloody murderers," Kerchner kept muttering to himself as he walked out the front door. After he had closed the store front door, the store owner made his statement more pronounced, "Those damn Yankee murderers! Just wait, they'll get the justice they deserve."

* * *

Just about five miles west from Kerchner's General Store, about half a mile off the King's Highway, an entirely different conversation was being held in Karl and Rebecca Heindrick's living room of their very substantial farm home constructed almost entirely of stone. Karl and Rebecca were relating for their fourteen year old son's, Walter, benefit about his grandfather Ulrich Heindrick. It seems that Karl's father, Ulrich, had been murdered and his wooden framed home had been torched to the ground during the famous November 12, 1757 massacre in the Mohawk valley when a collection of French and Indians staged a devastating raid into the valley. After returning from New Palatine's smithy shop and its general store, Karl and Rebecca discovered that Ulrich had been scalped and murdered, and his home burnt to ground. It was then and there that Karl vowed that they were going to remain on their property, but they would build a stone house which would be more fire resistant to such destruction; no more wooden buildings for him and his family.

"Tell me more about my grandfather Ulrich," requested Walter. "You have told me about the time his parents brought him here to America in the middle of 1710. As I recall, you had mentioned that he was only about nine years old."

"That's correct, my son," confirmed Karl. "Even though your grandfather was only a young boy, he would occasionally tell me that those years were extremely trying times. During those years you must remember that all of the Palatines, whom the British had shipped over to America, came as indentured servants of the British, who had total control in counting the amount of supplies and food issued to the Palatines. They were also the only ones who established the prices for which to charge the Palatines for the food and supplies they were supposedly issued. During those few years, all of the Palatines, children as well as adults, were forced to help with the British fanciful experiment to tap the pine trees for their tar to be used in sealing their naval ships' hulls in a place called Livingston Manor, New York, just about a hundred miles north of New York City. There they were also to harvest many tall pine trees for ships' masts and yard arms for the British naval ships. Our ancestors never knew much about the masts and yard arms collected, because they were busily tapping the pine trees and processing the pine resin into tar." As an after further thought, Karl continued, "after tapping all of those pine trees, perhaps that may have been one of the reasons your grandfather wanted to plant that long lane of maple trees from our home out to the Kings Highway. Your Grandfather Ulrich really enjoyed the process of tapping, collecting the maple sap, and boiling it down into maple syrup every Spring. As a matter of fact, you know that I do, too! Always will," he acknowledged as he reached for a small round flat cake of maple sugar lying in a pewter tray on the low table near his chair.

"That entire manufacturing of naval supplies project really didn't make much sense, when you think about it," stated Rebecca silently admitting that she, too, enjoyed the sugaring time. "First of all, the British wanted the resin from the pine trees. In the meanwhile, they were cutting down the same type of trees for ship masts and yard arms."

"Well, needless to say," explained Walter's father, "the experiment was not profitable, and became a total failure. The British had to chalk this endeavor up to experience. To their dismay, they still had their Palatine servants on their hands. On the 22nd day of September of 1712, the British announced that they were closing down the entire project, literally the British turned the Palatines loose from their bonds. Now, remember Walter, that was in the middle of September just when the frost was on the pumpkins and squash, and the apples were ready for harvesting; meaning the winter was just around the corner. Some of the Palatines had been attracted by William Penn's marketing scheme to settle in Pennsylvania. Others were lured to upstate New York and the Mohawk valley. As you can guess, your Grandfather Ulrich ventured to the Mohawk valley, and settled on this very land, which reminded him so much of his homeland. He had come from in Sandhausen, Baden, Germany."

"Occasionally, I have heard you refer to your brother," stated Walter. "As I understand it, Grandfather Ulrich had only one child. You!" He stared at his father, and asked, "What is the correct number? Did you have a brother?" asked the puzzled teenager.

"Karl, why don't you tell our son the entire story of your parents and your birth," suggested Walter's mother.

"You're right, Rebecca. I do believe that it's about time Walter hears the entire story," agreed the forty-six year old Palatine farmer and cheese maker. "Before I start let's serve ourselves with some hot cider, along with some of your mother's delicious maple sugar and hickory nut cookies."

"That sounds great!" declared Walter, following his parents to the sizable farm kitchen with its open fireplace.

While Rebecca was pouring the steaming hot cider from the cast iron kettle hanging in the fireplace, Walter and his father were busily helping themselves from Rebecca's earthenware cookie jar. As soon as they had satisfied their quest, they returned to the rustic living room with its dark, polished wooden furniture. Karl and Rebecca returned to their maple rocking chairs which Ulrich had fashioned during the long cold winters after his wife, Elizabeth, had died. Walter settled himself upon a thick, black bear rug spread in front of the fireplace. The fireplace's low glow sent dancing shadows on the wall behind them as they settled themselves around the fireplace.

"I guess I should go back to the time when my father, Ulrich, and my mother, Elizabeth, first met," started the proud Palatine father. "As I have already told you, everyone of the Palatines had to work in the Livingston Manor British naval supply project located in what I would call downstate in what is called the Catskill Mountains. That's when my parents first met; when they were in their very early teens. In fact, they were just about your present age," he added as he nibbled on a cookie, and took a sip of the warm cider. "Their attraction for each other continued, even after their parents had moved to the Mohawk valley. Needless to say, they continued to court each other over the years. In due time, they married. After nearly five years of married life, and never having any children. One day my mother surprised my father saying that she believed she was pregnant. After a week or so, my mother confirmed her pregnancy to my father. When my father heard my mother's words, he exclaimed that the Lord has blessed us in all ways possible, but now He has given us His ultimate gift."

Karl took another bite of his cookie, sipped his lukewarm cider, and returned to his story, "To make a long story short, my parents' neighbors, Herman and Louisa Schultz, and their servant, Miss Georgia Franklin, who had a two-month old son, agreed to assist my mother during her delivery period. Miss Franklin was a brown-skinned lady, and I understand she was a stately, rather attractive young lady in her early twenties; interestingly, her eyes were hazel-colored. When the day arrived, and my mother went into labor. In the middle of night, your grandfather jumped astride his old plow horse, and rode bareback three miles to the Schultz's farm. Mr. Schultz hustled up and hitched a horse to their buckboard, and Mrs. Schultz and Miss Franklin hopped into the backseat, and arrived our family home just as my mother was having regular contractions. While the ladies were with my mother, my father was having a nervous fit hearing my mother cry, and Herman Schultz tried to do whatever he could to assist and console my father. In fact, I wouldn't be surprised that they might have a sipped a little your grandfather's hard cider. After a few hours, the screaming and crying stopped. Suddenly, the men heard a different kind of cry. A baby's cry! Me! Then my father with Mr. Schultz rushed up the stairs into the bedroom. They saw Miss Franklin placing the baby in the cradle which my father had constructed years before. Then Miss Franklin rushed back to the bedside to assist Mrs. Schultz with my mother. Covered with perspiration, my mother was moaning and crying, and then she let out a sudden and loud yell. No one else in the room spoke a word! Occasionally, the silence was broken by my baby cries, or my mother's groans and moans. All the while my father was holding my mother's hand. I was never told what Herman Schultz was doing. He may have decided that it was best he just got lost. Frantically, Mrs. Schultz demanded my father go quickly and get some more clean sheets, and her husband to bring more hot water. This they did! They quickly returned, and gave the sheets and water to Mrs. Schultz and Miss Franklin. They both asked if there was anything more they could do. As my father told me much later, Mrs. Schultz said sharply, young man if you believe in the Lord Jesus Christ, you get right down on your knees, and pray for the Lord to help all of us. At the same time, my father has since told me, that he thought the night would never end. He prayed, prayed again, and again, while the women were frantically trying to staunch my mother's bleeding. After about three hours, the exhausted ladies came out of the bedroom with their heads lowered and arms dangling down along the sides of their blood-soaked dresses. They had tried their best, but it wasn't good enough. I guess it was God's will!" Karl lowered his head.

His son, Walter, asked, "How did Grampa Ulrich take care of you? How did he fed you?"

"At the time, my father told me that he was really beside himself," confessed Karl. "Fortunately, Mrs. Schultz and Miss Franklin had been discussing this possible problem, and Aunt Georgia, as I used to call Miss Franklin, had told my father that she would be mighty proud to wet nurse me, since she was already nursing her two month old son, George. In addition, both Herman and Louisa Schultz helped in every way possible. In reality, I never knew any mother other than Aunt Georgia. Everything and everybody acted as our arrangement was as natural as the pine needles and the pine cones hanging from the pine trees," Karl admitted. Stopping for a moment place another log on the dying embers of the fire and proceeded, and empty the remaining lukewarm cider in his mug. Leaning forward with his elbows on his knees, and bend toward his son, the very assured father said to his beloved son, "There's an old saying which I've heard many times. Perhaps your grandfather may have told me, regardless it goes something like this: *you never miss what you have never had.* I guess that is how I adjusted. As for your Grandfather Ulrich, his adjustment was much more different," Karl concluded.

"From that time on," inserted Walter's mother, "your father and Aunt Georgia's son, George, were raised as brothers."

"How?" quizzed Walter. "How can they be brothers? One is white and the other is black!"

"You see, my son," his father responded, "there's one basic rule your Grandfather Ulrich taught George and me which he thought everybody should be guided by, and that rule is: *We're all God's children.* He further explained this philosophy that *it doesn't make one bit of difference whether we're white, black, brown or yellow, we're still all God's children.* My father, your Grandfather Ulrich, and Aunt Georgia, God bless them, never let skin color differences ever enter into our discussions or decisions. In fact at times. I believe that my father and Aunt Georgia were as close as any husband and wife. We all loved and respected each other. I know for a fact that my brother George and I were color-blind as far as to the color of our skins was concerned.

"While living with my father and me, Aunt Georgia, told us many heart wrenching stories about how Negroes she knew had been treated. There's one story, which I especially remember, which happened in 1741 to a Spanish vessel, which was partly manned with Negroes. The ship had been brought into the New York City harbor as a prize, and all of these blacks were condemned in the Court of Admiralty as slaves, and were sold at a public auction. Some of these men demanded their freedom, because in their country they were considered *freemen*, and they protested that they should not be sold as slaves. Due to some unknown circumstances or other, a fire broke out in the house of one of the purchasers of one of the *Spanish Negroes*. Everyone started to yell the *Take up the Spanish Negroes*. Immediately, all of these *slaves* were all incarcerated. Since the fire had occurred in the house of a purchaser of one of the Negroes, rumors were spread about *that the wicked Spanish Negroes were trying to burn down the city.* They were brought swiftly to trial based upon the testimony of a *common informer* named Mary Burton, who later it was learned was rewarded a sum of one hundred dollars from the city authorities. The prisoners had no counsel, while the prosecuting Attorney General, who was assisted by two members of the bar, appeared against them. To say the least, the evidence against them had very little consistency and was very weak with only circumstantial evidence from Mary Burton the only witness. One of the prosecuting lawyers said to the jury:

> The monstrous ingratitude of the black tribe is what exceedingly aggravated their guilt; their slavery among us is generally oftened with great indulgence.

"The prisoners were immediately convicted, and were sentenced by the Court to a brutal punishment, to be burned to death. In ordering the prisoners to death, the Judge said, *You, abject wretches, the outcast of the nations of the earth, are treated here with tenderness and humanity!* The prisoners pleaded their innocence and absolutely denied any knowledge of any plot whatever, but when they were removed from the courtroom for execution at the stake, the poor creatures were extremely terrified. They were chained to the stake, and when the executioner was ready to apply the torch, they admitted all that was *required* of them. An feeble attempt was made to procure a reprieve; but by then a great multitude had assembled to witness the execution. Excitement had reached such a high-pitched pinnacle, that it was considered utterly impossible to risk returning the prisoners into prison. As they say, *the show must go on!* They were, accordingly, burned at the stake."

"I can't believe that such inhuman deeds were committed here in America," declared Walter. "Just because of their color of their skins."

"And these *noble* authorities," sarcastically Rebecca added, "probably call themselves *good Christians*. Dearest husband, please tell Walter the rest of the story about you and George Franklin."

"When George and I was about ten years old, George was just two months older than me, my father and I had a complete shock when we looked out one of our home's front windows and saw Aunt

Georgia and George walking down the long dirt, maple tree lined lane toward the King's Highway hand-in-hand with a dark man. You must remember George and I were brought up as brothers. We lived and acted like brothers. In fact, we made each other *as blood brothers in Indian fashion.* I was devastated to say the least! The only true friend and brother I'd ever had. And I'm certain that my father and Aunt Georgia had a special thing going," he concluded.

"Why didn't your father run out and ask them where and why they were going," asked Walter.

"You would have to understand how and what your grandfather believed," stated Karl. "He believed something like: *if it was God's will, and everything would be healed in due time.* Maybe someday we'll meet again," he added wistfully.

"The main reason your father and I wanted to discuss this story about your grandfather, his housekeeper, and her son," stated Walter's mother, "is that your father and I have been discussing the disagreeable turn of events and attitudes developing throughout part of the Mohawk valley."

"As you have heard the New Englanders have started a military conflict with the British in Lexington and Concord on April 19, 1775," added his father. "What your mother and I are concerned about is that this military action does not appear to be just between the British and the colonists. Rather from what we have heard in and around the hamlet from the persons we've been talking with, there appears to be strong divided loyalties even between families and neighbors, and even within families. And, don't forget the black population. In Albany County alone, ten percent of the county's total population of 40,000 is black, and if the New England affairs erupt into a massive military contest, I'm certain the blacks will play an important part. They're even talking about something that the New York Assembly calls *manumission* to be used as an incentive for the blacks to join the state's militia forces."

"That's better than what the Jews are allowed to do," Rebecca inserted. "I've read that in New Netherlands, and before its name was changed to New York City, the Jews were barred from joining the militia. What is further sad and unbelievable is the Jews were not allowed to own real estate, and yet some blacks were allowed and often did own their real estate. In fact, I understand that some *free blacks* are really free; they even have their own indentured servants." Rebecca placed her cider mug to her lips, then realized that there was no cider left, she longingly looked toward her husband. Karl read her silent message; went to the fireplace and refilled her empty mug. "You see, my son, some people can be and are very cruel. At times, I think that some people just enjoy finding wrong with some people, just to fill their own insecurity void. Some people may make fun of you by calling you naive, or plain stupid. Your father have always let the *Golden* Rule be our guide: *Do unto others, as you would them do unto you."*

"Thank you, mother and father, for sharing all of this information with me," Walter said as he drained the last drop of cold cider from his earthen mug. "You've given me a lot to digest. I think I'll take Grampa Ulrich's advise, and let the Lord show me the way. His advice may come like a bolt of lightning, or it may take as long as it took those maples trees he planted along both sides of the lane to the King's Highway."

SEVEN

END JUSTIFIES THE MEANS

In the Mohawk Valley
After the Lexington and Concord Scrimmages

If the scrimmages in and about Lexington and Concord were to be known as the proverbial *shots heard around the world,* the unexpected death of Sir William Johnson at eight o'clock in the evening of July 11, 1774 had sent just as powerful reverberations throughout the Loyalists' communities in the Mohawk valley, and even more devastating uneasiness throughout the Confederacy of the Six Nations.

At the time of his death, Sir William's was one of the largest British land holders in America. Of course, after July 11, 1774, his admitted son, Sir John Johnson, inherited Johnson Hall and the large surrounding estate, the lands around Onondaga Lake, beside most of his father's personal property. At the time, Sir John, who was thirty-two years of age, was a comparative stranger to the people, having lived much of his life with in Albany or New York City before and after his marriage to Miss Watts, an heiress and lady of fashion.

During these years, two-thirds of all of New York City was owned by Loyalists, consisting of wealthy merchants, proprietors of feudal manors, and adherents of the Church of England, which was more numerous than elsewhere.

Sir John's sisters, one of whom had married her cousin Guy Johnson of Guy Park, the other sister married Colonel Daniel Claus, each receiving 14,000 acres. Sir William's second wife whom he supposedly married Indian style, Miss Molly, as she was usually styled, was liberally provided for, and to each of his other admitted children, he bequeathed 1,500 pounds and 300 acres, and a like quantity of land to each of his four sisters and brothers, and to Joseph Brant and to Joseph's brother. In fact, there was an enormous quantity of land held by a few active Loyalists, which be parceled out among their followers.

Sir William was a completely different person than his son, Sir John. He was a frontiersman. Sir William started his life as a trader along the Mohawk valley. During the French and Indian War, he abandoned this profession to accept the position to manage Indian affairs for the British. His opinions concerning the Indians seemed to be guided by a single-minded philosophy, *we enjoy the most security when they (the Indians) are divided amongst themselves.* His feelings toward the Indians ran the spectrum from a friendly opinion to sheer pity. Generally, Sir William was considered a *white politician* who treated the Indians well and fairly with his decisions and trinkets, and often fighting their battles with governmental officials or between tribal disputes. Even though his primary loyalty was to his first love of land speculating, no one ever one questioned his loyalty to the king of England. This baronet, who was constantly working on *official duty on behalf of the Indians and on the authority of the king,* conducted a relatively secret personal life. Even though he never had a legal wife, he fathered three children with a rather quiet and undemanding young German servant girl named Catherine Weissenberg. It had been rumored that Sir William married her as she lay dying of tuberculosis on her deathbed in April, 1759.

Soon after Catherine's death Sir William did not waste much time before he met in Canajoharie, Joseph Brant's twenty-three or twenty-four year old attractive and very intelligent and energetic sister, Molly Brant. In addition to her beauty and intellect, Molly had numerous other attractions for this crude politician and land speculator. Her step-father, Brant, a sachem of the lordly Turtle clan and leader of the Mohawks, still possessed rich holdings of land along the Mohawk River and vast hunting grounds to the north. It took Sir William little time to recognize that he needed to cast his net over this jewel of an Indian maid who could accept his remoteness, and at time, his crude manner in living. He not only needed a housekeeper, but he needed a hostess who could makeup for his lack of social graces. In Molly Brant, Sir William believed that he had literally stuck a gold mine which would increase not only his value to himself, but also to King George the III and his Indian allies by opening new roads to political influence and personal wealth. Not surprisingly, Molly became pregnant and their son Peter was born in September, 1759. On December 22, 1760, Sir William, the Mohawks' *Affectionate Brother and Friend,* and Molly were invited to visit the Mohawks at Canajoharie. Shortly after they arrived, the Mohawks completed a land deed as their *wedding* present to Sir William and Molly, his legal wife as they envisioned their relationship. Their gift represented nearly eighty thousand acres, which was nearly all the land that the Canajoharie Mohawks had left and that bordered the Mohawk River. They assured Johnson that they wanted to grant him the land *Whilst it is in our power to give you this proof of our friendship, which we fear, will not be long, as our White Brethren are getting all our lands from us.*

From there on Sir William Johnson, his Miss Molly and her brother Joseph Brant would exercise authority and influence over the Mohawk Valley, especially over the Indians, on behalf of Sir William and King George the III. After conducting his last Indian Council on the blindly hot and humid July 11, 1774, Sir William who had been ill, managed to complete his speech and was assisted to his room in Johnson Hall.

According to British agent Claus, the sudden death of Sir William on the eve of what might be called a *civil war*, the *Iroquois scattered like a flock of helpless sheep.*

In their own minds, the Indians had lost their one and only *white* friend!

* * *

Earlier in 1774, the supervisor of Tryon County had flatly refused to take sides in any disputes between the Tories and Whigs, declaring their opinions, "that it did not appear to tend to be the violation of their religious rights, but merely regarded a single article of commerce which no person was compelled to purchase, and which persons of real virtue and resolution might easily have avoided or dispensed with." Continuing, the supervisor said, "They do therefore resolve to bear faithful and true allegiance to their lawful sovereign, King George III, and that in the true and plain sense of the words."

After Sir William's death, Guy Johnson, his nephew and younger son-in-law, assumed his father-in-law's business, as recommended by Sir William after his son, Sir John Johnson declined the position. With Guy's assumption of the position, and with the Indians' hearty support and enthusiasm, he was able to persuade the Iroquois to *keep the peace*. In so doing, Guy sent a message throughout the Iroquois nation vowing that the *fire still burns, and the road is open to this place (Johnson Hall)*. The Indians took Guy Johnson at his word, and scheduled a Council Meeting on September 12-18, 1775 where approximately 235 of them gathered, during which time they gave Guy a new name, Uraghquadirha, or "Rays of the Sun Enlightening the Earth." New Name or not. Guy had been well schooled by Sir William, and he had adopted Sir William's Indian policy: "to make friends with the Indians when you can, to redress their grievances when possible (and practicable), and to give them presents in public and in private," indeed, they had been on a regular dole for years. Bur mostly, Guy Johnson adopted Sir William's first and fast rule of conduct: *to divide and rule.*

After this Council Meeting at Johnson Hall, Guy, following his mentor's practice, detained six of the most *principal men* and gave them each a *handsome present.* Joseph Brant, Sir William's adopted son, was just beginning to gain not only Guy Johnson's attention and respect, but also that of the other Iroquois leaders with some degree of resentment. This burning resentment had been festering ever since a certain George Klock, a well-to-do-farmer of German extraction moved into their neighborhood. He had *purchased* out many of the claims of the Livingston Manor heirs. The Indians were always justly suspicious whenever white people and land were concerned. They would grow uneasy and frightened; expecting the worse to happen to them. To the Indians, George Klock confirmed all their fears about white men and land. Klock, a man of little formal education, was a formative man and was willing (and usually able) to stand his ground to any person he was facing, including the Superintendent of Indian Affairs.

There's a story told that Klock told Sir William to go and hang himself, confirming the fact that there was no love lost between the two individuals.

Indeed the Indians, especially the Mohawks, had something to worry about. In a moment of weakness, the Fort Hunter Indians, in varying degrees of drunkenness, had deeded their homesite where their village stood to the Corporation of Albany, which was controlled by Klock. In some fashion of other, a royal governor had later burned the deed, and had taken a similar deed to the king. The Corporation of Albany made no immediate claims, believing that the *Indians would die out,* but the *local whites* would periodically bring up the matter. This is where George Klock entered the picture. He was threatening to evict the white tenants from the land of the Upper Mohawks, who had for years been renting the land to them. Thus, Klock had endangered a seemingly peaceable arrangement for both the whites and the Indians.

Up to his usual mischief, Klock still kept the Canajoharie community in turmoil. Besides serving them with *writs of ejection* on the white tenants, who had regularly and faithfully paid their rented to the Indians, he had managed to divide the Indians themselves into quarreling factions by plying a few with drink and getting them to sign a deed in his favor for the disputed land. Sir William, the Indians' ever guardian and healer, was informed by the court that a *land patent* was valid title, so matter how obtained; even with evidence of fraud it was not even admissible at common law, and there were technical reasons why the suit could not be tried in chancery. The Indians' only hope lay in an appeal to the king of England. The king, through his ministers, and encouraged by Sir William Johnson wanted to know the seriousness of settling their land disputes with the whites.

To prove their sincerity, each of the Six Nations delegated one sachem, who could not read nor write English, to a Council Meeting held on November 5, 1768 at Fort Stanwix. Each sachem made his *mark* on the document, subsequently referred to as the Fort Stanwix Treaty. Without a question none of the sachems was aware of the seriousness of their commitment, nor of what they had actually signed over to the greedy and sanctimonious whites, who in tradition had filled their bellies with hardy, English rum. With their *marks*, the sachems of the Six Nations had handed over an incredible amount of land to the British, which included large parts of present-day Tennessee, Kentucky, West Virginia, Pennsylvania and New York states. The boundary began on the Ohio River at the mouth of the Tennessee River, followed the Ohio River up to Fort Pitt, proceeded on up this Allegheny River to Kittanning, then directly overland to the west branch of the Susquehanna River, continued down that river and thence by two smaller streams to the east branch of the Susquehanna and up to Owegy and then east to the upper Delaware River, went on up the Delaware and back again to the Susquehanna at Unadilla Castle and up the Unadilla River to its source, and then finally to a point on Wood Creek near Fort Stanwix. Simply stated, all the land south and east of this line, except for the land the Mohawks still owned, would be known as *white mans' country* thanks to the *generosity* of Sir William! For all of this land, the Indians received stacks of blankets, kettles, knives, and brooches which were laid on hither and yon on the common square in from of the fort, along with a few piles of currency on a table, all to be divided amongst the six sachems.

The total price tag?

Perhaps about the equivalent of present day fifty thousand dollars!

The Indians had forgotten one of their long standing principles, *never trust a white land trader.*

Joseph Brant, along with the six sachems, returned to their respective homes believing that the Ohio River could be considered a gift from the white traders, but it was perhaps too far away for them to consider.

As the years passed by, there was growing fear by the various claimants of the Canajoharie patent, in the very real danger that the Mohawks and even the entire Six Nations might go on the warpath. Another Council Meeting was called to settle the dispute. Everybody signed the release of the part of the patent the Indians actually occupied, except the *epitome of* unctuous, in the shadowy person of George Klock. This rather greasy, and affected person was, on one occasion, brought before the then New York State governor, Sir Henry Moore. On another occasion and before another governor, Joseph Brant attempted to settle the Klock controversy through the governor warning him; "Now, Brother, we rely on your justice for relief, and hope we may obtain it, so as to continue to live peaceably, as we have hitherto done. We are sensible that we are at present but a small number, but nevertheless our connections are powerful, and our alliances many & should any of these perceive that we who have been so remarkable for our fidelity and attachment to you, are ill used and defrauded, it may alarm them, and be productive of dangerous consequences." Brant's speech angered Governor William Tryon, but the governor promised to try to obtain some degree of justice for the Indians, all the while knowing that his power did not extend sufficiently far enough to assist the Indians.

The truth was the Indians had placed their entire faith in the royal crown and in Sir William Johnson. The only thing even Sir William could do was to sooth the Indians' emotions. Even though the king's ministers did wish to give justice to the Indians, there was little they could do. In reality, the Indians were victims of the squatters, landgrabbers, dishonest traders, and the malicious purveyors of gossip and even the murderers of Indians. The Indians were literally trapped between the swelling assortment of charlatans from all sides, including the British authorities, who initially may have meant well, but were ultimately operating on behalf and for the king who was relatively ignorant of the deceit and trickery foisted upon the Indians. Nor did it seem likely that the self-centered colonial legislatures would be able to even care to exercise greater authority to assist the Indians.

What it all boiled down to, the *whites,* both the Whigs and Tories, wanted almost all, if not all, of the land possessed by the Indians. Each exercising the principle: *the end justifies the means.* Later the Indians would discover that General George Washington knew from personal experience during the French and Indian War the potential value of the virgin lands in western New York, Pennsylvania, and other areas to the south and west. Washington believed that it was vital to conquer as much of this territory as possible before the pending conflict ever ended, if the United States was to amount to more than a narrow strip of coastal land. In his orders to General John Sullivan for the Indian campaign, Washington called for "the total destruction and devastation of the Indian settlements and the capture of as many prisoners of every sex and age as possible," Continuing that "it will be essential to ruin their crops in the ground and prevent their planting more."

* * *

In 1777, Governor Tryon visited the Mohawk Valley and wrote rapturously of the evident prosperity and contentment of the people, who were not seemingly pleased with the presence of the governor, than he with them. He reviewed the militia and reported that it exceeded 1,400 men under arms.

Either by happenstance or by design, both the British and the American communities had successfully followed Sir William's principle of "dividing and conquering." Through a series of maneuvers the once great Iroquois Confederacy of Six Nations had split its loyalty between the American Tories and the British on one side, and American Whigs and Rebel patriots on the other side. Plainly the differences in America's public and private opinions and beliefs had evolved into a controversy between two political factions of the same nation, which would eventually tear itself asunder, and erupting into open warfare between the two American political groups. America's first civil war!

EIGHT

YOU'RE MY BROTHER!

August 27, 1775 in a brick homestead facing the Mohawk River

Two middle-aged brothers sat in maple rocking chairs staring blankly toward the blazing log in the living room's massive stone fireplace sipping homemade brew from their pewter steins and discussing the loss of their Palatine refugee father, Johan Jost, who had died the previous day. The living room of the older brother's impressive two-story brick home with a gambrel roof built about 1752 near the *Little Falls* carrying place, served as an landmark to travelers, traders, and merchants seeking a place for board and lodging.

Their father, an emigrant from the Rhein-Pfalz or the Palatine of the Rhine, was probably the first white Palatine trader in German Flats. A fascinating folktale circulated around about their father soon after he had arrived in the Mohawk area. He was paddling his canoe searching for a desirable location to settle. Near a crevasse in the river he ventured ashore and scouted about for that *suitable* location to build a cabin, eventually, to cultivate a farm. After spying a small group of Mohawk Indians, he walked over to them, and asked for their consent to construct his cabin on the piece of land he was showing them. Abruptly, they refused his request. Nearby another group of Indians, who had been busily constructing a dugout canoe, had finished their chore. As could be expected, this burned-out log, capable of carrying a dozen or more warriors on hunting, fishing or war expeditions, was extremely heavy. They were struggling to slid their new burned-out canoe to the river's edge. Johan Jost suggested that all of them go to one end of the canoe, and that he would lift the other end. Laughing, joking, and smiling at such a ridiculous suggestion, the Mohawks, who were great admirers of strong and brave individuals, did as the *white* trader suggested. The group of Indians hoisted their end of the canoe, while Johan, Senior easily lifted his end and proceeded to lead them all, together with the canoe to the river. When they reached to river's edge, the canoe was tossed into the water splashing everybody. The Mohawks jumped and shouted with exhilaration to celebrate their accomplishment. Suddenly, one Mohawk yelled the word, "Kouari" (the bear). Then another repeated the word. Within a minute, all of the Mohawks were hollering "Kouari" and slapping their new found *bear* on the back. From that time on, the patriarch of this Palatine family in America, Johan Jost, Sr., was admired by the Mohawks. Quickly, the Mohawks granted Kouari permission to construct his cabin on the site he had selected, which eventually became known as Fort Herkimer, and referred to as Fort Kouari by the Indians. Having gained the confidence of the Indians, this resourceful Palatine acquired wealth, thus becoming one of the leading individuals in the region. In fact, according to some people of the day stated, "next to the Johnsons, Johan Jost, Sr.'s family was probably the most influential family in the Mohawk Valley."

To satisfy his oral craving, the 49 year old elder brother, a plain German farmer-trader, Bible-reading, and rough all-round good fellow, filled his clay pipe with fresh tobacco and struck a light, while his five-year younger brother, Johan Jost Jr., looked upon his nicotine, addicted brother with contempt. To further foster his contempt, some fifteen years ago, their father had given the older brother, Nicholas, a deed to 500 acres facing the ever picturesque and dependable, life-supporting Mohawk River. The river's dependability could be counted upon throughout the year. During the spring, the river would generally flood the low-flat, fertile lands along its shores. After the spring flooding, flat-bottom bateaux would travel east and west carrying furs from the western trapping grounds in exchange for finished eastern yards goods, and other manufactured products. Soon after the beginning of October or November, the Mohawk could be depended upon freezing over where many of the farmers would continue to travel on the river by boat or sled whichever was most appropriate. In addition to travel, winter was the time to harvest square cakes of ice, which were to be stored in *ice* houses and covered with sawdust or straw to serve as refrigeration for the valley's hot, humid summer, and the daily cooling and storage of the milk from their herds milch cows. On a winter's holiday, it was not uncommon to see crowds family friends watching, and even betting, as some of the farmers and their farm-hands raced their horses, and sleds on the ice.

"I can't believe what I'm hearing you say correctly, Nicholas," declared the startled forty-three year old younger brother who "*was considered to be a Man of very considerable Property,*" and was currently serving as a colonel in the 4th Battalion of the Tryon County Militia. Seeing that his brother who was five years his elder seemingly had not heard him, the younger brother repeated himself, "I can't believe what I'm hearing you say."

"What don't you understand, brother dear," his older brother stated in his broken English as he casually puffed his clay pipe.

"Here it is only one day after our father's death, and you're telling me that you are going to turn your back on our noble king to side with all those ruffians and rabble rousers."

"You have let the Johnsons influence you too much," responded the older brother. "You have let that Loyalist Sir John Johnson brainwash you of any common sense. Just because you are on friendly terms with him, it does not mean that he is always right," said the square-built, crusty brother with raven hair and dancing eyes, who was known fondly among friends and Indians alike as *old Honikol.* His younger brother, as well as all his friends and brothers, knew that Nicholas preferred to continue this discussion or any profound debate in his family's native German language, but he continued their conversation in his broken English to accommodate his younger brother. Nonchalantly, Nicholas leaned back in his rocking chair, stuffed more fresh tobacco in his pipe, struck a light, and blow a few smoke rings toward the ceiling's rough hewed cross-beams. As if he was ignoring his younger's brother remark, Nicholas watched the smoke rings evaporate as if he had just seen a wild, bobcat disappear into the undergrowth after being discovered.

"I don't believe our parents came over to America to be lead around like a pig with a ring in its nose by a person such as King George III," the rugged farmer and general of the Tryon County Militia said as his smoke rings silently evaporated from sight. "Our parents left the Palatine, and came to America for their *freedom.* Freedom to work as hard as we want. Freedom to speak what we want. Freedom to worship as we want. Freedom to escape the tyranny of a despot. Freedom to debate the politics we want to live by. Freedom to debate politics just as we are doing right here. I'd be the first to admit that it is impossible to find the consummate political system. But there is one thing for sure," the older brother stopped, tapped his pipe on a fireplace log, packed fresh, homegrown tobacco in its empty bowl, struck a light, and stared at his younger brother's growing irritation. "You must remember that the English brought our parents and our ancestors here as *indentured* servants. "And remember too, the British were not doing our people any favors, any more than they were when they were bringing the West Indians ashore here in America! Their motive was *greed,* not *freedom!*"

"But who paid for their transportation? Who fed them? Who furnished work tools and supplies?" asked the husband of Maria Van Allen and father of six young American children. He did not wait for his brother to respond. "I'll tell who not only paid for their transport, food, and other supplies, but also who saw them through their first brutal winter in Livingston Manor, or else they would have starved to death. It was the majesty of the British Empire."

"Johan, we don't owe the king or the queen a damn thing!" declared his older brother. "Our parents fulfilled their obligations in the British foolish venture to manufacture naval supplies downstate in Livingston Manor. In fact, our ancestors were charged for every tool they used, for almost all of the food they ate except for that inferior beer, which any respectable pig wouldn't drink. And do not forget all those promises of property, which the British made to our ancestors, but never kept." And quickly adding, "And it was no sin on the part of our ancestors that they could not read contracts and other the documents, which as you know were all recorded in the English. The British knew very well that the German language was the one and only language our ancestors could read or write. Since coming here to the Mohawk Valley, all of us have worked diligently to be productive and God-abiding citizens, and........."

Before the militia general could finish expressing his thoughts, his colonel brother interrupted, "Maria and I have talked about the politics which are beginning to divide us into two separate groups. The rabble-rousers call themselves Whigs; while those who are loyal to the British monarchy call themselves Tories. Personally, I'm sorry, Nicholas, I'm afraid the politics is even beginning to divide our family, as evident to the way our conversation is progressing right here and now. I guess the way our conversation is going I'd be labeled as a Tory, and you as a Whig. Personally, I don't want to be called one or the other. I just want my independence or freedom as you call it. I just want to be left alone to serve my family, my God, and my king."

"I totally agree totally with you, my brother," said the older brother as he leaned over toward his brother, and patted Johan Jost Jr.'s knee, "except when you say you want to serve the king," declared the French and Indian War veteran. "I do not understand why we have to be held accountable to some person or group of persons who are on the other side of the ocean and three thousand miles away, who wasn't voted into office and claims to be have been ordained king by God.

"Personally, I believe that I am unfortunate that I have some near relations who differs with me in sentiment about the politics of the times. I am determined to stick to my principle of freedom from Britain's tyranny. I will maintain this creed, and let the consequences be what they may be. As you know Maria and I have no children, but I do have deep concern for your wife and children," Nicholas confessed to his brother. "It is a difficult time to be alive," concluded the man known to the valley people as Old Honikol, "but I would not trade it for the world; life is exciting and certainly, with glorious challenges and opportunities."

"We are a young country, Nicholas," stated Johan, "we need England, just as a baby needs its mother........."

This time it was Nicholas who interrupted his brother, "But, my dear brother, even a baby must leave its mother's breast, cut the umbilical cord, and begin to shift upon its own. I do not mean that the child has to leave his mother entirely, but it does need its *freedom* to exercise his imagination and creativity; to spread his wings and to fly from the nest."

"To a certain degree I agree with you, Nicholas, about leaving the nest. However, there's a certain degree of comfort about being able to return to one's nest That's why I believe it is necessary for America to maintain its loyalty and support to King George III. And what's more, do you think that bunch of ruffians in the Continental Congress, especially those New Englanders, are going to be any more tolerant and understanding? The very name they call themselves, Whigs, is a good name for them. They should take off their Whigs so they can see the daylight, and what they'll be losing if they try to carry on by themselves.

"And my brother, even though you are older than I am, you and Maria do not have any children to worry about. You have nothing to lose."

This statement cut Nicholas worse than an Indian's scalping knife when he was reminded of his childless marriage. Like a wounded soldier, he said, "It's good, Johan, that you brought up that name," said the older brother as he tapped his clay pipe against the and-irons in the fireplace, and proceeded to stuff fresh tobacco in the warm pipe bowl, and struck a light. "Let's explore where these names, Whig and Tory, really did come from."

"What makes you such an authority of the subject," asked the younger brother in his occasional contemptuous mood.

"During the last few meetings of the Tryon County Committee of Safety we have been discussing various issues, and these same words were discussed," responded the still *wounded* brother in his broken English. He noticed that every time when he occasionally returned to his family's native language, that his younger brother would wince, and stick up his nose as if whatever he said was repugnant.

"I wish you would learn to speak English as you should. All of the king's subjects should speak only English!" Johan declared. He stopped a moment, then acquiesced, "Tell me the tales you heard from the *authorities* at the Safety Committee's meeting about how the names Whigs and Tories became part of our vocabulary."

Ignoring his brother's sarcastic remarks, Nicholas began.

"The name *Whig* is said to have been a reproachful name meaning *sour milk,* which first was given to the Presbyterians in Scotland when they were forced to flee from their homes, hungry and thirsty they often drank *buttermilk (Whig or whey),* which was given to them," Nicholas took two deep drafts on his pipe, blew smoke rings as usual toward the room's hewed ceiling rafters. After the smoke rings had disappeared, he continued to relate what he had heard at the committee's meetings. "The name Tories or high churchmen stood on the side of the King as being above the law. Their adversaries therefore gave them the name, referring to Irish robbers or highwaymen who lived upon plunder and were eager for any daring or villainous enterprise." Nicholas took a few more sips of beer, a couple deep puffs from his pipe, and concluded, "And so, the names Whig and Tory are used only with reference to their originals, from whence they are borrowed…..*sour milk* and highway robber. What really concerns me about you, Maria and your children is that the Committee of Safety is busily drafting credentials which will assist them in identifying all Tories………"

Before the general could finish his train of thought, his younger brother stood up and began pacing in front of the fireplace as if he were about to deliver a sermon. "The other day," he began, "I recently attended a town meeting conducted by this very knowledgeable person, Daniel Leonard, I suppose you would call him a Tory. He paid his respects to the Committee of Correspondence set up by Samuel Adams, who was also present in the following words: *This (committee) is the foulest, subtlest and most venomous serpent that ever issued from the eggs of sedition. It is the source of the rebellion. I saw the small seed when it was planted; it was a grain of mustard. I have watched the plant until it has become a great tree; the vilest reptiles that crawl upon the earth are concealed at the root; the foulest birds of the air rest upon its branches.*" Johan Jost Jr. paced momentarily with his hands in his pant's pockets just long enough to catch his breath and calm his inter-being, "As you very well know, Nicholas, Mr. Leonard has an equally as high opinion about Samuel Adams, who is like the poison venom of a snake!"

"If you continue to talk that way, I hope you will be careful to whom you say such things as you just told me." Becoming very serious, the older brother looked at his younger brother, and warned him, "You must be careful, Johan, with what you say and to whom you say it, or you may find yourself imprisoned in a patriot's jail. If I were you, I would be very careful about what you say, especially in public. Johan, you're my brother, and I love you dearly, but love can only protect you just so far," Nicholas said with pleading eyes. "I know as a fact, that some of the committee's members have been especially charged to watch you and your activities. Some of these people are supposed to be your friends. Regardless, they are ordered to report back to the committee, if they identify anything about you, or any other Loyalists You're my own brother, Johan, please don't give me or any other of your friends reason to report you to the committee. There's some on the Committee of Safety who'd like nothing better than to throw the militia general's younger brother in jail. Please," the militia's general pleaded, "do yourself and your family a favor, and keep your sentiments to yourself. If you must share them with someone, share them with Maria, she'll be good counsel."

"As long as you're preaching to me, Nicholas," said the infuriated younger brother, "I have something I've been wanting to tell you, and I guess this is as good time as any."

"Let's hear it," invited his brother.

"I think that you and your family have been, and are very sacrilegious!"

"I don't understand what you are saying," said the stunned general.

"Soon after our ancestors arrived here in America, we joined the Dutch Reformed Church. When Maria and I started taking an assessment of the local situation, we decided that we owe it to the crown to join the Anglican church."

"How stupid you sound!" said the older brother as he raised from his chair and tapped his pipe on an and-iron, returned to his chair to pack and light his pipe. He proceeded through his usual routine of blowing smoke rings toward the ceiling, which further incensed Johan Jost Jr. "The only thing you owe the crown is assuming your responsibility of raising your own family. I do admit that you owe the good Lord his respect," said the Dutch Reformed Church Bible reading militia general. "Another thing......," said Nicholas as he took another sip of his brew, puffed on his pipe, and blew the smoke rings while Junior inched forward in his rocking chair. "To continue my story of the Safety Committee's meeting, there was a story told there that went something like this: that every fool is not a Tory but every Tory is a fool. The man who maintains the divine right of kings to govern wrongly is a fool and also a genuine Tory."

Nicholas had no sooner finished his last sentence, than Johan quickly jumped up from his rocking chair, flipping it over on its back to the floor. "You damned *reformers* can plum go to hell, as far as I'm concerned," said Johan as he leaned over to upright the chair. The two brothers came face-to-face with each other as they simultaneously leaned to straighten the chair. As they stared toward one another, each knew that Nicholas's last remark had struck a critical stroke about their politics, their differing principles, and their own family relationships.

* * *

STEPS TOWARD FREEDOM

One of New Palatine's most charismatic and respected individuals was the valley's circuit rider preacher, Reverend Johan Stouffer, whose association with New Palatine started late one Saturday night as he arrived in the hamlet from Fort Stanwix. With sun about ready to settle beneath the western mountain, he stopped at the Heidelberg Tavern seeking nourishment and a place to sleep before he was to meet with the settlement's mayor on the following day to explore the possibility of establishing a church in New Palatine. As he was eating his sauerbraten, and soaking up the excess gravy with his dark pumpernickel crust, he sensed the fragrance of a female's presence. He looked up to see a sturdy, voluptuous blonde woman in her late forties towering over the roughly hewed wooden table with two huge steins filled with dark beer. In a rather breathy, deep voice, she pleasantly asked, "Do you mind if I join you with a drink?"

Stunned by this sudden intrusion, and looking around the relatively large dining room, the preacher realized that time had quickly passed him by, and he and this woman were the only persons in the tavern' dinning hall. He stretched his right arm, with its open palm facing the ceiling across the square, crudely constructed dinning table, "No! not at all," he responded, "I'm not one who fancies eating my evening meals alone, especially when there's a delightful lady near." The preacher stood up to greet her. In his usual courteous manner, he pulled a chair from beneath the table; extending his arm, he said to the beguiling stranger, "By all means, please join me."

"I guess it would be proper for me to introduce myself," said the matronly woman as she sat down and pushed one of the beer steins in front of the preacher. She extended her right hand, and said "I am Martha Butler, the proprietor of this tavern."

"I, too, should introduce myself," responded the preacher as they shook hands.. He felt her bone crushing grasp, and announced "My name is Reverend Johan Stouffer of the Dutch Reformed Church. My profession is that of a circuit riding preacher here in the Mohawk Valley. I'm scheduled to meet with New Palatine's mayor tomorrow to discuss the possibility of establishing a Dutch Reformed Church. My primary mission is establish the church here in New Palatine." He took another fork full of food from his plate, and said, "Please tell the cook that this sauerbraten is exceptional. He is to be complimented."

"You're talking to the cook, Reverend," the proud tavern owner declared.

"Oh, by the way," he added as he sipped his beer, "This beer is the kind I prefer. I love its dark color, and its bitter taste. It helps to warm one's heart on these chilly nights," he said as he looked beyond the tavern owner toward the huge fireplace with its blazing logs, as he rubbed his closely trimmed salt-and-pepper beard while his similarity colored hair lightly touched the shoulders of his homespun wool jacket.

"I'm glad that I can accommodate you, Reverend," she quickly added, "with our good food and grog. Don't let me interrupt your eating," as she observed his hearty appetite. Just the kind of appetite an man of his size should have, she thought as she examined his six-foot plus, stout frame. She had noticed that dust was still clinging to his threadbare pant legs, obscuring the original color of the dark wool fabric. His knee-high boots appeared to have had some attention given to them to remove the outside layer of mud. Yet despite his unimpressive appearance, his very presence and jovial manner, together with his pleasant, deep baritone voice which perfectly enunciated each word as if he were an actor, sounding and looking like one of those Shakespearian actors she had heard about over in England, Martha thought.

While the preacher continued to enjoy his meal, his hostess asked him, "Pray tell me why in the world did you and your church ever select New Palatine for a new church? I hope I don't offend you, but you sound and look more like an actor than a preacher."

The preacher leaned back in his chair, and let out a hearty laugh, "You haven't heard me preach or act! But, I do believe it helps to be an actor in order to be an effective preacher. I must admit that beside reading the Bible, I thoroughly enjoy reading Shakespeare's works," confessed the Reverend Stouffer. He placed his elbows on the table, and hoisted the half full stein to his lips, took a healthy draft, and smiled in a jovial manner, "Oh, I guess you could call me a sort of a half-assed actor, that is if it pleases you. I love acting, but the Lord has directed me, at least for the time being, to his pulpit."

"Well, if you had arrived a few months ago you would have been meeting with my husband," Martha stated. "But, thank God, he's not around here anymore. He ran off with some of his distant cousins named Butler. I suppose you've heard of Colonel John Butler and his wild-ass son Walter. Personally, I don't much like my married last name, especially the way those Tories are acting up with the Indians. Regardless, I've decided to keep his last name, because I can't prove whether he is dead or alive," she declared. "As far as those Tories, who live around here, are concerned, they're too darn snooty for me, and......" She stopped quickly, and asked, "Are you one of them? One of those Tories, I mean!"

"I'm one of God's messengers," the preacher said evading her direct question, and finished the last of his beer. "As I have told you, my mission in New Palatine is to establish a Dutch Reformed Church. I must admit that while I travel from Fort Stanwix, Fort Dayton, and to Fort Herkimer, and along the way I am able to find various pieces of information which might be helpful to those in need of such assistance.

"So, in time and by asking dumb questions, I have acquired a second mission," said the preacher as he stroked his beard, and smiled rather sheepishly. He stopped long enough to gain Martha's full attention. "You see I have chosen to fight for our freedom from the church pulpit. As you may know, the German Palatines and Dutch Reformed number only about two-hundred and fifty in the whole state of New York. We're far out numbered by the members of the Anglican Church in America. I've been quite a student of a pastor of the West Church in Boston. His name is Jonathan Mayhew, who has been called by Robert Treat Paine *the father of civil and religious liberty in Massachusetts and America.* His church was the first church in that religion to avow itself as Unitarian. The distinctive trait of Mayhew's work was intellectually, and he thought the Church of England with its sedate hierarchy was foreign to the new American nation and would, if established here, eventually ruin America with *a flood of Episcopacy.*"

Martha rescued herself from the intellectual trance the preacher had placed her in, and asked, "If your primary mission is to start a church here, I'll tell you what I'll do," as she stood up, picked up their empty steins, and headed toward the bar. Momentarily, the tavern proprietor returned with the two filled steins in one hand, and two small dishes with what appeared to be hot, steaming apple strudel. The preacher assisted Martha with the steins, as she placed the small dishes of strudel in their places. She repeated her last statement, "I'll tell what I'll do for you and your church! First of all, I agree with you that New Palatine needs a church, but there just isn't any appropriate existing building around."

Martha stopped talking, sampled her strudel, and sipped her beer. Meanwhile, the preacher was busily assessing the tavern and its owner. The two-story tavern, which had a huge stone fireplace located at one end of the large eating and drinking area. The large room's ceiling was constructed low with huge, hewed rafters, which occasionally required the preacher to lower his head to avoid hitting his head on some of the low-hanging rafters. If this building is similar to other taverns he had visited where the second floor was an open one-room affair used as sleeping quarters, he thought, as Martha continued her offer.

"Again, I'll tell you what I'll do," Martha repeated. "I want you to know that I'm saying this as much for myself as it is for you, your church, and our hamlet. You see, until you came in here with this idea about starting a church, I've been the nearest person this settlement has as a psychiatrist, advisor to the lovelorn, and mentor to the homeless and alcoholics. I don't expect you to patch up some knife wound, or sew up a ripped eye, or to remove a stray bullet from a *friend* in need, but you and your church just might help to relieve me of some of these various demands for my services.

"You see I've led kind of a choice life," Martha continued, "but ever since the politics of this valley has became so damn rotten and threatening, I've made up my mind that I'm going to contribute something to my community and to my country. But, this time it'll be more meaningful compared to my past life." She stood up and pointed around the sizable, yet a rather cozy and appealing room.

"You see this room? I'm offering this room to your," she corrected herself, "to *our* church for every Sunday until you have succeeded in constructing a free-standing church of your,….." she stopped, and corrected herself, "……of our own," she continued cheerfully.

"That's a very generous offering," the preacher acknowledged, "but how do you purpose to do such a thing?" Momentarily, the preacher experienced a mysterious emotion as he surveyed the tavern owner's dynamic presence and her enthusiastic emotional zeal about what they were talking. It was not any biological need he sought to satisfy, because in his one-room cabin near Fort Dayton was his Oneida princess, Red Bird, whom he had married in Indian fashion some years ago. Red Bird knew her man to be faithful in every way that counts. She knew, too, that *the Reverend* as she preferred to call him, appreciated her help, counsel, and encouragement, as well as her love to make his sometimes monotonous and tiring profession exciting. Just as suddenly as the preacher's mind had drifted away from Martha's generous offer, the preacher's mind reclaimed her nearness, and what she was offering his church.

"I understand that initially you are planning to preach here in New Palatine only every third Sunday. Am I correct?" she asked.

"That's correct Mrs. Butler," said the preacher.

She stood up, propped her right foot on the chair's seat, placed her elbows on her right knee, and leaned forward almost rubbing noses with Reverend Stouffer, and stated, "Let's get one thing straight right here and now, if we're going to be doing business together, my name is Martha.'

"Then you may call me Preacher," staring up towards her face, the Reverend Johan Stouffer said that name, because Red Bird had already claimed *Reverend* as her name for him.

"All right Preacher, I'm offering you and *our* church this very room every third Sunday morning until our church is constructed. I'll close down the bar exactly at midnight night." She sat down again in her chair, and continued, "After midnight, there'll be no more booze served, and then I'll have my ever ready-helper, and jack-of-all-trades, Mr. Harry Hunter, clean up the place and arrange the chairs in a church-like order. After that," she hesitated and smiled,

"I'll make sure that Harry doesn't find a soft spot on the floor where he can sleep his hang-over off."

"Harry sounds like his own man," smiled the Preacher. "I think I would like to meet him! Maybe we can become friends."

"Whatever the townspeople say about Harry," Martha stated, "he has been very loyal to me. Talking about loyalty," she continued, "Harry is not one of those Loyalists everyone is talking about. So if you've ever have something that you want to relate to me, just tell Harry Hunter, that is if I'm not here, and he is sober. Otherwise your news will be circulated all around the hamlet."

Weary from his long time in the saddle from Fort Stanwix, the preacher was beginning to nod at his charming and charitable hostess. Recognizing his condition, Martha suggested that she would clean up the table after she had shown the preacher to his sleeping quarters. She gathered and handed the preacher a straw-filled pillow along with two home-made quilts, and pointed him toward the narrow stairway to the tavern's loft. "I'm sure you can find an empty space somewhere up there. We don't have many guests staying over tonight. Coffee will be served anytime after six o'clock. You can have your breakfast at this very table. In fact," she smiled and added, "I may even join you for breakfast."

As Martha watched the preacher lumber up the stairs, she wondered who and what the good preacher really was. Was he as holy as he professed to be? Or, was he a Loyalist spy pretending to be here to establish a church, but all the while trying to learn information about the Rebels' cause and their strategy. On the other hand, he could be a member of Tryon County's Committee of Safety dispatched to ferret out Loyalists to the king's men. She knew that the Heidelberg Tavern had developed into the watering hole for both Tories and Whigs. But ever since the time, when her husband Jerome had disappeared, there were fewer Tories than usual. She had heard rumors that they had decided the Shoemaker's Tavern down the road was a safer place. She finished clearing the dinning table, and headed for the kitchen where Harry Hunter had found himself a soft spot to sleep *it off*. "Well," she said to herself, "he's all we've got to start with! The Lord must have chosen him for some reason or other. He's certainly been my faithful friend, so I should count my blessings and shut up! Certainly a lot better than traveling the ten miles every Sunday to German Flats just to go to their church."

* * *

In another part of the Mohawk valley a very different aggregation of brothers had been assembling. The sachems of the various tribes of the valley's Confederacy of Six Nations were continually meeting and being encouraged by representatives of the Tories and Whigs to give military aid and support to their respective sides. Initially, the Indians had no intention of taking sides with either group. As far as they were concerned, it was the *white* man's quarrel. As matters became more divisive between the white people, numerous Indians said that they could not hunt, or eat, or sleep, for worrying that a war might suddenly break-out between the whites who were becoming more openly belligerent toward each other. "O," wailed one poor Indian woman, "strange *Englishmen* kill one another. I think the world is coming to an end." Obviously, the Indians did not understand the Rebels cry of "Taxation without representation," but they certainly did understand there were unfriendly relationships developing between various groups of the white settlers. Indeed, the Indians did grasped that there were also religious implications in their strife. "O Britain! O North America!" exclaimed one of Chief Joseph Brant's former schoolmates in anguish, "can the heathens Say, Behold and See how those Christians love one another." Perhaps under the influence of Guy Johnson, Sir William Johnson's nephew and younger son-in-law, the Indians did not, at first, take the white peoples' troubles too seriously. Eventually, during the few years before 1775, not only the white people but the Indians, too, were trying to sort themselves out and taking sides with one or the other. By 1775, it was fast approaching time when each valley inhabitant, white or red, needed to choose between the Tories' long accustomed authority of Britain's king, and the Whigs' nonconformist opinions and actions.

The Indians were totally bewildered on whom to believe. They believed that they were receiving mixed messages, especially, from the *Christian* men of the clothe. The Reverend John Stuart,

Anglican missionary to the Mohawks, and the Reverend Samuel Kirkland, Presbyterian missionary to the Oneidas had not doubt who the Indians should support. Both men believed that they were not preaching politics; nevertheless, their sermons had a distinctive political ring to them. Reverend Stuart was an ardent Loyalist, while the Reverend Samuel Kirkland was just as an impassioned Whig. Through the preaching of their interpretations of the *Word of God*, these two men had utterly confused the *heathen* Indians, making them as pliable as a mound of fresh clay.

While the busy reverends were preaching the "word of God," Sir John Johnson, Sir William's oldest son, was genuinely bewildered to hear all the Indian and white people's talk about *liberty*. Almost totally ignorant to the dirt farmers and the Indians who had to scrape and scratch for their merger living, Sir John was busily protecting his inherited estate, and had grown accustomed to the good *elite life*. While discussing their life style with the valley's inhabitants and their lack of *liberty*, Sir John was astounded to learn that such an issue needed to be discussed. He said, "I have liberty!" And then arrogantly he asked his acquaintance, "Doesn't everybody have liberty?" He dismissed the subject, and strutted away from the group.

Daniel Claus, Sir William Johnson's elder son-in-law and deputy to the Indians of Canada for many years, was a completely different type of man who knew exactly what he stood for. But, he, too, was apparently oblivious to the strife and turmoil of the common man. Claus made it very clear to all who would take time to listen to him that he believed the "Rebels were stupid," and he suggested as early as October 1774 that his Indian charges "might easily be brought to fall out with them."

Early in 1775 the relations between the Whig Reverend Samuel Kirkland and the Loyalist Colonel Guy Johnson exploded into open conflict. Since 1766, Reverend Kirkland had been living with the Oneidas. He had managed to gain their confidence and affection without bribing them with presents and trinkets, as was the British custom. The industrious Oneidas were learning agriculture. They had even opened a smithy shop and erected two grain mills, as well as succeeded in constructing a church. One issue which antagonized Guy Johnson was Reverend Kirkland's interpretation of the Continental Congress's operations to the Oneidas, and as he expressed it, opening their eyes. Colonel Guy insisted that any kind of training and education about the valley's politics given to the Indians was shocking, wrong, and a waste of time. Believing, that ignorance was blissful, the colonel preferred to keep the Indians blissful. In short, the Indians didn't need to know such things! The less they knew about the whites, the better, he thought. Had Guy Johnson been more complacent about Kirkland's preaching and his extra-curricular activities, his commander Major General Thomas Gage would have ordered Colonel Guy to "get rid of the troublemaking missionaries." Unfortunately, Joseph Brant became involved with the colonel's difficulties with Reverend Kirkland, who was one of Brant's old friends. Joseph was very much under the colonel's influence, yet when a chance presented itself to save the preacher's life; Brant took advantage of it.

The time presented itself while both Brant and Kirkland were at Fort Stanwix when the preacher was attacked by hostile Indians. One Indian aimed a blow at Kirkland, and vowing to kill him. Quickly, Kirkland grabbed a chair and tried to protect himself. Just then Brant interrupted the disturbance, and seized the excited Indian. According to Kirkland's account of the story, Brant warned the attacking Indian, "He is our prisoner, and therefore not to be treated ill. We think him ungrateful to our King. He thinks he does his duty towards his country. Let him be considered as our enemy, but do not kill him while he is our prisoner...."

By the end of 1775, Tryon County and the Mohawk valley, in general, was fast becoming a keg of dynamite just waiting for someone to set it off. If the Whigs erected a *liberty* pole, the Loyalists would pull it down. If the Loyalists sent off messengers, the Whigs would stop and search them. If the Whigs gathered together for one purpose or another, the Loyalists would soon gather in larger numbers. One time, a group of Whigs adopted a declaration of grievances, and the Loyalists immediately drafted a declaration disavowing any of the Whigs' grievances. Interestingly, the word *peaceable* was a term which was used frequently describing their grievances. It caused a wide divergence of opinion between Guy Johnson and the Whigs as to its "true" meaning. Kirkland's teachings were beginning to come back and haunt Guy Johnson, especially when some Oneidas greeted him proudly at Fort Stanwix proclaiming their tribe's neutrality. Unknown to Johnson, the Massachusetts provincial Congress had urged Kirkland to exercise his influence to convince the Six Nations that they should enter the growing conflict on the side of the Rebels, but neutrality was the best the preacher could obtain from them.

Later, at Fort Ontario, approximately 1,458 Indians gathered in a council with Colonel Guy. Most of the Indians had come in quest for presents, including rum. Little Abraham of Fort Hunter, who attended the council, later told the Americans in Albany that Guy Johnson had advised the Indians to sit still and mind nothing but peace, and that the Indians had promised they would remain neutral. Johnson told a completely different account of the happenings to the British government. Guy Johnson, the wily Loyalist, the man whom the Indians called Uraghquadirha or "Rays of the Sun Enlightening the Earth," related how he had given the Indians a hatchet with which they were to cooperate with king's troops, and that the Indians had accepted his hatchet. To complete such an exchange, the acceptance of the hatchet meant that the Indians had agreed to go to war against the Whigs.

Not to be out performed, the Whigs of Tryon County were beseeching their friends in Albany and Schenectady for men and ammunition, "to save this County from Slaughter and Desolation." Meanwhile, Colonel Guy Johnson, together with Joseph Brant and Walter Butler, had landed in Montreal on July 17, 1775 just a few weeks after "the benighted Rebels had the folly and madness to join battle with the king's troops at Concord and Lexington. They were poised to invade Canada, where they knew the French peasants utterly refused to fight."

NINE

STRANGER WITHIN THE RANKS

August 27, 1775 Evening at Shoemaker's Tavern in New York State's Mohawk Valley

Wilhelm Kerchner was Teutonic in nature. He demanded and expected strict obedience and punctuality of everyone he came in contact with, especially of himself and his wife Sarah and child, Helena. This particular evening he was doing something he would not tolerate from any of his family and business associates, he was arriving late for the eight o'clock meeting, just because of that muscular dry-bones of a smithy, George Raab, and his own nibble-witted assistant manager, Harvey Perry. A hellva good pair, he thought with disdain of the men he had just left in his general store. Even though he thought the name Tory was very demeaning, silently he thanked the Lord that he didn't have to put up with these despicable Whigs with their nimble brains all the time. As silently as possible, he was living for the day when the Loyalists would defeat the Rebels. All this day, he had been looking forward to this meeting of people who believed as he did. Lately the Loyalists, as he preferred to be called, had been calling innumerable meetings usually held in a tavern or inn, where petitions, toasts, complaints, and plots would be discussed and planned. This night Samuel Shoemaker was the host, and was in the middle of a speech addressing about twenty or thirty well-dressed men seated around two of the tavern's long drinking tables. Shoemaker glanced toward the newcomer, and gave the front door guard, the high-sign of acceptance, and continued:

> I cannot say, but I wished some of my violent Countrymen, such as those we call Whigs, could have such an opportunity as I have had. I think they would be convinced that George the Third has not one grain of tyranny in his composition, and that he is not, he cannot be that blood-minded man the Whigs have so repeatedly and so illiberally called him. It is impossible, a man of his feelings, so good a husband, so kind a father cannot be such a tyrant.

Since it appeared that Shoemaker had finished, a well-dressed gentleman at the end of one of the long tables, stood up with his stein held high, and boldly proclaimed, "Here's to our King."

"Long live the King," raised another stein holder.

"To King George the Third, may he always reign over this bunch of heathen Whigs." toasted another.

As each attendee stood and gave a toast to the King, to England, and to the British Parliament, Shoemaker ordered the barkeeper to draw fresh steins for everyone.

"As you know, most of us emigrated to America from England," Shoemaker started, and most of us have a strong, emotional attachment to the British royalty, to its flag. Unquestionably, many of us still feel a native kinship, perhaps even a longing, for to our *homeland.* In all probability, when we left England, it was difficult to completely break all the families, and activities we left behind. I know there is one ceremony I thoroughly miss, that is the pomp and the pageantry of royalty, especially the *tattoo*, a military spectacle with its music, marching, and military exercises. It is certainly infinitely more colorful than the stark, dull colors of common democracy, the Whigs are trying to impose upon us. The British royalty has long been the unifying symbol of our faith, and of our country. And let us not ever forget that America is part of the great British Empire! These new ideals proclaimed by the Whigs have no comparable symbol. I am certain that all these impulses and attachments to our home country played an important part in each of us here in making your decision to attend this meeting."

"Here's to the British Empire," toasted a man dressed as a clerk. He continued, "To the British Empire, may it continue to rule from sea to shinning sea."

"To all of us Loyalists," pledged another, who appeared to be some kind of merchant as he raised his stein toward the tavern's ceiling, "and to hell with those shit-slinging farmers and their unpowdered Whigs."

Toasts to the royalty and to the empire continued with intermittent stories relating to what the attendees had learned or experienced since their last meeting.

After allowing everyone to voice his thoughts, once again, Shoemaker gained control of the meeting, and announced the purpose he had called this meeting. "One week from tonight at eight o'clock we are going to have a very special meeting which will be attended by one or two important members or representatives of the British military. It is part of the Crown's recruitment efforts throughout the Mohawk valley. I urge each and everyone of you to attend, and bring at least one or two loyal friends with you."

* * *

As Wilhelm Kerchner was riding his chestnut gelding home, he was trying to reconcile the reason why he had attended this meeting? Why he should consider attending the following week's meeting? He was a Palatine, not an Englishman. He was not sure how he fitted into this group of devoted king's men. He was even having a difficult time learning to speak their language. As far as he could figure, there were only two other Palatines present there besides himself. One was sort of a non-entity person named Hon-

GIL HERKIMER

Yost Schuyler. Apparently, Hon Yost, as most of the persons there referred to him, was General Nicholas' nephew, and was a man well known and respected by the Mohawks, who revered him as someone protected by the Great Spirit. The other Palatine was Johan Jost Jr., who was regarded to be a man of considerable property, and who served faithfully as a colonel in the Tryon County Militia. In addition, what was most unusual about Johan Jr.'s attendance was that his older brother, Nicholas, was the commanding general of the county's militia. However, it was widely accepted that Johan Jr. was on very friendly terms with the Loyalist leader, Sir John Johnson, as well as others including Daniel Claus, John and Walter Butler, Joseph Brant, and with at least two of Sir William's half-bred sons and other influential men. Johan Jr.'s arrangement appeared to Wilhelm Kerchner to be a strange contradiction. He reasoned, as he reined his horse into his home's stable, wiped down his horse, bedded him down with a wool blanket over his back, cleaned up the stall with fresh straw, gave one of his few admiring friends two forks full of timothy hay, closed the stable door, and headed toward his home's back door.

There were no lights on when he entered the kitchen, however, he did find a note from his wife Sarah attached to the inside door latch. The note informed Wilhelm that she had baked a mince pie in the evening, and it was located near the kitchen's fireplace. His wife was trying to be an amicable person, while he was out in the evening doing something that he knew would be distasteful to her. But, Wilhelm knew that he was doing something which was right! He was the man of the family! And, he had to make all the important decisions! He totally agreed with Shoemaker's remark that the pomp and the pageantry of royalty were infinitely more colorful, spectacular ...... and *orderly*. The keyword Kerchner was looking for was *orderly*, not all this rabble rousing the Whigs call democracy. Especially, those everlasting New England Town Meetings where everyone tries to shout down the other, until it was time to go home to milk the cows. From what he had heard, nothing every gets accomplished at these "democratic" meetings; the only apparent accomplishment is that everyone appears to have an opportunity to voice their opinions. A totally disorderly affair, and they call this type of yelling "democracy," he thought. I need everything orderly, he concluded, and sat down near the living room's smoldering fireplace eating his wife's mince pie, which wreaked with the smell of fine French brandy, and sipping lukewarm coffee which had been left over from the morning's meal.

The brandied pie and the strong coffee seemed to sharpen his imagination. Wilhelm had been impressed and captivated with the man named Alexander (just call me "Sandy") McKnight, whom Johan Jr. had introduced. He could relate to Sandy, a *real* person who believed that he had to do what was good for himself. Sandy informed Wilhelm that McKnight's father had been a member of the Scottish Highlanders. While Johan Jr, Wilhelm and Sandy conversed after the meeting, McKnight informed them that when he was twelve years old, his father had been transferred to the Boston area. Sandy beamed with joy when he talked about his father, who when a very young boy, he always fancied himself as a knight in King Arthur's court. Being realistic, his father knew that all those days had passed him by. As a result, his father had decided that the next best thing was to change his name from Samuel Mathews to Samuel McKnight and join the Scottish Highlanders together with their regimentation and bagpipes. Sandy gleamed when he admitted that his father really looked regal in his bright red jacket, black pants, shinny leather boots, and his tall black fur hat, which also had made an favorable impression on a young English lady, who eventually became Sandy's mother. When the McKnight family arrived in the Boston area, all three became involved members in the Anglican Church and loyal supporters of the British royalty.

During the French and Indian War, Sandy's father had been killed on the afternoon of July 9, 1758 when General Braddock offered his scarlet and blue coats in close ranks as perfect targets; they were not ambushed, but rather surprised by some 637 Indian Braves, about 150 French Canadian militia lead by about 72 French officers and regulars. Having never fought Indians, the British troops were completely unnerved could not see their attackers, but they could hear their loud and horrible war whoops. Toward sundown panic started to set in, after the largely unseen Indians had mowed down scores of the huddled and almost leaderless redcoats. General Braddock, shot in the lungs, had lost one horse after another while he rushed about trying to rally his troops, while his senior colonel and many other officers were killed. As George Washington recorded, the soldiers "broke and ran as sheep pursued by dogs," abandoning their wagons, artillery and even muskets. Fortunately, the Indians were too busy scalping, looting, and torturing prisoners to pursue deserting troops, or Braddock's entire fleeting column would have been massacred. As it was, of the 1,459 officers and men engaged, 977 were killed or wounded.

Fortuitously, young Sandy McKnight's father had neglected to march with his favorite set of bagpipes. As a memorandum, Sandy's mother gave her young son his father's bagpipes. In no time, young Sandy had mastered the bagpipes; thanks to his father's tutorage, he soon became a welcomed musician in a variety of social affairs in the Boston area. His mother had gallantly tried to reconstruct a meaningful life for Sandy and herself, but as the doctor told the young man in his middle twenties, "Your mother died of a broken heart."

After his mother's death, McKnight informed Johan Jr. and Wilhelm that he had kept busy in the carpentry trade, and supplementing his income playing the bagpipes for Boston's many dances, picnics, church affairs and other social activities. The one activity he had purposely avoided;..... the politics of the time, because he resented some of "rebel roosters" talking against England's monarchy. For a time this all changed. It seems that during one of social occasions, he was introduced to a young lady, who was about his own age and who was a member of a well-established family who traced their lineage back to the Mayflower. To the young impressible man, Sandy had thought that his "lady" would help to advance him up the social and political ladders. After a rather short courtship, yet relatively stormy and exciting romance, they married. Quick like a bunny, they had children one after the other. As if they did not know what caused his wife's pregnancies. Sandy continued to carry his loyalty to the British throne, and played his bagpipe any chance he could either at home or at a public affair.

Over the years, his wife and children became actively involved with school and church activities in the Congregational church, and began to associate primarily with rebellious Whig community. For a while, Sandy had endeavored to keep peace within his family, attending the church of his wife's choice. However, Sandy was beginning to feel torn between his responsibility to his family, and to his upbringing in the Anglican Church and the English monarchy; where he had solace and peace of mind. Gradually, music was his only retreat for this type of comfort, acceptance and relaxation. But this didn't always work! Whenever he played his bagpipes at home, his children used to make fun of "that funny sounding noise," and called him "Mr. Windbag." His wife, meanwhile, was relishing the increased attention she was receiving from her children, as well as, from the members of the Whig party. One day she stunned Sandy when she told him that her children and their country came before him; that was the last straw for Sandy, and he began to search more favorable surroundings.

Desperate for the love and attention he had once received from his family, Sandy realized that he had fallen out of step with the opinions of the majority in his New England community, especially with those of his family and their associates. Sadly, he became convinced that whenever he questioned the Rebels' logic and their "freedom seekers." Frequently, it appeared to Sandy that the Whig believers were purposely speaking with destain towards England's monarchy and Parliament in his presence. Regardless, he tried to reason with his wife, children and their friends, but they would look upon him as if he were the very Satan the Congregational preachers were warning their followers of. Like a few of his friends who were still sympathetic to the English cause, Sandy recognized the indefensibility of much of the legislation passed by Parliament and he had supported the repeal of the Stamp Act. However, he believed it was more important to maintain political order than to rebel against his mother country.

He distinctly remembered the time when his wife and children came home from church, relating to him what the Congregational preacher had warned the congregation: ...if Bishops should be sent to the Colonies, the people would generally turn Church-men, the Ecclesiastical state of things would soon be inverted, and the Episcopalians would quickly exceed the other denominations of Christians. If these Bishops should make use of their *Superiority*, as most probably they would, sooner or later, to influence our great men here, and much greater ones at home, to project, and endeavor to carry into execution, measures to force the growth of the Church, thus taking away the Christ given liberties which make men free." According to his family, the preacher concluded that if the Bishops and the Anglian Church grows out of its infant state so as to support and spread itself. He firmly believed that any non-Anglian church would not be able to propagate and proselyte according to their desire, their mission at least in the New England Colonies."

A few days later in 1776, Sandy had the opportunity to hear Samuel West deliver a Massachusetts Bay election sermon, during which he defended the logic of independence. In a long introduction, West explained the origins of society according to the Lockean principle of natural rights. His attitude toward government and his defense of revolution reflected the language and ides of Mayhew's essay against "unlimited submission." Samuel West then proceeded to relate natural rights to religious liberties and urged support of the Revolutionary leadership. At West's side stood David Jones of Pennsylvania who denied that Parliament had supremacy over the colonies, and suggested that *civil war* was an legitimate alternative to "abject submission." Jones qualified this statement by admitting that many colonists preferred to remain loyal to their king. However, he decried the British attempts to enslave the American subjects. As Sandy left the conference hall, he admitted to himself that New England was rapidly becoming a foreign place for him.

Realizing that his family was not going to change, Sandy concluded that he was left with just two choices. Stay and suffer the consequences, or pull up stakes and move out to a new environment. If he decided to move out, where would he go?

New York State was adjacent to Massachusetts, but Sandy knew there was no love lost between the residents of these states. Nevertheless, he had heard that there was a substantial number of Loyalists living in and about New York City. After considerable thought, he was determined to travel across the Hudson River and head for Albany; then pray that he would find some more "sensible" people. The next night he gathered his bagpipes, a few changes of shirts and socks, together with the Scottish Highlander medallion his father had given him, and stole away while his family were away at a political debate being held on the village's common.

TEN

THE RISK IS NOT TAKING ONE

August 30, 1775 in Johan Jost Jr.'s home on Fall Hill located on the south side of the Mohawk River in Tryon County

Johan Jost Jr. and his wife Maria sat in their rocking chairs facing the living room's newly constructed fireplace in the house on his mother's Burnetsfield Patent Lot #5 she had willed to him located on the south side of the Mohawk River. Maria had just finished hustling their seven children off to their beds. Being a very devoted and loving mother and wife, she knew that Johan had something very special he needed to discuss with her. Maria knew that they needed time together. While Maria was attending to children, Johan was busily stoking up a small fire in the fireplace. He knew that they really did not need to have a fire, but a burning log in the fireplace always helped to create a comfortable atmosphere for serious conversation. He had just finished pouring two mugs of hot buttered rum, as Maria entered into the room.

"What a welcoming sight," exclaimed Maria as she approached her favorite rocking chair. "This ambience you have concocted,

Johan, tells me that we have some serious talking to do." She raised her mug of hot, buttered rum to meet his raised mug.

"Here's to you, to us, and to ours," she toasted her weary husband, who was still trying to recover from his arduous conversation with his older brother Nicholas, and the meeting he had attended at Shoemaker's. "My love," he started, "I," he quickly corrected himself, "We have to make some serious decisions. Nicholas, in fact, warned me that if I continue to be so outspoken about my support of King George, that I'll not only lose my colonel's rank in the Tryon County Militia, but that the Safety Committee may put me in jail."

"How dare your brother make such a fraudulent statement to you," challenged Maria.

"I think because he loves me," seriously responded Johan. "I really believes he loves me, and does not want to see anything grave happen to me," he took of sip of the hot buttered rum, and continued. "I guess I should have said that he does not want to see anything perilous happen to our family."

"My dear Johan, how do you really feel about the politics of our country?" asked Maria as her thoughts hurriedly raced to their sleeping children. "Our oldest son George is fifteen years old," Maria stated, "maybe the war, if it does spread throughout the Mohawk valley, will be over by the time he will be drafted into service."

"You know, my dear, that I'm not a pacifist," declared Johan, "and I do not believe that George would hesitate to fight on the side of right as he sees it."

"Since you are a colonel in the Tryon County Militia, I have to believe that you, Johan, will fight with and for them."

"That's the problem, Maria," stated her troubled husband. "I honestly believe that Nicholas and my other brothers are being lead down the wrong path. Samuel Adams and Benjamin Franklin are just some loud-mouth politicians out to enhance their own future. I don't believe that Nicholas is that kind of person, but so many of those in the Whig party are nothing but opportunists."

"What makes you think those Tory leaders we know, do not believe in the same fashion?" asked Maria as she refilled their mugs with steaming hot buttered rum.

"Our king and his royal family come from a long line of traditions representing a considerable amount of stability and grandeur," Johan began as his mind pictured the regal presence of King George III and his Queen Charlotte in their golden carriage being drawn by three teams of white horses. He had heard George III was a tall, dignified man who worked hard taking his royal role seriously. Although as obstinate as the king sometimes was, Johan had heard that the king believed *that no one should be above confessing when they have been mistaken*. Johan had also heard that the king was deeply religious, and that he, unlike some kings before him was truly faithful to his wife. What Johan liked most about King George III was his sense of duty, both to the public and private, and his ability to speak to ordinary people. "I believe that our king has earned himself our well deserved respect and popularity."

"Just to be the devil's advocate," started Maria. "why do you feel so much loyalty to the Crown, when most of our friends and family are siding with the patriots and the Whigs.?

"Personally, we know," reasoned Johan, "that Britain's royalty has sustained itself for many centuries. The patriots and Whigs have virtually no track record. Whatever they have to demonstrate is far less than the record of our British monarchy. I do know whichever side we end up joining, it'll be a big risk." He stopped a moment and drank the last rum from his mug, and soberly stared toward his attractive wife of seventeen years. "Regardless of the side we eventually join, we risk to lose all we own, and perhaps even our lives," he added as an afterthought.

"The same is true for your brother Nicholas," stated Maria. "If both of our families chose the patriots, and the British defeat the patriots, both of our families will be declared traitors, and we'll lose everything; may even be tried and hanged as traitors."

"The same is true, if both families join forces with the British and the patriots win . Undoubtedly, we'll lose everything." stated Johan. "Just to assure that at least one of our families end up winning, perhaps Nicholas should continue with the Whigs and their rebel forces, and I'll switch from the Tryon County Militia to the British military," Johan continued half joking.

"You can't mean what you're saying," said his startled wife. "This is nothing to be joking about," she declared. "A few moments ago you were saying that there is a lot at risk. What is really at risk?"

"Well, first of all, we have this lovely, new house and barn sitting on 800 acres of some of the most fertile and beautiful land on the Mohawk River valley valued at somewhere near 2,850 pounds. We have at least forty head of horned cattle, 20 hogs, 20 horses, 60 sheep."

"You must not forget that we have seven slaves, also," sheepishly Maria her calculating husband.

"We're talking about nearly ten thousand pounds of value," Johan estimated. ignoring Maria's remarks about their slaves.. "That's a hellava lot of property to risk on one roll of the dice," Johan concluded.

"The greatest risk is if we do not take one at all, my dear," Maria seriously declared. "If you were to ask your heart, right now, which side would you like to fight for? What would you say?" Maria continued to egg her husband on toward a decision, "Which side comes immediately to your mind right now?"

Without hesitation, Johan responded to Maria's question, "The king's side of course!" To justify his choice, he continued, "I feel very comfortable fighting with the British, even though it may mean I'll be fighting against some of my neighbors, perhaps even against my siblings. The king and his troops have been very good to us, and I'm very proud to say I am a Loyalist, a Tory, if you prefer! Even with the British, I must admit there is some risk, but that's the risk I have to take," again he corrected himself, "We'll have to take. My love, we may lose everything," he concluded.

"On the other hand, we may be able to keep all the property we have right here," she smiled. "The most important part is that we keep our family together! Let's pray that His will be done."

* * *

Nicholas, as a widower had lost his first wife, Maria Dygert. He never dreamed that, if he were to remarry, that his second wife would have the identical name, Maria Dygert. But that is the way the circumstances worked themselves out. Unknown to Johan Jost Jr. and his wife Maria, Nicholas and his seventeen year old wife were having a similar discussion in the living room of their large brick mansion near a place commonly referred to as the "little falls" on the Mohawk River. As usual, there was a blazing log in the fireplace, Maria and Nicholas were sitting in their familiar rocking chairs which had been constructed by his father. But, unlike Nicholas's younger brother's taste for rum, Nicholas and his wife preferred drinking a hearty, dark beer at room temperature. To his brother's disgust, Nicholas's home always had a rank smell of burned pipe tobacco. Maria accepted Nicholas's pipe and all that went with it. He was her father figure, and she loved him dearly. Unlike Johan Jost Jr. and his Maria, who were constantly trying to improve their use of the English language, Nicholas and his Maria enjoyed speaking the guttural German language. Ironically, Johan Jost Jr. chose to keep the 18th century variant of his family name, and not to anglicize his family's name as his other brothers had. And much of the time Nicholas would forget that he was a Yankee, and would lapse over to speaking German much to his wife's displeasure. Before her marriage to Nicholas, Maria's family continued to intermittently speak German, but most of the time they tried to adopt the English language. Even though Nicholas was endeavoring to enhance his English, he felt more at ease speaking German.

"Yesterday, Johan and I had a serious discussion," confessed the general of the Tryon County Militia to his adoring wife. "Even though Johan is a colonel in the militia, I honestly believe that his heart and soul is with the king and his Redcoats."

"I'm sure that Johan likes the pageantry of the king's troops," observed his young wife, "and so does his wife. One day while I was watching our troops drilling on the field at Fort Dayton, I happened to overhear Johan's wife saying slanderous remarks about our militia. She was with some woman I did not know; I believe her last name was Shoemaker. Together they were laughing and calling our militia a bunch of country *yokels* in hunting jackets, who would retreat at the first sight of the British in their bright red jackets and shinny brass buttons."

"I guess I should not be surprised about what you are saying," declared Nicholas as he emptied the ash from his long clay pipe, and processed to fill it with fresh tobacco. He struck a light, blew a few smoke rings toward the living room's ceiling; his young wife was becoming use to this routine. "I have suspected that his wife wears the pants in Johan's household. Frequently, she puts the on appearance of someone who believes that her dung doesn't stink," the general stated rather contemptuously.

"Nicholas, you should not talk that way about your brother's wife! How would you like to have him say the something like that about you and me?"

"I know, my love, that you would not say anything like," confessed her admiring husband. "It was not too long ago when I was over at their home, and the three of us were discussing the political turmoil which appears to be developing in our colonies. Looking sternly at Johan and me, his wife said, *I'll tell you what our problem is. It's those damn immigrants. They should stay where they come from. We don't need them.*"

"Who does she think she is?" asked Nicholas's young wife. "The Native Americans were here centuries before the Dutch, the French, the West Indians, the British, and yes, even us Germans, for that matter, ever heard of America."

"Now, my dear, don't get your prettied little self all worked up over our foolish sister-in-law,' said her loving husband trying to console her in his interesting mixture of the German and English language, which was a sure sign that he needed a refill of his beer stein, and his pipe needed fresh tobacco. While Maria was refilling the steins, Nicholas attended to his pipe and tossed another log on the dying fire in the fireplace. Sparks from the fire seemed to jump up and welcome Maria as she returned with their two pewter filled steins, reminding her of the few times she had served as a waitress in the local tavern of her hometown.

After they had toasted themselves and their love, Nicholas confessed to Maria his beliefs regarding the simmering political undercurrent between the Whigs and the Tories. "Maria, my whole heart is with the Tryon County Militia. I believe to my very core in their cause. I also believe that the day will come when I may be fighting on the opposite sides of some my brothers. For some reason or another, I would not be surprised to hear that Johan had resigned from our militia, and to hear that he had accepted some rank in the British army, or other regiment loyal to King George III."

"You said that you believed in the militia's cause," stated Maria as her youth's curiosity radiated. "Please tell me just what is its cause."

"As I interpret the militia's cause," Nicholas began, "it intends to defeat the British military forces, and to be totally free of the British monarchy." He stopped talking, and took a couple of long drafts on his pipe. *He's starting his routine*, thought Maria, as she watched Nicholas blow the smoke rings toward the ceiling's hewed maple beams. "All of us want the *freedom* our ancestors came over here to America for," declared the weary general as he drank the last of his stein's contents. "I visualize an America free from the British royal, with all our mistakes and blunders, always being the beacon of freedom, charity, opportunity, and affection in to the point there many be many peoples who may envy us; perhaps even hate us, but if we want peoples of the world to like us, we must win their respect we need to be the best, the most consistent and most principled global citizens we can be."

"When you talk about freedom, Nicholas, do you include our slaves such as Dick, Sam, and Mary?" asked his wife hesitantly. She knew that this was one issue which she and her husband didn't always agreed upon. As long as Maria did not bring up the issue very often, he would tolerate the question, but the answer was always the same.

* * *

Colonel John Butler, the son of *Old Walter* and squire of "Butlersbury," sat meditating in his rambling two-story home overlooking the Mohawk River about seven miles from Johnstown, which his father Captain Walter Butler had acquired in 1760 for him. His father, *Old Walter,* as he was fondly called, reached the ripe old age of ninety after having served as a lieutenant in the British army for seventy years.

Colonel John Butler, who was born 1725 in New London, Connecticut, jokingly referred to Butlersbury frequently as *Old Walter's rum treaty acres*. When John was only a five-year old lad, his father had been transferred from Connecticut to take the command at Fort Hunter. Soon thereafter, his father arranged an afternoon meeting with New York's Governor William Cosby in Albany. As a result of the conference, John's father sent wampum belts to the sachems of Teantontalago, just across the Mohawk-Schoharie junction, and invited them to a *feast of brotherhood* at the fort. During that feast, which lasted three-days and eventually evolved into a jolly ole brawl, old Captain Walter Butler brought out the document, which Governor Cosby had read and approved the previous week, offering the Indians a huge gift of rum. As the Indians continued to consume generous quantities of the white man's rum, it became easier for them to scrawl their clan symbols on the bottom of the parchment. As a result, the recently relocated Connecticut resident magically became the sole owner of 86,000 acres of land at the Mohawk-Schoharie junction, minus 14,00 acres he granted to the governor as "finders fee." When Captain Butler discovered that a similar *rum feast* had secured the same results for George Klock's Corporation of Albany just a few weeks before, Butler had the Corporation's deed burned. At times, John had to question himself whether his father's treatment of the Indians was *Christian. Do unto others as you would they would do to you,* he would repeat to himself, then rationalize his fathers actions, *everyone else is doing it to the Indians*. So his thoughts ran to his good friend and mentor Sir William Johnson and to the beautiful and fruitful valley he lived in. Surprisingly, Sir William had nominated Colonel John Butler as the executor of his will, which caused the pronounced dislike, if not positive enmity, not only from Sir William's son, Sir John Johnson, but also of his two brothers-in-law, who were usually intimately associated with John Butler in their civil and military functions. Some will say their inherent dislike for John Butler was because he was born and bred in New England, that he possessed the New Englanders' cunningness and flattery which they used to dominate many situations.

The Mohawk Valley had been good for John Butler, his wife Catherine, and their five children. Walter, their oldest son was a law clerk with the firm of Silvester & Van Schaack in Albany. The three girls and the other son were being under the tutorage by the Reverend John Stuart, the Anglican missionary at Canajoharie. Devout church people, the Butlers held a pew at St. George's Church in Schenectady which was adjacent to Sir William Johnson's rarely used pew. John was one of Sir William's deputies in Indian Affairs along with Guy Johnson and Daniel Claus. John and his wife learned to keep much of Sir William's *wild Irish lusts* to themselves, yet they were aghast at the sequence of young Indian women who succeeded Catherine Weisenbergh as *housekeeper* at Johnson Hall. Often they had questioned themselves whether young Joseph Brant was truly Molly Brant's brother, or just another one of Sir William's half-bred offsprings. They wondered why Sir William had entrusted Joseph to the Moor's Indian Charity School in Connecticut and subsequentially sponsored him through the degree rituals at St. Patrick's Lodge of Masonary. Did the old man have a guilty conscience, or was he doing this *good turns* because he believed that Joseph Brant could assist him in future dealing with the Indians? John remembered hearing his wife Catherine saying *good riddance* when they had learned Reverend John Stuart had made Brant one of his assistants in translating the Scriptures from English to Mohawk. Butler also remembered Catherine's additional comment, "How is that preacher going to make a purse out of a sow's ear?"

As Colonel Butler remembered about Reverend Stuart, his thoughts went to thinking of *that other preacher*, Reverend Samuel Kirkland. Since 1766, this *Rebel lover* had been preaching to the Oneida, Tuscarora and eventually to the Onondaga, and had convinced them that they should proclaim a formal statement of *neutrality in this grievous struggle between our white brothers.*

The last straw as far as Colonel Butler was concerned was when he learned that Molly Brant was circulating the rumor that when Sir William Johnson lay on his deathbed, one of his last requests was to summon Joseph Brant to his side. At that time, Sir William entreated Brant to *Control your people. I am going away.* Shortly after Sir

William's death, the Crown appointed Sir William's nephew, Guy Johnson, as Superintendent of Indian Affairs. It has been *all down hill since then,* thought Colonel Butler. Regardless, he rationalized that someone, whether it was Molly or Joseph Brant it really didn't matter, the Mohawks have been convinced to join forces with the British.

In the middle of John Butler's mediation, his wife Catherine entered the room. "I apologize for waking you, my husband, but I just learned something which you might want to know."

Her dazed husband asked, "What have you learned, my dear? Has our noble king arrived on America's shore?" John queried jokingly as he rubbed his eyes.

"Now let's be serious, John," cautioned his wife, "I just learned from the reverend from our church in Schenectady that Guy Johnson has persuaded his wife and children to go to England *until the Rebels have been put down, perhaps four, certainly not more than six months.* I also learned that Daniel Claus and his family have settled temporarily in Montreal."

"It's interesting that you mention what the Johnsons and the Clauses have done, because I have had similar thoughts about you and our children," responded the colonel of a Loyalist regiment. "We just do not know how this disturbance will play out," he explained. "Like Guy Johnson, I expect that the entire affair will be over in less than six months, but while all this military conflict is being carried on, I want to be sure that you and the children will be safe and sound."

"John!" Catherine stated firmly, "The children and I will be absolutely safe right here in Butlersbury. Besides, you know perfectly well that I am a much better farm manager than you are.," she said smilingly, and gave her admiring husband a long, warm kiss on his lips. "Now tell me, my lover man," Catherine continued, "you're going to miss me when you and your rangers are out chasing the Rebels. With me back at Butlersbury to keep the farm fires burning, perhaps you could find some time to stop for a cup of tea, or maybe something else."

"Catherine, you are the dearest creature I've have ever known," the colonel confessed, "without you and the children I don't know what I would do. Talking about the children, I must confess that our eldest son, Walter, has me worried. It is his impetuousness and his nasty temper that has me concerned. I don't know how he will fit into any military force, to say nothing about the British type of European discipline. He has already asked my permission to join me when I report, in a few weeks, at Fort Niagara. Sometimes, I wonder if our right hand knows what our left hand is doing."

"I am not quite sure I understand what you are talking about, my dear," stated his concerned wife.

"I just recently received this letter from Colonel Mason Bolton, the commanding officer at Fort Niagara:

> I have drawn a bill of 14,760-9-5 pounds (roughly $75,000.) on account of sundries furnished Indians by Major Butler. Between us I am heartily sick of bills and accounts and if the other posts are as expensive to govern as this has been I think old England had done much better in letting the savages take possession of them than to have put herself to half the enormous sums She had been at in keeping them.

"As optimistic I as like to feel about this conflict," he said rather sadly. He quickly changed his entire demeanor, "I feel very strongly that the Tories and British will eventually prevail, but I will never underestimate the determination of the Whigs and their Indians allies. You see even though the Mohawks are with us, they are literally hemmed in on the east by the Whigs' Committees of Safety, and on the west by the Oneidas and Tuscaroras who that Rebel Reverend Kirkland convinced to *take the pledge of neutrality.*"

"You should be very grateful that Governor Sir Guy Carleton approved your formation of a regiment of the Loyalists Rangers," said Catherine trying to cheer up her husband.

"For that I am thankful," the colonel agreed with his wife, "as well as granting me the colonelcy. He even suggested that the "Butler Rangers," as he referred to my regiment, should wear the same green jackets with yellow trim, tan breeches, and a bucket-shaped leather headgear with a horned moon of brass near the crest, just like the uniform which the other Ranger regiments being formed at New York City and in New Jersey will be wearing." As an after thought, "We even agreed upon the strategy of frontier raids."

* * *

On a warm July 26, 1775 afternoon, Colonel John Butler, escorted by one hundred Mohawk Indians came to Fort Niagara's wharf, bringing America's first Civil War between the Tories and Whigs to Fort Niagara.

ELEVEN

STAND BY THE KING

Late March, 1777
At the home of Johan Jost Jr.

"The Tryon County Committee is after me," Johan Jost Jr. announced to his wife Maria as he burst through the front door of their comfortable home on the Mohawk, and rushed into the living room where wife was working on a patch-work quilt. "Thank the Lord that there's no full moon, or those ruffians could have trailed me," he exclaimed.

"Oh, my dear I'm so delighted to see you home. The children and I've missed you so much these past five or six months. How did you get here? How did you get out of the jail? Do you think they followed you here? I've missed you so very much ever since the Committee of Safety threw you into that awful jail in Albany last October. The children have missed you, too. They've been lost without you around home. How can I help? Can I get something for you to eat? You must be exhausted and starved," the excited and jubilant Maria said as she scrambled to abandon her quilting, and rushed to her husband's open arms.

"I don't think they followed me, but sooner or later they are sure to be looking here for me, my love," Johan stated as he looked into his wife's pleading eyes. "I hesitate to say what I'm going to say, but for all of our sakes; I believe I should leave immediately for Fort Niagara, and join the Loyalist forces there. As you may have learned from some of our Loyalists spies, after October and November, 1776 when the Tryon County Committee of Safety interrogated me, and threw me into the Albany *Gaol*, I have repeatedly tried to communicate with you."

"I did receive bits and pieces of news about you," responded his wife of nineteen years. "They told me where you were. I gave them written messages for you to let you know that we were alright, but I never heard from you."

"Well, the Rebels had me locked in solitary confinement, just because I was a brother to their General Nicholas." He thought a moment and added, "I do not believe that if Nicholas knew how badly they were treating me, that he would have allowed this type of torture. Right now, what is important is that I have been informed that the Rebels have just been reinforced by the arrival of fresh troops from New England, and they have gained almost full control of all of our public affairs. And, my dear," Johan Jost Jr. momentarily stopped to collect his thoughts. He stood erect, and addressed his wife as he would talk to the troops in his militia company. "These damn New Englanders did not fail to make relentless use of their power. One of their first acts was to disarm Colonel John Butler's tenants, and to reorganize the Tryon County Militia under officers whom they thought they could rely upon with implicitly. In order to assure the retention of every position, each and every militiaman was required to read and agree with the Articles of Association. Many agreed with the articles right away, for reason or other some were allowed a week to think about signing the "agreement." When my friends Colonel Frey, the Reverend John Stuart, and Henry Hare all flatly refused to sign the agreement, they were quickly hustled off to prison; that God awful jail the Rebels had me warehoused.

That's why I know that my time here is very short. As you recall, the Rebels gave me one week before they demanded that I either sign or else. After I refused, they tossed me into that dirty, stinking, filthy, rotten Albany gaol," he concluded by pinching the end of his wrinkled-up nose with right thumb and forefinger.

"I remember, my dear," responded Maria, "and we never believed that the Rebels would think of casting their militia general's brother into prison again. I just can't believe anyone who has known you and your family," she raised her arms outward, and grazed toward the ceiling, "why your family must be about the affluent and influential settlers in the valley. If it wasn't for Sir William Johnson, your father and your grandfather, this valley would still be back in the dark ages."

"My dear, I'm afraid it is too late to think about, or brood about how we wished circumstances were. We must be realistic, and plan for our immediate future before it's too late to have even the opportunity to plot our survival." He placed each hand on his hips, and stared toward his wife, "Maria, these men are deadly serious," stated Johan Jr. "From what I've heard, Sir John Johnson believed he was in a relatively strong position, and he told the committee that he would rather lose his head than to comply. Secretly, he has started to form a regiment for the support of the Crown. In fact, I just learned that Jerome Butler, the second mayor of New Palatine, and co-owner of the Heidelberg Tavern, has already joined forces with Sir John."

"Maybe that is what you should do, but I can not bare the thought of you being away from the children and me," regretfully Maria stated, and then she asked,"but what about Jerome Butler's wife, Martha? What is she going to do?"

"From what I have gathered," responded Johan Jr., "Martha Butler is going to continue to operate the Heidelberg Tavern. Hopefully, according to Sir John and Jerome, the tavern can possibly serve as a reservoir, an outpost for the collection of valuable political and military information. As you know, it presently serves as the valley's most popular watering hole where Whigs and Tories alike gather to

STEPS TOWARD FREEDOM

wet their whistle, and argue about who and how the conflict is going to win.

"But we, you and me," Johan continued very seriously as he sat in the rocking chair next to his wife's. "Very possibly, it will be tougher on you and the children than it will be upon me. We do know that John Butler's fears about his wife Catherine and their younger children were confirmed, when they the Rebels confiscated their home *Butlersbury* were taken *in custody* by the Provincial Congress *in lieu of John*'s bail bond. In addition, everything they owned has been completely plundered and destroyed. Why even the Continental officers have the nerve to be riding John Butler's horses in public. In addition, all of the Butler's sheep, cattle and hogs have been seized for the Rebel troops mess. Another thing, Colonel Butler's wife Catherine and all of the children, except their oldest son Walter, are being held under house arrest in Canajoharie. According to some rumors, I've heard that they may be all transferred to quarters in Albany. What we need right now are guns and Ranger uniforms," Johan resolved as he stood up in front of his wife's chair, knelt and placed his head in her lap. "My dearest wife, I know I must leave within the minute. I understand that Colonel John Butler and some of his Rangers are presently stationed at Fort Niagara, I know one of the ablest scouts, whom Colonel Butler trust implicitly, who can and will lead me to that fort. In fact, he had already agreed to meet me within the hour down by the *little falls*."

Maria and Johan quickly rustled up some food, and stuffed few extra pairs of clean socks, underwear, and other clothes into a knapsack, "Go quickly, my love, before the children awake, and I begin to cry," advised Maria, as the harried couple clung together in each other's arms wondering what the future would bring to their family. The back door of the Johan Jost Jr.'s house opened. His dark figure slipped out into the darkness, and melted into the night. Soon the Rebels' general's brother joined the Loyalist colonel's faithful friend and young adventurer, William Caldwell, who had successfully assisted Johan Jr. in escaping from the Albany jail, and was ready to guide Johan Jr. and his new found friend, Sandy McKnight through the wilderness to Fort Niagara. Together, the recently escaped Tory sympathizer, together with a stranger he had met at Shoemaker's Tavern, and their trustworthy guide headed for the *old Forbidden Path,* still a *terra incognita* to most white men, which would lead them through the Seneca country, and eventually toward Fort Niagara. Expecting to join forces with Butler's 's Rangers along with several other Palatines who had decided to "stand by the king," the next *friendly* person these three committed Loyalists would see would be Colonel John Butler and his son Walter at Fort Niagara. After arriving at Fort Niagara, Johan Jost Jr. was pleased to learn that his knowledge of and popularity among the Indians resulted in him being attached to the Indian Department with the rank of captain.

In time, Johan Jost Jr and Sandy McKnight.'s destiny was about to take a number of tumultuous turns eventually joining the King's Troops on the expedition against Fort Stanwix. As a captain, Johan Jr. would serve as an overseer of the detachment of bateaux and during the siege of Fort Stanwix, and Sandy was assigned to be his staff sergeant. More importantly, they would be a part of the detachment sent "in arms" to oppose the Rebel body of Tryon County Militia, which would be ordered to march west from Fort Dayton to relieve the Fort Stanwix's garrison.

TWELVE

A JOURNEYMAN'S TALE

Late March, 1777 En Route to Fort Niagara

It was about an hour or two before sundown. The guide, William Caldwell, sat around a small campfire with his two Loyalists friends, Johan Jost Jr. and Sandy McKnight, as they quietly discussed their evening's continued trek to Fort Niagara. The three had spent much of their daylight time resting, storing up energy and food in order to continue their travel swiftly during the evening. Since Caldwell was very familiar with this route, experience had taught him it best to travel during the darkness of night, and spend the daytime resting under cover, as well as gathering and cooking food stuff to enable them to travel more swiftly under cover of the night.

After they had completed their preparation for the evening's trek, Caldwell was the first to break their silence, "Sandy," he started as he poured the remaining luke warm, dark tea into their tin cups, "Johan Jr. tells me that you originally came from Boston area. How did you end up here in the Mohawk Valley? From what I hear most of the loyal Bostonians journeyed their way down to New York City. From what I've heard New York City is the American capital for Loyalists, with its fine harbor, the city is essentially serving as the depot behind the British armies, and is rapidly becoming a naval base for the Royal Navy."

"What you say about New York City is very true," acknowledged Sandy. "You see I was one of those Bostonians who journeyed to New York City, but to tell you the truth there were too much going on there which distributed me."

"Like what?" asked Johan Jr.

"Now you may think that I'm prejudiced against the Southerns. I am not," he stated emphatically, "but when they start talking about the black slaves in such disparaging manner, I could not take it. Sure we have slaves up in New England, but we treated them as human beings not like cattle.

"New York City attracts thousands of Loyalists, Tories as they are called in New York City," Sandy continued, "not just those who came from adjacent counties, but also refugees from every colony and every route. Many of us New Englanders who had served the king in Boston came to New York City by just following the British Army, as did the Marylanders and the Pennsylvanians. Therefore, it's not hard to believe that New York City has become the largest British garrison in the colonies with about fifteen thousand soldiers and sailors. In fact, I understand that New York's twenty-five thousand population is the nation's second largest city next to Philadelphia's forty thousand."

"What puzzles me," interrupted Caldwell, "why would a city slicker like you want to come up here in the north woods filled in the summer with black flies and the year around with all of these blood curdling Indians, rather than black slaves."

"The way I look at it," started Sandy, "we're all God's children. Each of us were reared in diverse philosophies by our parents and neighbors. We think differently; have different value-sets. We worship and are guided by distinct divine guidance. That's why I prefer having the British royal sovereignty as our divine guidance."

STEPS TOWARD FREEDOM

"At times you sound as if you favor the Rebels," inserted Johan, "when you talk about equality of people."

"I do believe in the equality of people," assured Sandy, "but there is a certain order of respect, and discipline which must be followed in a society. That's why I believe in the order our king provides for all of his subjects."

"Once, too, while I was in New York City," started Caldwell, "I met a Loyalist newspaper critic gentleman named Nicholas Cresswell, who had reached New York after eighteen months as a prisoner of the Rebels in Virginia. He and another persecuted Loyalist managed to steal a small sail boat, and were fortunate to be rescued by a British naval squadron. After his jail experience, this young English immigrant's initial high hopes and ambitions for America were beginning to wan after seeing New York City."

"From what I hear about New York City's harbor is jammed packed with very large number, of apparently prosperous sailing vessels from many ports-of-call waiting to crowd into its harbor, thus forming the kind of *liveliness* of most seaports," injected Johan Jr. He stopped a moment, and asked his companions, "Do need for me to describe what I mean about "seaport liveliness?"

"I don't how a backwoodsman like you, Johan, would know about seaport liveliness. Probably the nearest you ever got near to a seaport is time you had seen Albany," said Calwell.

"No, it wasn't it, was the time I visited Poughkeepsie, New York while they were towing whales up the Hudson River for processing," corrected Johan Jr.

"You're correct, Johan," agreed Caldwell, "I understand that New York City was once an flourishing, opulent and happy city, where everyone was doing everything they could do to assist each other, and the Whigs and Loyalists were equal gainers. But, now almost everyone is trying to cut each others' throats, and to destroy each others' property whenever the opportunity presents itself."

"It sure sounds like a civil war is going on there," observed Sandy.

"That's what I'm trying to say to both of you," Caldwell continued as studied his two charges, "that Cresswell had expressed to me some possible difficulties for us Loyalists. Many of us have frequently considered the Rebel General Washington as nothing but a Negro-driver with a rag-tag bunch of undisciplined farmers; the scum and refuse of the earth. But recently, this country bumpkin has been able to keep, as fine an army of veteran soldiers England has ever had on this continent, at bay or even at times in retreat. In fact, Cresswell predicted that Washington's great caution *would always prevent him from being made a prisoner to our inactive General Howe.*"

"Why do you sound so pessimistic about our cause?" asked Johan Jr.

"I'm not saying," started Caldwell, "that I believe what Cresswell said is the truth, or that I believe as he does. What I'm saying is that if we three truly believe in the Loyalist cause, we had better hurry our asses to Niagara, before Cresswell's pessimistic beliefs about the future of America begins to infect our loyal members of the New York population. I'm certain that many Loyalists are growing anxious about the campaign General John Burgoyne is planning to divide the New England and northern states from the southern colonies. Burgoyne's successful of this campaign will destroy all the Rebels' dreams they have of leaving the British Empire. Just imagine all of their personal sufferings the Rebels have endured in vain in the name of liberty and freedom. What I'm afraid of is that many of our Loyalists may be learning to hate and to despise not only the acts of terror, but also those who have supported and tolerated it."

"Do you have any doubt of Britain's commitment to the war," asked Johan Jr. "The reason why I'm asking you about Britain's commitment, is that I understand that Benjamin Franklin's illegitimate son, William Franklin who became the Governor of New Jersey, had remained in his office in search of conciliation until a revolutionary congress arrested him and sent him off to detention in Connecticut's Simsbury Mines, a cavern seventy feet underground where hundreds prisoners are housed in the abandoned shafts of a former mine. Later, the formerly conciliatory royal governor became embittered by his own maltreatment and the death of his wife, he gave up in despair, and became estranged both from America and from Britain.

Nevertheless, the younger Franklin stayed in New York complaining of Britain's failures of strategy and lack of resolve and proposing a ceaseless war against revolutionary America no matter what the cost. However, you have to give him one hellva lot of credit because under his leadership the Board of Associated Loyalists advocated and has carried out a policy of harassment and guerrilla raids against the Rebel territory all around New York City."

"Talking about raids," Caldwell interrupted without hesitation, "and that's all the more the urgency, why we have to get started toward Niagara."

The three Loyalists doused and buried their smoldering campfire embers, and let the North Star help lead them toward their destination.

Unknown to these northbound Loyalists, there were still some Loyalists in New York City opposed to Franklin's resort to war vengeance. Heading this aspect of the nation's first civil war was William Smith, a New York politician whose commitment to peace and the possibility of reconciliation kept him wavering between the Whigs and the Tories. Being a believer in New York City's mercantile community of practical trading men who retained a faith that America and Britain needed each other, and could yet resolve their differences. What most concerned Smith was that the exchange of guerrilla atrocities of the "civil" war, such as Franklin's Associated Loyalists, encouraged and could only stiffen resistance and poison relations between the warring parties. Rather, he argued for a more restrained military campaign.

What Smith had observed was that territorial control remained in dispute, destruction of property was as common as seizure. The Whigs and Tories continued to wage an *economic* war against each other in order to meet their own supply needs or to punish the other side. As the civil war proceeded, it appeared to Smith that the control over the countryside was generally maintained by the Rebels due to their flexibility and tenacious network of militias and Safety Committees. Often times, the net result of most of these seizures was either exile or imprisonment, and probably property confiscation whether the victim were either Whig or Tory, black or white.

Before the civil war started, slavery and the black population in the thirteen colonies had complicated the political issues for the Whigs and Tories. Loyalists to the Crown charged the Rebel slave-owners as *hypocrites.* The Rebels', many of whom were slave-owners and defenders of a society built upon slave-holding, vigorous talk of liberty, rights of man, representative government and resistance to the king's tyranny was merely a disguise, whereas some years earlier, the British had prohibited slavery. Throughout the war the British would offer freedom, first to slaves who would bear arms, then to any slave who fled Rebel owners and reached British territory. By the end of the conflict, escaped slaves were a vital minority in the Loyalist forces. Undoubtedly, these British efforts were in retaliation to the Rebels' *manumission laws* which granted free status to blacks who served in the states' militia.

Jeptha Simms, a New York frontiersman, relates an incident which occurred during one of General George Washington's visit to Albany:

> He [General George Washington] was walking the public street in company of Brower Banker, a respectable citizen, when a old Negro passing took off his hat and bowed to him; the great commander returned the compliment. Banker expressed surprise that his companion should notice a descendent of Ishmael, observing that it was not the custom of the place [Albany, New York] thus to notice slaves. *I cannot be less civil than a poor Negro,* replied the General.

Thomas Peters, a North Carolina slave who had fled from his owner's plantation in 1776, made his way to a British ship, which eventually carried him to New York City. There he enlisted in the Black Pioneers, a labor battalion of freed slaves, and served out the rest of the conflict in the New York City area. In three years Peters had earned the rank of sergeant, and married Sally, another escaped slave who had also joined the Black Pioneers. Thomas and Sally Peters were just two examples of black Loyalists out of thousands of slaves who sought happiness of liberty, which they believed that Tories and British belonged to the side most likely to offer these dangerous and eventful joys. Probably because the majority of colonies' black population was concentrated was located below in what is presently known as the Mason and Dixon line, perhaps this is the primary reason that the British were successful in attracting a vast number of black refugees in their military service, including many of George Washington's slaves from Mount Vernon.

THIRTEEN

THIS IS A FRATICIDAL WAR!

Spring 1777 After Butlersbury
was taken and plundered by Rebel forces

Walter Butler confirmed his father's, Colonel John Butler, worse fears about his wife, Catherine and his younger siblings. Butlersbury had been taken *in custody,* and plundered by the Continental Congress *in lieu of John Butler's bail bond.* All of the Butler's livestock including their cattle, sheep, and hogs became provisions for the Continental army. Initially, the Rebels allowed Mrs. Butler and their children to remain in their mansion in Canajoharie, but under house-arrest, knowing that they would soon be transferred to more secure quarters in Albany.

"This is a fratricidal war!" shouted Catherine Butler to the Continentals as proceeded to drive away all of their livestock. "It's a *civil war!"* she yelled louder as she and her children ran after the troops who were having trouble to herd the live stock in an orderly parade down their narrow farm road toward the King's Highway. Feeling desperately alone, even though her children were close by to give her moral support, Catherine Butler led her despondent family to what was left of their home.

When they arrived back to their home, the Butler's youngest child asked, "Mommy, what did you mean when you said that big word, fratricidal, to those bad men?"

"Fratricidal, my dear," Catherine responded to her youngest as her other children huddled about them to hear what she had to say. "Very simply, my dear, fratricidal is the act of killing one's own brother or sister, or the act of killing relatives or fellow-countrymen, as in a civil war."

"Will the bad people kill us?" asked the bright-eyed youngster.

"No, I'm sure they will not," assured the troubled mother.

"How about Daddy," asked the inquisitive youth. "Will the bad people kill my Daddy?"

"No, they will not kill your Daddy,"Catherine answered briskly, and immediately changed the subject. "Children, you all go and wash up, while I prepare our dinner."

As the John Butler family gathered about the dinner table with an empty chair at the head of the table, and as usual, Catherine lowered her head, but this time she suggested, "Children, let us all pray in our own words to God that this terrible war comes to a quick ending, and that all of us will soon be back together again."

* * *

It was not an easy task as Catherine Butler had desired when she tried to pacify her children. In reality, pro-Whig sons testified against pro-Tory fathers and brothers at the Committee of Safety hearings. Not surprisingly, Peter Van Schaack, the Albany attorney who had been Walter Butler's law teacher, was being held in jail as a Loyalist; simply because he was a friend of Catherine's notorious husband John, and their equally notorious son Walter Butler!

Even intermarriage did not assure similar political views. For approximately five generations, the Dutch had inhabited the Mohawk valley; they, too, were not immune to the civil strife which was flooding the valley. The Van Rensselaers, Clintons, Yates, and more hesitantly, the Livingstons had pledged themselves and their worldly goods to the Whigs' cause, whereas the Cuylers, De Lanceys,

Cartwrights were faithful Tory followers of the British monarchy, as did thousands of farmers, shopkeepers, traders and boatmen prayed for and joined the kings' men.

The Johnsons and Schuyler, too, had selected different sides. Sir William Johnson's son Sir John Johnson adopted his father's Tory side, while General Philip Schuyler chose the opposite side. Soon after Sir John arrived at Fort Niagara, on January 13, 1777, General Schuyler wrote him: *If Lady Johnson is at Johnson Hall, I wish she would retire... and therefore enclose passport... as I shall march my troops to that place without delay.* The Lady Johnson refused to accept the general's offer. As a result, General Schuyler arranged to meet with Sir Johnson on January 17th, when the Tory leader acquiesced to the Rebel general saying, "Hold myself at the order of your Congress, and not to support its enemies." Four months later in May, Sir John escaped parole, abandoning Lady Johnson, and fled to Fort Niagara where he met Johan Jr. At Fort Niagara, Sir John received a letter which Lady Johnson had smuggled out of Albany informing him that she and their baby were under house-arrest at General Schuyler's mansion, and that Johnson Hall had been plundered. She closed her letter telling her husband that their Highlanders, who had refused to flee, were either killed or shipped to the Connecticut cooper mines, which had become the Rebels' principal prison for *dangerous Tories.*

Sir John Johnson, too, was having his share of troubles with the Whigs. After a year of struggling with the Committee of Safety, he gave up and fled through the wilderness to Canada taking with him 170 of his loyal Scotch tenants. The committee believed that Sir John was corresponding with their enemies and was planning an Indian and Loyalist uprising, which indeed, he was, although that he had vowed that he would not. Sir John believed that the Rebels were getting ready to march against him, though they, too, vowed that they would not do such a despicable thing. Sir John could not understand what the civil strife was all about, and he had reason to flee, but it would cost him dearly.

Meanwhile, Catherine Johnson and their baby were being relocated, British frigates were escorting a fleet of transports and

STEPS TOWARD FREEDOM

merchantmen through the ice floes in the St. Lawrence River to Montreal with the dashing and the architect, Gentleman Johnny Burgoyne, of the British campaign designed to separate the colonies, and ultimately defeat the Rebels. It was Burgoyne with about 10,000 British Regulars and German mercenaries stuffed in below the ships' decks. Accompanying Burgoyne were one of Germany's leading generals, Baron Friedrich von Riedesel and his wife along with the three Loyalists' leaders including Guy Johnson, Daniel Claus, and Joseph Brant, who were returning from their mission to England. During July, Butler and Sir John had arranged a conference with the three Loyalists and the military officers. During this conference, Guy Johnson pledged *swarms of Six Nations warriors* to Burgoyne and von Riedesel for the execution of Gentleman Johnny's *Thoughts*. To guarantee this amount of support, Brant presented officers with some scalps he and other Mohawks had peeled from disarmed prisoners after the Continental's surrender at The Cedars a few weeks prior. While Joseph Brant was presenting evidence of his sincerity, his sister Molly Brant, Sir William's *wife*, was riding from castle to castle along the Finger Lakes, the Genesee and the Allegheny with a *red hatchet* in her saddle bag, stirring up rancorous hate toward the Rebels.

Throughout the summer and fall, Loyalist refugees came flooding through the gates to Fort Niagara. Among these refugees were Wilhelm Kerchner, the owner of New Palatine's only general store, together with his wife Sarah and their daughter Helena. An authoritarian of the first class, Kerchner could not stand the Rebel ruffians and their total disregard for authority and strict discipline. The British king's rule and respect was the nearest sign of authority and discipline since he had migrated from Germany.

With the arrival of each group, the lust for revenge grew within John and his son Walter's to match that of Sir John and his brother's-in-law. They watched the new arrivals, many of who were men and boys who were scarred by the horse-whipping, thumb-hangings, groin-kicks and testicle tortures that the Committees of Safety inquisitors inflicted upon them in order to force them to testify about *Tory spies* and *plans for the Johnson invasion.* Others among these refugees were two tattered and starving Negro slaves from Butlersbury escorted by Senecas. These men told of the looting and the imprisonment, eight to ten in a single cell, of Mrs. Johan Jost Jr. and other Loyalist wives. Guy Johnson had decided to send his wife and children to England "until the Rebels have been put down, perhaps four, certainly not more than six months." The Clauses had settled in Montreal in a *temporary* home. Unfortunately, Catherine Butler had refused all suggestions, and she and the Butler's children had believed that they would be perfectly safe in Butlersbury.

Throughout the balance of 1776, the threat of Colonel Gansevoort's troops at Fort Stanwix, as well as the severe winter, the Loyalists had been relatively content to delay any offensive action against the Rebels until spring. Joseph and Molly Brant, however, had been busily successfully recruiting some Senecas, Delawares, and Cayugas. Joseph took sufficient time off from his recruitment to lead some of his warriors off to interrupt Benedict Arnold's retreat down Lake Champlain, after his suicidal attack against the Burgoyne- von Riedesel fleet off Valcour Island on October 11th. During the early '76-'77 winter, Colonel Mason, with Governor Carleton's support had commandeered every refugee who could walk and every Indian who could be persuaded to work to carry supplies up from Montreal and strengthen the fortifications at Carleton Island. Near the end of winter, the Loyalists had selected one of the western Thousand Islands, constructed a blockhouse and wharf and named it Carleton Island in honor of the Governor, and garrisoned it with 1,500 of the Royal Highland Emigrants, Rangers and Quebec Militia. Needless to say, between Arnold's untimely interruption, and the valley's harsh winter conditions, Burgoyne's boast about "celebrating the New Year in the ruins of Albany" would be placed on hold until the following year, 1777. This period afforded the British time to fine-tune their strategy for Burgoyne's "Thoughts." It was resolved that Burgoyne and von Riedesel would the direct the main assault from Montreal and travel down Lake Champlain and Lake George. General Sir William Howe would leave New York City and sail up the Hudson River breaking through the chain of fort established by the Rebel General Israel Putnam at the Hudson Highlands. The third expedition, lead by Colonel Barry St. Leger, was designed to leave Montreal, sail down to Oswego, attack and capture Fort Stanwix, and follow the Mohawk valley to Albany. This force was composed of the Wurttemberg Chasseurs, the regiment of Royal Greens recruited by Sir John Johnson, plus any Indians who Joseph Brant could arouse This spur of Burgoyne's "Thoughts" was the one which would have most direct effect upon the Mohawk valley and its residents, and it was one of the most critical in Burgoyne's mind, because the Mohawk valley was the primary breadbasket which fed the Continental army; and the British needed the food produced in the valley ever as much as the Continentals. Burgoyne's plan appeared to be a masterfully designed campaign, but there were many variables which he had virtually not control over, such as the unpredictability of Indian support, the virtual no clear cut roads, the inclement weather, the undelivered orders to Howe. Consequently, General Howe was side-tracked in Philadelphia before he even headed his forces north. Perhaps the most important variable Burgoyne had miscalculated was the sheer determination of the Rebels to defeat the Loyalists and their British allies. To say the least about Burgoyne's own distraction caused by his commissary officer's wife, Fanny Loescher, the lady without the powdered wig.

* * *

During early July, 1777, Colonel John Butler arrived at Oswego from Niagara. When he learned from Molly Brant that she had only recruited about three hundred Senecas, and a few other Mississaugas, and Delawares had subsequently joined her; these were considerably fewer warriors than the five hundred warriors she had led him to expect. Butler made it very clearly to Molly how extremely disappointed he was.

"I can't believe that you and your brother were only able to scare up these few Indians," the colonel stated in disgust.

"I'm not making any apologies, colonel," responded Molly in her fluent, soft, and persuasive voice, "so many said they preferred to let the *white men* fight their own war. They wanted to remain neutral like their Onondaga brothers."

Irritated, Colonel Butler wrinkled up his face, and roughly told Molly, "You just go back and tell them that I'll give them ten beaver skins for each scalp they bring to me." The colonel looked at Molly's displeasing reaction to his offer. "In fact, Miss Molly," he said in a more pleasant voice, "I'll even give all the rum they can drink after the victory of capture of that damn little fort in the wilderness."

"I'm sure that will help to tempt them, especially if they can have some rum before they go into battle," suggested Molly Brant.

"Oh, hell!" exclaimed the exasperated Loyalist officer, "tell the sachems that we will provide plenty kegs of rum before they go on the warpath."

A few days later, Molly brother Joseph returned with about two hundred Cayugas from a recruiting mission along the Susquehanna valley. Thanks to the Brants' efforts, approximately seven hundred battle-ready warriors joined the St. Leger expedition to attack and capture Fort Stanwix, and from there to march through the exquisite, yet restless Mohawk valley.

The ever cautious and vigilant Molly Brant sent a Cayuga messenger with a letter to her brother Joseph informing him that she had received word from some Loyalists from either Palatine Bridge or Canajoharie, that the Tryon County Committee of Safety had recruited two regiments of militia from the valley, and that they intended to dispatched the regiments to relieve Colonel Gansevoort's garrison at Fort Stanwix. Last sentence in the Molly's letter stated that Joseph's former neighbor General Nicholas was charged with the responsibility to lead the Fort Stanwix relief regiments. Neighbor against neighbor, again!

* * *

Unknown to each brother, they, too, were going to be facing each other soon in battle. Johan Jost Jr. had succeeded in escaping from the Rebel jail and reaching Fort Niagara in March, 1777. In addition to Johan Jost Jr. serving with the Loyalists troops, a brother-in-law and a nephew were also marching with Sir John Johnson's Royal Greens. Most of the men serving in the Loyalists and the Tryon County Militia were old friends and neighbors who had worked together during the planting and harvesting times, on barn raising, at corn husking bees, and hop picking times. They and their children had socialized and courted each other, worshiped church services and enjoyed church picnics together. In fact, as in the case of Nicholas and his brother Johan Jost Jr. they had served and drilled together in the Tryon County Militia, and even left Oswego under the command of Sir William Johnson and Brigadier General John Prideaux with two thousand British regulars and the Colonial militia to besiege the Niagara forts held by the French.

* * *

On August 5, 1777, Brant and the Butlers, under St. Leger's orders, had taken the seven hundred Indian warriors downriver and established an ambush, as well as the siege lines around Fort Stanwix. John Butler had selected a wooded ravine two miles west of the Oneida's village of Oriska for the ambush. There the road dipped east down a slope to cross a creek and a marshy area with its dilapidated corduroy road before entering the western side of the ravine. Both Colonel John and Joseph Brant mentally thanked Molly Brant for her warning, they were preparing their forces for the ambush of the Rebel relief corps, as well the implementation the siege against the humble fort in the wilderness. This positioning of troops has been attributed to Brant, but Butler says it was a Seneca plan, while Claus and St. Leger say it was Sir John's plan. Regardless of whose plan it was, their warriors quietly lied in waiting until the relief force could be completely surrounded.

On the sultry, dark and early morning of August 6, 1777, as the eight or nine hundred Tryon County Militia trudged along the infamous King's Highway with their creaky oxen drawn carts under the cautious (some had accused him of cowardliness) command of General Nicholas. Some six miles east from the fort, the road crossed a marshy ravine, and here behind the bushes and willows were waiting the Loyalist and Indian Brant's forces.

Johan Jr. and Sandy stood behind a huge boulder near the western crest of the ravine affording them a relatively open view of the wilderness road's entrance through the ravine. What was unbelievable to them that the relief corps' Oneida scouts had not detected any signs of the ambush; Brant's warriors and Johnson's

Greens scattered behind trees, boulders and other hiding sites along both sides of the narrow route. As Johan Jr. and Sandy patiently waited in their vantage point, they suddenly saw a long straggly line of rag-tag men and young boys casually, as if they were on a hunting safari, carrying their rifles, knives and hatchets emerge from under the roads undergrowth followed by a number of ox drawn carts filled with supplies of various kinds.

"There must be at least two or three hundred men stumbling along that narrow and rocky road," Sandy whispered quietly.

"If they only knew what mischief awaited them hiding behind all those rocks and trees," observed Johan Jr., "they'd quickly high-tail it back toward where they came from," Just then Johan Jr. recognized the man in a military uniform riding an old white mare leading the column with a young lad carrying a silent drum along his side. "My God! Sandy, that's my older brother riding that white horse! He's leading all those men right into the trap, and sure as hell, he's going to be one of the first targets Johnson's Greens and Brant's warriors are going to aim for. My God! I remember drilling in the county's militia. I never thought that our difference would boil down to this kind of battle. Hell, I remember leaving Oswego with him under the command of Sir William Johnson and Brigadier General Prideaux with two thousand British regular and our county militia to besiege the Niagara forts held by the French.

Johan Jr, had no sooner finished telling Sandy about his discovery, than all hell broke loose. Even before the relief corps and its supply train had entered the ravine, some of the Indian warriors could contain their impatience no longer; they leaped from their hiding places, shouting their blood-curdling war whoops, like swarming bees charged the surprised Rebel forces, and began recklessly firing their guns. Once their muskets were empty, they either used their butts as clubs, or their tomahawks to attack their startled enemy. Suddenly, the once beautiful and peaceful woodland ravine was transformed into a tumultuous disorder of screams, curses, grunts and groans together with sharp reports of musketry, the clash of what few bayonets there filled the hot, muggy air. In addition to the clashing spears, tomahawks, knives, and Indian clubs, the unloaded rifle butts served as an instrument of death. The observing Senecas allowed themselves to be drawn into the fray, either because they enjoyed a good fight, or they wanted to survive themselves.

As Johan Jr. and Sandy watched a tomahawk crash into the skull of a Rebel near his brother's horse, Sandy declared, My God! those poor buggers don't have a ghost of a chance to survive this onslaught." As soon as an Indian saw a Rebel puff of musket fire, he would quickly jump upon the Rebel with the unloaded musket and proceed to scalp him. As the dead of both sides began to fill the swamp and cover the corduroy road, the result of musket fire, hatchet and tomahawk slashings, smashed skulls from rifle butts, and any other kind of weapon each individual could amass including rocks and branches. Soon the Indians began to emerge confidently, and at times carelessly, from the forest to claim their victims' scalps.

Johan Jr. saw his brother pointing toward the western slope near where he and Sandy were hiding, apparently directing a Rebel colonel to storm that very hill. As the Rebel troops advanced up the hill, they saw Johan Jr.'s brother's white horse leap up on her hind legs with his brother grappling to stay astride. As the obviously fatally wounded horse began to fall upon its rider, Johan Jr. saw his brother scramble and free himself from the saddle just as the mare appeared to nearly fall upon its rider.

The general's younger brother watched his brother as blood started to gush over the top of his boot. "Come on, Sandy," urged Johan Jr., "let's get the hell out of here before someone gets a line on us."

"Just a minute , Johan," said Sandy. "Do you remember the old Palatine storekeeper from New Palatine who used to attend many of our Loyalist meetings? I think his name was something like William Kerchner....."

"Sure, his name was Wilhelm," responded Johan Jr. showing signs of agitation, "but what's that got to do with the Rebels' general being shot? Any way, the battle's our, and their general is wounded."

Little they know that soon as thunderstorm would interrupt the fierce battle, and give the wounded general time to reorganize his troops into a *circle of death* and ultimately drive the Loyalist and Indian forces from their ambush site.

As the two scouts rushed from their observation post, Sandy finished telling Johan Jr, what he thought he had seen. "That fellow Kerchner, I just saw him and another one our Loyalists fighting with two Rebels who I've seen back there in New Palatine. One of them shot the Loyalist who was with Kerchner, and the other Palatine shot Kerchner right smack in the middle of his face sending his skull and brains to the winds. As they left the battle site, war whoops, screams, and musket fire kept echoing in their ears as they made their way to St. Leger's headquarters tent.

Years later, one of these young warriors, when an old man, declared that in the heat of that terrible battle "while we (were) doing of it, [it] feels no more [than] to kill the Beast, and killed most of all, the american (little "a") army." Colonel John wrote to Carleton a few days after the battle "the Indians shewed the greatest zeal for His Majesty's Cause, and had they not been a little too precipitate, scarcely a Rebel of the party had escaped," and added that their behavior "exceeded anything I could have expected from them."

The carnage was unbelievable with the ground littered with dead and dying of both sides. As far as the casualties, wounded and who won the battle is concerned the reader needs only to select whatever statistic suits himself or herself. The only thing the statistician can't prove is the truth. Historians, however, have stated that considering the relatively small number of men engaged, Oriskany was one of the bloodiest and most bitterly fought battles during this civil war.

St. Leger reported that four hundred Rebels lay dead on the field, and Butler and Claus as usual, could not agree on almost anything, estimated five hundred Rebel casualties. The Rebels themselves, however, admitted two hundred dead and a great number missing or wounded. Among the Loyalists fewer white men had fought, and suffered only about a dozen casualties, however, Sir John's brother-in-law was badly wounded and two of Indian department officers were killed. The heaviest of the Loyalists losses were incurred by the Indians totaling thirty-five killed and twenty-nine wounded, more than half of these casualties being among the Senecas, including several chiefs. Joseph Brant said later that his "poor Mohawks" also suffered heavily. The young half-breed, William Johnson, who had been with Brant's forces down on the Susquehanna, was killed. Rumor relates that as young Johnson lay with a broken leg, a wounded Rebel caught sight of him and struck the final blow.

Another source reports the following: after Brant's shrill whistle was sounded more than two hundred Rebels were killed in the next five minutes. After the thunder storm which interrupted the battle, the Rebel relief force lost another two hundred men. The Senecas lost a hundred and Johnson's Royal Greens lost another fifty.

One fact which no one would contest is that General Nicholas was shot through his left leg, and with the assistance of a thirteen year old lad from Schenectady, Jan Van Eps, the general was able to reach a beech tree. There he was placed astride his dead horse's saddle, he calmly smoked his clay pipe, and gave his troops orders which ultimately drove the Loyalist and their Indian allies in retreat.

This battle at Oriskany not only stopped the British and Indian forces' siege of Fort Stanwix by sending them retreating back to Canada, but it also was demonstrated that a gallant and determined collection of farmers, clerks, smithies, and whoever, when properly lead, could successfully exchange and even out match the well-trained British forces.

The next night or two, General Horatio Gates commander of the defense against Burgoyne's campaign, ordered General Benedict Arnold to take one hundred of Morgan's Virginia Riflemen and two hundred New England militia to the relief of Fort Stanwix.

At about the same time, Walter Butler received St. Leger's approval to take a patrol down the Mohawk valley and recruit for the Royal Greens. Sir John and St. Leger collaborated in writing a proclamation which ordered all of the "Rebels in the Mohawk Valley to lay down their arms,' and invited "supporters of the King's cause" to join Sir John's Royal Greens. By August 12th, young Butler and fifteen Royal Greens had reached German Flats, commandeered the home of a Loyalist named Shoemaker, exchanged their green uniforms for farm clothes, then sent Shoemaker's sons out to announce a series of meetings "for the King's men." Butler and his men made no effort to keep their meetings secret and claimed later that he was carrying "a flag of truce."

Over one-hundred of the valley's settlers had refused to march with General Nicholas and the Tryon County Militia to relieve Fort Stanwix, believing that it was not of their concern. But the massacre at Oriskany together with Walter Butler's, true to form, audacity angered them into action. These non-combatants surrounded Shoemaker's building, gunned down the Loyalists' sentries, and captured Walter Butler and everyone else in the house including a person named John Jost Schuyler, a nephew of General Nicholas, locally referred to as Hon Jost. He was considered a half-wit, but perhaps he was not quite as crazy as some of his neighbors believed. Son of the general's sister, Maria, Hon Jost was considered to be shrewd, resolute, and well versed in the language and custom of the Indians, and one whom the Indians had known for moons and trusted implicitly. Soon, he would become a useful pawn to assist the ingenious General Benedict Arnold in running off not only the embattled Indians, but also the defeated British and their Loyalist troops.

FOURTEEN

SUBJECT OR CITIZEN?

*Early Evening of August 27, 1777
at the Heidelberg Tavern in New Palatine*

The sun had set below the western horizon, and maple trees shadows were dancing about giving the sign for Harvey Perry to close down Kerchner's General Store, and for George Raab to stoke the coals near the anvil in his smithy shop; since the Battle of Oriskany, this had become their routine. After a lager or two along with some *intensive discussions* with some of their cronies at Martha Butler's Heidelberg Tavern, promptly at seven o'clock they would excuse themselves, and walk the short distances in opposite directions to their homes located within *the mid-settlement* of New Palatine where they knew their faithful wives would have a delicious traditional Palatine dinner, rich pastry, and their last stein of dark beer for the evening. As they entered the tavern, they were greeted by their friend and Karl Heindrick's assistant, Cal Swartz, gesturing them to join him at the heavy planked serving table where he was sitting at with some other familiar faces. Seeing the two enter, Harry

Hunter, the tavern owner's jack-of-all-trades, drew two steins of dark lager, and set them before the pair.

Cal Swartz was the first to speak, "Karl told me to tell you gentlemen that it'll be some time before he'll be able to join us here. He says that his leg is feeling much better, but the awkward splint which Old Doc Petrie, the general's only physician, put on his wounded leg makes it virtually impossible for him to walk, so I've been doing most of the cheese making business."

"Talking of cheese making," the smithy suggested, "I think we should have some of this famous Mohawk valley cheddar cheese, and some of Martha's fresh pumpernickel bread to go with our lager."

"What's this I hear about cheese and bread," asked the smiling tavern owner, as she carried four huge, empty steins past their table.

"Ya, Martha, you heard right," said the short, muscular smithy with his hairy chest proudly displayed between his unbuttoned leather jacket, "would you please ask Harry bring us a big chunk of cheese and a loaf of bread to help us sop up our lager?"

"I'll have Harry come right over here," the voluptuous proprietor assured her friends of their prompt service, "after he has filled these steins for me," she added. Martha stopped a moment, rested the empty steins against her bountiful bosoms, and asked, "What's this I hear about my former husband's young nephew, Walter Butler?"

"The other day," started Harvey Perry, "somebody was in Kerchner's store telling my wife, that young Walter is walking around as if he were the cock-of-the-walk claiming that the British defeated our militia at Oriskany, and that they were about ready to capture Fort Stanwix."

"Oh, hell!" declared a tall, skinny woodsman probably dressed in the same smelly, leather hunting jacket he had worn three weeks ago during the battle at Oriskany against Brant, his warriors, and their Loyalist allies. "That's so much bullshit," the woodsman continued as he emptied his stein. "Everyone knows that by the time the day was over, the only Loyalists or Indians left on that battlefield were dead ones. It was our militia who left the battle scene in a relatively orderly fashion, even though there were fewer of us leaving than when arrived there. We sure as hell were beat up, but we trimmed their asses," he concluded with his first-hand knowledge snicker on his whiskered face.

"I hear tell that we killed about one hundred of Sir John's Royal Greens out along that forest lane called the King's Highway this side of Fort Stanwix," stated a farmer from near the *little falls* on the Mohawk. "On top of that Brant and his Indian allies lost at least another one hundred before they left us alone at Oriskany."

"What is more important is not about who lost how many," Harvey attempted to return to the subject he believed his friends should be aware of, "is that young Butler is making no secret that he and a few of his Royal Green buddies are conducting meetings in the valley, and trying to recruit new members to join their regiment. They claim that a lot of our farmers and neighbors had refused to go along with Old Honikol to relieve our soldiers at Fort Stanwix, so they believe now that many of these men will join with their Loyalists forces."

"Sounds something like your old boss, Wilhelm Kerchner, only in reverse," said a bearded trapper from the carrying place near the Wood Creek, and wearing his coonskin hat looking at Harvey Perry. "Only's your old boss, Harvey, done took off for Fort Niagara before our battle at Oriskany."

Before the trapper could continue opinions on any further, George Raab stood up and motioned for Martha and Harry for refills. The smithy was attempting to rescue his friend Harvey from the embarrassment of telling the story, or hearing the story, told again how he had discovered that he had killed his former boss, Wilhelm Kerchner, with a musket shot straight into his face in the heat of battle at Oriskany.

Picking up on his friend's lead, Harvey Perry said, "I'll tell, you gentlemen, a couple things which helped to turn the tide in our favor that day," began the rather stout, and mild mannered Perry. "First of all, when our general *Old Honikol* got his horse shot out from under him, we were fortunate that that thirteen year-old kid, Jan Van Eps from Schenectady, and Karl Heindrick's son and our drummer-boy

Walter Heindrick, were there to help to set the general astride of his dead horse's saddle on that knoll beneath the beech tree. Then I think the Lord must have surly been with our side when He brought down that tremendous thunderstorm. As most of you know, we all got drenched to the skin, gun powder all wet, and everything else was wet a sop. However, while we all were trying to keep reasonably dry, Old Honikol's brain was busily cooking up ideas for a new strategy against those Indians and Loyalists. Before the thunderstorm and during the early morning's shooting, he had observed something that gave him the idea for his great idea of the *circle of death,* which was certainly novel and proved very practical."

Before Harvey could finish his thoughts, the bearded trapper said, "What I liked the most was when Old Honikol told us to team up into pairs of *two's,* and ordered each pair to hide behind big trees, large rocks, knolls, bushes, or whatever which could serve shields for us."

"That's when he told us that one of us was supposed to shoot while the other reloads his own rifle," chimed in Harry Hunter with a chuckle as he eavesdropped in on the conversation. "I sure as hell liked shootin' those Indians and their damn traitor friends of ours."

Ignoring Harry's remark, Cal Swartz said as he chewed on some of the very same cheese he and Karl Heindrick had manufactured some months before the Oriskany battle, "What was so great about the general's quiet manner, is that before the thunderstorm while Old Honikol was quietly sitting there on his saddle and smoking his clay pipe, he must have noticed that those damn Indians and Royals would, as soon as one of them saw one of us shoot toward them, they would immediately rush toward that shooter, and kill him either with a gun, a hatchet, a rifle butt, and sometimes even scalp him before he could even attempt to reload. That cagey old farmer must have seen the Indians pull that trick many times, so that's why he ordered us to team up in pair's, so one of us could reload while the other was shooting. I'm telling you men, that I'd never want to go through that living hell again, but I know for damn well sure I'm mighty proud, and thankful that Old Honikol was our leader." He stopped a moment, smiled and uttered, "Stubborn old Dutchman!

He's convinced me, if we want our freedom, we've gotta earn it, and fight for it to keep it!"

"What I regret the most about this whole experience," stated Martha Butler as she brought refills for the men's empty steins, "is that Old Honikol lost his life, and the freedom for which he had so gallantly fought defending his beloved Mohawk valley. We're all going to miss him."

"Yah, poor old Dutchman," said the skinny farmer who was beginning to feel the effects of the lager he'd been drinking. He smiled and continued, "Poor old fart, he first lost his horse, then he lost his leg which was shattered by the same musket ball which killed his horse, and finally, he lost his life. And so it goes, who ever said that life was fair?" he concluded as he laid his head on his arm, which was stretched out on the table.

True to form, Martha motioned Harry Hunter to help her with the inebriated customer up the staircase to the tavern's public loft filled with crushed straw. "This is what I don't like about running a tavern," she said. "You know I don't mind the drinking to have fun and good conversation, but sometimes some people just don't know when they've had enough. Part of my job is to make sure that it doesn't happen too often. I thank you men for cooperating with me, "she said as she strolled about the other tables with customers drinking, eating, laughing, but none too boisterous, especially as she roamed throughout the crowd.

"We've all been talking about Old Honikol," said a somber George Raab as he finished chewing the end piece of the pumpernickel loaf, "Doesn't it make you think what a peculiar set of circumstances we are witnessing here? Here we were his friends and neighbors, but now Old Honikol's younger brother Johan Jost Jr. was actually out there at Oriskany fighting along with Sir John's Royal Greens against his own brother."

"When you stop to think about it," the trapper with the coonskin hat, which was beginning to show signs of years' rough wear, said, "I'll betcha that there's many of us who were fighting against either our parents, siblings, or neighbors. All we know for a fact is that Oriskany was a damn bloody battle. I hear tell that one of our scouts recently visited the site. When he returned, he told some of us that entire battle site it was the most shocking spectacle he'd ever seen. There were dead Indians and white men still clinging together just as they had fallen. Some still held the weapons they were using, while other bodies had been torn to pieces by wild beasts."

"I think that about one of the funniest stories which occurred a few days after the battle was when Colonel Benedict Arnold was ordered by General Philip Schuyler to relieve Fort Stanwix. Arnold devised a trick to fool St. Leger and his gang," began Harvey Perry. "Arnold had learned about the capture of John Joost Schuyler, a nephew of Old Honikol's. Hon Yost, as most of us know him, is considered by many of us as a half-wit. But Arnold had learned that Hon Yost was not as crazy as some of us valley people believed him to be. In fact, he learned that Hon Yost was known to be shrewd, resolute, and well versed in the language and customs of the Indians. Arnold also learned that the Indians held Hon Yost in high esteem and reverence— *the way they treat all fools and lunatics.* Before leaving for Fort Stanwix, Arnold concocted a scheme to frighten the enemy, especially the Indians. After some friendly persuasion with Hon Yost and his mother, Arnold had Yost take off his jacket, then some soldiers shot holes in the jacket until it was riddled and torn with holes, and while his father and brother allowed themselves to be held as hostages until Hon Yost returned after a successful venture. Then Arnold ordered Hon Yost, together with a friendly Oneida sachem, to head for the Indians' camp with a *wild story about hundreds of Continental troops fast approaching Fort Stanwix.* Separately, they burst into the Indian council. First, Hon Yost told the Indians a story which completely exaggerated the size of Arnold's advancing troops. Very shortly, the wild-eyed sachem entered the council ring confirming Yost's *tall tale.* Their reports spread rapidly through the Indians' camps, ultimately reaching General Barry St. Leger, who was responsible for the capture and defeat of Fort Stanwix. The ingenious Oneida sachem intentionally mingled with some friendly Indians; with their assistance he spread alarms throughout the entire area that the fearsome *Dark Eagle,* as Benedict Arnold was known as among the Indians, had filled the valley swarming with at least a thousand men, ... *more than the number of leaves on the trees,* as Yost waved his arms toward the sky, and pointing to the trees which were beginning to show the first signs of frost with their bright orange and red colors. Between Hon Yost and the sachem, they convinced the Indians that they were not going to continue to fight any futile battles for the British that day; *let the white men fight their own battles* was their decision. Believing their Indian chiefs, as well as Hon Yost and the Oneida sachem, St. Leger and Sir John wasted little time in heading for Oneida Lake and Canada. As Arnold had instructed, a few young Indian warriors chased after the retreating officers, shouting, and yelling *"They are coming! They are coming!"* Meanwhile, some of the Canadian Missisague Indians, who had been fighting with the British, drank the officers' liquor, and soon became so thoroughly drunk that they began releasing their frustrations by attacking and robbing the British, Hessian and Loyalist troops. After St. Leger and Johnson arrived at Onondaga Falls, they learned about Arnold's deception, but by then both were willing to concede the western frontier to our Rebel troops. As the British and Loyalist troops headed toward Canada, St. Leger and Johnson, were startled to learn how poorly some of their troops were equipped; many of their men were without shoes and other personal equipment, as well as military supplies, which could be obtained only in Montreal."

"I understand that Karl Heindrick's black *blood brother,* George Jefferson, marched along with Benedict Arnold to Fort Stanwix, is that correct Cal?" asked the tall skinny farmer from the carrying place near Wood Creek.

"Yes," agreed Heindrick's assistant, "In fact, right now he's staying at the Heindricks trying to catch up on their lost years. As I understand it, in a few days Arnold is planning to march some of his troops his troops back to Fort Dayton, while Sergeant Jefferson is supposed to be recruiting volunteers from our New Palatine area, and then march his recruits to meet Arnold at either Fort Dayton or Fort Herkimer."

"I move that we adjourn this cheerful meeting," said Harvey Perry, "I've got to go back home or my wife will not let me in the house, and I'll have to sleep in Kerchner's store. "One word of caution though, before I leave," Harvey continued as he drained his stein, "let's all of us be on the lookout for young Butler and his Royal Green recruiters, and let's remember that we're all *free citizens*, and not just some of King George's *subjects*."

"I tell you," began Martha Butler, "if that young whipper-snapper nephew of my former husband wants to recruit Loyalist sympathizers, I'll tell him to go down to New York City. I hear tell that most of our rural country up north here in New York, and along the Mohawk is mostly controlled by our Rebel committees and county militia. I admit that we can easily identify the few isolated Loyalists. But, if Walter truly wants a bunch of Redcoat sympathizers, he should go down to the big city where I understand there is a whole nest of Loyalists, ever since the British were run out of Boston. My word of caution to all of us is that we should keep a watchful eye on that Loyalist pawn, Walter Butler."

Martha took a healthy drink from her stein, and continued, "Just a few days ago a Tory sympathizer stopped into the tavern. From what he told me that down in New York City, there are numerous units of New York royal sympathizers, who actually helped to conduct raids upon their own home region. Some even helped to destroy their own homes. He said that by the end of this summer, that the British hoped to have some of the provincial regiments so well organized that they will play a very important role in their effort to keep General Washington and his Continental Army on the run. He also said, that the British regulars' biggest problem was to learn the irregular tactics and skirmishing skills required to do battle in the upstate New York terrain. To help to solve this problem, the British were able to recruit and attach Loyalist sympathizers as guides and scouts to their regiments. Finally, he said many of these Loyalist *volunteers* were slowly, but surely beginning to accept a sense of exile for themselves and their families, as well as from their hometowns. He told me, that in order to survive, most of these *turncoats* have established new commitments to the *royal* cause to replace their *rooted* American ties. In fact, he said most of them have ceased to consider themselves Americans, rather they have pledged themselves and their families to the king and all he stands for."

"He concluded," said the concerned tavern owner, "that this war is not a revolution. Rather, he considered it a *civil war*. It was being fought by Americans with two different viewpoints and beliefs. The Tories believe that the colonies need to retain the support of the king and his Parliament, while the Whigs believe that *freedom* from the monarchy's tyrannical rule, three thousand miles across the ocean, is absolutely non-essential. In fact, he said something that really made to think twice. He said that us Whigs, Rebels or whatever we call ourselves have been busily talking our desire for *freedom*. Then, he asked me if we believed in *liberty*. I told him that our main concern and desire was our *freedom*. Then he made a very profound question when asked me, what the difference was between the two words? Our conclusion was that freedom and liberty were synonymous. It all boils down, my friends," said the thoughtful provocative and fascinating tavern proprietor as she stood up, and strutted before her audience, and announced that she believed that we want both freedom and liberty from old George III, and his royal guards!"

"Gentlemen," Martha said as her friends raised their steins to hers, "I learned all this information by just being a good listener, while a some lonely Tory customer was enjoying his brew." She hesitated before she left her friends presence, and said, "I'm so sure he was a Tory, or just someone who likes a stimulating discussion, along with his lager."

"He probably was one of those lost souls, he was telling you about," said Harry Hunter as her rapidly collected the empty steins, and brushed the bread and cheese crumbs on to the floor. His remaining friends, as well as Martha, stared at him with disdain. "Oh, what the hell," he said as he shrugged off their scornful expressions, "you all know the boss-lady is expecting me to sweep up this floor before we close down!"

BOOK TWO

FREEDOM!

ONE

THE BEGINNING OF THE END

December 5, 1777
In French Foreign Minister Vergennes's Paris Quarters

"Mr. Franklin, you drive a hard bargain," stated King Louis XVI's talented foreign minister, the Comte de Vergennes, as he reached for the half-full crystal wine glass of burgundy, pushed his plush straight-back chair from his desk, and raised his glass to toast Benjamin Franklin's raised empty glass. Before anything was spoken, Vergennes filled each of their pieces of crystal, and toasted, "Here's to our alliance between King Louis XVI's France and your new United States of America."

"Long may our alliance live, and be beneficial to both parties," replied Franklin as his glass touched his friend's glass. "Now my good friend, Vergennes, about that slanderous remark you made stating that I drive a hard bargain," Franklin said as he peered over his wire-rimmed glasses while his heavy jowls crept over his white starched collar. "You know, my dear sir, that France is just as anxious to defeat England as America," as Franklin's cunning smile betrayed triumph.

Both men were well acquainted with the American Continental Congress's efforts to seek foreign aid. It had started way back in November of 1775, when Benjamin Franklin along with Thithler Silas Deane and Arthur Lee were appointed members of a *secret* committee to communicate with such *interested parties* in Great Britain, Ireland, and *other parts of the world*, implying France. The primary mission of this committee was to acquire munitions, and to convince certain *interested parties* of the advantages of direct support to the virgin country's resistance against the tyrannical rule of King George III and his Parliament. Over a period of time, and unknown to Franklin and his fellow committee members, Vergennes had developed an enthusiastic interest in the developments of the American *experiment*. This interest was nurtured through his readings of Thomas Paine's provocative book *Common Sense.* Vergennes was so intrigued with Paine's writings, that he succeeded in placing the middle-class English Quaker on a secret French payroll. It was no secret to anyone, especially to Franklin and Vergennes, that all France condoned the American *civil* war, where the Loyalists and their allies were supported by England. Franklin knew, too, that King Louis and all of his people were still smarting the loss of their *New France* in North America. He also knew, that for a generation France's dominant intellectuals' primary efforts were to reconstruct it's own society. Even King Louis XVI's finance minister had written that America's experiment was *the hope of the world.* In fact many Frenchmen believed that America's model could well serve as an excellent model for any country desiring governmental change. The crafty and wily Franklin kept all these thoughts to himself while he waited for Vergennes's response.

"My good friend, Mr. Franklin, I must admit that you have successfully enamored all the gay, sophisticated, and the Roman Catholic society of the French court with your homely witticism, but you have not fully convinced me that France should join forces with America to fight England. Your General George Washington and his Continental Army have not shown sufficient fire power, military savvy, and determination to combat and defeat the Loyalists and their English and Indian allies. From what I've heard about your General Washington has either been delaying direct contact with the enemy, or relocating his troops for a more favorable site to encounter them. We Europeans have a more direct method to fight our battles. We pick a favorable location to face the enemy, then engage them, and then pray to God that the best army may be victorious, and……..."

Before Vergennes could finish his thoughts, Franklin interrupted him, "But you French, as well as General James Braddock, learned that the traditional European military tactics are not practical in American. Soon, we will all learn of a major American victory."

"Soon?" questioned the Frenchman as he raised from his chair to refresh their wine glasses. "You want money and munitions, and probably sooner or later you and your upstart Rebels will also be expecting France to furnish you with troops. You know very well that we just finished a war with the British. How can you expect France to fill its exchequer so rapidly, and dole out armaments to you?" Before Franklin could respond to his question, Vergennes added, "But I must admit our escalating group of industrialists are clamoring for entry into what they perceive as a highly potential growth market in America." He raised his wine glass to Franklin's, and said with a chuckle, "Who knows, but what you and your bloody bunch of shit- slingers and horse traders may end up defeating the English lobsterbacks and their savage allies."

"I'd like to be serious for a moment," Franklin said as he endeavored to change the subject.

"Haven't we always been serious and truthful with each?" asked Vergennes as he rolled his glass of burgundy beneath his nose, and enjoying the wine's fine bouquet.

"I agree totally with you," agreed Franklin as he watched his longtime French acquaintance. "I know both of us have long enjoyed each other's company, even when we jest with each other, but I seriously want talk about what I think is about to happen to change the whole atmosphere of the American civil war."

"Oh, now you're calling a *civil* war!" exclaimed Vergennes. "All the while, us Frenchmen have been calling your war the great *American Revolution, the great American experiment!*"

"Truthfully, this conflict started within the colonists' ranks," stated Franklin. "Some who called themselves Loyalists or Tories wanted to retain allegiance with England and its king, while others who referred to themselves as Whigs, even Rebels or Patriots wanted to be free and independent of England, even including its haughty Church of England. Simply speaking, this conflict is frequently brother against brother, father against son, son against son, and any other combination of family relationships. The one situation, which makes America's conflict different, is that England has chosen to join forces and with the loyalist Tories against our rebel Whigs."

By this time Vergennes, too, wanted to return to Franklin's initial thought about being serious. "What were you thinking of, when you said you had something very serious to converse with me about?"

"Oh, yes, yes," replied America's cleverest diplomat in Europe. "Recently, I guess it was about six months ago, I heard rumors about the planning of a major campaign to be staged by the British and their Loyalist and Indian allies against an area in the mid-section of New York state called the Mohawk Valley."

"What's so attractive about that wilderness area?" asked the Frenchman who was rapidly gaining interest in Franklin's discussion. "I would think that the British would be more interested in capturing some of America's important seaports like Boston, New York City, even Philadelphia or Charleston," he added as an afterthought.

"I think that this campaign, if it is staged and attempted, could really split the states," Franklin mused as he sipped the last of his wine, and moved the empty glass toward his French friend. "From what I've read and heard about the British plan, which incidentally was conceived a most intriguing individual named General John Burgoyne."

"Oh! I've heard of him," exclaimed Vergennes as he emptied the wine bottle, and chuckled when he said, "He's the one they call *Gentleman Johnny.* Isn't he? I understand that he has quite a way with the women. As matter of fact, I've also heard that you, my friend, have an enticing manner with those of the opposite sex," he smiled as raised his glass, and added, "and may you always be your charming and sophisticated self."

"Thank you for your compliments," Franklin responded raising his glass towards his friend. "But, this Gentleman Johnny, as you call him is no ordinary English general." He carefully placed his wine glass on the glossy ebony table top," As an illegitimate son of a distinguished family, Burgoyne has raised up relatively fast within the British military ranks. Even has direct access to King George III and his secretary of state Lord George Germain. I understand that Burgoyne had developed a military campaign which he calls his *Thoughts*, formally entitled *Thoughts for Conducting the War from the Side of Canada*. Burgoyne has no doubts about the soundness of his plan. He also knows that his friend King George is desperate for a victory, and Burgoyne believed that he and his *Thoughts* were just the combination which the king needed to stave out and defeat the rabble-rousers; thus bring America back his sovereign rule."

"Pray tell me more about this man Burgoyne's *Thoughts,"* urged Vergennes as his man-servant opened another bottle of burgundy. "He sounds like an interesting person, someone I'd like to meet."

"You don't have to proclaim this to intimates, but I believe that Burgoyne has devised a strategically outstanding plan," advised Franklin, "there are two elements which will prove critical to the success or defeat of his plan. First, the weather. As you probably know the winters in upstate New York can be very severe. A summer campaign would probably be the best even though his troops would have to put with millions of knats, black flies, and mosquitoes. Secondly, the leadership ability of the American general who faces Burgoyne's troops." As an afterthought, "I just hope that General Washington doesn't place that ignoramus General Horatio Gates in charge. He'd rather just sit on some place high on a mountain, and direct his troops from a far. He's not an in-fighter, he's a no-fighter period."

Very fortuitously, Franklin would not be surprised to learn that in 1780 Gates was appointed by Congress took command of the Southern Division over De Kalb's and against Washington's advice.

When Gates under took to capture the commons at Hillsboro, he decided to advance against on Camden. Against everyone's advice, Gates insisted on taking the direct route through the pine barrens where there wasn't enough food to support a hog, instead of following the longer wagon road along which there were many farms and well-affected people. To make matters worse, this march was accompanied by hunger and dysentery. Near Camden, Gates's army with between 2600 and 3000 men fit for duty - only 1000 of them Continentals- was attacked by British troops led by their beloved and outstanding leader Lord Cornwallis with an inferior number of British regulars; some Rawdon's Volunteers of Ireland, and Royal North Carolinians. On August 16, 1780, the Battle of Camden, New Jersey was fiercely fought between the professionally led British forces who had mounted a fierce bayonet charge. Even though the famished American militia panicked at the first bayonet charge, the Rebel forces courageously stood their ground until De Kalb was mortally wounded. After Major John Eager Howard's threescore had cut their way out, and he was shortly after captured or killed. Seeing all of this disaster, the *gallant* Gates mounted one of his Virginia thorough-breds, galloped at the head of the fleeing militia and never stopped until he reached Charlotte, North Carolina, sixty miles from the battlefield finishing Gates's army career and scattering most of his troops to the woods and swamps.

"You don't sound very optimistic about America's chances against General Burgoyne," observed Vergennes.

"It all depends upon the roll of the dice," Franklin stated, "which American general or generals Burgoyne encounters. For example, Washington has assembled some very talented men with considerable amount of experience fighting in the unfamiliar environment to the British forces. General Philip Schuyler should have the command of the American Northern army, but the New England troops refused to serve under him. Another excellent example of fearsome military knowledge is Brigadier Benedict Arnold. He should have received his second star for his brilliant work in the Canadian campaign, but he was denied this promotion because New England's allowance of major generals was already filled."

"Sounds to me, my dear friend, that your New Englanders seem to be ruling the roost," observed Vergennes. "I thought you told me that you were pleased with the way Washington was commanding the troops."

"I am very satisfied," Franklin said as he pounded the palm of his hand the top of the table nearly tipping his wine glass over.

"If you're so pleased with Washington, where's his victories? America's victories? You know very well that justification of your persistent pursuit for our support must be demonstrated with battlefield victories over the British. We must see evidence that France will not be pouring our money down the proverbial rat hole," Vergennes stated flatly. "In fact," Vergennes continued, "from what you tell me about this fellow Gentleman Johnny, your forces sound to be rather doomed. When is his *Thoughts* campaign supposed to be waged?"

"From what I understand," said the freemason diplomat whose suit was unadorned with gold lace because he had not received the money for court dress, and his unpowdered hair had made a great hit before Louis XVI as the embodiment of republican simplicity, "Burgoyne was scheduled to leave Montreal and take the lake route south toward Albany, General William Howe was to leave New York City and go up the Hudson River, and a Brigadier General named Barry St. Leger was to leave Montreal down the St. Lawrence River to Oswego and cut across the Mohawk Valley. The beginnings of these three individual campaigns were to be synchronized to begin during the latter part of July, so they could converge sometime in October in Albany before the bitter Adirondack winter sets in."

"What's this Adirondack winter stuff you're talking about," said the Frenchman as he wrinkled his nose as if he was smelling some foul tasting cheese."

"The Adirondack Mountains are America's version of Siberia," stated the urban Philadelphian. "The Adirondacks is nothing but a huge cluster of high mountains covered with dark and dense forests with virtually no roads as we know them cut through them. About the only thing which may resemble a road, are a few well-trod trails which were once Indian footpaths. Some of these trails have graduated," Franklin smiled as he added, "to wagon paths. I would not envy Burgoyne or anyone else, as far as that is concerned, to make their way south from Montreal to Albany. If the British did decide to take that route, our Rebel forces would chop trees across their path. If they tried to float down a creek or river, our Rebel forces would fill the waterways with trees. No civilized individual would live there. That's why only Indians and a few daring Palatines, serving the British as a buffer against the Indians, live there."

"Sounds like a charming place to stay away from," stated Vergennes as he drained their second bottle of burgundy, and called his butler for another bottle. "Oh, by the way," he added, "Do they have wine there? I understand that Gentleman Johnny Burgoyne is not only a charmer with the women, but is also a connoisseur of fine French champagne."

"Don't be ridiculous, my friend, probably about the nearest alcoholic beverage you could find in those backwoods is the homebrew the Palatines make for their own enjoyment….." Franklin stopped in the middle of his sentence, then chuckled to himself, and added, "If Burgoyne wants anything besides the Palatines' homebrew, he could either share the British's rum and gin with the Indians, or he'll have to bring along his own champagne……." Again the clever diplomat stopped, took a sip of wine, and said, "I would not be a bit surprise that Johnny would load up a wagon or two with French wine for himself and whatever lady he finds along the way."

Just then the beautifully hand-crafted paneled, cherry-wood door burst open startling both Vergennes and his American friend, hearing the smiling intruder announcing, "I have wonderful news for you gentlemen from America."

Without announcing who he was, the youthful and plainly dressed individual headed straight toward Benjamin Franklin. "Vergennes this is my right hand, my clerk of the court, and my jack-of-all-trades, Master Josiah Quincy, who claims to be only a long distance relative to our friend John Adams."

Master Quincy stepped toward Franklin's host, and extended his hand, "Monsieur Vergennes I am delighted to meet you."

"Comte de Vergennes," the Frenchman corrected Franklin's clerk. "I'm sure you are a valuable asset to my good friend Doctor Franklin. I, too, am pleased to make your acquaintance," Vergennes said rather briskly, trying to hide his irritation ignited by his wine-filled brain, because he and Franklin had been so discourteously interrupted.

"What is the wonderful news you have for us, Josiah," his mentor asked in a mannerly fashion?

"On October 17, 1777, General John Burgoyne surrendered himself and his British forces to our General Horatio Gates at Saratoga. We've saved the Mohawk Valley from the British," declared the ecstatic and devoted clerk."

"Well, my friend Vergennes, earlier today you were asking when our forces were going to give a victory to verify our willingness and ability to defeat the mighty British war machine. Now, you have heard that our Rebel forces have defeated the British military genius, Gentleman Johnny Burgoyne," Franklin said with reservations. He did not want of gloat about the so-called victory, for he had serious doubts about the military leadership ability of Horatio Gates, the politicians' favorite general. Franklin addressed his attention directly to Master Quincy, and asked, "Have you heard any of the particulars about the campaign, and what lead to the American victory?"

"Before Master Quincy gives you the detail," stated the reserved and sober French foreign minister, "if it is true what Master Quincy has just related to us, I must admit this type of news is just what I and my associates have been patiently waiting for."

"Good! Now a Rebel victory and a British defeat has been recorded, please give us a little more detail of Burgoyne's famous *Thoughts* campaign," asked the seventy-plus year old first man of science in the colonies who had for years been hailed by the intelligentsia of Europe for his electrical experiments.

"While being interrogated by the American command, Burgoyne told his interrogators that he came very close to defeating General Gates, if it had not been for the fortuitous intervention of General Benedict Arnold who changed to whole history of the war. Adding, that Arnold had risked everything, because he was lead to believe that the British Generals Howe and Clinton, too, were willing to take the same risk."

"I've heard that Burgoyne was a gambler, as well as a womanizer. As far as womanizer is concerned, and his over-blown affair with the commissary's wife Fanny Loescher, I don't believe that he was any worse or better than most men in his class and times," smilingly stated the experienced Franklin. "What I admire about Burgoyne, however, I must caution you is that I never met the man. All I can tell about him is what I've heard how much his troops respect him."

"One of his sergeants, a Sergeant Lamb, is reported as saying that during the conflict Burgoyne behaved with great personal bravery. According to Lamb, Burgoyne shunned no danger; his mere presence and conduct animated his troops, for they greatly loved him. He delivered his orders with precision and coolness, and in the heat, danger, and fury of the fight, maintained the true characteristics of the soldier- serenity, fortitude, and undaunted intrepidity."

"Burgoyne sounds just like your famous General Horatio Gates," Vergennes joked as he asked to butler to fill the wine glasses. After offering young Quincy a glass of wine, which he cheerfully accepted, Vergennes asked Master Quincy what Benedict Arnold had done to receive such lustrous accolades from a defeated general.

"After receiving Gates's reluctant approval to see what all the firing was about, Arnold rushed astride his black stallion, Warren, yelling *Victory or death*, as he spurred into Warren's flanks, losing no time in joining his troops, who were already drawn up in ranks and impatiently asking his orders. At the sight of Arnold astride his horse yelling his war-call, Gates became fidgety, and quickly ordered his aide Major John Armstrong to recall Arnold. Fortunately for our troops, Armstrong's fast horse following a wagon trail between trees never did overtake Arnold, who was by this time was far ahead again plunging his spurs into to the flanks of his big charger until they cleared a sally port. Then he briskly rode into the woods rounding up stragglers, turning them around, and leading them cheeringly toward the enemy. Then, Arnold and the men he had rounded up in the woods joined forces with Colonel Daniel Morgan's men, who were assaulting the light infantry. Meanwhile at the edge of the forest, Learned's smoke-streaked men had paused for at a stream to drink, with their cheering faces these en hurried after Arnold, who was calling, *Come on, brave boys, come!* His horse leaped the stream, while Arnold urged it up the exposed hillside toward the Hessian troops. Suddenly, as the Hessians fired, he realized that he was alone; Learned's men had broken, and run back towards the woods. Wheeling his horse about, Arnold returned to the stream, rallied his men for another charge. This time, the Hessians broke and ran, fleeing from this *madman,* leaving his Rebel troops in possession of a cornfield littered with bodies.

Quincy continued, "At the time when General Arnold saw the Learned brigade's situation, he galloped across the line exposing himself, as some have said, with great folly. Arnold galloped on flourishing his sword to encourage the troops, and in a state of furious distraction, struck Captain Bell of Dearborn's infantry on the head. Bell's first impulse was, apparently, to shoot Arnold; he raised his musket and collecting himself was to remonstrate when Arnold raced off to another part of the field, galloping again across the line of fire. Appearing both deranged and exhilarated, Arnold barreled down hill on his big stallion, with his sword flailing, literally taking command of Learned's men, many of whom were neighbors of his back from back in Connecticut. Needless to say, the enemy was caught by surprise at the sudden appearance of the Americans, but did not fire except from the cannon, until our forces were within forty-five yards. Then the Hessians opened up a tremendous fire from the whole line, falling a few of our attackers. Seeing that the Massachusetts infantry had taken cover at the first discharge, Arnold, rushed along the line, snatched up fifteen to twenty riflemen, and turned his horse, galloped across the clearing towards the redoubt two hundred yards away. Riding and giving orders everywhere, Arnold and his command, with their overwhelming force, won the redoubt that otherwise might have resisted their assault. The Hessians were terrorized, and hastily abandoned the redoubt. Seeing his men retreating or surrendering, their Hessian General von Breymann struck down those who attempted to leave their post with his sword."

Quincy took a deep breath to continue his story, but before he could continue his mentor said, "What a daring and fascinating victory," declared Franklin to his host as he raised his wine glass to his host's glass. "How say you, my dear friend Vergennes?"

Before the French foreign minister could reply, Quincy said, "Oh! but gentlemen there's more."

Stunned, Vergennes asked, "How could there be more? This sounds like a Shakespeare play!"

'I don't think even Shakespeare could have had this much imagination," continued the young clerk. "Seeing the Hessian general slaying some of his retreating soldiers was too much for one of his men, this chivalric soldier raised his rifle and killed his own general. Meanwhile, another wounded Hessian soldier, lying on the ground, seeing an American officer on a horse charging in his direction, raised his rifle, and shot the horse at point blank range. The big black charger rolled over, pinioning its rider, General Benedict Arnold, to the ground and breaking his left leg, the same leg he had broken the previous year in the Battle of Quebec. While Colonel Brooks and his men were mounting the redoubt, one of his soldiers took aim to kill the Hessian, who had felled Arnold. Arnold called out loudly, '"Don't hurt him, he is a fine fellow! He only did his duty.'" When Dearborn came close to Arnold, he asked where were you hit? Arnold whispered, in the same leg; I wish it had been my heart."

Quincy ended his report. Stunned and overwhelmed, the room's occupants were in a trance. Their imaginations racing from their presence to the Freeman's Farm battlefield near Saratoga. Visualizing dead and dying bodies lying namelessly over the blood soaked fields, and the gallant American leader lying beneath his dead charger. Quincy broke the silence, "Do you have any questions concerning Burgoyne's defeat?"

Ignoring Quincy's question, Vergennes reached for the half filled wine bottle. As he circled about the table filling the empty wine glasses, he stated, "Let's toast America's famous and daring general, Benedict Arnold."

"Hear! Hear!," agreed the whig-less Americans, Franklin and Quincy. "To Benedict Arnold and his black charger Warren."

TWO

CONCERNS

Early Morning of December 6, 1777
In French Foreign Minister Vergennes's Paris Headquarters

Ever since he had been in Paris, Benjamin Franklin took special care to develop an image of a unpretentious republican. He never was driven about Paris waving his arms and soliciting cheers. He did, however, enjoy holding receptions at his lodgings in Passy, dining with courtiers, and enjoying the fact that he was becoming a living legend in a foreign country. He once wrote of France that he had spent several years in the sweet society of a people, whose conversation is instructive, whose manners are highly pleasing, and who above all the nations of the world had perfected the greatest art of making themselves beloved by strangers. But, everyone who heard him brag about the amicable French, knew that Franklin could not have experienced this belief without his genuine love of people.

As Franklin was entering the quarters of Comte de Vergennes, the butler interrupted his task of preparing the morning meal, and greeted the cheerful and familiar rather pudgy figure, "Good morning, Dr. Franklin. It is a pleasure seeing you so bright on such a snowy morning; Monsieur Vergennes will be with us shortly." Proceeding to finish the morning meal, the butler placed a bountiful array of fresh fruit, cheeses, preserves, and the famous French croissants together with silver coffee server filled with a rich, dark brew. After being served a steaming cup of his favorite sweetened cafe' au lais, Franklin stared in amazement at the abundant assortment of food. He thought to himself, I just hope that Vergennes has had sufficient time to consider how much assistance, and money France would be willing to give or even loan to America. While Franklin was in a rather daydream recalling his clerk's report of the American victory over the British at Saratoga; he stood in a trace seeing the bounty of foods before him, and suddenly he visualized Benedict Arnold charging against the Hessians on his black stallion, fearlessly swinging his sword, and encouragingly yelling for his troops to follow him, only to be startled by Vergennes's entrance into the room.

"Good morning, my friend," Vergennes said, "I didn't mean to surprise you."

"Oh! Good morning to you, my friend," Franklin said dismissing his thoughts of Saratoga, and reminding himself was here in Paris, France. "I was just standing, and admiring the generous display of tasties. I must admit it dumfounded me, and it sent me into a trance. Suddenly, it seemed I was transported to the battlefield at Freeman's Farm near Saratoga trying to visualize General Benedict Arnold on his big, black stallion, fiercely swinging is sword above his head, and leading our troops against the Hessians."

Vergennes handed Franklin a flowered decorated, bone china plate, and encouraged him to help himself to the beautifully displayed fruits, cheeses, meats, preserves and pastries. Vergennes followed suit, and each returned to the same chairs they had occupied the previous day, seating across from each other at the shiny, cherry-red table. Vergennes was the first one to break the silence. "Benjamin, I could not sleep very well last night."

"Are you disappointed about the American victory at Saratoga," asked Franklin? "I thought the news of that victory would be joyfully received."

"Well, in a way you're correct. I am very pleased that the British and their Hessian friends were soundly defeated by Arnold and his aroused troops," Vergennes said as he placed his bone china cup to its matching saucer. "In fact," he continued, "this very morning King Louis XVI declared his recognition of the United States of America. However," Vergennes responding to Franklin's comments, "Arnold's very victory was responsible for keeping me awake most of the night. While you've been busily visualizing Arnold on his charger, I've been engaged trying to figure what the British, especially Lord North will do once he has learned that his *gentleman prince charming* lost New York State to your Rebel troops."

"I'm not quite sure what you mean," Franklin said quizzically staring toward his friend as they enjoyed the fruits of the bountiful buffet. Franklin was, especially, enjoying the soft-ripened brie cheese; the nearest cheese he had ever tasted as delicious as the Limburger cheese, without its aroma, he had sampled once from the New York's Mohawk Valley.

"Well, I've trying to imagine what Lord North will do. I would not be a bit surprised if that easy-going foreign minister dreamed up some sort of extravagant offer to the Continental Congress, and those clowns in your capital city would joyfully accept his offer. Very simply, with just a throw of the dice, the British Empire would then be restored, and us Frenchmen and you and your frivolous Rebels will all be thrown in jail as traitors or be driven out of the country, while the Redcoats and their Loyal Tories divide up all of their bounty amongst themselves."

"I can not believe I'm hearing you correctly, my friend," said the startled Franklin. "You must have had a bad nightmare to even have had such thoughts. I know many of those Rebels, as you say, very well. Everyone of them have literally placed not only their lives, but everything they own on winning this civil war. On a single roll of the dice, as you suggested."

STEPS TOWARD FREEDOM

"We all know that! The Loyalist Tories have done exactly the same thing," countered Vergennes, "they have, however, placed their whole future on the British and their king."

"But, my dear friend," started Franklin as he sipped his tepid cafe' au lais, "There is another thing different why the Rebels, as you call them, have the inbred desire to defeat the British and their Indians allies, as well as their hired Hessian troops. They have had the taste of freedom, ……..of democracy and liberty. Of plowing their own ground, planting their own fields, harvesting their own crops, and experiencing the rewards of their efforts. Yes, in fact, even the penalties of their losses. The big thing is that our people do not, and will not revere a God ordained monarch with its tyrannic rule. You see, my friend, most of these Rebels, especially the Palatines from Germany, were misled by the British even before they consented to board the British vessels to America. They were lead to believe that each of them would receive a forty acre plot of land where they could establish their own farms. However, when they arrived in New York City harbor, and transported north to Livingston Manor, they discovered that they were truly British *indentured servants* destined to work in their *masters'* foolhardy experiment of tapping resin from the pine trees, as well as trimming these same pine trees for masts and yard- arms for their navy. Plainly speaking, most of the rebellious Palatines in the Mohawk Valley believed that they had been deceived by the British monarchy and its Parliament. The fact is that today's Palatines believe that their ancestors were truly mislead by the British, and they have not been able to remove that stigma from their gullet. Very simply, these people believe that these battles along the Mohawk Valley are their long awaited *steps toward freedom.*"

* * *

Lord North did, in fact, do just as Vergennes had predicted. Soon after North had learned of Burgoyne's defeat, he quickly developed an acquiescent bill, and promptly submitted it to Parliament. This bill, if punctually passed, might have changed America's whole entire chronology as well as Britain's; in fact, probably the entire world. But this virtuous body of morality and efficiency was more concerned about their Christmas and New Year holidays, and all that's related to these events. In addition, North dispatched an *unofficial* emissary of American birth, Paul Wentworth, to talk with Franklin in Paris. Wentworth's mission was to steer the Americans away from an alliance with the French. But the results of Wentworth's mission turned out to accomplish just the opposite. The perceptive Franklin played him off against the French. By the time North's *secret emissary* reached Paris, King Louis XVI had authorized Vergennes to continue treaty negotiations, despite his concerns of possible bankruptcy and revolution. France's foreign ministry's young men had been eagerly awaiting for the day when the balance of power would right itself, and restore France to her greatness. Though considered a brilliant statesman, Comte de Vergennes was endowed with patience which groped its way through the tangled politics of the nations towards his goal *to seize the opportunity to raise France from her degradation. 'If she neglected it, if fear overcame duty, she would add debasement to humiliation, and become an object of contempt to her own century and to all future peoples'.*

Franklin, equally motivated, did not let the holidays interfere with his mission in France. Nor, did he ignore Vergennes's warning about Lord North's possible maneuver to seek reconciliation with America, in order to restore Britain's sovereignty to its colonies. Franklin had been known for his famous utterance he quoted in the mid-seventeen hundreds: *Early to bed and early to rise, makes a man health, wealthy and wise.* But, during holiday period Franklin also kept in mind: *He that riseth late, must trot all day, and shall scare overtake his business at night.* To these memorable quotations, He added: *An empty bag cannot stand upright.* Fearful of the French making accommodations with Britain, or Britain making amendments with the colonies, Franklin made up his mind that he was not going to Vergennes with an empty bag. Feverishly, he toiled with the English language. Selecting words and phrases, testing on himself, and again with his friend Vergennes. After meaning full and exhausting day and nights, the two gentlemen had completed two treaties; one of friendship and commerce, and the second a military alliance. To each other's credit, Vergennes permitted Franklin to

STEPS TOWARD FREEDOM

compose his own terms, which resulted in favorable provisions for America. The primary mission of these treaties was a pledge that neither nation would lay down their arms until Great Britain recognized America's independence. Surprisingly, France renounced interest in annexing Canada, providing for the possibility for Canada to become America's fourteenth state. For this concession, America would promise to recognize France's sole possession of the West Indian colonies she held at the time, while commerce was to be conducted on the foundation of *most favored nation*. As diligent these two gentlemen were in preparing the treaties, unfortunately, they had neglected to include anything about the amount or kind of military aid to be provided by France; and if provided, the financial arrangements for repayment by America.

On February 6, 1778, Vergennes and Franklin signed these two documents. Eleven days later on February 17, 1778, the British Parliament approved Lord North's conciliatory bill offering more than the Second Continental Congress had demanded. About three months later on May 2, 1778, the news of the French treaties finally reached New York City. Six days later on May 8.1778, Lord North relieved General Sir William Howe of his command and assigned General Sir Henry Clinton the command with orders to evacuate Philadelphia, to concentrate on New York, and be prepared to fight a French expeditionary force. Franklin and his friend Vergennes played a key role in the alliance between America and France. Formal peace negotiations began in Paris in April 1782 between Franklin and Richard Oswald, a liberal Scots merchant sent over by the Earl of Shelborne. When John Jay arrived in June 23rd, he raised the objections to the wording of Oswald's commission, "To treat with the Thirteen Colonies.....or any parts thereof." He insisted on Oswald's obtaining a new commission to treat with "The United States of America. The preliminary treaty of peace was signed on November 30, 1782, more than thirteen months after Lord Cornwallis's surrender at Yorktown.

Franklin, who was relieved by Thomas Jefferson as American minister to France in 1784, had completed his mission in France. Together with Burgoyne's defeat at Saratoga were the turning points of America's first civil war. General Horatio Gates, as appointed lead general, had received most of the praise for the Saratoga victory over the British and their hired Hessians. The British and their Tory and Indian allies were reduced to a plague of a series of hit-and-run raids throughout the Mohawk valley to Fort Niagara, which would be taken care of by the Sullivan/Clinton expedition into the Indian country the following year.

Everyone one seemed to be satisfied with the Saratoga victory except General Benedict Arnold. While Burgoyne was living in General Philip Schuyler's Albany mansion, Schuyler escorted Burgoyne to the hospital to visit his *real conqueror*, as Burgoyne had painfully and candidly admitted that he lost the Battle of Saratoga on October 7th only because of decisive, eleventh-hour leadership exerted by General Benedict Arnold. This acclaim, together with those awarded him by his own troops and others, helped to make Arnold think that just maybe his talents would probably be better appreciated by King George III and his Parliament rather the Continental Congress, especially after its members had rejected his promotion. Some of Arnold's critics claim that the seed for his defection was planted by Burgoyne during their private meetings in the hospital. Not only was Arnold not thinking of treason at the time, but Gentleman Johnny would not tolerate any such talk. Several years later while Arnold was living on the half-pay of a retired British brigadier, the two men came face-to-face in a London club. Gentleman Johnny turned on his heel and stalked off without speaking.

THREE

HE MERITS UNRESTRAINED CONFIDENCE

February 6, 1778
Valley Forge Washington's Encampment

On February 6, 1778 while Benjamin Franklin and Comte de Vergennes were toasting and celebrating the signing of the two treaties with Louis XVI, and the ladies and gentlemen of the royal court, quite a different mood was being experienced by Washington's troops headquartered in Valley Forge, Pennsylvania.

On October 5, 1777, Washington attempted to exploit British General William Howe's perceived temporary weakness in Philadelphia by attacking Howe's main encampment at Germantown. Everything that could go wrong in an assault, went wrong at Germantown. After losing over 1000 men, Washington decided to withdraw and winter at nearby Valley Forge. There were numerous reasons why Valley Forge was selected as recorded by Albigence Waldo:

........1st There is plenty of Wood & Water. 2dly There are but few families for the soldiery to Steal from-tho' far be it from a Soldier to Steal. (Author's note: the writer did not record a 3rd reason) 4ly There are warm sides of Hills to rect huts on. 5ly They will be heavenly Minded like Jonah when in the Belly of a Great Fish. 6ly They will not become home Sick as is sometimes the Case when Men live in the Open World—since the reflections which will naturally arise from their present habitation, will lead them to the more noble thoughts of employing their leisure hours in filling their knapsacks with such materials as may be necessary on the Journey to another Home

Two weeks later after his crushing defeat at Germantown, Washington learned of and, shared the triumphant news of General Burgoyne's surrender at Saratoga with his officers and troops. Thus, started what became known as the Conway cabal, General Horatio Gates was hailed as a hero, and promoted by a few general officers and members of Congress to replace the retreating Washington. But, when the true identity of Gates's character was finally unveiled, the entire intriguing plot fizzled out, and nobody thereafter would ever admit having anything to do with the plot. The fact is that the army and the country chose to stand with Washington; no other major revolution has a loser of so many battles been supported to the point where he could win. A genuine credit for a truly great man, but this great man knew that wars were fought with weapons, but wars are won by men. He also knew that the spirit of the men who follow, and of the man who leads that gains the victory.

True to his principle, Washington chose to honor the *Honorable Congress*'s setting apart December 18, 1777 for public Thanksgiving and Praise to devoutly to express our grateful acknowledgements to God for the manifold blessings He has granted us. The General directed "that the army remain in its's present quarters, and that the Chaplains perform divine service with their several corps and brigades. And earnestly, he encouraged all officers and soldiers, whose absence is not indispensably necessary, to attend with reverence the solemnities of the day."

On the day of the nation's first Universal Thanksgiving, Albigence Waldo, a twenty-seven year old Connecticut surgeon appointed to the Connecticut Continental regiment, recorded in his diary:

>……..a Roasted pig at Night. God be thanked for my health which I have pretty well recovered. How much better should I feel, were I assured my family were in health. But the same good Being who graciously preserves me, is able to preserve them & bring me to the ardently wish'd for enjoyment of them again.
>
>Rank and Precedence make a good deal of disturbance & confusion in the American Army. The Army are poorly supplied with Provision, occasioned it is said by the Neglect of the Commissary of Purchases. Much talk among Officers about discharges. Money has become of too little consequence. The Congress have not made their Commissions valuable Enough. Heaven avert the bad consequences of these things!
>
>Our brethren who are unfortunately prisoners in Philadelphia meet with the most savage and inhumane treatments that Barbarians are Capable of inflicting. Our Enemies do not knock them in the head or burn them with torches to death, or flee them alive, or gradually dismember them till they die, which is customary among Savages & Barbarians. No, they are worse by far. They suffer them to starve, to linger out their lives in extreme hunger. One of these poor unhappy men, drove to the extreme by the rage of hunger, eat his own fingers up to the first joint from the hand, before he died. Others eat the Clay, the Lime, the Stones of the Prison Walls. Several who died in the Yard had pieces of Bark, Wood, Clay & Stones in their mouths, which the ravings of hunger

had caused them to take in for food in the last Agonies of Life! These are thy mercies, O Britain!

* * *

The diligent Waldo records the following concerning the food the soldiers were fed while at Valley Forge:

> ……..A general cry thro' the Camp among the Soldiers, "No Meat! No Meat!"—- the Distant vales Echo'd back the melancholy sound—- "No Meat! No Meat! Imitating the noise of Crows & Owls, also, made a part of the confused Musick.

Waldo asked the cooks, "What do you have for dinner?" They responded, "Nothing but Fire Cake & Water." At night he asked, "Gentlemen the Supper is ready, what is your Supper lads?" They responded as before, "Fire Cake & Water." Then next morning Waldo asks, "What you got for Breakfast, Lads?" "Fire Cakes & Water," was their answer. Waldo said, "The Lord send that our Commissary of Purchases may live on Fire Cake & Water, 'till their glutted Gutts are turned to Pasteboard.

Apparently many of the Continental troops considered the cooks' fire cakes one of the gastronomic distresses they had to endure while they were in a newly formed camp, such as Valley Forge at this time. Usually, once a permanent camp was established fresh baked bread was a luxury. But, in most temporary camps the fire cake was one of the staples of most meals. The recipe was very simple. Flour was placed on a flat rock and cold water was added. The mixture was stirred into a paste, then daubed on another flat stone and set upright near the fire. The fire cake was thereby charred on the outside, leaving raw dough inside. Here was a dish that only the stoutest or hungriest Continental could relish.

After a hearty breakfast of fire cakes and water, and anything else the cooks were able to scare up, Waldo and his division were placed on marching orders. On the march, Waldo stated that he was ashamed to say it, but he was tempted to steal Fowls if he could find them, or even a whole Hog, for he felt as if he could eat one.

After surveying the countryside, he realized that the Improverish'd Country about them, afforded but little matter to employ a Thief, or keep a Clever Fellow good in good humor. But, he reasoned, why do I talk of hunger & hard usage, when so many in the World have not even fire cakes & water to eat.

On Christmas Day, he records that they were still in tents, when they should have been in huts much earlier. Cold & Smoke make us fret; the Sick suffer much in Tents this cold Weather. But they are treated differently from what they used to be at home, under the inspection of Old Women and Doct. Bolus Linctus. Here they are given Mutton & Grogg and a Capital Medicine once in While, to start the Disease from its foundation at once. We avoid Piddling Pills, Powders, Bolus's Linctus's Cordials and all such insignificant matters whose powers are Only render'd important by causing the Patient to vomit up his money instead of his disease. But he did admit a very few of the sick Men Die.

One of Waldo's greatest concerns was the frequent officer resignations primarily because their families were being neglected at home. Their wages will not by considerable, purchase a few trifling comfortables here in camp. & maintain their families at home while such extravagant prices are demanded for the common necessaries. Waldo summarizes the circumstances of the soldier is better by far than the officers, for a family of the soldier is provided for at the public expense if the articles they want are above the common price, but the officer's family is obliged not only to beg in the most humble manner for the necessaries of life, but also to pay for them afterwards at the most exorbitant rates. One home-bound wife wrote to her officer husband that she was able to procure a little bread for herself and children. Concluding with expressions bordering on despair of procuring a sufficiency of food to keep soul & body through the winter; that her money is of very little consequence to her, and begs of him to understand that Charity begins at home, and not allow his family to suffer to perish with want in the midst of plenty. There was so much talk of officers resigning that his Excellency (General Washington) expressed his fears of being left alone with the soldiers only. Waldo thought it strange that Congress would not exert themselves for his support, and save the good, great man from entertaining the least anxious doubt of their virtue and perseverance in supporting a cause of such unparallel'd importance!

* * *

On January 14, 1778, John Laurens, volunteer aide to General George Washington wrote to his father Henry Laurens, who had helped to organize defense of Charleston against British attack in 1776, also served as delegate to the Continental Congress 1777-80, and served as its president from November 1777 to December 1778, that he wished had a foundation to ask for an extraordinary addition to those favors which he had already received from his father. These favors were that his father would:

> ……..cede me a number of your able bodied men Slaves, instead of leaving me a fortune. I would bring about a two-fold good, first I would advance those who are unjustly deprived of the Rights of Mankind to State which would be a proper Gradation between Slavery and perfect Liberty, and besides I would reinforce the Defenders of Liberty with a number of gallant Soldiers, Men who have the habit of Subordination almost indelibly impress'd on them, would have one very essential qualification of Soldiers. I am persuaded that if I could obtain authority for the purpose I would have a Corps of such men trained, uniformly clad, equip'd and ready in every respect to act at the opening of the next Campaign. The Ridicule that may be thrown on the Colour I despise, because I am sure of rendering essential Service to my Country. I am tired of the Languor with which so scared a War as this, is carried on. My circumstances prevent me from writing so long a Letter as I expected and wish'd to have done on a subject which I have much at heart. I entreat you to give a favorable Answer.
>
> Your most affectionate

Two days before Franklin and Vergennes signed the two treaties between France and the United States on February 2, 1778, John Laurens again was sitting on the edge of the bottom level of his army bunk bed writing a response to his father's reply, which expressed his belief that men reconciled by long habit to the miseries of their Condition would prefer their ignominious bonds to the untasted Sweets of Liberty, especially under the terms his son had proposed concerning the enlistment of slaves into the Continental Army. John Laurens, however, took exception to his father's response:

.....I confess indeed that the minds of this unhappy species must be debased by a Servitude from which they can hope for no Relief but Death, and that every motive to action but Fear, must be nearly extinguished in them, but do you think they are so perfectly moulded to their State as to be insensible that a better exists. Will the galling comparison between themselves and their masters leave them unenlighten'd in this respect, can their Self-Love be so totally annihilated as not frequently to induce ardent wishes for a change.

You will accuse me perhaps my dearest friend of consulting my own feeling too much, but I am tempted to believe that this trampled people race so much human left in them, as to be capable of aspiring to the rights of men by noble exertions, of some friend to mankind would point the Road, and give them a prospect of Success. If I am mistaken in this, I would avail myself even of their weakness, and conquering one fear by another, produce equal good to the Public. You will ask in this view how do you consult the benefit of the Slaves. I answer that like other men, they are the Creatures of habit, their Cowardly Ideas will be gradually effaced, and they will be modified anew, their being rescued from a State of perpetual humiliation, and being advance as it were in the Scale of being will compensate the dangers incident to their new State. The hope that will spring in each man's mind respecting his own escape will prevent his being miserable, those who fall in battle will not lose much, those who survive will obtain their Reward.

John Laurens stopped writing for a moment trying to rationalize his thinking before finishing his letter. He knew that his own resources would be small, on account of the proportion of women and children. He acknowledged their soldierly qualifications which these men possessed in an eminent degrees including their patience under fatigues, sufferings and privations of every kind. He admitted to himself that his ultimate plan was to give freedom to the Negroes and gain Soldiers to the States. In case he could reach concurrence, he reasoned that he could sacrifice of Private interest to Justice and the Public Good, he would chose to change the women and children for able bodied men; the more of these he could obtain the better, but he decided that forty might be a good foundation to begin with. John Laurens was convinced that a well chosen body of 5,000 black men properly officer'd to act as light troops in addition to our present establishment, might give the Continental Army decisive success in its next campaign.

Admitting to himself and in the letter to his father:

…….I have long deplored the wretched State of these men and considered in their history, the bloody wars excited in Africa to furnish America with Slaves, the Groans of despairing for the Luxuries of Merciless Tyrants. I have had the pleasure of conversing with you sometimes upon the means of restoring them to their rights. When can it be better done, than when their enfranchisement may be made conducive to the Public Good, and be so modified as not to overpower their weak minds.

response to his father's question about General Washington's opinion concerning this subject, Laurens responded:

> ....he (Washington) is convinced that the numerous tribes of blacks in the Southern parts of the Continent offer a resource to us that should not be neglected. With respect to my particular Plan, he only objects to with the arguments of Pity, for a man who would be less rich than he might be.

* * *

In his letter of May 7, 1778 letter to his father, John Laurens wrote that yesterday we celebrated the new alliance with as much splendor as the short notice would allow:

> ....divine service preceded the rejoicing, after a proper pause, the several brigades marched by their right to their posts in order of battle, and the line was formed with admirable rapidity and precision, three salutes of artillery, thirteen each, and three general discharges of a running fire by the musketry, were given in honor of the King of France, the friendly European powers and the United American States (with) loud huzzas.

Laurens gave special tribute to Baron de Steuben who had planned and trained the marital appearance of the troops to a beautifully planned effect of the running fire which was executed to perfection. The whole exhibition was managed by Steuben with only a few signals, which warranted to him for his unwearied attention and to the visible progress which the troops have improved under his discipline. Laurens added:

> ....a cold collation was given afterwards at which all the officers of the Army & some Ladies of the neighborhood were present. Triumph beamed in every countenance. The greatness of mind and policy of Louis XVI were extol'd and his long life toasted with as much sincerity as that of the British King

used to be in former times. The General (Washington) received such proofs of the love and attachments of his officers as must have given him the most exquisite feelings....

But amid all this inundation of Joy, there is a conduct observed towards him by certain great men which as it is humiliating must abate his happiness...... I think then the Commander in chief of this Army is not sufficiently informed of all that is known by Congress of European Affairs. Is it not a galling circumstance for him to collect the most important intelligence piece-meal and as they choose to give it from Gentlemen who come from York, apart the chagrin which he must necessarily feel at such an appearance of Slight. It should be considered that in order to settle his plan of operations for the ensuing campaign, he should take into view the present state of European Affairs, and Congress should not leave him in the dark. If ever there was man in the world whose moderation and Patriotism fitted him for the command of a Republican Army he is, and he merits an unrestrained confidence.

FOUR

A NEW WORLD'S A COMING!

Sunday, May 31, 1778 at
New Palatine's Dutch Reformed Church

News of the signing of the two treaties forming a friendship and commercial alliance between France and the United States of America did not reach the hamlet of New Palatine until nearly two weeks after it had been announced to Washington's troops at Valley Forge. Reverend Johan Stouffer seized upon this long-sought news to develop his sermon for the last Sunday in May.

Karl and Rebecca Heindrick, in their four-wheel buck-board wagon, were joined with Karl's black blood brother, George Jefferson, dressed in his familiar army sergeant uniform, was riding along astride on his chestnut horse, the five miles east to New Palatine to attend the community's recently completed Dutch Reformed Church. As a veteran of the Oriskany and Saratoga campaigns, George, who reported directly to General Philip Schyuler in his Albany headquarters, had been assigned to help recruit volunteers for the Tryon County militia, and to assist in its training. The community had grown accustomed to seeing Karl and his black blood-brother together. Each had earned the community's respect during and shortly after the Oriskany campaign when Karl's left leg had been seriously injured. It was during this campaign that the two grown men had finally met each other after some twenty years of separation. Now the only thing which kept them apart was their respective families and the war. Each had heard rumors about a pending campaign west into the Indian country. But this morning, the three friends were looking forward to hearing their favorite preacher, and seeing and reminiscing with old friends.

Until the completion of the stone church building, Martha Butler's Heidelberg Tavern had for years served as the community's house of worship. Reverend Stouffer, the former circuit-riding preacher for the western Mohawk Valley, and Martha Butler had been the driving forces leading to the construction of the new church located on the opposite side of the village's commons directly across from the hamlet's only tavern. The church was truly the pride of the settlement, especially after Reverend Stouffer and his Indian princess wife, Red Bird, had agreed to move from their small abode in Fort Dayton into the apartment in the back of the church. Since then, *The Preacher,* as Red Bird proudly referred to her husband, was spending less time being a circuit-rider and quasi-collector of *important* information, he was able to devote more time and energy in building the church's congregation. Red Bird, dressed in her tribe's regalia of soft doeskin and colorful beads and moccasins, was especially helpful with the younger members of the community, especially spending enormous amount of time teaching the white children about nature lore and the ways of the Indian. One of her next goals was to invite Indian children to join their meetings to enable each to learn about each others' culture and religion.

During the heavy winter snows, the Heindricks had not been able to attend church as faithfully as they preferred, but the early signs of Spring and the visitation of Karl's blood-brother encouraged them to venture the five miles.

This particular morning was an exceptionally beautiful early spring morning, one which the Heindricks and their blood brother appreciated. To add to the joys of the Spring season, they were thankful that Burgoyne's British and Loyalist forces together with their Hessian mercenaries had surrendered at Saratoga to the incompetent General Horatio Gates, much to the dismay of General Benedict Arnold and his supporters.

"All's right with the world," announced Karl as he pointed to a swampy area with husky, brown cattails waving in the breeze and serving as the look-out posts for a lone red-wing black bird as he scrutinized the swamp for his early morning breakfast, "That's surely a definite sign of Spring," he concluded just as Rebecca called their attention to the other side the narrow wagon road known as the King's Highway.

"Those forsythia, too, are one the most welcome signs of Spring," declared Rebecca. "Now, George," she pressed her point, "don't you believe that those bright yellow, bell-shaped flowers are a more beautiful significant sign of Spring, as compared to that foolish red-wing black-bird sitting atop of a cattail? Incidentally, I understand that the forsythia are a genus of the shrubs of the olive family. Isn't that interesting?"

George realized that if he were not very careful, he would be in the midst of a family argument. Instead of siding with either of his dear friends, he was going to completely change the subject. "I think the news we recently heard about the United States and France signing an alliance is an excellent way to start our Spring. We must give that cagey old gent, Ben Franklin, a lot of credit. Without even carrying a gun, he is able to accomplish victories, which we as military individuals could never achieve."

After the introduction of this subject, the three friends turned their conversations to trying to project the future without war with British and their allies, and trying to envision a country without a British monarch. Before they realized it, they were entering the quaint hamlet of New Palatine. As they approached the center of town, they were proud of the hamlet's common pastoral setting located directly in the middle of the settlement with a few scattered black-faced sheep grazing on its lush green grass. "Look!" declared Karl, "no snow!" They laughed when they remembered the mountains of snow piled along the main street just a few weeks earlier, along with the hard packed, frozen snow on the dirt road, which facilitated the horse drawn sleds filled with milk cans traveling to the Heindrick's cheese factory. To their left was the old faithful Heidelberg Tavern, and directly across the common was the large, empty pasture where the new stone church proudly stood. As they directed their horses into field, they could see the portly and jovial Reverend Stouffer and his fascinating wife Red Bird welcoming their congregation into the village's only church. After George had tethered his horse and Karl and Rebecca had parked their horse and wagon in the long, white wooden stable with its shingled roof, they walked toward the church's front door where the Stouffers were cheerfully greeting the worshipers. Karl observed, "There must be something special going on here today with all these wagons and horses tethered either in the pasture or in the stable."

"Maybe they all knew, that you and I were coming out of our winter's hibernation," smiled Rebecca as she squeezed her husband's arm as proceeded toward the Stouffers.

"See I told you that that red-wing black bird sitting atop of that cattail is a sure sign of Spring," Karl reminded his wife and George.

Before George could relate his thoughts about this beautiful Spring day, he felt the preacher's strong, thick and rather rough right hand grasp his right hand. "Welcome, Sergeant Jefferson," greeted the former circuit-riding preacher. "We haven't seen you since last August when you were here recruiting volunteers for General Benedict Arnold's march to Fort Stanwix."

"That's correct, sir, I remember that time very well," George acknowledged, as he was welcomed by the preacher's Indian princess. George thought to himself that Red Bird was nearly as beautiful as his wife Julia; George believed himself the most blessed person to be stationed in Albany near his home, wife, and their son Benjamin, who was one of Karl's son, Walter's, best friend. Both, he and Benjamin, felt very fortunate to be reporting to one of the most ablest of the Continental Army's general. Presently, Walter Heindrick and Benjamin Jefferson were on a special assignment with General John Sullivan west of Fort Stanwix into Indian country.

After Preacher Stouffer had exchanged a few cheerful remarks with the Heindricks, he surveyed the pasture and the stables. Recognizing that apparently all the congregation had entered the church, which were going in, he escorted Red Bird to her favorite pew next to Martha Butler on the left side of the church near the front; the Heindricks and George Jefferson sat in the same pew, to the right of the ladies. Preacher Stouffer then returned to the back of the church to its center aisle. He crossed himself and reverently bowed his head. He held his worn leather-bound Bible tightly over his heart with both hands. Solemnly, he walked straight up the aisle until he reached the kneeling rail. He turned around, faced his flock, glanced toward the church's ceiling, crossed himself, and greeted his parishioners with a hearty, "Good morning!" In unison, they responded with a cheerful "Good Morning!"

"And 'tis, a joyous Spring morning. In fact," he added, "I saw my first sign of Spring." He hesitated a moment. Throughout the congregation people were staring at each other wondering what the preacher was going to identify as his *first sign of Spring.* During that moment of silence, Rebecca exchanged glances with Karl, each guessing what the Reverend was about to say. Then Preacher Stouffer identified his first sign of Spring as the pussy-willow with its large, silvery catkins. "This time of the year is truly a new beginning for all of us," he declared as he placed his Bible in his left hand. "To think that our gallant militia and Continental Army have defeated the British at Saratoga, and added to that stunning victory we have recently received the joyous news that Benjamin Franklin was successful in persuading the French to join an mutual assistance alliance with our United States of America." Still grasping his Bible, he rubbed his closely cropped salt-and pepper beard with his right hand, smiled as if he were a young child again with a special secret. Then assuming one of his favorite poses, that of Moses as he lead the Israelites across the dry Red Sea. "My friends," he began, "I wish I describe the joy I feel for this day. Our victories at Oriskany and Saratoga, and now the good news of France joining with our country to fight the British and their Loyalist and Indian allies. It truly is like the beginning of another of God's Spring, giving us all a fresh breath to our lives. The ancient Greek philosopher, Homer, had a beautiful saying which I'd would like to share with you:

> A generation of men is like a generation of leaves: the wind scatters some leaves upon the ground, while others the burgeoning wood brings forth— and the season of Spring comes on. So of men one generation springs forth and another ceases.

"and so it is our generation's responsibility to assume the leadership role in helping us to remove the chains of oppression from the tyrannic rule of not only of Britain's monarchy, anyone else who oppresses any of his human-kind."

He looked toward the pulpit, and rejected the idea of ascending to the elevated pulpit to preach his sermon. In fact, he did not like to use the word *sermon,* rather, he preferred to just *talk* with his congregation. As long as he had preached in the new church, he much preferred to stand on the slightly raised kneeling platform, instead of *Lording it over his flock from the formal pulpit.* As he often stated; it was more like the Heidelberg Tavern with everybody on the same level. It was not unusual for the chesty preacher to roam down the center aisle, and to speak directly to any particular parishioner. As he would occasionally say, he like to mingle among his flock. Unlike the Anglican priests with their long robes, Reverend Stouffer chose to wear his home-spun, dark wool suit with its turned-around collar. Still with his Bible in his left hand, he stepped down from the raised platform, and stood by the first row of pews, and continued his remarks:

"When we think about of our many variety of ancestors, many of which were brought to this country as indentured servants and expected to serve their masters for a certain number of years. After serving these required years, they would theoretically be turned *free.* At last, they would realize the *freedom* they were long seeking. Still others, were brought to this *land of freedom* as slaves. Just as the Israelites were taken into Egypt to be slaves for the Egyptians, many of our white ancestors, as well as our African-Americans and Native-Americans, were either brought one way or another to the shores of this great land to serve as slaves or servants to the behest of their Dutch and English masters. As John Locke, the famous philosopher, stated that at the time, the English surely viewed themselves as among the most civilized people on earth. What led them to believe themselves above most other peoples of the world may have been the result of their early explorations into Africa, which lead them to believe of their *covenant*."

He switched the Bible from his left hand to his right hand, and held it loosely at his side as he roamed back near the raised kneeling platform. Then he starred directly toward his wife and George Jefferson, and with an emotional dramatic soft voice, he continued, "In Africa, the English had encountered *other* people, who had an identifiable and shocking difference to their *norm*; they were black and *non-Christians*. To the early English settlers of this great continent, as well as in other foreign lands, Christianity was the essential element of civilization in order to be classified as *civilized*. Add to this, one's *whiteness* completed the Englishman's *norm*. To many, their established whiteness or their non-color was symbolically representing purity and beauty. To their way of reasoning, being black or some other non-white color symbolized evil and filth. Frequently, these early white English, and propertied Christian settlers envisioned themselves at the top of the pyramid of human beings. When the English came to America, and discovered the Native American, a new people whose skin was not white, black, or yellow, and who were not Christians. The categorization of human beings and the assignment of rank order to them was a natural cultural activity for the Englishmen, especially for those who first settled in Virginia.

"Some of those beings who did not fill all of their established parameters to be classified as civilized human beings were identified as targets to be Christianized. Still others, who did not fill the *whiteness* requirement, and were pigeon-holed as servants, and or slaves to white masters.. What has developed here in America, as I see it, are two separate groups of people; those who consider themselves at the top of the human pyramid, and those who follow the Lord's Golden Rule: *Do unto others, as you have do unto you."*

He paused, rubbed his beard, and plainly uttered each word, "These two groups are fundamentally at odds with each other. Unfortunately, the elemental arbiter of these differences usually develops into violence or the threat of it.

"Presently," he continued, "many of our fellow Patriots are making great sacrifices on our behalf. In turn, it is your and my responsibilities to become the most understanding and considerate individuals that we can be within our own abilities. We must able to walk with the gentry, yet never lose our common touch. Humility, one might define this approach. But, I say humility with empathy toward others."

He stopped a moment, lowing his head as if in prayer, then as if he had been struck by a bolt of lightening, he raised his face gazing toward the congregation. What the congregation saw was that their preacher's facial expression had became transfixed and illuminated; the same expression they envisioned Moses' face may have looked after he presented the Ten Commandments to the Israelites. Recovering from his trance, he rugged his closely cropped beard, and thoughtfully stated, "After this conflict is over, and we gain our freedom from Britain, I envision an enlightened, democratic country, which allows us to have the freedom we have all strived for, ….to do, and be what we want to be; as long as we do not infringe upon others' God given rights. But, my friends, there is a price we all must pay for this privilege! And that price of freedom is eternal vigilance, and the development and maintenance of personal and national strength in times of war, as well as during peace and tranquility."

Grasping his worn, leather-bound Bible with both hands, the preacher lowered his head, as if in prayer. The resulting silence throughout the church was deafening! A few moments later, the Reverend raised his ashen face looking as if he had just seen a ghost; through his clouded eyes he looked up toward the church's rafted ceiling. Still somewhat seemingly under a spell, he lowered his face, and rather blankly stared toward his flock, "Unfortunately, my friends, as far as this war is concerned, I, personally believe that the elemental arbiter, of which I have just mentioned has passed us by, in fact, we have probably reached the point-of-no-return," he sighed rather despondently. "But, I have good news for all of us. As a result of this present conflict and its results, I believe that a new world's a coming!" Suddenly his face brightened, and a smile came upon his face, as he raised his arms with his Bible in his right hand. "All we have to do is keep Psalm 121 in our mind. He closed his eyes toward the ceiling, and extended his enormous arms as if he were parting the Red Sea. He assumed his favored Shakespearean poise, and began reciting with the feeling of a dying Rabbi:

"I will lift up mine eyes unto the hills, from whence cometh my help. My help cometh from the Lord, which made heaven and earth. He will not suffer thy foot to be moved: he that keepeth thee will not slumber. Behold, he that keepth Israel shall neither slumber nor sleep. The Lord is thy keeper: the Lord is thy shade upon thy right hand. The sun shall not smite thee by day: nor the moon by night. The Lord shall preserve thee from all evil: He shall preserve thy soul. The Lord shall preserve thy going out and thy coming in from this time forth, and even for evermore."

He took a deep breath. He placed his Bible in his right hand over his heart. He, then, opened his closed eyes, and let them roam about the congregation as he repeated the Psalm's last phrase, "The Lord shall preserve thy going out and thy coming in from this time forth, and even for evermore." He crossed himself, and suggested that everyone "Go in peace."

Again, silence penetrated the congregation. The worshipers sat stunned as the Reverend Johan Stouffer solemnly strolled down the center aisle toward the church's front door. As he reached the door, Red Bird was there to meet him. They lovingly joined hands, and began exchanging greetings with the church's parishioners

* * *

On the very same morning, May 31, 1778, Ambrose Serle journalized his thoughts about the unsettling events in the British colonies. He had arrived in New York from London on July 12, 1776, to serve the private secretary to Admiral Lord Howe, who had been appointed as a peace commissioner for the colonies. While in New York City, Serle wrote articles for the Loyalist *New York Gazette,* and became well acquainted with numerous prominent Loyalists there and in Philadelphia. Before he was recalled to England on July 22, 1778, Serle recorded the following in his journal:

> This morning the D. (Duke) of Cumberland Packet arrived, & brought Advices to the 4th. of April from England. A general War appeared inevitable in Europe; and no more Forces are to be sent out to America, but Part of them to be withdrawn.—- This News perplexed the Friends of Govt. here, & and induced them to think seriously of a negotiation with the present Powers. My Friend Mr. G. (Galloway) much distressed upon the Subject. I hinted to him, that probably by making his Peace now, he might have it in his Power, with other Friends, when the madness of the Times was abated, to be a mediator between the two Countries, whose Interests being really one, and bring about a happy Union of Constitution & Policy. At present he could only be to them a ruined Enemy, & to us an inefficient Friend.—— He seemed to form his Resolution accordingly.

Prior to this journal entry, apparently Serle could see the handwriting on the wall, the following are some entries, which might help to confirm this statement:

> Wednesday, 20th. May. (1778)- Early this morning, a Detachment of 4,000 Men marched out to attack the Marquis de la Fayette, who with about the same number of Rebels had ventured over the Schuylkill (River) to a Spot within about 12 miles of Philadelphia; but, through some mistake on our

Side or Information given the Rebels, they ran off & forded the River before our People could come up with them. The commanding officer exceedingly blamed by the army.

Thursday, 21st. (May, 1778)- ...... Upon representing the Uneasiness which prevailed among the loyal Subjects on Account of the Rebels, the Genl. (Sir William Howe) advised him "to make his Peace with the States, who, he supposed would not treat them harshly; for that it was probable, on Account of the French War, the Troops would be withdrawn." This was soon circulated about the Town & filled all our Friends with melancholy on the Apprehension of being speedily deserted, now a Rope was (as it were) about their necks, & all their Property subject to Confiscation.—- The Information chilled me with Horror, and with some Indignation when I reflected upon the miserable Circumstances of the Rebels, &c.

Friday, 22d. (May, 1778)- ...... and now to wander like Cain upon the Earth without Home, without Property. Many others are involved in the like dismal Case for the same Reason—- attachment to their King & Country, & opposition to a Set of daring Rebels, who might soon be crushed by spirited Exertions.—- I now look upon the Contest as at an End. No man can be expected to declare for us, when he cannot be assured of a Fortnight's Protection. Every man, on the contrary, whatever might have been this primary Inclinations, will find it his Interest to oppose & drive us out of the Country.—- I endeavored to console, as well as to advise my Friend. I felt for him & with him. Nothing remains for him but to attempt Reconciliation with (what I may *now* venture to call) *the United States of America;* wch probably may not succeed, as they have attained him in Body & Goods by an Act of the Legislature of Pennsylvania.—- O Thou righteous GOD, where will all this Villainy end!

Mr. G. summoned the magistrates of the Town, & imparted the sad news, wch filled many an honest & loyal Heart with Grief & Despair.

Sunday, 24th. May. (1778)- This Day the Genl Sr. Wm. Howe departed from Philadelphia, & the Command devolved upon Sr. H. (Henry) Clinton), who presently afterwards sent a message by Col. Innes to my friend Mr. G. expressing his Desire to see him. .... I sat down in the Evening, & suggested in writing 13 (as I think) cogent Reasons, for Mr. G. to use with Sr. Henry, against the Abandonment of this central Province, wch appeared so convincing to us, that we recd. a Gleam of Hope that this terrible measure my be averted.

Monday, 25th. (May, 1778)- My Friend Mr. G. had two long Conferences with Sr. H. Clinton, in wch he imparted every Intelligence of their Country in His Power, & much to his Satisfaction. From the Tenor of these Conferences our minds seemed more satisfied than before, that no imprudent Steps wd. be taken. .... The poor Inhabitants still distressed, & preparing for Flight.

FIVE

CIVIL WAR WITHIN THE IROQUOIS

September 15, 1777 Quebec
Sir Guy Carleton's Headquarters

Unlike Johan Jost Jr. and Sandy McKnight, who immediately headed for Fort Niagara as soon as it was evident that the Rebels were victors at Oriskany, Colonel John Butler, too, wasted no time, but in opposite directions. Instead of heading to the western boundaries of New York State, Butler chose to go directly north across the Canadian border to Quebec accompanied with three principal Iroquois chiefs to Governor Sir Guy Carleton's headquarters. Their mission was to present to the governor Butler's renewed proposal to raise a battalion, the basic building unit of a division, of *rangers* to serve with the Indians. Still smarting from the British defeat at Oriskany, Governor Carleton quickly recognized Butler's plan as an appropriate sequel to that defeat, and readily approved and furnished Butler with *beating orders* for the enlistment of eight companies, each composed of a captain, a lieutenant, three sergeants, three corporals, and fifty privates. Carleton did, however, make a few suggestions as to the composition of troops. First, he advised Colonel Butler that two of these companies be staffed of *people speaking the Indian language and acquainted with their customs and manner of making war.* The governor informed Butler, that the rangers were to receive four shillings, New York currency, a day. He also recommended that the remaining companies *to be composed of people well acquainted with the woods, in consideration of the fateague they are liable to undergo;* they were to receive but two shillings per day. Carleton informed Butler that Canada had only limited finances, consequently, all of the recruits of the battalions would be required to clothe and arm themselves entirely at their own expense. The governor also informed Colonel Butler that this was extremely high pay, and that General Haldimand had estimated that these eight companies of rangers would cost the Canadian government as much as twenty companies of regular infantry.

On that same day, Governor Carleton gave Colonel Butler orders to march immediately with the number of rangers and Indians as he had already enlisted, and he advised him to continue to recruit while in march. In addition, Butler was ordered to collect as large a body of Indians as he could gather together without exposing their country to attack. Butler's mission was to form a junction with General John Burgoyne and his troops, and to proceed south from Montreal along New York State's lake region toward Albany.

En route to complete his assigned mission, Colonel Butler was faced with numerous disappointments. First, the Indians protested soundly against the withdrawal of the British troops from Oswego, claiming they were being abandoned to their enemies contrary to the pledges they had received from the British. In addition, Butler received two extremely disappointing messages. First, it was reported that sickness had reached such an epidemic stage at Fort Niagara, that the garrison had been reduced to seventy-five men *fit for duty.* When this fact had been learned by General Philip Schuyler, he seized the opportune moment while the Indians were still fuming with disappointment, and invited them to meet with him at the German Flats *to settle what was past and renew their former chain of friendship,* adding that he, *did not blame them for what had happened, but he had long ago told them that Colonel Butler would lead them to ruin.* General Schuyler also requested that the Indians to *deliver him (Butler) and not follow his wicked counsels any more.* Schuyler, further, expressed intention to taking Oswego, and asserted that if he found that Butler had gone to Fort Niagara, he would follow him thither, and if he had gone to Montreal he would intercept him on his return.

Butler received a letter from a friendly trader in Niagara informing him that some of the Senecas were much displeased with him, and that the loyal alarmed chiefs were anxious for his speedy return. While at Carleton Island, Butler received some other disturbing news, that the Oneidas, Onondagas and Tuscaroras had indeed *buried the hatchet* with General Philip Schuyler, and had proven their friendship to the Rebel forces by taking some Loyalists as prisoners, with Colonel Butler's ten-age son among the prisoners, while they passed through their country. With his son Walter and two other Loyalist officers confined, heavily ironed, and *cruelly* treated in an Albany jail, Colonel Butler intended to proceed overland from Oswego to Niagara, passing through all the principal Indian villages on his way, recruiting and engaging warriors for his proposed battalion. However, after he was warned that the overland route would be very dangerous, he decided to travel to Fort Niagara by water. When he arrived at Niagara, again Butler received some most disheartening information; Gentleman Johnny Burgoyne had surrendered his entire British army along with their allies to General Horatio Gates in Saratoga. Consequently, he reasoned that the orders he had most recently received were no longer valid, or even practicable. Instead after the siege of Fort Stanwix, he ordered most of his rangers to march overland to the Susquehanna river with orders to drive cattle from the Susquehanna settlements to Fort Niagara for the maintenance of the fort's garrison. Unfortunately, again, Butler heard nothing from these adventurers after the forest had swallowed them.

* * *

Johan Jost Jr. and Sandy McKnight were among the first to greet Colonel John Butler and his rangers after they arrived in Fort Niagara. Johan and Sandy also met the relentless and optimistic Chief Joseph Brant as he left a general meeting of the entire Iroquois confederacy at Ononadaga, during which a turbulent argument ensued over their future policy. The majority of the Senecas and Cayugas were determined to stay on friendly term with the British, and at their suggestion Butler boldly summoned the other tribes to join him and deliver the *hatchet* they had accepted from General Schuyler. To his pleasant surprise, all the chiefs of the Tuscaroras and Onondagas humbly promised to follow Colonel Butler's advise, and quickly surrendered their hatchet and war belt.

* * *

Perhaps America's first civil war had more direct and catastrophic impact on the Iroquois, and their territory than on the Loyalists and Rebel "whites" and their settlements. America's first civil war demolished the ancient Iroquois Confederacy bringing brothers against brothers, and these vicious border conflicts disrupted the *normal* patterns of Iroquois civility. In addition, the Rebel invaders broke into the Iroquois castles and villages destroying their crops and burning their villages causing most of the refugees to flee to the British for protection. To demonstrate the impact of this civil war upon the Indians, the story of the Oquaga or Onoquaga castle, one of the most important communities in the area serving as a melting pot for the Six Nations, reflects the pandemonium and anguish of the Iroquois experienced, reminding us that in a civil war the lines of allegiance are not always neatly drawn. Further, this type of political strife demonstrates that such conflicts over church and state are not confined exclusively to the *white* Americas. King George III is reputed as having said that the Revolution was nothing more than "a Presbyterian rebellion." If this were true, this Presbyterian rebellion had calamitous consequences at Oquaga, one of the four main Oneida villages located on the banks of the Susquehanna River in what was formerly known as the Susquehannock hunting territory, and a frontier crossroads straddling major Indian trails and at the junction of the Susquehanna and Delaware rivers near present-day

Windsor in Broome County, New York state. During the peak of its existence, Oquaga consisted of thousands of acres of cleared land, where its inhabitants cultivated fruit trees, peas, pumpkins, and *an abundance of Indian corn.* The Oquaga castle served as one of the main meeting places where the Indians from the south and west met traders from Albany and Schenectady. In fact, the Tuscarora displaced from their Carolina homes as the result of the Tuscarora War in 1713, migrated north accepted shelter, and subordinate status with their Iroquois relatives. It was, too, in this proximity where British Indian superintendent Sir William Johnson after making a trading expedition in 1739, said the Indians mostly wanted alcohol. (He had already identified alcohol as a useful and handy tool to effectively negotiate treaties with the Indians, especially those dealing with land ownership.) By the mid-1750's, Oquaga was not of one distinct tribe, rather it served as the castle for Tuscaroras, Mahicans, Shawnees, as well as the Oneidas, primarily because it served as a haven attracting refugees displaced by the *white man's war.* In 1758, the Indian superintendent reported that there were people from almost every one of the Six Nations settled at Oquaga. Soon thereafter in 1759, the Indians formally requested Johnson for a trading post *which would not only add greatly to our happiness, but would also increase our numbers, as it would draw Indians from all parts within 100 miles of us, to settle among us. .*

Due to the depleted region's beaver population, trapping and the fur trade in general needed to be replaced with a new type of economy. As a result of the unsavory (to the gullible Indians) Treaty of Fort Stanwix in 1768, more land was opened to settlement toward the west, especially energizing many landlords and their German and Scotch-Irish tenants to settle in these virgin forests. The development of an "advanced agrarian" economy by the white settlers required clearing fields, running fences, building farms with barns and other out-buildings, erecting saw mills, grain mills, cutting roads, operating ferries, and other infrastructure requirements caused a major disruption in the native Indian subsistence patterns. By the time the *white man's war* started, the people of the Oquaga were trading pelts for food. These fundamental changes in the Indians' culture elevating the warriors at the expense of sachems, making them vulnerable to other European imports, especially alcohol and Christianity.

In Oquaga, religious and political factionalism that had developed by the beginning of the *white mans' war* was not a simple division of *Christian* versus *pagan*. Rather, a dispute between the established religion of the Church of England, and the *new light* religion of New England Presbyterians and Congregationalists, which was already complicated by the existing divisions between traditionalists and Christians polarizing the communities. During 1751, a minister stated that the people at Oquaga had recently *made religion their main concern, rather than war, or worldly affairs*. This minister envisioned Oquaga as a potential center for missionary endeavors. By 1756, Sir William Johnson ordered a fort or blockhouse built at Oquaga, which supported the British during the French and Indian War. In 1761, however, Peter Agwrondougwas, an Oneida chief of the Eel clan also better known as Good Peter, requested that the fort "be pull'd down & kick'd out of the way," claiming that "these Forts which are built among us disturb our Peace, & are a great hurt to Religion, because some of our Warriors are foolish & some of our Brothers soldiers don't fear God." Interestingly, Joseph Brant, who had spent two years in Eleazar Wheelock's Indian School sponsored by Sir William, met his first wife and his future father-in-law in Oquaga, told Sir William that he was "determined to follow the Words of Jesus Christ as near as I can." Although Brant's's home was at Canajoharie, he reminisced after white mans' war, that he once owned a farm at Oquaga with a comfortable log house, fifty acres of cleared land, an orchard, and small herd of livestock.

Before America's first civil war, all appeared to be progressing relatively well for Oquaga. The Indians even planned to build a church there, and Reverend Samuel Kirkland glorified in seeing crowded congregations, and "a savage wolf of the Desert transformed into the Lamb of Christ." An Indian priest named Issac Dekayenensere, better known as Old Issac, complained to Sir William Johnson that many of Oquaga's Tuscarora residents refused to use the Church of England's Book of Common Prayer, and were averse to the word of

STEPS TOWARD FREEDOM

"God." Johnson's reaction was to urge the Indians at Oquaga "to live united," and warned the Tuscaroras to follow Old Issac's advice.

In 1771, Reverend Eleazar Mosely, a Presbyterian missionary who had came from Boston resigned his post as missionary in Oquaga, because he found life in the Indian castle was very lonely having "no suitable companion for society, nor housekeeper to wash my dishes." He relinquished his post to Reverend Aaron Crosby. Reverend Kirkland became concerned about what he was hearing, that the Oneidas in Oquaga were concerned that engrain tribal rivalries had transformed the "one true religion" into two rather uncertain religions. When Kirkland heard this report, he became depressed fearing that the "Prince of Darkness" reigned in Oquaga. In March 1773, the Reverend Kirkland made an exhausting trip on snowshoes to assist the Congregationalist minister, Reverend Aaron Crosby, a Harvard graduate and protege of Eleazar Wheelock, who he learned after arriving in Oquaga that Crosby had refused to use the Church of England's service, thus confusing the Mohawks who had learned to used that denomination's rites in their Fort Hunter home. In addition, Reverend Crosby refused to baptize children, whose parents led what he thought were immoral lives. Kirkland discovered that most of the residents of Oquaga were lost in continual turmoil, except Good Peter. Thanks to this Oneida chieftain, "who hath long been distinguished for his Piety & good sense," the Indians seemed to believe that leading exemplary lives and learning the Ten Commandments by heart was all they needed to secure eternal life. Kirkland was shocked to learn that the Indians "had no other idea of repentance than mere oral confession." He was convinced that the powers behind the turmoil were the Johnson family and Joseph Brant. The Johnsons were Anglicans, and Sir William had encouraged the establishment of Reverend John Stuart's Church of England among the Mohawks. Sir William had been concerned for years about the weak state of the Church of England in his area of the country, and feared that "the Number of Dissenters and the measures they pursue threaten more than our Religious liberties if not timely prevented." Sir William predicted that, unless he could remove Kirkland, the entire Iroquois Confederacy would be "set to quarreling," Religion was now entangled with local power struggles, and Oquaga was pulled between Kirkland's Presbyterian mission at Kanawalohale and the Anglicanism of Johnson and Brant. Not only did the missionaries have two different words for their congregations, but "the Word and the War" were also becoming "intimately entwined."

During the winter of 1777-1778, most of the Loyalists and Indians needed shelter and substance in Fort Niagara, but a goodly number of Indians and "disaffected Scotch Inhabitants" remained at Oquaga and Unadilla to alarm the settlers of Cherry Valley. Some abandoned their farms and pursued safety down country. Meanwhile, those who stayed behind petitioned Governor Clinton for rangers to guard the frontiers. By September, it was estimated that there was between four and six hundred Indians in the area, with the majority located in and around Oquaga, which was serving as a the staging area for summer raids against the Rebel settlers. By this time, Oquaga was now a prime military target for the Rebel forces. That same month, Governor Clinton wrote to Colonel John Cantine that he could see no prospect of peace on the frontier "until the Straggling Indians and Tories who infest it are exterminated, and drove back & their Settlements destroyed. If, therefore, you can destroy the Settlement of Achquago it will in my Opinion be a good Piece of Service." The next month Clinton called General Washington's attention to the situation, stating that the frontiers could never be safe, so long as Oquaga existed. Washington concurred, and ordered Lieutenant Colonel William Butler of the Fourth Pennsylvania Regiment to march against the settlement. In October, the Rebel colonel led his expedition, as Washington had commanded. against Oquaga and Unadilla. His forces met no resistance as they crossed the Susquehanna entering Oquaga during the night, "the Enemy having that day left the Town, in the greatest Confusion." Butler reported that, "It was the finest Indian town I ever saw, on both sides of the River, there was about 40 good houses, Square logs, Shingles & stone Chimneys, good Floors, glass windows &c. &c." The next morning, the American forces burned the town, and destroyed some two thousand bushels of corn. The troops's destruction, which left only one house standing, which probably belonged to the friendly

Oneida chief, Good Peter. Unadilla shared the same fate as Oquaga, thus depriving Chief Joseph Brant of his forward base, although Brant returned periodically during subsequent border raids. Later Good Peter admitted that many Oquagas might have been "misled by Want and false Insinuations" to act against the Americans, but he hoped that the Oneidas had seen their error and "make them hearty Friends to the United States." Seventeen Indians from Oquaga took refuge with the Oneidas; the rest dispersed "for other parts of the Indian country." More than 150 Oquagas joined fellow Iroquois refugees at Fort Niagara, campaigning with the British and Loyalists stationed there. A few people returned to the Oquaga region after the war, but many Oquagas retreated even farther from home after the war, joining new communities on the Grand River in Ontario, Canada. Those who had joined forces with the losers found themselves driven from their lands to new homes in Canada. Despite repeated treaty guarantees that the Indians would not be deprived of their lands, most of their Oneida neighbors who had backed the Rebels also found themselves pushed from their lands to new homes in Wisconsin and Ontario. After the *white mans' civil war,* the Oneidas split up into two separate communities: the warriors of Christian party of Shenandoah at Kanoalohale, and the chiefs or pagan party at Oriske. Later, they separated even further, the warriors moving to Wisconsin and the sachems to Ontario, "where each asserted beliefs consonant with their political objectives. Still other, Oneidas chose to live in their New York homelands. Eventually, the pro-American Oneidas petitioned the United States Congress to compensate them for losses that included frame houses, wagons, livestock, farm equipment, kitchen utensils, clothing, teacups and saucers, punch bowls, rugs, looking glasses, jewelry, and other items large and small that constituted the material culture of their once-flourishing communities. Eventually, Congress provided financial compensation, but by that time, most of the Oneidas' lands, together with those of the Oquaga relatives, friends, and enemies, had been swallowed up by private land speculators, the State of New York, and the United States of America. Oquaga reflected the Iroquois Confederacy as a haven for many diversified people, but once it lost its basic "cohesiveness" due to its religious and political stress, its relative tranquillity was torn apart amid the pressures of America's first civil war.

SIX

ALONG THE MOHAWK TRAIL

Last Week of September, 1778
at Fort Dayton located east of Fort Stanwix

Throughout the summer of 1778, intelligence reports were mounting upon Colonel Peter Bellinger's desk as fast as the brilliant orange, red and yellow autumn leaves were falling from the valley's maple trees. For the past three months reports, which were supplied by an effective network of informants and scouts, kept informing Fort Dayton's commander that Chief Joseph Brant and his warriors were planning to attack German Flats. Frequently, Bellinger was criticized by some of his staff of becoming nearly the point of being paranoid. According to one of the latest reports delivered informed him that, "Ever since July, we've been hearing that Brant and his warriors were about ready to attack German Flats. However, there is another thing we know is that Brant's warriors did attack and destroy Andrustown and Springfield. But, Brant must believe that we'll be ready for any of his raids, since it is common knowledge that rumors of his pending attack on German Flats have been circulated for the past three months."

On the morning of September 14, 1778, Colonel Bellinger, following his own gut feelings, dispatched a scouting party of nine Rangers to either confirm or deny these rumors. Unfortunately, near some land owned by a Major Edmonston on the head waters of the Unadilla River, Bellinger's Rangers stumbled upon a force of 150 Indian braves and 300 Tories under the command of William Caldwell. This mixed force chased the Rangers into the river, killing two, while the others scattered in all directions.

Under the cover of night and unknown to Bellinger, Brant and Caldwell had led their force of Indian warriors and Tories to the home of a well-known Tory, a Mr. Rudolph Shoemaker. About two miles down the Mohawk River, Brant and Caldwell's mixed forces hid in a ravine. Having given up on Colonel John Butler ever joining them, at approximately six o'clock in the morning, true to form Brant along with Caldwell led their force up the Unadilla River, where they hoped to pass unnoticed by the Rebels. Unfortunately for the mixed force, one of Bellinger's Rangers, who had escaped the ambush checked into Fort Dayton, and reported to Colonel Bellinger that he had last seen Brant's warriors only nine miles from the fort. Immediately, the colonel ordered an express rider to notify Colonel Jacob Klock, who had worked with Bellinger during the battle at Oriskany, and urgently requested reinforcements to his regiment. To Bellinger's dismay; no reinforcements appeared. However, he was becoming used to disappointment and adversities. One day while Bellinger was on sentinel duty, he spotted an Indian on the hill northwest of Fort Dayton. The Indian was running with a rifle. Bellinger aimed and fired, but the distance was too great and the Indian dropped behind a stump. While watching for the Indian to reappear, Bellinger's head and shoulders were visible above the pickets, and the Indian shot him through the left shoulder. The shoulder was a long time healing, and it was said that nearly thirty pieces of bone and three pieces of metal worked out of the wound. Meanwhile, the Indian left the hillside experienced and unharmed, but without a white man's scalp.

Three days later on September 17th, in a driving rain, Brant and Caldwell led their raiders to their target. To their disappointment, there was not one captive available to be taken, and any material valuables were as scarce as chickens' teeth. So as not to be a totally fruitless venture, Brant and Caldwell attacked Fort Dayton on the north side of the Mohawk River and began burning homes, barns, and outbuildings in the village of German Flats. Two Rebels were killed and one was wounded, but the stubborn fort withstood the assault leaving only two houses and the community's only church still standing.

Brant and Caldwell's forces continued their assault on the south side of the river about six miles above Fort Herkimer; from there, they continued their destruction down to the fort where the Indians and Tories were just starting to burn a barn. At that time, their mixed attacking force was caught red-handed by one of Colonel Bellinger's sally, which Bellinger believed could be spared from the fort, scattering the Indians and Tories into the forest. After Brant and Caldwel called the end of their attack, they returned to the Susquehanna area; their destruction totaled three defenders killed, 63 homes burned to the ground, 57 barns loaded with grain and fodder were nothing but charred remnants of a fruitful harvest, and 3 grist mills were completed destroyed, along with one saw mill and a great number of outhouses. In addition, a countless number of swine, as well as 235 horses, 229 cattle, and 269 sheep were either killed or driven away, some destined for the garrison at Fort Stanwix. As had been the custom, the Rebel militia was completely disorganized; totally ineffective running about in circles, responding to all kinds of rumors, not knowing which way to go, and making no effective pursuit. Colonel Bellinger, sympathetic to those who had lost their household goods and provisions, did order his aide-de-camp at Fort Dayton to furnish these victims with supplies from the military stores. Many of these people were left with nothing; and voicing their discouragement and intentions of leaving the Mohawk valley permanently. Knowing that abandonment of this frontier settlement would be a serious blow to the American war effort, Colonel Bellinger did everything he could humanly possible to persuade them to stay and rebuild.

Caldwell and Brant's devastating assaults and plundering was getting too close for the comfort of the Oneidas. They believed that these disastrous attacks upon the Rebel settlements would eventually jeopardize their neutral status, even though there were a number of Oneidas fighting with Washington's army.

* * *

After the German Flats campaign, Chief Joseph Brant and Captain William Caldwell decided to prepare for another sally, changing their attention toward the Delaware Valley instead of the Mohawk Valley leaving his Unadilla castle vulnerable to Rebel Colonel William Butler and Colonel Daniel Morgan's famous Virginia Riflemen, who were recruited from the back country of Pennsylvania. Maryland, and Virginia. On October 2nd, Morgan and Butler's troops were dispatched to march to Schoharie on a *punitive* expedition against the Indian castle at Unadilla, which was not the usual collection of huts and wigwams. Rather, Unadilla was like its neighboring Oquaga castle with its framed stone buildings, brick chimneys and glazed windows. Over the period of sixteen days, the Rebel forces had reduced in and around the Indian paradigm castle to nothing but a pile of rubble.

On their return from the German Flats campaign, Brant and his warriors stumbled upon the small Rebel settlement of Peenpack, which had three small forts located on the Neversink River. Meeting no resistance, Brant's braves seized one fort filling and capturing a few of the fort's defenders, while the other two forts were successfully repelling the Indian attackers. Fortuitously for the Peenpack residents, heavy rains had filled the stream to overflowing, so Brant's warriors were unable to drive the captured cattle away. With the captives minus the livestock, Brant led his braves back to his Oquaga castle where he was expecting to meet Colonel John Butler's young son, Captain Walter Butler. His scouts returned with devastating news! They exclaimed, "There is no Oquaga to go back to!" Upon investigating the devastated castle, Brant discovered that not only had he lost the Oquaga castle, but also his Unadilla castle.

He also learned that the Rebel forces could plunder, burn, and scalp as efficiently, quickly, neatly, and nearly as effectively as any of his braves. With the devastation of these two paragon castles, which had served as a rest haven for Tories fleeing to Canada, Brant's and his followers had lost their home base along with their well-filled warehouses. With the exception of seventeen Oquaga residents loyal to the Rebel cause, who fled to Oneida, most of Brant's Indian and Tory supporters who had lost their homes, fled to other parts of the Indian country. Brant realized that winter was fast approaching, and he was determined to make at least one more raid before New York's severe winter's snows began making a raiding party's footprints easier to track. However, he had forgotten that Indians, like the British did not like to go on the war path during the winter. After traveling steadily for about nine days from Peenpack, Brant and his warriors finally met Captain Walter Butler at Oswego near the end of the Forbidden Path on October 22nd. En route from Niagara, Butler had recruited a mixed force of some 300 Indians, a detail of approximately 50 volunteers from the King's regiment, including Johan Jost Jr. and Sandy McKnight, plus 50 or so of Rangers, who had recently escaped from the destruction of the Oquaga and Unadilla villages. On November 6th, nearly two weeks after Brant and Captain Butler's joined forces and identified their next target, the commander of Fort Stanwix sent an urgent messenger to Colonel Ichabod Alden, who commanded the Cherry Valley garrison of 250 Continentals, warning them of an imminent Indian attack on their settlement. Alden acknowledged receiving the warning, but he choose to disregard it stating, "These Oneida spies have long been crying wolf." For more than two years, the residents of Cherry Valley had been receiving warning after warning. Fortunately, Alden, not being a frontiersman, gave the latest rumors considerable thought. Becoming very suspicious, the former Massachusetts regiment commander, ordered a scouting party to reconnoiter the area, and promised the residents of Cherry Valley that he would furnish them ample warning if an attack was about to take place.

    According to the survivors of the eventual attack, Colonel Alden, his officers, and their families found the conveniences at the

Wells, home some 400 yards away from the fort, more pleasing than the bunks and salt pork mess available at the fort. In fact, the New Englander sat tight, denying the villagers the right to take refuge in the fort. "When we were first attacked," one of the men testified the following December, "we had not a pound of bread per man in the garrison. Had it not been for a barrel of gun powder and half a box of cartridges belonging to the town, the garrison's own ammunition would have failed us."

Brant and Butler had identified Cherry Valley as a target just ripe for picking with its bumper crop of more than 100,000 bushels of wheat ready for the flailing floors. By early November and after numerous arguments and disagreements, Brant and Butler finally resolved their differences, and navigated far up the west side of the Susquehanna River as far as the mouth of the Schenevus Creek; there they crossed the creek by ford, and proceeded up the east side. On November 9th, the Brant and Butler forces stumbled upon the tracks of Colonel Alden's scouting party, who had recklessly lain down to sleep beside a blazing campfire. All nine of the Rebel party were either captured or killed; not one escaped to carry the warning to the sleeping town, and the fort's bedraggled garrison and its commander.

The following day, the Brant and Butler's forces camped on a hill in the shelter of evergreens about six miles from Cherry Valley. Cherry Valley was the principle and most elegant settlement with its 300 residents on New York State's entire western frontier south of the Mohawk River. From their captive scouts, Brant and Butler learned that Colonel Alden and some of his officers were lodged with the amiable and good-hearted surveyor, Robert Wells, and his family's home near the fort. They also learned that some of the fort's officers were lodged with other families, who were lived close to the fort. In fact, the entire Wells family was well respected, living no more extraordinary a life than any other family in the beautiful community. In fact unknown to many, Robert Wells was one of Joseph Brant's Loyalist friends, who had traveled with him and Peggie, Brant's wife, and baby on a journey down the Susquehanna River in 1769. Brant knew, too, that he would have to do everything within his power to halt the Senecas from reaching the Wells home before he did, or all hell would break loose against every resident in the Wells household.

During the evening of November 11, 1778, a sleet storm turned to mushy snow. Even the Indians were lying down in the cold, under their hastily thrown together shelters without campfires, and feasting upon parched corn or whatever other food they could scrape together. One thing about the Indians, which Brant was fully aware of, was their many nurtured, and hidden animosities. Unlike Brant, Butler did not comprehend the extent of the Indians' venomous passions. Accordingly, Brant proposed that he, his warriors, together with about 50 white Tories, including Captain Johan Jost Jr. and Sandy McKnight, would attack all the houses, and capture or kill the Rebel soldiers.

Meanwhile that evening, Colonel Alden, Lieutenant Colonel Stacy, Major Whiting, and several other officers were leisurely enjoying the hospitality of the Wells' home. Suddenly, some of Brant's warriors, after running over plowed ground, violently smashed in the front door of the Wells' home before Brant was able to reach the house. Shocked, Cherry Valley's fort commander fled toward the fort, and was quickly killed; meanwhile, Lieutenant Colonel Stacy surrendered. Major Whiting, however, was more fortunate; he jumped through one of the Wells house's windows, reached the fort, and took command.

As previously agreed, Walter Butler commanded the attack upon the fort, ordering Brant and his Indians to destroy the settlement. After the attack, Butler stated that he had ordered Brant to *permit your warriors to attack only armed men.* That, however, was not the way it worked out! The Indian and Tory siege of Cherry Valley's fort lasted about three hours, and failed. At three-thirty in the afternoon, Captain Butler decided to order his Loyalist forces to withdraw from the attack on the fort, thus giving Brant's warriors an opportunity destroy the settlement. When Johan Jost Jr. and his buddy, Sandy McKnight were in the process of withdrawing their attention to the fort, they were totally shocked at the site of the havoc, which the Indians and the many Loyalists dressed as Indians, were inflicting upon the once cultivated and elegantly beautiful settlement. The warriors and their allies were all over the landscape plundering homes, out-buildings, barns, and finally, burning all standing building, capturing and driving away all livestock, even burning the wheat that they were unable to carry. Meanwhile, other raiders were occupied killing, scalping and taking prisoners.

"I can not believe what I'm seeing," exclaimed Johan Jost Jr. "I would have never believed that human-beings would be able to inflict such cruelty upon other humans."

"Sort of practicing what the *good book* says, *Do unto others, as you would they do unto you,*" said Sandy, as he leaned over a huge rock, and regurgitating his latest meal of undigested corn, and smoked venison.

"Do you feel up to completing our assignment Captain Butler gave us?" asked Johan Jost Jr. his buddy. The assignment, which the captain had given them, was to take an inventory of the burnings, killings, captives, plus any other statistical or operational information they thought would be meaningful to his superior officer.

"Oh, I'll make it, Johan, but I'm telling you I didn't expect any such massacre and devastation," admitted the Scotsman. "As far as I'm concerned, I've had enough of this bloody war."

Trying to ignore McKnight's last remark, Johan Jost Jr. urged his buddy to assist in following their Captain's orders. When they had finished their tally of the destruction, their report stated that 35 women, children and unarmed men had been scalped, 40 homes had been set afire, and 40 settlers including Lieutenant Colonel Stacy, Mrs. Campbell and her four children, Mrs. James Moore and her three children were captured and guarded by Captain McDonnell at the headquarters company of the Rangers. Captain Walter Butler included these statistics in his report, which told how a major, a few soldiers and Indians were able to enter the Cherry Valley fort, and how the fort's officers and their guards were either captured or killed. Though it rained that night incessantly, Butler and Brant's forces remained in the same location until late in the evening, and then their entire detachment retired about a mile away where they spent the remainder of the night. The next morning, Captain Butler dispatched Captain McDonald with 60 Rangers, and Chief Brant with 50 braves to *complete* the destruction of the *"Place,"* while the other Indians and the weaker Rangers drove off the cattle. Meanwhile, Captain Butler, Captain Johan Jost Jr. and Sandy McKnight watched the fort while *the Garrison all the while coop'd within their Breast-Works remained Spectators of our Depredations which they made no Attempts to interrupt.* Finally, after admitting that his Loyalist and Indian troops were not able to take the fort, the bewildered Captain Butler asked Johan Jost Jr. and Sandy McKnight, "Well, gentlemen, I think we should retire, and leave the fort *the only remaining Building amidst the Ruins of the Place."* Butler continued, "I have much to lament, that not withstanding my utmost precaution, and endeavors to save the women and children, I could not prevent some of them falling unhappy victims to the fury of the savages. These barbarians have carried off many the inhabitants prisoners, and killed more." He stopped a moment, perhaps lamenting the *shame* of the massacre, never did he admit guilt, rather he continued, "Many of our Indians and Rangers were unable to distinguish between the Loyalists, and who were the Rebels. Consequently," he continued, "all 13 of the Loyalist Wells family members were killed. From what I've heard, Seneca chief, Little Beard, was responsible of the Wells murders. In retaliation, some the Rebel soldiers fired back at Little Beard wounding three of his warriors; in return, Little Beard ordered his warriors to *put men, women, & children, to death."*

While Captain Butler was commiserating with Johan Jost Jr. and Sandy McKnight, one of Rangers, a Lieutenant Hare, approached the three with a smile of satisfaction upon his face, "Captain Butler, I just want you to know that my squad have been successful in rescuing an old minister and his young daughter, who we believe to be a Loyalists. We found the daughter trying to protect her dead mother from being scalped."

"That has been one of the problems here," inserted Johan Jost Jr. All eyes of his audience were focused upon Johan Jost Jr., wondering what words of wisdom he was about to proclaim. "It just appears to me, that most of the Indians are ignorant of peoples' loyalty; confused about who is Loyalist or who is a Rebel. Their reasoning is that this is a *white man's* war; a civil war! They seem willing to fight on the side of the ones, who give them the most liquor, trinkets, and promises."

"Me thinks," as Sandy McKnight in his Scottish brogue injected his unsolicited observation, "it be wise if we have no more service when the savages constitute the main force of our army."

* * *

Captain Walter Butler never went out on such an expedition again, and Johan Jost Jr. and Sandy McKnight were dispatched to Fort Niagara.

* * *

One day later during the evening of November 12, 1778, the news of the Cherry Valley massacre reached Schenectady, Immediately, 1,000 Continentals, including Sergeant George Jefferson, who had been stationed near Albany since Burgoyne's surrender at Saratoga, were dispatched to pursue butchery's raiders. The Rebel troops chased the attackers past Otsego and across the Chenango hills capturing only one of Butler's Ranger officers, who was waving a truce flag. This officer was carrying a letter from Captain Walter Butler addressed to General Philip Schuyler requesting *Mrs. (Walter) Butler and family* plus others named on an attached list *be permitted to go to Canada* in exchange for *an equal number of prisoners of yours taken either by the Rangers or the Indians.* After a passionate denial that *I wage war with Women and Children,* Butler closed his letter with the threat that *If you preserve in detaining my Father's family with you, we shall no longer take the same pains to restrain the Indians from prisoners, Women and Children that we have hitherto done.*

SEVEN

CANADA, A NEIGHBORLY BORDER?

Middle of December, 1778
at Fort Niagara

After being dispatched by Captain Walter Butler to Fort Niagara, Johan Jost Jr. and Sandy McKnight arrived at the fort during the middle of December, 1778 just in time for Colonel John Butler to assign them to one of the six companies of Butler's Rangers the colonel was currently organizing. After each ranger had received their clothing issue, each were assigned to a company, which was assigned to one of the cluster of log buildings, known as the *Rangers' Barracks*. These buildings, which were constructed under the supervision of Colonel Butler during the autumn on the west side of the St. Lawrence River, served as the companies' winter quarters. The uniform designed specify for the Rangers was of dark green cloth, trimmed with scarlet, very similar to the present rifle uniform, with a low, flat cap, having a brass plate in the front bearing the monogram "G.R." encircled by the words "Butler's Rangers." Initially, It was intended that they Rangers should be armed with rifles, but since each ranger was expected to provide his own gun, they brought with them a great assortment of firearms, which they were able to secure or seize, consequently many of the arms proved to be improper for the kind of service expected by Colonel Bolton, commander of Fort Niagara. To help fill the need for uniformity in arms, Bolton *lent* the Rangers one hundred "firelocks" from the fort's magazine, but he confessed that there was not a single good flint to be found in the entire fort.

After scrutinizing the enormous expense incurred and estimated more would be required to recruit, establish, train, garrison and feed the new regiment, plus the considerable amount of problems incurred in furnishing these and other requirements, the Rangers and the refugee Loyalists, Governor General Haldimand was convinced that it would be to the British advantage to establish a permanent settlement for these troops at Niagara. The sole credit of the project may be fairly attributed to Haldimand. For over a dozen years, he had found that the military gardens he had established at Oswego and Niagara had been noted for their size had the fine quality of the vegetables produced in them; specimens of which the officers occasionally sent down to astonish their friends in Montreal and Albany. The governor was influenced by the fertility of the area's soil, and believed that its cultivation might be at least part of the solution to the maintenance of the garrison, and perhaps even the Loyalist and Indian residents. On October 7, 1778, the governor wrote to Colonel Bolton suggesting that the refugees might be usefully employed in tilling land near the fort. Bolton, who was in poor health, emphatically despised the location. To make matters less promising, initially, he was not truly interested in the project; he was just not a damned farmer, at least of the caliber of Governor Haldimand. Secretly, he did not hold out much hopes of the project, when he believed that the troops should be out chasing the Rebel forces Consequently, Bolton responded, "It would require seven years to bring the land under cultivation to supply the garrison. We must be cautious how we encroach on the land of the Six Nations," the commander warned Governor Haldimand, "as we informed them that the Great King never deprived them of an acre since 1759, when we drove the French away." A few months later, Haldimand responded to Bolton, "The gentlemen I have consulted think, both from the soil and situation, the west side of the river, (the proposed land site belongs to the Missassaugas and the Government of Canada,) is by far more preferable than the east side where these none of those concerns will arise." The governor expressed his belief and those of others he had consulted, that he project offered an opportunity to make a beginning by encouraging some of the distressed Loyalists lately arrived at this post for His Majesty's protection. Expressing with the limited number of livestock they have brought offered an excellent start, and projected that the second year they might possibly be able support themselves and families. By the third year, the governor expected improved production for the post. "From that point," the governor forecast, "the increase would be considerable, so that in six or seven years such a plan would be serviceable to the Government, and the individuals that would undertake it."

Meanwhile, the governor repeatedly prevailed upon Colonel John Butler concerning the necessity of provisioning and protecting Niagara from attack at all hazards. "Your own knowledge of the importance of Niagara will suggest the necessity of your corps, and that people (the Indians) having a constant eye to the designs of the Rebels, and in case of need of throwing yourselves into that place to join in its defense….. The great expense and difficulty of transporting provisions to Niagara makes it desirable that cattle should be driven in, or any other articles sent in to Colonel Bolton, who would pay a reasonable price for them." In response, Colonel Butler assured the governor that although the Rangers, having no other means of subsistence, generally consumed most of the captured cattle, more than a hundred head had been brought in by them. To this Haldimand heartily approved, but he fervently objected to and condemned the cruelty of the Indians. Based upon the report, he had received from Captain Walter Butler, the governor wrote, "the success (at Cherry Valley) of which would have afforded the greatest satisfaction, if his (Captain Walter Butler) endeavors to prevent the excesses of which the Indians, in their fury, are so apt to run had proved effectual." Continuing, Governor Haldimand wrote, "that it is, however, very much to his credit that he gave proofs of his disapprobation of such proceedings, and I trust that you and every officer serving with the savages, will never cease your exhortations till you shall at length convince them, that such indiscriminate vengeance taken even upon the treacherous and cruel enemy, they are engaged with is as useless and disreputable as it is contrary to the disposition and maxims of their King, in whose cause they are fighting."

The Governor reminding Colonel Butler that he revered Butler and his Rangers' assistance as indispensable as ever. "I am confident," he assured Colonel Butler, "no pains or trouble will be spared on your part to keep the different tribes in the humor of acting for the service of the Crown, and that every argument will be made use of by you to convince them how severely they would feel the contrary behavior."

During the winter, the Indians declared themselves to be in great fear of a Rebel attack. To ease their distress, Colonel Butler assured them that Congress had its emissaries everywhere, and that they were using every tactic to attract the Indians to their side. In fact, by some hook or crook, the Continental Congress was successful in converting some of the Onondagas, using them to persuade others to join the Rebel forces. Throughout the severe winter, scouts were tirelessly patrolling the vast surrounding area in every direction, while the main body of Butler's Rangers were retained within the fort's enclosure in perpetual readiness to march wherever they might be needed. Their scouting efforts extended to keeping watch upon the Rebels in and around the Wyoming county area from which daily reports were communicated back to Niagara. Several scouting parties were dispatched to survey the road between Fort Stanwix and German Flats. There they were ordered to intercept, if possible, any of the Rebels' express. On this route, an Indian made his way, from this point, to Albany, and observed what preparations were taking place. As a result, a scouting party was ordered towards the Minisink to observe the enemy's situation. There a Seneca chief promised to have some of his young warriors continually out scouting the area, and to forward any information they were able to discover. With all of this surveillance, Fort Niagara's command believed it almost impossible for the Rebels to wage the smallest of movement upon the fort, before the garrison was alerted.

As Spring approached, every scout and messenger brought news of assembling of Rebel troops. At Fort Pitt, it was discovered there was a numerous force preparing boats for some unknown purpose. At Wyoming, meanwhile, a formidable army was gathering, and a spy returning from the Mohawk valley disclosed that he had seen at least 700 men in camp at Canajoharie. In addition, it was reported that a vanguard was leading an army of approximately 3,000 troops advancing from the Canajoharie area against the Indians. In addition, it was reported that 600 hundred men from Fort Stanwix had waged an attack on Ononadaga, where three Indian villages were burnt, 38 women and children captured, and a few killed. Since the Ononadaga tribe was already friendly to the Americans, this attack only served to alienate them, and exasperate the remainder of the Indians. The Indians were fast becoming convinced that their enemies intended nothing less than their extermination and total annihilation. Meanwhile, Colonel Butler made every exertion to prepare the Rangers for instantaneous service.

* * *

While Governor Haldimand, Colonel Bolton and Colonel Butler were busily trying to shore-up their fort's defense, and make provisions for feeding and supplying the fort's garrison, their dependents, the Indians, and others who were expecting shelter, and substance from the fort's facilities, General George Washington was seriously evaluating a proposal he had received recommending that the Americans stage an invasion against Canada. During his deliberations with his confidential staff members, they recalled two major battles which were waged against Canada. The first major siege against Canada, was the heroic British campaign waged against the French forces stationed at Quebec, and commanded by King Louis XV's chosen career soldier, Louis Joseph, Marquis de Montcalm-Gozon de Saint-Veran, who had spent decades traveling throughout Europe with the army, and wanted to stay close to his family and his estates in Provence, but like any good soldier, he obeyed his orders. The British command selected Major General James Wolfe, who had helped to take Louisburg, to strike the blow against Montcalm and Quebec. Wolfe, a slight man in his early 30's with flaming red hair, a receding chin and a delicate constitution, didn't look the part of a commander to say nothing about being a hero. Quebec was a walled *Upper Town* adorned in the grandeur of the time with narrow gates giving the only passage into the old city high on cliff above the St. Lawrence River. At the foot of the cliff was the teeming *Lower Town*, a preserve of storekeepers and sailors, where ships docked at nearby wharves, while adjacent pubs and inns echoed with rough boasts. After making an unsuccessful attack on Montcalm's forces at Beauport east of Quebec, Wolfe came up with a daring plan. At 4:00 o'clock on the rainy morning of September 13, 1759, Wolfe and his advance party scrambled up the cliffs, surprising a small group of French defenders at the top. The rest Wolfe's attack force streamed up the cliff face behind the advance party, and by dawn more than 3,000 British soldiers stood in battle formation on the Plains of Abraham. Poorly trained, the French militia reinforcements advanced too quickly against the British troops, and began shooting before they were close enough to hit any of the British troops. After their ill-advised firing, these French-Canadian sharpshooters dropped to the ground to reload, getting in the way of the regulars who were following closely behind them. When Wolfe judged that the French were close enough, he gave the order to fire. Panic spread throughout Montcalm's soldiers as their members began to fall. Wolfe gave the order to charge, and the French soldiers retreated to the safe walls of the city, and to nearby Beauport. Montcalm, borne along by the crowd, commanded his soldiers to regroup, and keep fighting. No one heeded his commands. As his defeated army reached the port Saint-Louis (Saint Louis Gate), Montcalm was shot twice, and some of his soldiers rushed him to the home of a surgeon, who saw that he could do very little for the dying general. The British lost their commander as well. General Wolfe had been shot through a lung near the beginning of the battle. His soldiers carried him back behind the lines, but Wolfe died within minutes. Four days after the Battle of the Plains of Abraham, Jean-Baptiste-Nicolas-Roch de Ramezay, the governor's second-in-command, handed Quebec over to the British. He signed the terms of Quebec's capitulation in a house at 25 rue Saint-Louis, not far from the Ursuline convent.

The second campaign against Canada, which Washington and his staff studied, was the expedition led by Generals Robert Montgomery and Benedict Arnold. This expedition began off with a good start, but crashed against the rocks of Quebec. General Montgomery lead a force of about 1,000 New Englanders up the Hudson River and Lake Champlain route, and captured Montreal on November 12,1775. Benedict Arnold lead a group of 600 Yankees, who had marched through the Maine wilderness to the St. Lawrence opposite Quebec, where they rendezvoused with Montgomery. On the evening of December 31st, the snow, which had been falling lightly suddenly developed into a blizzard. Marching his force into the driving snowstorm, Arnold lead his men toward the Lower Town from the northeast, while Montgomery's forces proceeded from the southwest. Just as the two forces approached the entry to the Lower Town, a rocket cut through the air, followed by two more. (It was New Year's Eve!) This was the signal for all the church bells in Quebec to start ringing. Arnold waved his sword, spurring his men to a charge, they began working their way into a narrow street in Lower Town. There Arnold knew that at the top of this street was a barricade where the British had planted a cannon well equipped with canister shot (hunks of iron, nails, and other lethal objects), which could be mow down an advancing column much more effectively than a single cannon ball. He also knew, that he would have to take this cannon before he could move on to the Upper Town. So, he ordered a charge! He could see the flash of the cannon powder seconds before the explosion roared down, accompanied by flying bits of metal. Amazingly, Arnold was untouched, and predictably, he shouted to his men to follow him. Suddenly, musket fire poured down on all sides of his force from the surrounding houses. He was almost at the barricade when a sharp pain seared his lower left leg. Thinking he might have been grazed, he continued the charge, but suddenly he could move no further. He leaned against a house, and yelled to his men, "Go on, God damn it, lads!" With blood oozed over the top of his boot, he ordered his troops, "Follow (Colonel Daniel) Morgan and take the town!" Morgan and his troops stormed another barricade, only to be thrown back by musket and cannon fire. Morgan's only hope lay in the immediate arrival of Montgomery's forces, with which the Americans conceivably could have battered their way into the Upper Town and victory. Unfortunately for the Rebel attackers, Montgomery's fate was briefer than Morgan's. After cutting their way through two barricades, Montgomery's men followed their general past a blockhouse toward what appeared to be a fortified house. In his eagerness, Montgomery did not wait for the rest of his troops to pull themselves through the breached barricades and snowdrifts. He and two dozen of his men cautiously moved forward, oblivious that all the while they were being watched by the British and American Loyalist volunteers. When Montgomery, Aaron Burr, and several other officers were within a few yards of the house; all hell broke loose! Cannon and muskets poured canister shot and bullets into the Americans, immediately, killing Montgomery along with a dozen others. Fortuitously, Aaron Burr and two or three others escaped unhurt. Meanwhile, Colonel Morgan and his men were surrounded by British troops advancing with their dreaded bayonets, ordering them to throw down their arms and surrender. True to form, Morgan, with his back against a wall and tears of impotent rage streaming down his craggy face, waved his sword at the advancing bayonets, and hoarsely yelled, "If you want my sword, you'll have to take it from me!" When the British threatened to shoot him, Morgan's men pleaded with their leader not to throw away his life. Just then, the towering Virginian spotted a priest in the crowd, called him forward, and asked him, "Are you a priest?" The priest gave Morgan an affirmative nod. Accepting the nod, Morgan said, "Then I give my sword to you. But not a scoundrel of these cowards shall take it out of my hands."

Washington had learned much from these two campaigns. The first thing he learned was that very military campaign requires the leadership of a daring, experienced, yet intelligent and alert leader. He believed that he had found such a leader as a result of the New

Year's Eve campaign. Surprised by what he had found at Quebec, General David Wooster, who had been assigned Arnold's command while he was recuperating from his wound, wrote to General George Washington, "General Arnold has, to his great honour, kept up the blockade with such a handful of men that the story, when told hereafter, will be scarcely credited." Continuing Wooster said, "throw him into the midst of a battle, and no matter how heavy the odds against him, Benedict Arnold's determination, inevitable radiated enthusiasm, and his renewed vigor to his tattered troops. Due to his energy and positive attitude, Arnold achieved miracles. His march, which ended nearly capturing Quebec, probably would have been accorded as one of the most famous military campaigns in American history. In fact, after learning of what Arnold had achieved at Quebec, Joseph Warren, one of the imposing Sons of Liberty, wrote to Samuel Adams, "Arnold has made a march that may be compared to Hannibal's or Xenophon's; after hearing the evidence, Thomas Jefferson rapidly concurred with Warren's appraisal. On June 18, 1776, Arnold, the last American to leave Canadian soil, stood by the shore of St. John's, waiting until he heard the thundering hoofs of the British advance cavalry. In the distance, Arnold could see Redcoats and their flashing steel. He removed the saddle from his horse, placed it in a canoe, put his gun to his horse's head, shooting his faithful animal dead, rather than have it fall into British hands. In his mind, defeated yet victorious, Arnold, demonstrating his defiance, paddled his way south from St. John's down the river, and into Lake Champlain.

In November, 1778, after much consternation and numerous consultations about the proposed expedition against Canada, Washington responded to his friend Henry Laurens, who was serving as the president of the Continental Congress:

>........I have one objection to it, untouched in my public letter, which is in my estimation, insurmountable, and alarms all my feelings for the true and permanent interest of my country. This is the introduction of a large body of French troops into Canada, and putting them in possession of the

capital of that Province, attached to them by all the ties of blood, Habits, manners, religion and former connexion of government. I fear this would be too great a temptation, to be resisted by any power actuated by the common maxims of national policy.

Let us realize for a moment the striking advantages France would derive from the possession of Canada; the acquisition of an extensive territory abounding in supplies for the use of her Islands; the opening a vast source of the most beneficial commerce with the Indian nations, which she might then monopolize; the having ports of her own on this continent independent on the precarious good will of an ally; the engrossing the whole trade of New found land whenever she pleased, the finest nursery of seamen in the world; the security afforded to her Islands; and finally, the facility of awing and controlling these states, the natural and most formidable rival of every maritime power in Europe. Canada would be a solid acquisition to France on all these accounts and because of the numerous inhabitants, subjects to her by inclination, who would aid in preserving it under her power against any attempt of every other.

France acknowledged for some time past the most powerful monarchy in Europe by land, able to now to dispute the empire of the sea with Great Britain, and if joined with Spain, may say certainly superior, possessed of New Orleans, on our Right, Canada on our left, and seconded by the numerous tribes of Indians on your Rear from one extremity to the other, a people, so generally friendly to her and whom she knows so well how to conciliate' would, it is much to be apprehended have it her power to give law to these states.

STEPS TOWARD FREEDOM

Let us suppose, that when the five thousand French troops (and under the idea of that number twice as many might be introduced,) were entered the city of Quebec; they should declare an intention to hold Canada, as a pledge and surety for the debts due to France from the United States, or, under other specious pretenses hold the place till they can find a bone of contention, and in the meanwhile should excite the Canadians to engage in supporting their pretenses and claims; what should we be able to say with only four or five thousand men to carry on the dispute? It may be supposed that France would not choose to renounce our friendship by a step of this kind as the consequence would probably be reunion with England on some terms or other; and the loss of what she had acquired, in so violent and unjustifiable a manner, with all the advantages of an Alliance with us. This is in my opinion is too slender a security against the measure to be relied on. The truth of the position will entirely depend on navel events. If France and Spain should unit and obtain a decided superiority by Sea, a reunion with England would avail very little and might be set at defiance. France, with numerous army at command might throw in what number of land forces she thought proper to support her pretensions; and England without men, without money, and inferior on her favorite element could give no effectual aid to oppose them.

......I am heartily disposed to entertain the most favorable sentiments of our new ally and to cherish them in others to a reasonable degree; but it is a maxim founded on the universal experience of mankind, that no nation is to be trusted farther than its bound by its interest; and no prudent statesman or politician will venture to depart from it. In our circumstances we ought to be particularly cautious; for we have not yet attained sufficient vigor and maturity to recover from the shock of any false step into which we may unwarily fall.

If France should even engage in the scheme, in the first instance with the purest of intentions, there is the greatest danger that, in the progress of the business, invited to it by circumstances and, perhaps, urged on by the solicitations and wishes of the Canadians, she would alter her views.

As the Marquis clothed his proposition when he spoke of it to me, it would seem to originate wholly with himself; but it is far from impossible that it had its birth in the Cabinet of France and was put into this artful dress, to give it the readier currency. I fancy that I read in the countenances of some people on this occasion, more than the disinterested zeal of allies. I hope I am mistaken and that my fears of mischief make me refine too much, and awaken jealousies that have no sufficient foundation. But upon the whole, Sir, to wave every other consideration; I do not like to add to the number of our national obligations. I would wish as much as possible to avoid giving a foreign power new claims of merit for services performed, to the United States, and would ask no assistance that is not indispensable. I am, etc.

* * *

You know that these two nations [France and England] have been at war over a few acres of snow near Canada, and that they are spending on this fine struggle more than Canada itself is worth.

Voltaire [Francois Marie Arouet]
Candide, 1759

EIGHT

HERE'S YOUR MARCHING ORDERS!

December, 1778
Washington's Philadelphia Headquarters

Even before he had gathered his select group of advisors, Washington had diligently developed his assessment of America's military situation. In his letter to Henry Laurens, he had completly ruled out an offensive campaign into Canada. Based upon his perception, he reasoned that an offensive expedition into and throughout the Iroquois country would produce more beneficial results. In preparation for the conference of his advisors, he wrote his appraisal of American's condition:

> Our affairs are in a more distressed, ruinous and deplorable condition than they have been since the commencement of the war.... to continue defensive action along the Atlantic coastline, however, I intend to dispatch one-third of the entire Continental Army

on a series of strikes into the heartland of the Iroquois homeland in an effort to completely destroy their settlements and the fields.

This statement served as Washington's opening statement when, in the opening weeks of February, 1779, he gathered his select group of officers including General Philip Schuyler, General George Clinton, Colonel Goose Van Schaick, Colonel Marinus Willet, and Major General John Sullivan, together with a few other seasoned, well respected, and loyal Iroquois scouts and experts. After sifting through numerous surveys, questionnaires, interviews, letters, and other overt and subvert information collected about the Iroquois and their homeland, together with other relevant details that would assist them in planning their campaign strategy into the Six Nations territory, Washington believed he and his council were prepared for their strategic meeting. Following a series of council meetings, Washington presented a plan, which he and his council totally supported, to the Continental Congress stating that: "The council is fully sensitive of the importance of success in the present expedition, and the fatal mischiefs which would attend a defeat. We should perhaps lose an army and our frontier would be deluged in blood." In essence, Washington was willing to gamble one-third of the colonies' army on this one campaign. On February 27, 1779, Congress authorized Washington to organize the expedition into the Iroquois homeland. His first task was to identify and commission the commander-in-chief of the expedition. He felt obligated to initially to offer the post to General Horatio Gates, the recipient of General John Burgoyne's sword at after the British defeat at Bemis Heights. However, he was not over-overjoyed in making such a proposal to Gates, because he was not impressed with his rather ineffectual performance during the entire Saratoga campaign. Once he had offered Gates the position, Washington's prayers were answered; Gates declined the command! Expecting his refusal, Washington had already decided to offer the command to Major General John Sullivan. This stocky, thirty-nine year old ex-lawyer from Summerswoth, New Hampshire readily accepted the command post. Just as readily, Washington gave Sullivan his responsibility, *"Lay waste to all the settlements around, so that the Indian country may not only be overrun, but destroyed."*

General Sullivan had a varied military background. On August 26, 1776, Sir General William Howe's British forces attacked Sullivan's troops on the left wing in the Battle of Long Island. A day later, Howe's forces surprised the Continental force with an attack that hit the American's left flank and rear guard, crushing Sullivan's forces and sending them fleeing; Sullivan's forces suffered a shattering defeat. For a short time, Sullivan and about 400 of his men exhibited a stubborn resistance, but in the end, they surrendered waiting for another day. Some officers blamed Sullivan for the defeat, while others believed he did not deserve censure. Apparently, the primary reason the Rebel forces loss this encounter was due to the relative inexperience of their officers and soldiers compared to the highly disciplined British regulars. The Rebel prisoners, especially General Sullivan, were treated fairly well by General Howe, meanwhile, this peace advocate British general was insisting that he and the British were anxious to make a reconciliation with Americans. Accordingly, the British paroled Sullivan to travel to Philadelphia, and carry such a reconciliatory message to the Congressional leaders. This he did, but Congress did not believe that Howe could or would grant acceptable terms. Once again, while Sullivan's intentions were noble, he was soundly criticized. Regardless, and unlike General Benedict Arnold one of his discouraged fellow officers, Sullivan's endeavors were moral, giving no thought of deserting the American cause. His problem was that he naively believed that the nation's independence could be achieved in this manner. Shortly after this incident, Sullivan was exchanged for a British prisoner, and soon Washington placed him in command of the several brigades that formed one part of the attack force on Trenton, New Jersey. Despite the cold, icy, winter day of December 26, 1776, the Rebels forces enjoyed winning a solid victory at Trenton. Later, on January 3, 1777, Sullivan performed well, commanding the American main units at the Battle of Princeton. His role in this victory demonstrated that he was a brave fighter and a determined leader.

***

On May 31, 1779, a smiling and relieved General Washington greeted his guest in his headquarters office, and extended his right hand in gratitude saying, "I knew that I could count on you, my dear friend, to accept the command of our expedition into the Indian country."

The confident and relaxed thirty-nine year old Major General John Sullivan smiled at his much admired commander-in-chief, and responded, "I am very proud and pleased that you have selected me to command this exceptionally critical expedition."

Even before Sullivan had completed his statement, Washington had slipped behind his military issued desk, opened the narrow oak drawer, and pulled out a clean white envelop. Handing the envelop to Sullivan, Washington said, "These are your marching orders! I expect you, your staff, and your troops to follow them implicitly."

This expedition you are appointed to command is to be directed against the hostile tribes of the Six Nations of Indians with their associates and adherents. The immediate objects are the total destruction and devastation of their settlements and the capture of as many prisoners of every sex and age as possible. It will be essential to ruin their crops in the ground and prevent their planting more.

While Sullivan was thoroughly study his marching orders, Washington's thoughts about America were racing well ahead of Sullivan's expedition. Washington's pincer movements were designed to be much more than a punishment of the Iroquois, and the eradication of Fort Niagara's *hornet's nest*. In Washington's mind, the ultimate purpose of his orders to Sullivan was a declaration that the 1768 Fort Stanwix Treaty's boundary line between the *White man's* territory and the *Red man's* territory had been trashed, and that America stood ready to settle the boundary line, as Washington stated: *"Where it damn well pleased, even clear to the Mississippi River."*

***

Spurred by General Haldimand's latest letter to the Six Nations, the Indian chiefs at their council meeting in Canadesaga were reminded that they were not fighting the king's battle solely, but were also defending the line of 1768. The Americans, Haldimand added aim to take the whole continent from you and the king's people. He also brought to their attention that the Rebels could not give the Indians anything since they had nothing, and were "getting poorer every day." He urged the Indians to prove themselves worthy descendants of your brave ancestors. Defend the conquests of the land which your forefathers made, and you will regain the same awe and veneration which they enjoyed. With this inspiration, the Indians were rejuvenated to new energy level and purpose.

In late June, 1779, Chief Joseph Brant and about sixty warriors had left Niagara Falls. En route towards Detroit, he received disturbing message from an Indian runner (later found to be false) that the Americans were on their way to attack the Cayugas. Immediately, he hurried back to Niagara. Knowing that Major John Butler was already there, Brant and his cadre set out in the opposite direction into the Indian country. Colonel Bolten, as soon as, he had heard of the Rebels attack on Onondaga, ordered Butler, ill health or not, to go to the aid of the Indians. Butler had about four hundred Rangers and warriors. Among the Rangers were Captain Johan Jost Jr. and his Scottish buddy, Sandy McKnight, their last contact with the Rebels had been at Oriskany, where Johan Jost Jr., had seen his oldest brother shot. Later, he had learned that his brother's left leg was amputated, eventually, causing his death. Between the battle at Oriskany and this expedition, Captain Johan Jost Jr., because of his knowledge of and popularity with the Indians, was attached to the Indians Department at Fort Niagara. To his advantage, he was permitted to select his own adjutant; not surprisingly he selected Sandy McKnight.

Butler and his force had continued receiving reports from everyone of his scouts and spies that two Rebel armies were poised, one down the Susquehanna near Wyoming, and one up the Susquehanna River at Otsego Lake. The Indians, who had been living in these areas, reported to the scouts and spies that the

Rebels were as numerous as the leaves on the trees. Butler did not ignore the Indians' warning, rather he did not trust the validity of their information, because he knew that the Indians always tended to exaggerate the true circumstances. So! How could there be that many enemy forces? How could the Rebels have, so quickly, raised that many men? In reality, Butler and his force of Indians and Loyalists had more pressing concerns than imaginary numbers of Rebel forces or their targets. His forces had been endeavoring to live off the land, but the hunting and fishing were extremely poor; they had almost exhausted their food, and were virtually near the stage of starving with nothing to eat. Since the provision fleet, which was expected any day, had not arrived, Colonel Bolton had not been able to transport any foodstuffs to the field. The frustrated Colonel Butler delayed as long as he could, till he realized that some of his men were becoming very ill. At that point, Butler ordered that most of his forces go to Genesee Falls, where he believed the fishing was better. Desperate for food and fully aware that the fort was also in short supply, Butler pleaded to the fort's commander, Colonel Bolton, for some relief. About all that Colonel Bolton could gather together was a few bags of flour, peas and oatmeal, plus a very, very little amount of pork. When the famished troops discovered the food, which had been delivered, they acted like children with candy treats running and jumping "whooping & hallowing & skipping about as if they had lost their senses." The Indians looked upon the troops' antics without any new food supply. They, too, were just as hungry, if not hungrier. They had been living on roots and greens gathered in the woods, and using up precious ammunition by firing at every small bird or squirrel they saw. They had long since eaten the previous year's crop, and the current year's crop was not ready for harvesting. Some of Butler's troops caught the Indians stealing a small calf, which the Rangers had been trying to fatten. Needless to say, Butler's men were furious. "May their first morsel choke them!" one Ranger exclaimed. "That such reptiles should enjoy such delicious bit," was another's tormented cry.

Meanwhile, numerous groups of Indians and soldiers were dispatched to disperse into small groups to search for any kind of food stuffs, including any kind of live stock such as cattle, sheep, pigs and chickens. Joseph Brant led one such search group. Remembering that a Rebel force was stationed at Lake Otsego, Brant was hesitant to attempt to drive cattle from either the Mohawk or Schoharie areas, and he also knew that there was nothing to be had on the from the ruined sites of the Indian castles of Oquaga and Unadilla near the Susquehanna. Then he remembered hearing about a small settlement, called Minisink, down on the Delaware River. As he had learned, the relatively small community of Minisink had earned a fine reputation as a thriving neighborhood. Even though it was a long distance to go from he and his warriors were located, Brant decided that rewards there would be worth the long trip through some of the roughest country he had ever traveled. Even though rumors had had Brant all over the Indian country, this expedition would be his first of the season, except for a few small scouting expeditions from Fort Niagara.

On July 8, Brant and his warriors reached Chemung, an Indian settlement on the Chemung River. At the time, there was a widely circulated story about a man named Moabary Owen, who was known as a *double deserter*; one who was once from a Rebel regiment, and once again from one of Brant's supporters. While *working* for the Rebels, Owen is reported to have informed Rebel authorities at Goshen that Joseph Brant had with him about sixty warriors and twenty-seven Loyalists, and that he, Owen, had "Heard Said Brant gave Orders that they Should not Kill any woman or Children, and if they Knew any person to be a Tory not to Kill them, and any that would Deliver them Selves up to Take them prisoners, but any person Running from them to Kill them." Owen also stated that Brant expected more Tories to join his force, then they planned to destroy Catskill, and that an army from Canada was coming south to take Fort Stanwix. Needless to say, most people who had heard this story did not give much credibility to his remarks, but some of Owen's reports probably had some spark of truth for Owen was able to name very accurately about thirteen of Joseph's white Volunteers. One of whom was Johan Jost Jr.'s friend, Sandy McKnight, who was faithfully carrying his bagpipes with him.

About two weeks later near midday on July 20th, Brant and his men reached their Minisink destination. Their arrival time was a disappointment, because Brant had wanted to attack before daybreak. Regardless, there was virtually no resistance, and the raiders brunt some houses and proceeded to round up the cattle. A second obstacle helped to frustrate the attackers; most of the cattle were scattered throughout the surrounding woods. Another impediment was reported by Brant himself in these words: "We have burnt all the Settlement called Minisink, one Fort excepted, round which we lay before about an Hour, & had one man killed and one wounded. We destroyed several small stockaded Forts, and took four Scalps & three Prisoners, but did not in the least injure Women or Children, The Reason that we could not take more of them, was owing to the many Forts about the Place, into which they were always ready to run like Ground-Hogs." These many forts Brant reported about probably included Freeland's Fort and Northumberland, which General John Sullivan eventually learned about.

As the Minisink massacre was slowly drawing toward a close, an incident occurred which Chief Joseph Brant had no knowledge of, which would have a lasting impact upon not only some of his braves, but also on some of the Rebels he and his warriors were to encounter. Just after two of his braves, Thunder Cloud and Red Squirrel, had finished torching one of the few remaining farm houses in Minisink, they heard cries of children in the house. Knowing that Brant was emphatic about not killing women and children, Thunder Cloud urged his friend, Red Squirrel, to rush into the burning house and rescue the children. Once in the house, they found two black youths. With an eye for beauty, Thunder Cloud grabbed the attractive, teen-aged mulatto girl, while Red Squirrel seized the young boy. Once outside the house, Red Squirrel, in a split second, scalped the darker of the two children with his tomahawk, and threw the limp body of the youth on the ground, as he would discard a piece of rotten meat, and stalked away toward his pony.

"Why did you do that?" demanded his astounded partner, Thunder Cloud. "You know very well that Chief Brant doesn't encourage the killing of children. He's no more than ten or twelve years old," stated the sensitive Mohawk.

"He's not dead!" shrugged the arrogant Red Squirrel. "He's just got a little headache, which should go away some way or other by morning!" declared cocky twenty-year old Indian brave. Red Squirrel had acquired his name while, in his early teens, he had made a practice of chasing after red squirrels, catching them, and then strangling them with a brisk twist of his wrist. "Regardless, he'll look better without that tight, head of curly black hair."

Meanwhile, the light-colored, older girl was nearly delirious as she watched the turn of events with her brother. Embarrassed by what his companion had committed, Thunder Cloud tried to calm his captive who had long, black wavy hair reaching down to the middle of her back, by assuring her that he meant no harm to her. Red Squirrel, on the other hand, had jumped astride of his Indian pony, and was racing toward another still-standing house. Thunder Cloud hoisted his captive on his pony, and headed to his chief. After reaching Chief Joseph's council fire, Thunder Cloud jumped to the ground, and proudly helped his captive down. After explaining what had occurred in the Minisink farm house, Brant complimented Thunder Cloud for using discretion with his tomahawk, but then he asked the young warrior, "What do you plan to do with this charming young lady? You know very well that you'll not be able to keep her to yourself," he concluded was he wistfully appraised the youth's captive.

"You know, Chief, that I'm not married," declared the Indian warrior, who appeared to be about five or six years older than his captive. "She's beautiful, almost the same color as we are," he added.

"Color doesn't mean a thing," asserted his leader and godfather. "It's not what they look like on the outside that counts, rather it's what's on the inside of a person which establishes their value." As an after thought, Brant said with almost a sneer, "Her mother was probably some slave owner's mistress. Oh, what the heck!" he added, after thinking about the subject. "Probably something like my own lineage, only in reverse. I guess a little white stock in each of us, might eventually help us all get along better."

Brant assessed his godson, and asked, "Something seems to be troubling you, my son, do you want to talk about it?"

Thunder Cloud accepted Brant's invitation, and explained about Red Squirrel's scalping of his captive's apparent younger brother.

"That's my problem and his, assured his godfather. "You take care of the girl, and I'll take care of Red Squirrel."

As the sun began to creep beneath the near western mountain, Thunder Cloud slowly walked his captive to a suitable place where he spread out his blanket. He settled himself on the ground nearby, while his fellow braves looked on with envy.

Knowing the local county militia were becoming more effective, and expecting them at any moment, Brant and his warriors vacated Minisink early the following morning. Brant was correct in his calculations concerning the militia. News of the massacre at Minisink spread throughout the valleys, as a result militia from Orange and Ulster counties, and even some from New Jersey responded to Minisink's terror.

About noon after Brant's forces had vacated the massacre site, Benjamin Jefferson and Walter Heindrick, who had been assigned to the Orange County Militia, were detailed to survey the ruins of Minisink for any possible survivors. The two teen-aged, blood-brothers, who had just recently served respectively as fifer and drummer as mounted messengers for General Benedict Arnold and Colonel Daniel Morgan during the Saratoga campaign. Walter Heindrick, too, had served as one of General Nicholas Herkimer's youngest drummers during the battle at Oriskany. It was after the Oriskany battle, that Benjamin Jefferson's father, George, had located his long lost white blood-brother. The two sons, Benjamin and Walter, became very close friends, eventually, exercising the Indian ritual making themselves blood-brothers, just as their fathers had performed nearly thirty years previously in Walter's father home in New Palatine located about fifty miles east of the Oriskany battle site. At the time when the two fathers, Karl Heindrick and George Jefferson, finally did meet, the two Jefferson men were serving the

Rebel forces under their friend General Philip Schuyler. While not serving in either the Continental army or the Tryon County militia, George Jefferson and his son Benjamin were permitted reside in their home in Albany where George's wife and Benjamin's mother, Julia, had a rewarding home-baking business. After spending what seemed like two fruitless hours of searching throughout the devastated settlement, the two blood-brothers almost stumbled over the limp body of the young Negro boy who Red Squirrel had left for dead.

"My God! What a beastly sight," said Benjamin as he knelt over the lifeless body seeking the youth's pulse rate. Momentarily, he looked up into the hopeful eyes of his blood-brother, and smiled. "He's alive!" he declared. "Quickly, Walter, we must get him to a medic."

"You stay here with him," suggested Walter, "and I'll ride over, and bring back with me one of our medics."

After about ten or fifteen minutes, Walter returned with a medic, who nearly fainted after seeing the young lad's hideous bleeding, and hairless skull. The first thing the medic did was to quote Dr. Benjamin Rush's observation *too much cannot be said in favor of cleanliness.* After thoroughly washing the youth's bloody head with lye soap, he slapped on a handful of bear grease, then taking a relatively clean strip of cloth, he tightly wrapped the youngster's head, and promptly excused himself and headed toward another call. Benjamin and Walter then made a stretcher with their rifles and hunting shirts, and transported the comatose juvenile to their base camp; vowing to visit him daily.

After determining the direction in which Brant's forces had fled, and throwing caution to the wind, the confident and high spirited militia raced in hot pursuit of their quarry. The fleeing Iroquois lead their pursuers through animal infested badlands, After two days of traveling approximately 27 miles through vine entangled, rocky terrain, the hunted and the hunters were in sufficient proximity to be cognizant of the others' presence. It was a wild and haunting location for two adversaries to be perched in before a battle. To their right a mountain rose and stood vigil, while to their left rapidly flowed the crystal clear Delaware River. As a background to this scene loomed the far-ranging Catskill Mountains. As one observer stated, *"There was not a wilder, lonelier place on the whole frontier, a place where the wolves gathered by night but men were seldom seen."*

Shortly, the Rebel hunters caught sight of Brant's men at a ford, where they were transporting their plunder across the river. It was evident that all of the Iroquois were preparing to escape across the river deep into their territory. A small group of hunters set out to thwart their Indian quarry at the ford by getting in front of them. After reaching their desired position, the militiamen began firing rifle shots toward the fleeing Iroquois; each exchanging their first shots.

Hearing the rifle discharges, Brant, who was in the rear of his raiders, sensed the Rebels' maneuver. Together with about 40 warriors, Brant crept through the underbrush and, reaching the Rebels' rear guard, managed to ambush the ambushers. This skillful tactic caught the Americans totally off-guard. Part of the Rebel militia, mostly those who had come from Goshen, Connecticut, were cut off from their comrades. Those who were not trapped, disgracefully retreated to safer grounds.

This skirmish, which raged for rest of the entire day, was reported to have been as fierce, and hardest fought bloody battles as the one at Oriskany. The hunters pursuing the hunted up and down the heavily foliaged mountain, and in and out of the blood-filled cool river. Fortunately for Brant, whose men numbered only about 85 Tories and Indians as compared to 120 militiamen, the day-long battle was waged *Indian style,* every man for himself, behind and around rocks and trees, shooting and clubbing, and using whatever weapons one could easily defeat his opponent. Finally, Brant's troops gained the upper hand. Both the hunters and hunted had nearly exhausted their supply of ammunition, with the militia running out of shot sooner than the Indians and Tories. So, the militia lost yet another day! They knew though that there would be another day! Maybe!

Unfortunately, the *hunters* ended up being the losers, and were unable to save themselves; some being shot while trying to swim the Delaware. On the other hand, the Tory and Indian *hunted,* alike, who carried off 40 scalps and only one prisoner, were in no mood for the burden of prisoners. The wounded were clubbed, tomahawked, or both while begging for their lives, a merciful fate, essentially, since they could not have been carried to Fort Niagara, and there was no way they could ever return to their homes. The one prisoner who was not killed, a Captain John Wood, gave the Masonic sign of distress, and for this reason Brant personally intervened and saved his life. Eventually, after Brant found out that Wood was not really a fellow Mason, he treated Wood with the contempt he thought he deserved. The same day, as Joseph Brant related afterwards, he found a man on the battlefield who was wounded past any hope of recovery. Night was falling, and darkness would only bring out the wolves. Joseph engaged the wounded soldier in a solemn conversation, and then distracting the soldier's attention, Brant quickly dispatched the wounded man with his tomahawk. This was Brant's idea of humanity!

When Brant and his troop of Indians and Tories left the battlefield at Minisink, they left ten of their own wounded and three dead on the blood drenched grounds. One of their wounded was named Captain John, a Tuscarora, who was one of Joseph's great friends. Brant deeply mourned the loss of his friend, calling him his "trusty chief," and wondering what he'd ever do without him. As for the vanquished Rebels, so many citizens were killed that their neighbors and families at home could not believe the disastrous results. Some families like to believe that some were taken as prisoners to Canada, not realizing that the Iroquois preferred not being troubled with prisoners. Most waited in vain for many months.

From Minisink, Brant and his well-seasoned warriors travel up the river by way of Cochecton and Cokeose (present-day Deposit, New York), and then over to the Susquehanna. At the ruins of the old Iroquois castle at Oquaga, Brant wrote an official report of his troops' operation. From Oquaga, he sent most of his force, believing they were fortunate to escape with their lives, to Chemung. According to one of his Rangers, Brant had sent his few prisoners up into the Indian country where they were cruelly beaten; probably forced to run the gauntlet, while Brant, with a small detail of warriors, headed for Lake Otsego to discover what the Rebels were doing. This expedition was especially dangerous for Brant, because the Americans had placed a *bounty* on his head by the highest Rebel authority, General George Washington, himself. In a desperate attempt to bring peace to the area, Washington even suggested that some of the captured Onondagas might be persuaded to kidnap Brant or Colonel Butler. Anyone who brought either one in as a captive could expect to be handsomely rewarded. Washington also stated that such an act would be "a most essential piece of service, which will meet with suitable encouragement."

* * *

All of these dastardly deeds which Sandy McKnight had witnessed, and had faint-heartedly participated in were indelibly imprinted on his brain, raising question what was his true mission of life. Was it his freedom, or some one else's? If it is his freedom, is it really worth it to participate in all of these killings, and slaughter? If it is for some elese's freedom, why should he worry about some one else's desires? Placing his elbows on this knees in the position the sculptor's "Thinker," he quickly stood up, walked straight to his bagpipes, lost himself in his love of music and his constant nagging and conflicting thoughts of the futility of war. "To the hell with 'em all," he announced to the majestic oak tree he was standing under. Closing his eyes, he took another *taste* of scotch whiskey, and began to make music for himself and the stately tree.

NINE

FREEDOM IN CANADA

Early July, 1779
Fort Niagara, New York

It was early evening when Captain Johan Jost Jr. leisurely strolled from the officers' mess hall, when he faintly heard a familiar musical sound vibrating through the hot, humid air which had engulfed the fort's very existence. The captain readily recognized the sound of bagpipes. Instead of walking directly toward his barracks, he changed the direction he was walking, and headed straight toward the familiar sound. The one troubling thought he had continued along trying to side-step over and around some of the huge mud-puddles remaining on the ground from the afternoon's drenching thundershower. How he wished that his friend, Sandy McKnight had returned from Brant and Colonel Butler's campaign to retrieve food supplies for themselves and fort's garrison and Indians. Besides his love of a "touch" of scotch whisky, there was nothing Sandy loved more than playing his pipes. But, this couldn't be Sandy playing his pipes; he usually played nothing be *happy* music. This music sounded so mournful; something like what one would hear coming from a group of blacks in the cotton fields of Virginia. As Johan Jost Jr. approached the common wall tent, which measured about six and half feet square, and five feet high, he saw a number of soldiers standing in front, and around the tent where the sorrowful music was flowing from. Johan quicken his pace, and thrust himself through the group of soldiers blocking the tent's entrance. There sitting on a cot was his friend, Sandy McKnight playing his pipes to his heart's delight; his eyes closed, and his head was waving back and forth as if he were playing in some kind of hypnotic trance. Occasionally, Sandy set his bagpipes aside and then, in his deep baritone voice , he sang haunting phrases which apparently were in a strange language than his usual broken English. Johan Jost Jr. had never seen Sandy perform like this, even when, at times, he had had too much scotch to drink. Johan Jost Jr. dashed over to his friend, whose eyes were still closed, and he was blowing away on the pipes. Without announcing himself, Johan rapped his arms around his friend, who had been away from the fort for many weeks. Startled from his stupor, Sandy exclaimed, "What the hell's going on?" as he stared blankly toward his friend.

"Sandy, it's me, Johan Jost Jr." declared the captain he had befriended after Sandy had left the New England area, and eager to join the Loyalists forces.

Puzzled, Sandy continued to stare toward the *stranger* standing before him, whom he had stood together with witnessing the captain's brother being wounded during the battle of Oriskany. It was then that the two buddies had first had observed men killing other men. But, unknown to Johan Jost Jr., Sandy had not only witnessed many inhumane atrocities, but had actually participated in one of the most brutal massacres beyond one's imagination. In addition, Sandy had become entangled in an internal conflict against his own people, and struggling not to turn his back from his loyalty to his king, he had found solace through his love of music and playing the bagpipes, where he could express his innermost feelings of remorse and guilt. Recognizing this problem, Johan Jost Jr. decided he was going seek out the fort's chaplin to assist Sandy in regaining his mental and spiritual faculties.

* * *

In addition to Sandy McKnight's serious condition, something else on a happier note occurred on July 12, 1779, which was to change Captain Johan Jost Jr.'s entire future. That day his wife, Maria, applied to the Albany County Board for permission to join her husband in Canada. The Board stated that it had no authority to grant such a request, but it would refer her application to Governor George Clinton. The Governor, however, had declared that permission would not be granted to the wives and families of Loyalists to move from the State, until the women and children captured by Butler and Brant in their raids on Cherry Valley and other forays on the frontier had been returned.

By the Act of October 22, 1779, passed by the New York Legislature Johan Jost Jr. and a number of other prominent Loyalists were attained losing their civil rights, and all of their properties were declared forfeited to the State of New York. This Act further stated that *"each and every [one] of them who shall at any time hereafter be found in any part of this State, shall be, and are hereby adjudged and declared guilty of felony, and shall suffer Death as in cases of felony without Benefit of Clergy."* Johan Jost Jr.'s property and personal effects, with the exception of one sheep allowed for each child, were eventually sold for 2195.10.0 currency. By the end of 1779, the Johan Jost Jr. family were joyfully reunited at Fort Niagara.

In February, 1780, General Haldimand directed that a King's store be established at Coteau du Lac for the forwarding of provisions and supplies to Carleton Island, and the upper posts. Later on July 6, 1780, the general ordered the formation of a company of bateaumen from among those Loyalists who wished to be of service to the king, but not as soldiers. Captain Johan Jost Jr. was designated commander of the company, under the direction of Captain Jacob Maurer, Inspector of Bateaux, with his headquarters located at Coteau du Lac. While enlisting recruits for his company, who wanted to contribute their service to their king, Captain Johan Jost

Jr. may have taken his instructions "not as soldiers" too literally. To complete his draft requirements, the relatively inexperienced young captain added a number of old men, women, and children, many from Machiche. When Haldimand heard of Johan Jost Jr.'s actions, he ordered Captain Maurer to Coteau du Lac in October to inspect the company. Maurer's reported that a number of the men were not "fit" (supposing they even were not willing) to handle either setting pole or axe." Maurer's report of conditions was naturally displeasing to Haldimand, who directed Maurer to take charge of the recruiting and to discharge all those unfit for service. Once the company became properly organized, however, it rendered good service under Captain Johan Jost Jr. until it was disbanded along with other Provincial troops on December 24, 1783. Johan Jost Jr. was also placed in charge of the stores at Coteau du Lac from March 1781.

One year later in 1782, Captain Johan Jost Jr. again incurred the displeasure of General Haldimand. The reason for Haldimand's annoyance started in April, 1781 when Davis Abeel of Catskill (New York) was taken prisoner by a party of Indians and Loyalists, and was sent to Fort Niagara. During the fall of that year, Abeel was transferred to the prison at Coteau du Lac, from which he escaped. On December 20, 1781, Abeel made an affidavit, which was circulated in the patriot press reporting of an alleged conversation between himself and Captain Johan Jost Jr. at the Cedars regarding the negotiations then in progress between Haldimand and the State of Vermont. Captain Robert Matthews, General Haldimand's secretary, wrote to Captain Joseph Anderson, who commanded the post at Coteau du Lac, on April 18, 1782, stating that the Commander-in-Chief desired him to reprimand Captain Johan Jost Jr. "very severely, acquainting him that if ever anything of the kind should again happen, it will not be looked over, as the consequences, not the motives for such indiscreet conduct will be attended to." Captain Anderson, in his reply to Matthews, stated he had reprimanded Captain Johan Jost Jr., who denied ever discussing the negotiations with Abeel. Admitting, he had done nothing more than inquire "of him about the situation of Mr. Tenbrook's family, they being his near relations, and Abeel a near neighbor of theirs."

Sometime between 1784 and 1785, Captain Johan Jost Jr. and his family settled in a town then called Cataraqui, and eventually named Kingston in 1788. The land granted him for his rank and family amounted to 3,450 acres, all located within the township of Kingston, and two lots in Kingston proper. Captain Johan Jost Jr., who named was one of "the Benefactors of the Members of the English Congregation for erecting a Church in Kingston" (St. George's), died in Kingston in August, 1795. His wife, Mary (Maria?) died also in Kingston ten years later in August. Captain Johan Jost Jr. and his wife had four sons: George, Lawrence, Nicholas, and Jacob together with three daughters: Mary, Jane, and Catherine.

George, Captain Johan Jost Jr.'s eldest son, was appointed a first lieutenant in Butler's Rangers on December 26, 1779, and died at Detroit, apparently before termination of the Revolution, for his name does not appear in the list of officers of that regiment at the time of the reduction in June 1784. In 1789, his father applied to the Land Committee of the Executive Council of Quebec for "lands which he supposed his deceased son would have obtained had he lived," and asked that a "Lieutenant's quota may be laid off for him (as heir to his son) on the Isle Foret." The Committee stated that "without entering into the consideration of the merits of the petitioner's claim for lands which his son, a reduced Lieutenant of a Provincial corps was entitled to, they think it necessary (at present) only to observe that the Petitioner cannot have lands on the Isle Foret as that Island is claimed by the Messessaga Indians."

During the winter of 1788-89, Philip R. Frey, U. E. (United Empire) Deputy Surveyor, Province of Quebec, a nephew of Captain Johan Jost Jr., surveyed the township of Binbrook (No. 11), laying it out in blocks of 1000 acres, and entered upon the plan the names of certain deceased officers of Butler's Rangers and the Indian Department, without issuing the necessary certificates for the land. The name of Lieutenant George was placed on Block No. 2, concession 1. On June 13, 1810, the question of the legality of these locations came before the Land Committee of the Executive

Council of Upper Canada. Chewett and Ridout, the Acting Surveyors General, after suggesting the locations had been made for the benefit of creditors of the deceased officers, recommended that "as it does not appear by His Majesty's Instructions of Genl. Haldimand, that the Royal Bounty was held out to Dead Men, and Absentees..... the whole thereof is open for Location, whenever His Excelly. the Lieut. Governor may be pleased to grant the same;" hence, the Committee, with the approval of the Lieutenant Governor, ordered some of the locations thrown open for settlement. The matter of the remaining locations, among which was that of Lieutenant George, was considered on June 14, 1781, and the Land Committee ordered that a notice should be inserted in the *York Kingston,* and *Quebec Gazettes* that the locations were to be "thrown open for Grant to other Persons, unless within Six months from this date, they severally appear, by themselves or Agents, to establish their claims and sue out their Patients." Lieutenant George's brother, Lawrence, put in a claim before the Heir and Devisee Commission on March 11, 1812, as the heir to his brother, for the 1000 acres of land located in the name of Lieutenant George, but the claims was disallowed.

Although Lawrence was appointed a captain in the First Regiment of Frontenac militia on July 25, 1812, he did not take an active part during the War of 1812. He was a magistrate, a commissioner of the court of requests for the Midland district, a trustee of the Midland District School Society, and one of the shareholders in the *Frontenac,* the first steamboat on Lake Ontario. In 1816, he released to the Crown two lots in Kingston, numbers 92 and 101, which were to form part of the "The Premises reserved for the Government House" there, and received in exchange two lots in the south and east corners of the Market Street.

Lawrence, who had married Elizabeth Kirby daughter of John Kirby Sr. of Crown Point, New York and was born in Yorkshire, England, died at the age of 54 in Kingston on October 14, 1819, and was buried "on his own farm." Elizabeth died also in Kingston at the age of 61 years.

Johan Jost Jr's. third son, Nicholas, became a farmer and settled at Herkimer's Point near Kingston where he was murdered in the autumn of 1809 by Samuel and Gurdon Rogers, who had broke jail, and thus escaped the penalty of the law. Nicholas had married Charlotte Purdy, daughter of Gilbert Purdy, Sr., U. E. (United Empire loyalist). Sometime after his death, his widow married Robert Abernethy, and died near Collin's Bay on September 3, 1843.

Johan Jost Jr.'s youngest son, Jacob, moved from Kingston to the town of York (Toronto) about 1797, and became a merchant there. He was the tax collector for the town of York and the townships of York, Scarborough and Etobicoke in 1800, and a town warden of the Town of York in 1801. He was drowned in the wreck of the schooner Speedy, off Presque Isle, on the north shore of Lake Ontario, on the night of October 8, 1804. Prior to 1803, Jacob had "several children" by a woman of the Credit Chippewas. Their youngest son, The Rev. William (Oominwahjewun), was a Methodist missionary among the Indians from 1843-1874, where he died in the New Credit Mission in his seventy-fifth year on October 3, 1875. Whenever the Rev. William had an occasion to visit Kingston in the course of his work as a missionary to the Indians, the Rev. William Macaulay Herchmer "readily claimed him as his kinsman, received him into his family, and subsequently showed him every attention." Jacob married, as his second (or first) wife, Margaret Hickman England, daughter of Captain Poole England, 47th Regiment, at York, on July 1, 1803. This wedding was not without interest to the Rev. John Strachan, who had come to Kingston in 1799 as tutor in the Cartwright family, for a manuscript book of poetry preserved in the Strachan Papers in the Ontario Archives reveals a love affair between the Scot (Strachan), who was to become the first Bishop of Toronto, and Miss Margaret England. The first poem in which Strachan shows his affection for Miss England is one of twenty-one stanzas entitled, "The following verses were written as a task impos'e by M:E: (standing for Margaret England), who not liking the measure I did not correct them, July 1st 1801." At the end of the poem is, "Transcribed July 29th 1802," the date Strachan began to keep the book of poetry. Under the date October 21, 1802, is a poem of thirty-eight lines entitled, "For Laura's Birth Day." (Margaret England, the gift of the name of *Laura* from the Greek, Laurel, "The Cloistered" may have been due to a parental objection to the poor young tutor, or Strachan may have had in mind the poet Petrarch and his incomparable Laura.) At the end of the poem, Strachan attached the following note, "Prevented from delivering it (the poem) till the 25th four days too late." At an assembly held in Kingston on St. Andrew's Day, 1802, Strachan had apparently danced more than once with a "Nymph of lively glance," for which his "Laura" had reprimanded him. By the following Christmas Day, he had written a poem entitled "Philo and Laura- A dialogue,:as his answer, representing himself as "Philo" (from the Greek, Philon, "Love").

Strachan was appointed officiating minister of Cornwall on May 22, 1803, and shortly after entered on his ministry there. While he was in Cornwall, "Laura," in spite of her understanding with Strachan, married Jacob Herchmer in York on July 1, 1803. When Strachan heard the news of the marriage, he wrote a poem which he headed as follows: "Written July 29, 1803—On finding that a Lady had deceived her lover after coming under the most solemn engagements and married a man she had formerly despised, Jacob Herchmer because of his previous connection with the Indian lady. Mrs. Margaret H. Herchmer married, secondly on October 11, 1809, Colonel (later Major-General) the Hon. AEneas Shaw, U.E., and thirdly, on January 13, 1823, the Rev. William Leeming, Rector of Chippawa. Thus, the lady who had jilted Strachan and married Jacob Herchmer for "a little and only a little money" found herself in later years married to a clergyman in the same diocese of which Strachan was bishop. She died at Chippawa on April 6, 1853, in the 76th year of her age, without issue by any one of her three husbands

Mary, one of the daughters of Captain Johan Jost Jr., firstly married Neil McLean of Kingston, and secondly, the Hon. Robert Hamilton of Queenston, who had been a close friend and business adviser of her first husband. Mary died January 26, 1808 in Queenston. Mary's first husband, Neil McLean served in the Commissariat Department for thirty-four years, and was Assistant Commissary General at Carleton Island during the Revolutionary War. In 1783, he was *reduced,* and in the following year settled at Cataraqui, where he acted as Deputy Inspector of Loyalists. He was one of the first

Justices of Peace in the area which became Upper Canada, a Judge of the Court of Common Pleas in 1788, and a member of the first Land Board of Mecklenburg (later Midland) District, 1788-1794. Neil McLean died without issue by his wife Mary Herchmer, and was buried in Kingston on September 1, 1795.

Mary's second husband, Hon. Robert Hamilton, was a son of the Rev. John Hamilton, minister of Bolton, in Haddington, Scotland, had arrived in America during the Revolutionary War. He was a merchant and trader; first at Carleton Island, and subsequently at Niagara and Cataraqui, and, in partnership with the Hon. Richard Cartwright, U.E. At the dissolution of the partnership, Hamilton settled in Niagara, and became the founder of Queenston. Acquiring wealth and position as a merchant, he became interested in land speculation and in his day was undoubtedly the largest individual owner of land in Upper Canada. He was one of the first members of the Legislative Council of Canada, a member of the Land Board of the District of Nassau, and holder of other public offices. Hamilton died at Queenston on March 8, 1809. By his first wife, Catherine, daughter of John Askin of Detroit, and widow of Captain Samuel Robertson, he had five sons and one daughter; and by his second wife, Mary Herchmer McLean, Hamilton had three sons and one daughter.

Jane, another daughter of Captain Johan Jost Jr., married Captain Joseph Anderson, of the first battalion, King's Royal Regiment of New York, and she died in her 87th year in Kingston on April 1850. Her husband, Joseph Anderson was a son of Benjamin Anderson of Bush Mills, County Antrim, Ireland, who emigrated to America in 1720, and settled in Boston about 1735 along with his brother Captain Samuel Anderson, U.E. of Cornwall. At the outbreak of the Revolution, Joseph Anderson resided in Pownall, Vermont. He was elected one of the representatives from the Manor of Rensselaerwyck to the "Patriot" Committee of Correspondence at Albany, and attended a number of meeting from May to July, 1775, but withdrew when the Committee determined on violent measures in their opposition to England. In March, 1776, Joseph went to Canada with a detachment of reinforcements for the force under General Benedict Arnold at Quebec, but paid a 40 pounds to deliver information regarding their intentions to Sir Guy Carleton. In May, 1776 along with a number of other Loyalists, he came under the observation of the Albany Committee, who ordered that, should he be found in the neighborhood of Johnson Hall, he was to be taken prisoner. With his brother, Samuel Anderson, John Munro, and others, Joseph Anderson was detected in an attempt to gather recruits to go to Canada, and on July 13, 1776 he was ordered placed in close confinement in the "Tory Gaol" at Albany. He was held there until August 1, 1776, when he was then shipped to Hartford, Connecticut, where he remained until the end of 1776. Soon after the turn of the year, Joseph Anderson escaped to New York, where he received an appointment as a Lieutenant in the first battalion of the King's Royal Regiment of New York. The following spring, 1777, Joseph was dispatched to Quebec. There he purchased command of the company of Captain Stephen Watts, brother-in-law of Sir John Johnson, who was permitted to dispose of it by Sir Guy Carleton in consequence of severe wounds received at the Battle of Oriskany in August, 1777. Early in 1782, Captain Anderson commanded the prison post at Coteau du Lac, and in December of that year, after a disagreement with certain officers of the Royal Yorkers, he was granted permission by General Haldimand to sell his captaincy in the Regiment. He resided for some years at Lachine, and about 1789 he went to Kingston, where he served as coroner of the Midland District until his death, which occurred on June 11, 1813; he also held the position of Collector of Customs for the Port of Kingston. Joseph Anderson's only child, Charles Anderson, served successively as Interpreter, Lieutenant and Captain in the Indian Department during the War of 1812, and was mentioned in despatches for the part he played in the actions of Sackett's Harbour in May, 1813, and for Crysler's Farm in November, 1813. Charles was appointed Major in the First Regiment of Frontenac militia on August 22, 1821, and was for many years a justice of the peace for the Midland District. His death took place at his residence on Rice Lake, in the township of Otonabee, on January 12, 1844, at the age of 58 years. Major Anderson, by marriage and by what seems to have been a natural attribute of the Herchmers, exerted a great deal of influence over the Indians in the vicinity of Rice Lake.

Catherine, another daughter of Captain Johan Jost Jr., married Thomas Markland, U.E., who was born in the American Colonies, and after "having sacrificed large possessions on the Mohawk River" at the close of the Revolutionary War, came to Cataraqui in 1784. There, Thomas Markland appears to have been connected, probably in a business way with Robert Dickson, for they received a joint "location ticket" from Alexander Aitken, Deputy Provincial Surveyor, dated Kingston, October 17, 1789, for lot 6, concession 4, township of Pittsburg. Thomas Markland was one of the leading merchants of Upper Canada, as well as a magistrate and for number of years was chairman of the Court of General Quarter Sessions of the Peace for the Midland District. On January 26,1796, he was appointed Treasurer of the Midland District, a position he held for over forty years. During the War of 1812, he served as captain of a flank company of the First Regiment of Frontenac militia, and on August 20, 1821, was appointed Colonel of the Regiment. He was member of the second Land Board of the Midland District from 1819 to 1826. Thomas Markland was Judge of the Surrogate Court of this district from June 10, 1830, until his death, in Kingston, on January 31,1840 in his 85th year receiving the acclaim as "the last of the patriotic band of U. E. (United Empire Loyalists)" who settled in the town of Kingston. Thomas and Catherine had only one child, the Hon. George Herchmer Markland, who was appointed Lieutenant Colonel of the Frontenac militia Regiment upon its formation in August 1821. He served as Inspector General of the Public Provincial Accounts for Upper Canada from March 5, 1833 until he resigned on October 1, 1838, when he retired from public life in Kingston until his death there on May 19, 1862; wife, his Anna, having died in Kingston on May 27, 1847. One of the positions, which he held and cherished, was that of a trustee of the Six Nation Indians.

* * *

On May 31, 1779, one month and eleven days before Captain Johan Jost Jr's wife, Maria, applied to the Albany County Board for permission to join her husband in Canada, a smiling and relieved

General George Washington extended his right hand to Major General John Sullivan, who had agreed to accept Washington's offer to command the Rebels' expedition into the Indian country against the Iroquois, the Loyalists and their British allies. After telling his friend, "Thank you, General, I know I could depend upon you," Washington headed directly to his desk's drawer from which he pulled out a clean white envelope. Walking straight back to General Sullivan, Washington said, "These are your marching orders. I expect you, your staff, and your troops to follow them implicity."

This expedition you are appointed to command is to be directed against the hostile tribes of the Six Nations of Indians with their associates and adherents. The immediate objects are the total destruction and devastation of their settlements and the capture of as many prisoners of every sex and age as possible. It will be essential to ruin their crops in the ground and prevent their planting more.

While Sullivan was reading his orders, Washington's thoughts were racing well ahead of Sullivan's expedition. He was focusing upon his overall strategy for America's future. His planned pincer movements in the Indian country were designed to be much more than a punishment of the Iroquois, and the eradication of Fort Niagara's *hornet's nest*. The ultimate purpose of Washington's orders to Sullivan was his declaration that the Fort Stanwix boundary line between the *White man's* territory and the *Redman's* territory had been trashed, and that America intended to settle, as Washington stated: *"Where it damn well pleased, even clear to the Mississippi River."*

TEN

SEARCH AND RECOVER

August, 1779
In the Mohawk Valley near Little Falls

On August 2nd, while Brant and his small group of warriors were traveling toward Lake Otsego along the Mohawk River looking for sources of food and other useful tools and weapons, they came upon a small white settlement, Brant called Onawatoge, in the proximity of Little Falls. This was familiar territory for Brant; it was where he had resided on a farm as a neighbor to the fallen General Nicholas Herkimer during their battle at Oriskany. From Onawatoge, he and his braves captured two Rebel prisoners, who informed Brant that the Rebel army had boats and provisions, and were preparing to invade the Iroquois country. After a short interlude, a Rebel scouting cadre of the local militia engaged Brant's small band in a skirmish. Brant was slightly wounded in the foot, and his coat and breechcloth were riddled with buckshot, regardless he successfully retained possession of his prisoners. One of the prisoners, a man named John House, became lame when the braves made him march without shoes, and tied his feet into a forked stick at night. The Indians debated whether they should kill him. Fortunately, for the prisoner and Brant, they discovered that House was friend of Colonel John Butler. After this discovery, Brant convinced him to sign a neutrality oath, and turned him loose.

Shortly afterwards, House was discovered by a American scout, who immediately escorted him directly to the American army headquarters of General James Clinton at Lake Otsego. That same afternoon, the general had issued orders to Sergeant George Jefferson to commence conducting a reconnaissance mission into the Iroquois country. General Clinton was very restless, it was well into the first week of August, and he had not received his orders from General Sullivan. As Clinton and his faithful sergeant were in the process of identifying their desired goals and objectives for the sergeant's mission, an American scout came bursting into the general's tent with the Brant's former prisoner, John House.

"Sir," automatically saluting his general, the exhausted scout started, "This man's name is John House. I found him hidden in the underbrush. He has a very interesting story to tell, which I believe you should hear."

"Tell your story to me, my good man," demanded the grinning general. With a quick glance toward Sergeant Jefferson, "Sergeant, I want you to stay, and listen Mr. House's story, because his information maybe helpful to you and your mission."

"Thank you, sir," agreed Jefferson as he settled down on a wooden, ladder-back chair, after he had offered similar chairs to the prisoner and scout.

The general quickly, but politely, introduced the men, and demanded, "Tell your story to us, Mr. House." "And I warn you, sir, don't give us any bullshit!" The general then settled in his army-issued desk chair, and relaxed behind his desk keeping with a very skeptical, but open mind to hear what the prisoner had to say. "I guess, Mr. House, you should start from the beginning," suggested the general respectfully, but with authority.

"I was a part of the American militia that was chasing after Chief Brant and his warriors," started the battered militiaman dressed in

STEPS TOWARD FREEDOM

a bloody, leather hunting shirt. "We, finally, caught up with Brant and his braves, and engaged them in a skirmish. I know that Brant was wounded, because when I last saw him, he was lame. While his warriors were discussing whether to kill a fellow prisoner, Brant convinced me it would be to my advantage if I signed an oath of neutrality. As I was signing the oath, three of his braves came back, and handed him a scalp dripping with fresh blood. With scalp in his hand, Brant told me I'd better keep my oath; if I didn't, he cautioned me that he would be holding my scalp."

"Do you believe Brant has any idea as to what we are preparing to do?" asked Clinton, as the general offered House a drink of brandy.

"I honestly don't know, sir," responded the spent prisoner. "We all know that Brant is a very intelligent individual, with an enormous amount of common sense. Sir, I wouldn't be a bit surprised if he or some of his scouts were right out there in the forest watching our every move.

"The only thing I'm sure of, sir," House continued, "is the fact that I'm here, and alive to tell you my experience. I've heard stories about Brant claiming he did not approve the common practice of torturing prisoners, and also claiming that he had saved several not only from torture, but from being killed. One thing for sure is that Brant did mention to me, is that he is very suspicious of us Americans, believing that we were as likely to kill Indians prisoners, as we were to look at them. One thing I know for sure, general, is that I'm very grateful for his benevolence."

General Clinton and Sergeant Jefferson continued their debriefing process for another half an hour before House and the scout were excused. After the scout had located quarters for the wounded House, the general and sergeant continued mapping their strategy for Jefferson's mission into the Indian country, more specially into Brant's camp. One fact was obvious, Brant was now sure that the Americans were planning to invade his territory. Jefferson's mission, for his friend General Philip Schuyler, as well as General Clinton, was to locate and identify the Indians' strength and weaknesses. That night, Jefferson and his usual trusted cadre, the group he had worked with long before under Schuyler's direction, ventured from their separate tents under the cover of night in quest of their assigned mission.

Less than a week later, General James Clinton received his long awaited orders from General John Sullivan to move out on August 9th, and to expect to receive some of Sullivan's light troops *to favour and secure your march.* On that day, General Clinton and his troops promptly proceeded from Schenectady to Lake Otsego. From there Sullivan informed Clinton that he and his troops should await for further orders, before continuing with his army. Fortunately, Benjamin Jefferson and Walter Heindrick together with their wounded black youth were able to report back to Colonel's Willet's brigade, under General Clinton's command. Colonel Willet assigned the two youths the duty of caring for him, and trying to learn as much as they could about his attackers, and where he believed they were headed.

From the time Benjamin and Walter had found the scalped youth, the young men had grown accustomed to each other, which helped to expedite the youth's recovery. The young man's name was Samuel Montgomery. Samuel told his new found friends that when a colored women's child reached the age of three years, usually, the baby was solemnly presented on the first New Year's day following to the owner's son, daughter, or other relative, who was the same sex as the baby. The infant to whom the young colored was given, immediately presented the toddler with some money and a pair of shoes, and from that day forward a strong attachment grew between the *child domestic,* and its destined owner.

Samuel's owner was Master Gunther Haas. Samuel and his sister, Marie, had been sent out into the field to pick blackberries. While picking berries, they noticed smoke and flames raising from the settlement of Minisink. They had no sooner arrived at their master's home, than they discovered that the entire Haas family had been brutally massacred. They began screaming and crying, and were suddenly attacked by two Indian warriors. Samuel told his rescuers that the first thing one brave did was scalp him, and then ride off. The other brave was much kinder to Marie, "I guess," he bashfully, but proudly said, "because she is a beautiful looking girl. The Indian who took Marie placed her on his Indian pony, and I guess, together they he rode off to join the other braves. After I saw them ride off, I probably passed out, because I don't remember anything after seeing Marie and the Indian ride away." He stopped and rubbed the bandage, which was wrapped around his head, and continued, "I really don't remember much of anything until long after you two rescued me, for which I'm very grateful."

"One of the things we must do first is to find where the Iroquois have taken Marie Montgomery," suggested Benjamin.

"I think Samuel should describe to us what Marie looks like," advised Walter. "How are we going to recognize her, unless Samuel tells us what she looks like?"

"Good observation!" agreed Benjamin.

"Marie is about seventeen-years old," Samuel told his friends.

"Just a year younger than me," smiled Benjamin.

"And the same age as me," chimed in Walter.

"Don't forget, you've already have a girl friend, Helena Kerchner," Benjamin jokingly reminded Walter.

Another thing Benjamin and Walter learned was that Marie and Samuel were step-children. Samuel's father was colored, and Marie's father was Master Haas. After hearing more about their history, Walter asked, "What was Marie wearing at the time of her capture?" This Samuel described, and then the two blood-brothers, and their new found friend reported to Colonel Willet, who had summoned Sergeant George Jefferson to his office.

"George, I need your help," the colonel greeted Benjamin's father. "It appears that your son and his blood-brother Walter Heindrick, have rescued and nursed this young slave lad, Samuel Montgomery, back to reasonable health after his scalping. He's still wearing a head dressing with its bear grease, otherwise he appears like a pretty healthy youngster. After the raid on Minisink, he and his family were some of the legion of casualties. Samuel is one of the fortunate ones. He's still alive! Thanks to Benjamin and Walter. However, Samuel's sister, Marie, we believe is still alive, but has been taken captive by one of Brant's warriors. As far as we know, the rest of his family and their master's family were murdered. What I'd like you and your cadre to do, is to scout out the location for Marie Montgomery. I'm convinced once we find her, we'll find a nest of Brant's braves," he stopped a moment, then smiled and added, "maybe you'll even find their lord and master, Chief Joseph Brant, himself."

"Sounds like an interesting assignment, sir," eagerly replied the ebony colored sergeant. Knowing the colonel's answer in advance, but out of courtesy, the sergeant asked, "How soon do you want us to start?"

"You know the routine, George. We've worked this kind of detail before. Since you and your usual cadre will be working with your son, his friend, and the wounded young slave, it may take a little longer than usual to get yourselves organized," observed Colonel Willet, but I expect you to be on the trail by sundown this evening."

"One word of warning, sergeant," added Colonel Willet as he grasped his dependable sergeant's calloused hands, "we may be moving from here toward Otsego before you return. I think we'll be headed for Canajoharie in a very few days, so that's the place to start looking for us, if we're not here."

George Jefferson clipped his heels together, and gave his good friend and commanding officer a sharp salute. Walter and Benjamin followed his example, while Samuel, wearing a dark colored turban type of bandage, tried to mimic his companions' gestures, and followed the sergeant to his common tent.

* * *

General Clinton's march was through an unbroken wilderness with no roads. His troops were required to load their provisions on a number of bateaux, and then float them down the various streams they saw fit to travel by. In all cases, whether the troops carrying freight, boats, their wounded or just themselves, all the bateaux were carried by the men to the head-waters of another stream, or from one side of a *crossing* to the other side in order to float their bateaux down or up an adjoining stream. General Clinton and his troops incurred a considerable amount of trouble until they reached Otsego Lake, and from this point they expected very little problems as far as crossings and shallow water were concerned. At this junction was the lake's outlet, which gave birth of the mighty Susquehanna River.

It was on the Susquehanna, that Clinton expected to join forces with General John Sullivan. But the weather was hot and humid, and for many weeks there had been no rain. The mighty Susquehanna was river no longer mighty, rather there was not sufficient water to float the bateaux, and for a time Clinton thought he would have to retrace his steps, and start on a different route to meet Sullivan.

Rather suddenly, Clinton's imagination took reign. He remembered as a young lad, whiie he and his buddies were trapping beavers, in order to get the beavers' attention, they would remove sticks with which the beavers' dam was constructed. Once the beavers discovered that water was draining out from their pond, they would quickly go to site of the breach, and begin reconstructing the dam. With this experience in mind, Clinton decided that he would have his men do exactly the reverse of the beavers' activities. He ordered his soldiers to construct a huge dam across the lake's outlet. Unquestionably, his troops followed his orders. They began by rolling huge boulders from the neighboring fields, filled in the spaces between with brush and clay. Soon water was not able to flow through or over the dam, and the lake began to fill. In three weeks time, the lake was six feet above its summer level. A few days before August 9th, Clinton's troops were about to learn what their commander had in mind. Clinton ordered his men to ready their bateaux with provisions and men aboard. Once the troops and provisions were aboard the bateaux, and a small detail of men were charged with the responsibility of opening the dam. As soon as this group of men finished opening the dam, they quickly jumped aboard a bateau. The water began flooding the lake's outlet's narrow banks, and racing down into the mouth of the once again mighty Susquehanna River. Swiftly, Sullivan's entire force and its supplies were carried down to the place where they were to meet Sullivan's's troops.

During the last weeks of July prior to Clinton's damming of the river, the Indians, who were calmly living along the along the river, suddenly became alarmed when their *great river, the source of their existence,* unusually, began to dry up during August. Soon after August 9th, the *unexpected* happened. The Indians witnessed another strange happening to their great river, almost instantly, the river began to rise to nearly the levels they would expect during the spring floods. Needless to say, they could not understand, first the dry river bottom, and then the sudden surge of water, the flooding. Needless to say, they became frightened, and fearful; reasoning that there had been no rain, and the only way they could account for the flooding of the river banks was that the Great Spirit had sent the waters to help the white men. In the greatest of alarm and anxiety, they fled in every direction.

General Clinton's forces did not meet one enemy until they joined forces with Sullivan's men. Their combined army met no opposition until they reached the settlement where the city of Elmira now exists. Here a battle took place, in which the Iroquois and their Loyalist allies were defeated. An unfortunate event occurred at this location. When Sullivan and his forces returned from their successful campaign in the Indian territory, Sullivan was obliged to order the soldiers to kill his horses for want of forage; the place, where the horses' skulls lay for a long time, has since been called "Horseheads."

* * *

While General Clinton and his troops were floating down the rapidly flowing Susquehanna to keep their date with General Sullivan at Tioga, Sergeant Jefferson and his cadre were having some degree of success in locating the raiders of Minisink. They discovered that Brant and his small band of braves had made their way, traveling mostly under the cover of night, down to their Chemung castle. Jefferson's group reasoned that Brant's objective was to join forces with the remainder of their Tory and Indian allies. Fortunately, the sergeant's cadre knew the close proximity of both Clinton and Brant's forces.

"The two forces are too close for comfort," admitted the concerned sergeant. "We must alert General Clinton that Brant and his warriors are bivouacked near Chemung." In a second breath, he added, "That's near to the location where Clinton had planned his rendezvous with General Sullivan," acknowledging the necessity to warn Sullivan as well as Clinton.

Out of his cadre of eight soldiers, including his son Benjamin and Walter Heindrick, Sergeant Jefferson selected four soldiers. He detailed two men to search for General Clinton, report their findings directly to the general, and quickly return to Jefferson's squad. He ordered the other two soldiers to perform the identical assignment warning General Sullivan. Once the four scouts were on the trail, Jefferson reviewed the strategy required to the two remaining soldiers, his son and his blood-brother, as well as the wounded youth, Samuel Montgomery. Walter and Benjamin were detailed the responsibility of guarding Samuel, while the remaining two soldiers were to attempt close surveillance of Brant and his band.

It was August 11th, and as he and his remaining men were preparing to review their assignments, one of the Jefferson's scouts discovered what he believed looked like fresh Indian tracks. "Good God!" he exclaimed to himself, and called his sergeant to evaluate his findings. "Hell, none of us know much about each others' activities," he declared as the sergeant rushed over to examine the scout's findings.

The sergeant cautioned his experienced scouts, "We have one advantage over Brant. I have a sneaking suspicion that he doesn't know how close he is to General Clinton's troops, or for that matter how close he is to us. "In fact," he added, "Brant probably doesn't even know that Clinton and his troops are riding down the Susquehanna, but I'll bet you that Brant is even ahead of Clinton, I want you two scouts to survey the situation, and communicate your findings quickly to Clinton so he wont run into an ambush. Benjamin, Walter, Samuel, and I will look around here, and see what we can find out about these fresh tracks. Do you, gentlemen, have any questions?"

"I don't want to be a dead hero," said one of the scouts, "but if we can divert a disastrous ambush on our forces, and prevent a calamity, we'll have met our mission."

'There's one thing, you men, must know about me by now," advised the sergeant. "I don't favor heroics for heroics sake. General Clinton assigned us to our mission. First, we're to find out what Brant and his men are up to, and secondly, we were to locate, and rescue

Samuel's sister, Marie. One thing is for sure," asserted Jefferson, "if either of you guys get killed, neither of you will be able to warn Clinton, which can mean only one thing, he'll be getting closer to Sullivan's army. Sooner or later, there's bound to be a great, big battle. So, watch your asses! And," he smiled and patted their rear-ends, "God bless both of you."

It appeared obvious to Jefferson and his remaining cadre, that Brant and his raiders were traveling south as fast as they could believing that they were escaping General Clinton's forces, yet, in fact, they were rushing toward General Sullivan and his troops who had reached Tioga on August 11th. The next day, unaware of Brant's close proximity, Sullivan ordered a detail of his troops to march west, and seek out Indian settlements. On August 13th, Sullivan's western contingent approached the lower section of the Iroquois castle at Chemung, and ended up burning all the settlement's houses, corn, and any other objects which were combustible, as well as frightening the settlement's residents into fleeing from the destruction. Many of Sullivan's marauders were farmers, by occupation, and were completely flabbergasted to see the size and quality of the Indians' corn and vegetables. In fact, many debated whether they should harvest the crops themselves; however, *common sense* prevailed. They decided to burn rather than be bogged down with a large supply of farm products; this decision they would remember when they were placed on rations. Reluctantly, they set about their orders to *burn everything combustible*, but they did report to General Sullivan their amazing discovery of the Indians' agricultural capabilities. The next day, on August 14th, Brant and his band of Tories and Indian warriors reached the northern section of the Chemung castle, and silently, watched as Sullivan's men carried out their destruction. Some of the Indians with itchy fingers took a few random musket shots at the Rebel raiders resulting with a few casualties on both sides. After quelling his warriors, and convincing them that their current efforts would be futile because, based upon the hundreds of enemy campfires lighting up the night, Brant estimated Sullivan's troops far out numbered his forces. He, therefore, suggested, "It is best to wait until we're better prepared to attack, rather than to risk more losses here." Convinced, Brant's frustrated warriors withdrew from the scene except for a few scouts, who trailed the American forces to Tioga.

* * *

From a distance near in the Chemung area, Jefferson's scouts were watching, and counting numerous small bands of Iroquois and Tories as they slowly assembled around Brant's council fire. By August 19th, Jefferson's scouts estimated Brant had gathered a force of approximately 300. What Jefferson or his scouts did not know was that specific evening, Brant had carefully wrote a cheerful letter to Colonel Mason Bolton, and gave the letter to one of his fleet-footed couriers, who immediately started out for Fort Niagara. Brant's letter was to inform Bolton that he had been engaged in a skirmish on the Mohawk, and that he had been wounded but was recovering very well. Brant wanted Bolton to learn of his wound directly from him, and to assure him that everything was proceeding according to their plan. He also informed Bolton that his warriors had captured two Rebel prisoners from whom he learned that the Americans were gathering in great numbers, and were intent on invading the Iroquois country. Brant wrote that most of his warriors were in *good spirits,* and he was certain that they were going to win the forth coming battle. Even though Brant was expecting Colonel John Butler and the Seneca chief, Sayengaraghta, with a number of Rangers and Senecas on the following day, Brant acknowledged that he was *a little afraid we shall have hard work to drive the Enemy back, for our Friends are too slow in joining us.* Brant pleaded to Bolton to "drive all Indians from Fort Niagara, and not suffer a man of them to go to Canada." In closing his letter to Colonel Bolton, Brant predicted, *If we beat the Rebel Army, they will never invade our Country again.*

Immediately after dispatching the courier with his letter to Bolton, Brant settled down, and wrote an entirely different kind of letter to his friend, Claus, with whom he had always maintained intimate, and honest communications. Colonel Daniel Claus, Sir William Johnson's first son-in-law was an interesting person; a complete antithesis of Chief Joseph Brant. He was a quiet German, who had married the baronet's eldest daughter, Ann, in 1762. He served as deputy agent to the Canadian Indians, but he was more and more an agent in absentia, and left his comfortable Williamsburg only part of the year. With this Sir William appeared to be satisfied, and the Caughnawagas and other Indians to the north not dissatisfied. Daniel Claus loved his family, and loved to eat; he was overweight, and a bit lethargic; playing his fiddle was his solace, and the life of a country squire his greatest delight. Destiny could have no special plans for such a person. Nevertheless, Brant trusted Claus. In his letter, Brant expressed his heart-felt feelings, and anxieties about the outcome of the forthcoming battles stating that the Rebels with their thousands, were only eight miles from his castle and his only a few hundreds of braves and Tories. He, then confessed to Claus that he believed to the bottom of his soul, that the Americans intended nothing less than the extermination of the Iroquois nation. Further, he expressed belief that his forces would be engaged in a decisive battle almost any day. *"Then,"* he wrote, lapsing into the ancient figures of speech, which sounded so strange coming from such a valiant chief as Brant, *"we shall begin to know what is to befall us the People of the Long House."*

As Colonel Claus finished reading Brant's confessional, he knew Brant was too intelligent not to realize that the prospects for the British and Tory forces were equally bleak.

Colonel John Butler, who commanded the green coated forces known as Butler's Rangers comprised of Loyalists and Tories who had left their homes in the Mohawk Valley, like Chief Brant was convinced that the Americans were nearly ready to invade the Iroquois country. What surprised Butler was that the Rebels were dispatching forces to stop Sir Henry Clinton's progress up the Hudson River to relieve General Burgoyne. In those days everyone, except Sir General Henry Clinton, thought he was to bring his force up the Hudson; rather, his mind-set was upon taking the city of Philadelphia. Meanwhile, Butler who was parleying with the Indians in the Seneca country was looking forward to joining Clinton and his troops, too.

Like Butler, too, Brant believed the Indians at Niagara should be commanded to stop their idling, and *get off their asses* to join forces with Butler and himself. Butler, too, wrote Bolton urging all warriors in the vicinity of Niagara to be immediately dispatched to him. He even urged Bolton to require the Indians to march night and day until they joined forces with Brant and him. Attaching to his request, Bolton added that he hoped *that Such as so not Come, may not be allowed Provisions nor any thing Else, nor be looked upon as Friends, and this we desire you will tell them.*

In response to Butler and Brant's appeals, Colonel Bolton dared to send only one company of the 8th Regiment to support their troops. Meanwhile, Governor Haldimand ordered Guy Johnson to go *uplake to rouse your Indians.* But only 300 Senecas and Cayugas joined with the 250 Rangers and 50 regulars on the hills overlooking the site of Elmira.

On August 16th, Colonel Butler was ready to lead his forces toward Canadesaga (modern-day Geneva), but true to form the local Senecas refused to budge. Believing their only hope for a victory was to perform their traditional war dance, and feast from their meager food supplies. They demanded at least one day's delay. After that detainment, they promised they would not let Butler and his white Rangers start to march without them. After hearing the Senecas' demands, an aggravated Ranger declared, *Such another tardy Set never was known. The enemy if they had known it might have overrun their country before they got together.*

Throughout the next day, Sergeant Jefferson and his cadre watched Butler's forces. They noticed that many Indians appeared too exhausted; or more appropriately they were recovering from their hangovers developed during their festivities thus delaying the merging of the newly arrived Indians with Butler's main force. Under constant vigilance of Clinton's scouting cadre, Butler's forces reached a small Indian village, called Chucknut, on the Chemung River, about one mile from the larger village of Newtown, (modern-day Elmira, New York), where Brant and his troops of Tories and Indians were camped. Collectively, Butler and Brant's detachment totaled about 600 armed men. Or these, 180 were white men; most were Rangers and members of the Indian department, and with a small group from the King's regiment; the remaining 420 included all the Indians and white Tory volunteers Brant had been able to assemble. What puzzled both Butler and Brant was the poor response of the Indians. Brant was especially disappointed. Remembering his mentor and guardian and his sister Molly's husband, Sir William Johnson, telling him that according to his last census he had calculated that the Senecas had at least 1,000 warriors fit for battle, and the Cayuagas had about 250. He knew that the Indians had suffered many casualties in the battles, especially the one at Oriskany. They had never learned from Bolton how many Indians were safely housed within or just outside the confines of Fort Niagara. Among the Indians at Niagara, they did know the Canadian Missisaugas spent much of their time in and around the confines of the fort. Whatever the Indians population at Niagara, Bolton could only persuade 44 warriors to join Brant and Butler. The Delawares, many of whom lived in the Chemung-Susquehanna area, had supplied less than 30 fighters, even though they had promised to furnish 200 warriors. What perplexed Butler and Brant the most was the Indian philosophy of survival. It was virtually impossible to convince Indians from one tribe to come to the aid of another; according to their beliefs, the saving of the Senecas and Cayuga country was up to the Senecas and Cayugas. While Butler and Brant were trying to assemble their forces, they learned that an American force under the command of Colonel Daniel Brodhead was laying waste to the Indian settlements on the upper Allegheny River.

To complicate the Indians' situation, the Delawares wanted to preserve their settlement of Newtown, thus encouraged Butler and Brant to prepare an ambush well beyond their village. Sayengaraghta and his Senecas agreed with the Delawares, but Butler opposed their plan. Quickly, Butler communicated with Bolton informing him his troops were so outnumbered he proposed a retreat to a more favorable location, and to dispatch raiding parties to keep the Rebels in a continuous panic. Also, he informed Bolton that Brant agreed with his plan. Bolton, however, was beginning to notice that the white people respected Brant as an outstanding Indian leader;

STEPS TOWARD FREEDOM

ironically, the more the whites appreciated and respected Brant, the more the Indians tended to discredit him, some even detested him. Interestingly, Colonel John Butler's son, Captain Walter Butler, made an astute observation about Brant *...has been more notice taken of him than has been good for his own interest with his own people.* Time proved young Butler correct, Joseph's getting so much attention paid to him was the reason that Sayengaraghta and the Senecas could not forgive.

* * *

For the entire day, Sergeant George Jefferson and his cadre were spying on Butler and Brant's camp. So far, they had been able to keep Generals Sullivan and Clinton appraised of the activities in the British and Indian camps. Obviously, they were not aware of the disagreements among the Indians, but they did realize the Americans far outnumbered the combined forces of the British and Indians. During the day, the Jefferson cadre started evaluating their progress.

"So far, we've accomplished General Clinton's first objective by keeping him, and Sullivan informed daily of the enemy's operations," stated the sergeant with the hot August sun bringing out ripples of shinning perspiration from his ebony flesh. "Now comes the difficult task, to rescue Samuel's sister."

"We don't even know which tent or tepee she is kept in," declared one of Colonel Daniel Morgan's former rifleman. "She may even be sleeping out under the blue," smiled the rifleman.

"We don't even know whether she's dead or alive," observed the other Virginian as he looked apologetically toward Samuel Montgomery.

"I know that is possible, but I hope and pray she's still alive," acknowledged Samuel, with a tear in his eye.

"We all do, too," assured Walter Heindrick.

"I'll bet anything she's alive," Benjamin chimed in. "They'll keep her alive as a hostage, a bargaining chip for something they may want."

"Out first task," stated the sergeant, "is to find her location." Turning toward Samuel, he asked, "Samuel, do you remember what either of the two warriors looked like? Were their heads shaved? Were their faces painted, if so what color, and how? Did they carry anything unusual? What did they wear?"

Before Jefferson could ask another question, Samuel said, "The short, stocky Indian who hit me had a limp with his right leg, like he couldn't straighten it out." He hesitated a moment, and began to smile as he itched his turban head bandage, "He wore a dark red breech cloth, very muscular, even though he had a limp, he was fast, or I guess I'm rather slow compared to him," smiled the confident youth.

"How about the Indian who captured Marie?" asked Benjamin, "Was he shorter or taller than the one who attacked you?"

"Oh!" exclaimed Samuel, "He was about six inches taller than the other one, and he looked a few years younger. He wore long, leather breeches. One of the last things I remember about him or his buddy was that he did carry a long spear with turkey feathers on the opposite end of the spearhead. He also had a knife in his belt, but he didn't carry a tomahawk."

"You haven't said anything about their hair or headdress," observed a scout who had served with Sergeant Jefferson under General Benedict Arnold during the battles in and around Saratoga.

"The man who attacked me, had his head completely shaved except for some hair which stuck up straight down the middle of his head with one white feather hanging down across his right ear. Oh, yes!" Samuel said excitedly, "right near the feather he wore a large white colored earring hanging down from his right ear. He was really a tough, rugged man, while the one who captured Marie was a slimmer, and more handsome."

"The slimmer one must have had some degree of compassion," declared the tall, skinny soldier in a hunting shirt who had played his fiddle with Walter and Benjamin while they played a drum and fife during the Saratoga campaign against General "Gentleman Johnny" Burgoyne. For this mission, Slim, as well as Benjamin and Walter had left their instruments back at the base camp with General Clinton's aide-de-camp.

"Not necessarily," said the fiddler's buddy who still hadn't unpacked his harmonica, "I betcha he is a young buck lookin' for someone to keep him warm during the winter. You know it's not unusual for Indians to take some of their female captives as their squaws. We all know the story about Mary Jemison. Hell! she's been living with them Senecas ever since 1764. I hear tell them Redskins all treat her with kindness and affection. They even adopted her into their tribe. Eventually, she married some warrior, and I understand they've had at least one son."

"Mary Jemison, the famous white woman of the Genesee Valley did marry an Indian warrior," confirmed the sergeant. "His name was Hiakatoo known for his fierce fighting, his strength, and amazing fleetness of foot. It has been rumored that he travels regularly with Joseph Brant participating in many raids."

"You mean she had a half-bred kid, and she's shacking-up with a murderer of whites?' sneered Slim's traveling companion with the harmonica.

"I don't want any of that kind of talk in my squad," flatly demanded their sergeant.

Benjamin and Walter, immediately thought of White Tail's Aunt Mary. Before they could say anything to defend a woman such as Mary Jemison, Sergeant Jefferson exerted his authority saying, "I don't want any of these kinds of disparaging remarks made in my squad. Our business right now, is to find and rescue Marie Montgomery, and then to get the hell back to General Clinton's army. We don't need any distractions. If any of you have any more belittling remarks, please keep them to yourselves. Is that clear?"

Everyone knew that the sergeant had handpicked his cadre for their special talents, and they had been successful working together on numerous special assignments during the Saratoga campaign; no one wanted to jeopardize their record, nor their close-knit camaraderie. In their secluded hideout, they plotted their strategy to seek out Marie's captors, and to watch for signs of her presence. One thing they agreed upon, that the designated rescuers needed to be disguised so, if necessary, they could blend into the Indians' camp. The entire day was spent spying from various positions surrounding the camp site, until Slim sent out a message to Sergeant Jefferson that he had spotted a brave with a lame right leg. After young Samuel confirmed that the identified brave was his attacker, half of the cadre was assigned to survey the Indians' activities. While watching the lame warrior, a tall Indian wearing long, leather breeches met with him and together they entered a tepee located near the outside rim of the circle of the camp. Quietly and anxiously the cadre members watched their prey. The younger brave left the tepee carrying a gourd, and went toward what appeared to be a common food container. After filling the gourd, he carried it back to the tepee where his partner awaited; hopefully, there was where Marie Montgomery was their prisoner. The rest of the day was spent in identifying the rescuers, and how they would carry out their respective assignments. The two Virginians who had conducted such missions of Colonel Daniel Morgan, volunteered for the rescue duty, while Jefferson and the others identified their roles for the evening's daring deliverance of the Indians' captive. Something had changed since they had first located the enemy camp; the main camp, during the day and night, seemed to be sparely populated with very little activity.

* * *

For two days, Butler and Brant's forces waited in ambush on a ridge about half a mile from the Rebels' main camp, protected by a bend in the river. To their right was the river, on their left a mountain, and in front of them a wandering creek. Brant and his warriors, together with some Rangers, were situated near the river. Butler with a few Indians and regulars, together with the main body of Rangers were stationed in the center, while the rest of the Indians, by far the greatest number, were located on the left. To the rear lay the village of Newtown. The selected sight for the ambush was highly favored by the Indians. Reluctantly, Butler agreed upon the location. It was Butler and Brant's conjecture that the unsuspecting Americans would be coming along the river's towpath with their entire right flank exposed.

On the first day of Sergeant Jefferson's cadre's surveillance, Butler's Rangers left their breastwork and retired, due to a false alarm caused by two Delawares shooting deer on the mountain.

When the Rangers discovered the cause of the shots, they quickly returned to their posts. During their second day, Butler endeavored to persuade the Indians to move a few miles up the river, but they would not consider his suggestion. He was beginning to believe that regardless what he wanted the Indians to perform, they would damnwell do what they wanted to do! Finally, on the third day, August 29, 1779, Butler received word that the Americans were approaching. About this time the Indians took it upon themselves to change their position on the ambush line, sloping the line it toward the mountain in such a way as to give the enemy room for a flanking movement.

Evening's shadows came creeping over the Indian's camp, while the Indians' maneuverings were going on. Under the cover of darkness, one skinny Virginian with vermillion painted over his face, wearing long, leather leggings, and carrying a Kentucky rifle disguised as an Indian spear with a white feather attached on its end, together with a shorter muscular Virginian dressed in nothing but a ragged, dark red breechcloth, and carrying a tomahawk along with his camouflaged Kentucky rifle, crept into a tepee near the outer perimeter of the Indians' camp. Moments later, two similar figures ghost-like silently appeared from the entrance of the same tepee, escorting what appeared to be a young, long, dark-haired girl dressed like most white girls; unlike most young Indian girls of her age. These three figures silently, and swiftly evaporate into the surrounding murky forest, while Colonel Butler and Brant, and the Cayuga chief ineffectively urged the Indians to move up the hill.

ELEVEN

MOVE UP THE HILL!

The Later Weeks of August, 1779
Colonel Butler's Rangers along the Mohawk

When Captain Johan Jost Jr. and his adjutant and best friend, Sandy McKnight, returned with Butler's Rangers and Brant's warriors, Johan had realized that Sandy was not the same individual, who he had left with to join Butler and Brant just two previous months in June, 1779. Because of his knowledge of and popularity with the Indians, Johan Jr. had just been attached to the Indian Department at Fort Niagara. Before he could even start his duties in the department, Colonel Bolton, who had heard of the Americans' attack on Onondaga, had ordered him and Sandy to immediately join Major John Butler and Chief Joseph Brant and their combined force of approximately four hundred Rangers and warriors.

Neither Johan Jr. or Sandy would ever forget that July 20th in Minisink. It was their first time either had ever experienced seeing white men conducting themselves as cruelly and savagely as the Indians; they had previously branded as inhuman and merciless.

Each groups were executing the savagery of scalping and burning with equal repugnant and sickening expertness. All of these dastardly deeds, which Johan Jr. and Sandy had witnessed and had faint-heartily participated in, became indelibly imprinted in both of their minds, raising questions about what were they doing in this cruel and futile civil war between so-called civilized people. These same people, who frequently looked upon the *Redman* with destain, aghast learning of the activities *those barbaric Redmen* committed. Suddenly, these very same "white" people were racing around after each other, catching one another, slaughtering former family members and neighbors with little or no conscience, and inconsequential concern as to the brutality they were committing. All of these repugnant encounters and experiences were rapidly eroding Johan Jr. and Sandy's utopian and idealistic visions of life of freedom in America. Instead in time of war, they were learning how cruel, greedy, and carnivorous people, who call themselves civilized human beings, can perform and can act unconsciously like vultures feeding upon the helpless and innocent.

But, their quixotic state of mind would have to wait. Not to their surprise, an almost mutinous state within their ranks was fermenting. The warriors, such as had turned out, and the white Loyalists were not on the best of terms. The Indians were angry and sullen because General Haldimand had not captured the post at Oswego (a thing they much desired to enable them to collect the bounty due them), nor did their friends, the British, appear to be sending them any aid. The Loyalists, for their part, found it difficult, even distasteful, to work with the Indians. It was a well known fact that most of the Loyalists had a bitter contempt for the Indians. First of all, the whites did not understand the culture of the Indians, nor did most of them attempt to learn about it. Survival, alone made these two different cultures and their instinct for survival, was the common motivation which created humanity allies of these two diverse peoples.

A great deal of mutual antagonism lay behind that line of hastily cut brush and logs used to camouflage their ambush. The Delawares, because they wanted to preserve their settlement of Newtown, had insisted the ambush be prepared beyond that village.

Sayengaraghta and his Senecas supported their reasoning. On the other hand, Colonel Butler opposed the Indians' strategy, because his forces were outnumbered. Butler and Brant wanted to retreat to a more favorable location, and to dispatch strong raiding parties to harass the enemy. In retrospect, Butler's idea appears to have been an opportunity to improve the British and Indians' position.

Neither, Butler and Brant were experiencing great popularity among the Indians. Butler was a white man, and white men were not held in high esteem among the Indians. Brant too, although an Indian, was encountering similar destain and was just as likely to antagonize the Indians as to favorably influence them. While most white people thought Brant as an outstanding Indian leader, it appeared that the more respect Brant received in the eyes of the whites, it appeared that the greater the desire for the Indians to destroy his reputation. Butler's son, Captain Walter Butler probably was correct, when he stated the Brant's getting so much attention paid to him by the *whites* was a deficiency that Sayengaraghta and the Senecas could not ignore nor forgive him.

On the first day in their ambush, there was a false alarm caused by two Delawares shooting at the deer on the mountain. Thinking that the Rebels were attacking, the Rangers left their breastwork and retired, intending to get ahead of the enemy and gain the heights. When the Rangers discovered what had happened, they returned to the breastwork to the hooting and yelling of insults from the Indians. The next day, Butler tired to persuade the Indians to move miles up the Chemung River.

On the third day, August 29th, the British and Indians discovered clear evidence that the American troops were very close to their breastwork. At the same time this was discovered, one Indian took upon himself to change their part of the line, sloping it toward the mountain in such a way as to give the enemy room for a flanking movement on that side. When this was called to the attention of the chiefs, they refused to change their positioning. Along about two o'clock in the afternoon, as the American forces, lead by Sullivan and Clinton, first appeared firing at the Ranger and Indians' breastwork. Immediately, Colonel John Butler, Chief Joseph Brant and the Cayuga chiefs tried ineffectually to persuade the Indians to move up the hill.

The American forces, too, were operating under numerous difficulties. First of all, they hardly knew where they were going. Out of the twenty-five Oneidas, who had first volunteered to show the way through the white man's *terra incognita,* commonly referred to as the Forbidden Path, there were only two remained along with a Stockbridge Indian from Massachusetts, who undoubtedly knew even less about the local terrain than the Oneidas. To the untrained eye, it may have appeared that these troops were advancing recklessly, but most of them were well seasoned and disciplined Continental soldiers. Carefully and steadily Sullivan's troops never let their guard down, stopping only to burn whatever Indian settlements and their under harvested grains they found along the way. Late in the afternoon of August 29th, while the sun was beginning to set in the west, an advance group of Continental scouts discovered the hidden breastworks behind which Butler and Brant had finally permitted their mixed force to station themselves. One of the American scouts had climbed a tree and spied some brilliantly painted near-naked bodies shinning in the late summer's hot and humid sun glow. Momentarily, the American advance force began to fire from behind the trees and creek banks, and very soon thereafter, their artillery soon began training their fire power toward the demoralized vermillion painted bodies. With every kind of missile available; shells, grapeshot, harrow teeth, iron spikes, etc., randomly falling about them, the Indians, as John Butler told the story to Bolton in his official report, thought they were surrounded. Terrorized, most of the warriors broke ranks and fled; some of the Senecas not stopping until they reached their homes on the Genesee. Butler himself, with the Rangers and the few remaining Indians retreated to the mountain, where he and Brant wanted to be in the first place. But, as he expected, Butler and his force soon were confronted with Sullivan's American troops who were trying to outflank Butler's left. After a fierce running battle, the greatly outnumbered Loyalists exhausted by all their inter-disciplinary ventures, arguments, and indecisions, fled across the river or along the mountain. Finally, they were able to converge, about ten miles away, for the night. It was very late in the evening, and the Loyalist and Indian forces were caught in one of the area's renowned and sudden thunder-showers. Soaked to the skin, Ranger and Indians alike, had had nothing to eat since daybreak, and then only a few ears of corn.

A number of the troops were becoming ill with the ague, while others were wounded and being carried or dragged along cradled in a blanket between two poles. One of the critically wounded was Sandy McKnight, whose left leg had been so critically mangled from grapeshot and iron spikes, that before their retreat he had asked his fellow Rangers to leave him on the field of battle. Somehow or other, Sandy and Johan Jr. had been separated. In their desperate attempt to escape sure death, Sandy's fellow soldiers took his advice and left him on the battlefield in a conspicuous location. They believed this to be an appropriate decision, because they had heard from some of their other wounded comrades, that the Americans were relatively compassionate with wounded enemy, especially the whites.

All these factors considered, Butler believed he had nothing for which to apologize. "Both Officers and Men," he noted proudly, "Behaved with Much Spirit, but the Efforts of Such a hand full were of little avail against the Force they had to oppose."

Virtually all of the Americans, who had been engaged with the Indians on the mountain, confirmed that most of the Indians fought bravely. John Norton, Brant's white friend, who wrote many years later, and that contrary to Brant's advice, the courage of the warriors had been allowed to *cool* too long behind their entrenchment; that he, Brant, favored a less cautious course. Later after the battle, Butler admitted: "Joseph Brant's Conduct through the Whole of this affair does him much honor, he with Kianagarachta and Several Other Chiefs and Indians remained with us to the last. In their flight, part of Butler's troops got separated from the main body; there is some evidence that Brant was one of these, and that he spent that dark and lowering night despondently hiding in a tree. But, there is also evidence that after the battle, Brant took the wounded to a place of safety up the Chemung River. Perhaps he did both!

When General Washington heard of Sullivan and Clinton's success, his reaction was swift and predictable. "The advantages we have already gained over the Indians, in the destruction of so many of their settlements," Washington wrote to Sullivan, "is very flattering to the expedition. But to make it as conclusive as the state of your provisions and the safety of your army will countenance," he continued, "I would mention two points I may not have sufficiently expressed in my general instructions, or if I have, which I wish to repeat." The two elements which Washington wanted to repeat and emphasize to Sullivan were as follows: "The one is the necessity of pushing the Indians to the greatest practicable distance from their own settlements and our frontiers; to the throwing them wholly on the British enemy. The other is the making the destruction of their settlements so final and complete as to put it out of their power to derive the smallest succor from them in case they should attempt to return this season."

It was rumored about, if anyone was to ask Washington to name his favorite peoples, Indians would have been far down the list. Evidently, the events he had experienced during his youth when he had fought the French and their *savages*, were very clear in his mind. To Washington, Indians were enemies, crafty, diabolical, and cruel. He once likened them to "wolves," and in a quarter of a century he had not changed.

As the wounded Sandy McKnight lay on a blanket, which some thoughtful Loyalist soldier had draped over a few pine boughs to make he laid more comfortable, and placed his ever-loving bagpipes along his side. The sun was beginning to set in the west, and Sandy was becoming concerned that with the coming of night there would be a pack or so of hungry wolves coming around. After about an hour or so, he heard faintly in the distance what sounded like a host of Crusaders singing and marching in his direction celebrating their victory over the Loyalists and their Indian allies. As they neared to where he laid in a near comatose state, he took a deep breath, and began yelling, "Help! Help!" and waving his arms. By the time some of the American soldiers located him, Sandy had relapsed into a deep coma.

TWELVE

DREAMS OF THE FUTURE

Late November 1779
In Sergeant Jefferson's Albany Home

By the end of November, Samuel and Marie Montgomery had received their emancipation from their former and deceased master, Gunther Haas, of Minisink much to the thanks to the persistence and determination of General Philip Schuyler and his friend and New York Governor, George Clinton. To further assist in expediting the process, Sergeant Jefferson's service under the general had helped to build a mutual respect and friendship between the two, as well as, the fact the sergeant was also in partnership with the one of the general's brother Hans Schuyler in a Albany smithy shop and livery stable business also helped in expediting the emancipation process. Not only did the ex-slaves receive their freedom, but they also became foster children of Mr. and Mrs. George Jefferson of Albany, New York, who just happened to be the parents of young Benjamin Jefferson, blood brother of Walter Heindrick of New Palatine. Julia Jefferson, who had established a renown reputation as an accomplished home-baker, was delighted to learn that her foster daughter was also interested in learning the baking skills. Of course, Benjamin, who was approximately the same age as Marie Montgomery, looked forward to sharpening his baking abilities.

"I have an idea," declared George Jefferson, who was on a short leave from the Continental Army, as his enlarged family ate their evening meal in front of the large kitchen's stone fireplace, "with all the blessings we have been showered with this year, and seeing the end of November is fast approaching, I propose that we celebrate a Thanksgiving Day with our friends, the Heindricks and the Kerchners."

"What a wonderful and thoughtful idea, my dear," agreed Julia, knowing full well the heavy burden of preparing the meal would fall upon her shoulders. "You know for as long as you have known Karl Heindrick and his family, I have never met them. You have often talked about your blood-brother Karl with whom you lived your first ten or twelve years. I've also heard about their son, Walter, from you and Benjamin, especially while you three were serving with Generals Schuyler and Arnold."

"Don't forget, mother," Benjamin inserted, "about Walter's girl friend, Helena Kerchner, and her mother. Remember me telling you that Mr. Kerchner, suddenly announced to his wife and daughter that they were headed for Fort Niagara, where he intended to join the Loyalist Army? After a few weeks, Helena managed to escape, and returned to New Palatine to live with the Heindricks. After Mrs. Kerchner learned that her husband was killed during the Battle of Oriskany, she, too, returned to New Palatine, and to the settlement's only general store they had owned. Fortunately, for the Kerchners the store's assistant manager Harvey Perry had taken excellent care of the store. After realizing how well he and his wife had managed the store, Mrs. Kerchner made them equal partners with her."

"This sounds like we'll be having an good old-fashioned Thanksgiving dinner, as well as our own family reunion," observed George.

The two Montgomery children looked at their new foster parents, and their step-brother in amazement. Each thought that what they were hearing couldn't be happening to them. They were going to be a part of a family! Not that their former master's family had treated them badly, but they had never been in on the excitement of planning a festive occasion; their roles were usually the preparation and cleaning-up chores.

"Father," asked Benjamin, "were not you supposed to report back to Fort Dayton in a couple days?"

"That's correct son," responded his father, "why do you ask?"

"What do you think of the idea that I ride along with you? You stay at the fort and report to Colonel Willet, and I'll ride west to New Palatine to invite the Heindrick and Kerchners for our reunion."

Silently, Marie Montgomery wished that she, too, could ride along with them, especially with Benjamin to New Palatine where she could renew her friendship with one of her rescuers, Walter Heindrick. Walter had treated her and her brother with such wonderful care and respect, and had told them what a wonderful young lady Helena Kerchner was; she was anxious to meet her. Oh! how she prayed that some of her wishes could come true. She made up her mind that she must be patient, and be grateful.... thankful for all the blessings which she and Samuel had received so far. Samuel broke the silence

"Sergeant Jefferson, sir, could I ride along with you and Benjamin to that fort you're talking about?" asked Marie's excited ten-year old brother, who was just beginning to grow back some hair from his scalping. "I'd love to see the fort, and I'd like to know what the western frontier, you've always been talking about, looks like. Do you think we'll see any Indians? If we do, do you think they'll attack us?" He was about to ask another question, when his foster father glanced toward his wife, and saw her consenting acknowledgement.

"Samuel, I think that's a wonderful idea. Benjamin, do you have any problem with Samuel riding along?" asked his father.

"I agree with you, father. I'd enjoy having someone accompany me to New Palatine," replied Benjamin.

Once again the old green monster, jealousy, clawed at Marie, but Benjamin's mother helped to relieve the young lady's pain.

"I have any idea, Marie," announced Julia, "we'll let the men go ahead and do their men's thing." Silently, Marie, was wondering what her foster mother was going to suggest; she knew it would not be as nice as riding along the tree lined, narrow road referred to as the King's Highway to New Palatine with Benjamin Jefferson. "For the past few months, I have been performing volunteer nursing work at the military hospital here in Albany," stated Julia. "Tomorrow is my day to go on duty. Perhaps you'd enjoy seeing what we can do to assist in the healing and rehabilitation of the wounded soldiers."

"That sounds interesting!" responded Marie with less excitement than Samuel had exhibited when he learned about riding west. "At least, I'll be getting a different perspective of the war, than the one I've seen lately. Yes, Mrs. Jefferson, I'd love to accompany you to the hospital."

"Oh!, there's one thing more, George and I would like you and Samuel do for us," Julia caught their attention.

"What's that?" the eager ten year-old brother asked, while his more mature and sensitive sister patiently waited to hear what her new foster mother was going to say.

"George and I have been talking about how polite you two have been with us in a kind formal manner. Since we are now your foster parents, we would prefer being called something less formal as Sergeant Jefferson and Mrs. Jefferson. We'd much prefer mother and father. If those names don't come easy to you, just call us Mom and Dad, or something similar," Julia stopped and took a deep breath, and continued, "you don't have to start right now, just when you're ready to accept us as your parents would be fine with us."

* * *

The next morning the Jefferson men, including the newly adopted ten-year old foster son, Samuel Montgomery, who would probably be wearing this skull cap for the rest of his life the same way as many a Mohawk Valley farmer or his wife who had managed to survive the Indians' scalping knife, traveled the ever-rutted, narrow and winding King's Highway toward Sergeant Jefferson's appointment with Colonel Willet at Fort Dayton. The King's Highway followed the Mohawk River relatively closely from Schenectady to Fort Dayton westward past New Palatine and Fort Stanwix, eventually leading to Fort Oswego. Very early in the 1700's, this entire area of the young New York colony was settled by the Dutch and the Palatines from Germany. After the failure of the disastrous British experiment to establish a naval supply and tar manufacturing enterprise just north of New York City, many of the Palatines migrated north to the Mohawk Valley, establishing a relatively prosperous agricultural business, and eventually becoming known as the Continental Army's "breadbasket," and occasionally a food source for the British, Indians and their allies. Most of the Palatines, who chose not to migrate to the Mohawk Valley. were attracted by William Penn's publicity campaign to Pennsylvania, where they eventually became known as "Pennsylvania Dutch."

Since there were no bridges over the Mohawk River, travelers who were carrying any amount of freight would have to haul their cargo across at various "carrying places," which were strategically located on a narrow strip of land between bodies of water. Depending upon the time of the year, some of the carrying places were so shallow, and the rifts so rough that one could not ferry any more than a two-ton load at a time. Sergeant Jefferson and his two boys were not going to be troubled with fording the river this time of the year. In fact, most of small streams and the river usually were beginning to freeze over by late November. As the sun began to set in the west, the sergeant remembered a sign which had concerned him the pervious night. He has seen *rings around the moon;* to him this was a sure sign in the north country of a heavy snowfall. Shortly, they arrived at the site where he had camped before. After leading their horses to an open area in the creek which was not frozen over, each set about preforming their prearranged night chores. George started constructing a lean-to under which he piled a thick layer of pine and hemlock boughs on the ground, arranging for additional boughs to serve as insulation for their bed rolls.

While the sergeant was preparing the campsite, Benjamin and Samuel were surveying the creek. It was partially frozen over, but rather risky to try cross to the opposite side, because where the creek flowed swiftly, the ice was deceivingly thin. As they followed the creek down steam, they came to an unfrozen opening about five-feet across and twenty-five feet long where the rushing water had kept the creek open. Benjamin reached into his hip pocket, and pulled out some venison jerky, fastened it to a fish hook and line he had taken from his canteen kit which held other eating and cooking utensils.

"Boy! Benjamin," exclaimed Samuel, "you think of everything."

"Not me," responded Benjamin, "the army issues this cloth bag that holds many kitchen utensils. Many of the things in this bag come in handy whenever anyone is out on a scouting mission, or like right now, maybe we'll be lucky and catch ourselves some fish for tonight's supper." Benjamin tossed a small piece of venison jerky into the middle of the unfrozen creek. Suddenly, a fish, larger than the rainbow trout they were expecting swished by, grabbed the jerky and disappeared.

"If there's one fish here, I'll betcha," said Samuel, "there's another."

"I believe you're right, Samuel," agreed Benjamin as he tossed in the fish hook with some of the jerky baited upon it. "If there is, he'd better hurry and come up soon, because it's started to become pretty dark. Father is going to think we are lost." His words were sooner out of his mouth, than the baited hook was attacked in the icy, cold, clear water. Benjamin let the sizable fish nibble for a moment, then quickly jerked the hook up, and along came the hungry fish fighting to keep from becoming the boys' supper.

Benjamin carefully grabbed the fish. It had an enormous hard, flat black head with what looked like horns sticking out from the side of its head.

"He looks scary," Samuel said as he stood away from the slippery fish.

"He is scary," confirmed Benjamin. "This fish is called a *bullhead*. My father tells me that bullheads and another kind of fish called a *sucker* are only good to eat during the cold months. When the weather and water becomes warm,. he told me these kind of fish are not good eating; too soft, and tasteless."

Carefully, Benjamin removed the fish hook from the fish's mouth, and tossed the hook to Samuel. "Here Samuel, catch this hook and line," Benjamin said as he began to dress the bullhead for their evening meal. "We'll need another fish tonight," declared Benjamin, "if we're all going to have fish with whatever our mother stuffed into our saddle bags."

Like magic, minutes after Samuel had thrown the baited hook into the stream, he became almost hypnotized as he watched another fish attack the bait. This fish did not gently nibble the bait; he quickly attacked the bait. Just as rapidly, the fish swam away to circle the bait as if he was trying to decide whether Samuel's offering was something he wanted. A moments later, the fish returned to the bait, and nibbled just long enough to allow Samuel sufficient time to jerk up the hook, and start pulling this different kind of fish ashore.

"Benjamin! Benjamin! I caught a fish! I caught a fish!" exclaimed Samuel. "Only it's a different kind than the one you caught."

With his seasoned eye, Benjamin quickly recognized the fish Samuel was pulling in was a brown trout. "Father is going to love you for the beautiful fish you have there." declared Benjamin.

Puzzled, Samuel asked, "Why do you say that? I know that he loves me now. Why should he love me more, just because I caught this fish? We're just doing our job."

"I agree with you, Samuel, but that fish is a brown trout, which has a very delicate taste. It's one of father's favorite fish. Unhook the fish, and toss it to me, and I'll promptly dress it."

Within a few minutes, the two boys were headed to the campsite where their father was kneeling and feeding a few more dead sticks on the campfire. Their father stood up and said, "I was beginning to worry about you guys. I didn't know whether you had decided to roam the fields for rabbits, or go through the woods looking for squirrels, or just what you had decided to do."

"We,....." Benjamin quickly responded. "I decided to follow the creek, and we came to a large open area, which was not frozen over....."

Before Benjamin could finish his story, Samuel proudly said, "Father! Father! We caught two fish, and Benjamin has them all ready for the frying pan."

While the men were sitting around the fire, and enjoying the fish George had pan-fried with some fat-back, and some roasted potatoes which he had tossed in a small hole in the ground beneath the wood even before he had started the fire. Man-to-man, each were enjoying their hot and freshly prepared victuals, along with Julia's dependable and tasty johnnie cake; topped off with some steaming hot coffee strong enough to melt a metal spoon.

"We should be at Fort Herkimer no later than noon tomorrow," commented the men's father as he poured a second cup of coffee, and started on another piece of his wife's johnnie cake while light from the campfire danced about on his face. "We'll make a quick stop there, and find out if they have anything they want delivered to Fort Dayton. If we're lucky, we should arrive at Fort Dayton just before sunset. I suggest that you two stay overnight at Fort Dayton, have a good supper and a sound night's sleep. Then you'll be bright-eyed and bushy-tail in the morning, and ready for a hearty breakfast. After that you'll be ready for a full day's ride to New Palatine."

"Sounds great to me," declared Benjamin. "How about you, Samuel?"

"Sounds good for me," responded his foster brother. "I'm really looking forward to seeing Walter Heindrick again. I remember when you and Walter saved me from those Indians." He rubbed his scarred head, which was just beginning to show feeble signs of his hair growing back.

"Father," Benjamin said almost apologetically, "I, too, am looking forward to seeing Walter, but more to see the person who has been in my mind most recently, especially while we were riding on the western campaign."

"I can't imagine any person you'd like to see more than Walter, unless it's Helena Kerchner," his father said with a huge grin on his face, "but I know, and you know my son that she's already spoken for by Walter."

"You know that I love both of them very dearly, but the person I have dreamed about is White Tail's Aunt Mary. I'm afraid something has happened to her. If I can talk Walter, and even Helena, to ride west with Samuel and me to Aunt Mary's village, then I can release her from my dreaded dreams."

"Son, if you can persuade Walter and Helena, if she wants, to go with you two., I have no problem." George said sympathetically to his troubled son and cautioned him, "But, don't you forget there are still a few Indians, as well as Loyalist troops, roaming around this area. If you meet any Indians, I'm sure most will be friendly Oneidas. Nevertheless, I want you to exercise extreme caution." After this somber discussion, George suggested, "before we sack down for the night, I'd like you boys take a quick check on the horses while I stoke the fire, and then we can finally hit the sack, so we can be on the road soon after daybreak."

The evening's quiet and light snowfall served only as an additional blanket for the three as they slept; each venturing into their own dreams of the future and where it would lead them.

THIRTEEN

THE LADY DOTH VOLUNTEER!

Same Day in Late November 1779
at Jefferson's in Albany, New York

Moments after Sergeant George Jefferson, his son Benjamin, and foster son Samuel Montgomery had saddled their horses and began their two-day ride to Fort Dayton, Julia Jefferson shared some of her motherly instincts upon her nearly acquired foster daughter, Marie Montgomery, telling her about volunteering at the local military hospital. Marie was having a difficult time concentrating on what her well-intended foster mother was saying, because she so much preferred to have ridden along with the boys to see country west of Albany. Julia was inviting Marie to accompany her to visit the local military hospital where Julia had been regularly volunteering to assist in the care of the wounded and sick militia and army soldiers.

While Julia and Marie were cleaning up the kitchen, which served also as Julia's retail bakery, Julia began orienting Marie to the history and activities of the hospital. "Soon after the war began the Continental Congress called for a hospital plan for its nearly twenty thousand soldier army. Congress recommended that all military hospitals be managed by a Director General and Chief Physician. Incidentally, they were to be paid at the rate of four dollars for every day they worked. In addition to these two positions, the hospital was to staffed with four surgeons, one apothecary, twenty surgeon's mates, and one nurse for every ten patients. Some of these nurses, who lived in and about the camp, are paid regular pay. To supplement the duties the nurses were asked to perform, the Director General has asked the community to furnish volunteer ladies to assist in any manner they could. Usually, I have been assigned to perform my volunteer work in the surgery area, where I have been assisting the chief surgeon, Dr. Blake McDuff, as one of his *surgery cleaner-uppers.*" She laughed after, she had told Marie her job title. Marie, too, was amused at the job title, asked rather whimsically, "Is that really the title of your job position?"

"Oh, no!," responded Julia, "it's the name I gave to what I do for the hospital, and Dr. McDuff. It helps me to get through the day after seeing some of the wounded and sick. You, see Marie, we not only give care to our military, but occasionally we are asked to render care to wounded Loyalist and British soldiers. For example, just the other day a rather interesting man was admitted. He's a Scotsman from Boston; left Boston to join the Loyalist troops here in New York. What so interesting about him is that whenever he's up and around, he's usually playing his bagpipes. He loves to entertain the staff, as well as the patients. You'll love to hear his Scotch accent brogue; in fact you'll have to listen very carefully to understand everything he's talking about. He tells me that speaks pure English." Julia chuckled, then added, "I guess maybe that's the reason I have difficulty understanding him, after being born and brought up in North Carolina with a southern accent."

"What was he admitted for, and how old is he?" Marie took a deep breath, and asked, "Is he good looking? What's his name?"

"I can answer only three of your questions, Marie. First, his name is Alexander McKnight. He prefers to be called just plain *Sandy*, and yes, he is rather handsome, with a bit of a ruddy complexion." Julia stopped for a moment before she responded to Marie's question concerning McKnight's reason for being admitted to the hospital. "As to reason why he was admitted to the hospital, he was found on August 29th in a near comatose state with a badly wounded left leg on the battlefield just beyond Minisink."

"Minisink!," blurted out Marie. "That's where Samuel and I used to live as slaves, and that is near where Benjamin, Walter, Samuel and Benjamin's father found me."

"Well, I guess you and Sandy will have something to talk about. As to how I met Mr. McKnight; as I've already told you, occasionally, Dr. McDuff has asked for my assistance. When the two surgeon mates carried Mr. McKnight into the hospital operating room, Dr. McDuff recognized the seriousness of McKnight's condition, and he remembered that I had assisted him with a similar case. So!" Julia took a deep breath, "and Dr. McDuff summoned me to come in, and assist him and his surgeon mates. You see, Marie, the doctor recognized that the patient's left leg was so critically mangled from grapeshot and iron spikes, that he believed he was going to have to amputate the leg. The one thing you must know, Marie; nowadays, when a doctor amputates either an arm or leg, the stump is always washed with hot tar. This most painful procedure cauterizes the wound to staunch the bleeding, and sterilizes the avulsion."

"That must have been painful," said Marie as her body made slight shiver of pain. "Did they use anything to ease his pain? Did he yell or scream?"

"Yes, he did yell and scream. He even cried for his mother who still lives in Scotland," replied Julia. "You see, Marie, in our hospital, the only thing we do to ease the patient's pain is to require the patient to chew a lead bullet. As you may know, this does not ease the patient's pain, but it does prevent the patient from crying out, and from biting his tongue.

"Basically," continued Julia, "there are three operative procedures practiced by the Continental Army surgeons. Most of our surgeons do not perform any surgery which requires opening any body cavities, but occasionally, I have seen Dr. McDuff perform an extremely delicate surgery upon a wounded soldier in order to remove a musket ball. In this kind case, Dr. McDuff would try to remove the musket ball with his finger tips. If the bullet was beyond the reach of his finger, he would use forceps to grasp the lead sphere. If the musket ball was lodged further under the patient's skin, I have seen him make an incision in the skin to remove the ball. After that, Dr. McDuff would apply the usual hot tar wash procedure to the open wound.

Still trying to familiarize Marie to new science of surgical medicine, Julia continued, "Another type of surgery which is performed in our surgical unit is called *trephining*. When performing this procedure, a cylindrical saw is used to remove a disc of bone, usually from under the skull. That's when blood clots and pressure under the bone could be released through the hole made by this special small crown saw instrument called a *trephine* to remove a circular section, as of bone from the skull. After the completion of this surgical procedure, the wound is usually brought together with plaster and bandage. Afterwards, a dressing of soft flannel is dipped in oil and applied to the wound, followed by a poultice of bread and milk. "Oh, yes, I nearly forgot," exclaimed Julia, "the inevitable bloodletting, gentile laxatives, warm baths and opium are frequently used with many of the patients."

"Mother Julia, you have really stirred up my interest in seeing the hospital," said Marie as she began putting her winter coat and scarf. "How far is the hospital from here?"

"Just a good healthy walking distance. The cold, crisp air will awake both of us by the time we reach the hospital. I just happened to think, last night while George and I were taking our nightly walk, we noticed the beautiful, hazy yellow ring around the full moon. When we would see such as site, George would always remind me that his Daddy forever told him that during the winter, if there was a ring around the moon at night, it meant that it was going to snow that very night. That means tonight!"

"Can you imagine our men out there sleeping in the open with snow falling all over them?" asked Marie.

"I know one thing that I wouldn't enjoy such a thing, but I do know that men being men they will probably be looking forward such an experience," replied Marie's new foster mother as she pulled her snow boots on, and headed to the Jefferson's front porch. There was no snow on the ground, but the forbidding circle around the moon still was warning the early risers of the coming snow storm.

Julia and Marie walked along the side of the narrow, dirt main street, and as they passed an impressive mansion, Marie asked, "Who lives in that house? That family must be important!" she exclaimed.

"That is home of General Philip Schuyler and his family. While the British General John Burgoyne was a captive of the American Army after his surrender at Saratoga, General Burgoyne was confined in that house as a *prisoner*. It is sorta ironic that earlier during the war, General Burgoyne and his forces had burned General Schuyler's Saratoga mansion down to the ground. After that, our General Horatio Gates's ordered his soldiers replace the mansion; the timber was cut out and the house completed within fifteen days."

"I have often heard Sergeant Jefferson," Marie stopped and quickly corrected herself, "I have often heard Father George speak highly of General Schuyler. Is he really all that important?"

"First of all, Marie," started Julia, your step-father is in partnership in a livery business with General Schuyler's brother, Hans Schuyler, and the three of them have often worked together, as well as the numerous time Father George reported directly to General Philp on special assignments. Whenever the general wanted some kind of special rather risky venture performed, such as the research and recover reconnaissance project our men were on when they recused you, he would frequently would call upon your step-father and his small cadre to perform the task. That's how you and Samuel were rescued." Abruptly Julia stopped, and pointed to the large, white wooden building that had some of the architectural features of General Schuyler's mansion, situated on plot of land twice the size of General Schuyler's. "You see that building?" asked Julia. "That's Albany's military hospital. It's the same hospital where General Burgoyne visited his nemesis, General Benedict Arnold. Gentleman Johnnie Burgoyne used to call General Arnold his *real conqueror,* not General Gates to whom he had surrender his sword at Saratoga. Both the victor and the vanquished entertained great professional respect for each other, and spent about half-day together. Initially, General Schuyler was present for the first part of the time, but left the pair together while he went off to attend to private business.

"I understand that Burgoyne and Arnold talked at length about the technical aspects of the battle they fought against each other in the Saratoga area. In their privacy of Arnold's hospital room, they admitted that they had been the primary principals in the action at Saratoga, while the American General Horatio Gates had played a minor role, and yet he received all the credit for the American victory. Besides General Gates's incompetency, Burgoyne and Arnold discussed the European versa American methods of warfare, and finally wound up finding agreement on what Burgoyne called "the philosophy of war and the necessity for its avoidance."

The entrance to the hospital building was a stark difference to General Schuyler's manicured grounds, and the mansion's circular drive with its stately maples planted along the wagon path as it approached the mansion's front porch, which continued its semi-circle back to Albany's main street. Rather, the hospital's main entrance looked more like an aristocrat's front porch, which was just wide enough to allow sitting chairs room between the building's outside wall, and the edge of the porch.

"In comparison to General Schuyler's mansion, this building looks naked, and rather shabby with that smaller building built with rough logs," declared Marie as she wrinkled-up her nose.

"But first, Marie, you must remember that the building which we call the hospital is relatively new since the war started. Before the war in our Mohawk Valley, the isolation of the valley's settlements and farms prevented most of the serious illness from spreading. In addition, the valley's extremely severe cold winters, also helped to thwart many of the contagious diseases. And then came the war. When soldiers from all of the thirteen states, as well as those from the British Empire and their hired Hessians met in great clusters and camps, it was then that infectious disease went on rampages throughout American and British army camps. Many of these soldiers were under the age of twenty and were more receptive to many of these diseases common to the young, and were fair game to most of

STEPS TOWARD FREEDOM

the contagious diseases. Those soldiers who were over thirty years of age, usually were able to withstand most of these diseases, due to the immunity they had acquired from previous contacts. Initially, the hospital and the assigned physicians there were able to render little consolation to the ill soldier, because the physicians' knowledge of various diseases was very limited. They knew little or nothing about bacteria and viruses. When physicians ever discovered a formation pus in a wound, their sterilization techniques were primitive indeed. And because the method of how the disease was spread was almost impossible to diagnosis and cure. I must say that our hospitals and doctors have much to learn and implement, but," qualified Julia, "our practice of medicine has vastly improved even since the start of the war, thanks to the doctors who give tireless hours and care in military hospitals such as this one."

Julia dismissed the subject, and returned to Marie's initial question. "As far as that loosely constructed log arrangement is concerned, it's rather easy to explain the purpose of that type of *building*. During the early stages of the war, most of the hospital became a "catch-all" for various kinds of disease. Frequently lying heel to head, desperately ill patients were stuffed into small rooms. As a result, they shared each others' germs with the damp and dirty clothing, and waited out their misery on unchanged straw. Fortunate was the soldier, who could leave the hospital alive, and free of some new malady. By 1777, the large overcrowded general hospital was replaced by a host of smaller loosely constructed log buildings. Even though these buildings do not look attractive, they served their purpose. The loose structure provided free circulation of air, and the series of isolated units prevented man-to-man infection. Not surprisingly, as soon as the patients received explanation of the building's structure, they cheerfully accepted their cold room and the dirt floor. Incidentally, the typhus-carrying lice could no longer spread the dreaded jail fever and ague......"

"I've heard about some really queer names, such as *jail fever* and *ague;* what are they?" asked Marie.

"I must admit they do sound rather unusual. Jail fever is sometimes called hospital fever, or putrid fever; it is a progressive fever, rose-colored spots on chest and abdomen, delirium and coma. It is believed to be spread by fly excrement on food, clothing. bedding. In fact, typhus has similar signs, but with a generalized petechial or hemorrhagic rash, perhaps spread by the body louse. As far as ague is concerned, the patient usually has chills, with intermittently spiking fever finally ending with profuse sweating probably spread by mosquito bites, then entering the patient's red blood cells. Scurvy is another disease you should be familiar with. Doctors have discovered that scurvy responds almost promptly with a health diet of fresh greens and ripe fruit, preferably, citrus fruit," Julia took a deep breath, and continued enthusiastically. "Gradually, cleanliness has became an accepted, and required treatment for all patients. For example, when a patient dies or is discharged, the bedding is washed and aired, and the straw burned. By just performing these few sanitary precautions, as a result diarrhea caused by typhoid-contaminated bedding and clothes has become less frequent. Recovery from fevers was facilitated and dysenteries were minimized, when the patients were moved away from the cold walls, less crowding meant fewer coughs, and sneezes to spread "pleurisy" (pneumonia)."

Marie was captivated with Julia's knowledge about this hospital, asked "How did you learn so much about this hospital? I must admit that you have made this morning interesting. Oh! by the way," Marie said in amazement, "I've just noticed that that small building does not have any chimneys. How do they heat that building?"

"You're very observant my dear," appreciated Julia. "Well, the medical and nursing staff keep experimenting with improvements of the hospital. Eventually, they discovered that the facility is best served to have open fires, without chimneys. The smoke is allowed to escape through those spaces between the logs, and on the ridge of the roof. The staff believed that the "free smoke" in the room could purify the "putrid" air. Additionally, twice a week sulfur, pitch, tar or gunpowder is burned in the hope of ridding the air of germs. Incidentally, by this time, the military recommended "more realistic" staffing with one surgeon and five surgery mates for every one thousand patients. That's a vast increase from the original staffing of four surgeons and twenty surgery mates for every 20,000 patients."

"I hope I haven't bored you, Marie," Julia said apologetically, "as you can probably guess, I'm very proud of this hospital, and equally proud of the care it and the doctors give to it's patients. Once you're in the building with all of its doctors and staff, it literally radiates warmth and caring," proclaimed Julia as the two women walked up the steep, narrow wooden log steps toward the building's main door.

As they approached the hospital's front door, they were greeted by a imposing looking middle-aged woman who looked like a drill sergeant with her blonde hair pulled back in a bun on the top of her head; what made her so attractive was her smile which would melt butter on a cold plate. "Mrs. Riedesel, I'd like to introduce you to my new step-daughter, Marie." Looking directly at Marie, Julia said, "Mrs. Riedesel is the director of all the hospital volunteers." Casting her attention back toward the director of volunteers, Julia continued, "Marie has heard me say so many interesting things about the hospital, so she made up her mind to come along with me, and examine for herself what the hospital is all about."

"I'm delighted to meet you, Marie," Mrs. Riedesel said as she silently, but rather thoroughly examined, and questioned to herself why would a lady so reserved as Mrs Jefferson want to adopt a teenager as beautiful as this one, she asked, "Are you from around here, Marie?"

"Marie, is from a town called Minisink, where she was a slave along with her brother, Samuel. Our son, Benjamin and his blood-brother Walter, rescued both of them, and General Schuyler is helping George and me to adopt them."

"Its a pleasure meeting you, Marie," Mrs. Riedesel said rather hurriedly. "Oh!, by the way, Julia, Dr. McDuff was asking about you. He remembered that today was your day in the hospital, and I understand he had scheduled something for the two you to do. Incidentally, Marie, while we're talking about assignments, I think I may have some patients in the rehabilitation area where you could be of great help. The patients in the rehabilitation ward are in all sort of stages. Some will never be released, they are just waiting to die of one thing or another. Some patients have finished the initial recovery from surgery, and are in various phases convalescence. Those patients who have contacted small-pox are patient quarantined from the rest of the hospital. You see, Marie, until 1777 when small-pox vaccinations became routine in the Continental Army, smallpox could thin the ranks of the military quicker than bullets or even shrapnel from cannons." Mrs. Riedesel stopped incidentally, and stared directly at Marie, and asked "Have you been vaccinated for small-pox, Marie?"

"No, I haven't, Mrs. Riedesel," answered Marie.

"You must remind me, before you and Julia leave the hospital today, I'll see that you receive a small-pox shot. With this vaccination, you become immunized, and the chances of dying from pox are relatively small; say about one in four hundred. Prior to the vaccination, sixty out of hundred would surely lose their lives when this dread disease came into a setting. After the vaccinations began, that the old saying, *A pox on you!* no longer held that dreadful meaning it had during the pre-vaccination years."

As they approached the area referred to the rehabilitation ward, Marie observed, "I have noticed, Mrs. Riedesel, that the hospital appears to be relatively clean and orderly."

"I like your awareness and appreciation of orderliness and cleanliness, Marie," commented the hospital's director of volunteers. "I have been told that by Dr. Benjamin Rush, who observed, *Too much cannot be said in favor of cleanliness. If it were possible to convert every blade of grass on the continent into an American Soldier, the want of cleanliness would reduce them in two or three campaigns to a handful of men.* Dr. Rush recommended that the soldiers wash their hands and face at last once daily, and the whole body two or three times weekly. Frequent changes of clean linen, he said, were equally important."

As Mrs. Riedesel and Marie entered the rehabilitation area, which reassembled the small flat loosely log attachment to the main hospital, which Julia had called Marie's attention to as they approached the hospital from their home. "You'll notice that in this building we have open fireplaces without chimneys. The smoke escapes through those holes in the roof," calling Marie's attention to the holes in the rough. "You see, it is believed that the free smoke in the room helps to purify the room's air. Twice week we require sulfur, pitch, tar or gunpowder to be burned in this room. We think that process also helps to kill and help to rid the hospital of germs, and hopefully, these and other similar measures will assist in keeping other diseases from entering the hospital."

While Mrs. Riedesel had been explaining the mechanics of the ventilation system, an unusual musical sound came drifting through the room. The haunting tone mystified Marie. She asked Mrs. Riedesel, "What is that eerie sound I hear? It's rather weird, but the song is rather enchanting, and pleasing to hear."

"Oh! that's our enthusiastic, and always good natured Loyalist soldier. His parents were born in Scotland. They moved to Boston. He had always admired the English manner of life and fashion, but when the Rebels dumped the English tea into Boston's harbor, he didn't much approve. So, he up and packed his bagpipes, and he headed this way to join Butler's Rangers. He and some person, who claims to be the brother of General Nicholas Herkimer who led the Tryon County militia against Butler and Brant's forces at Oriskany. All of this may be true, and far as his story about his friend being the brother of General Herkimer," she hesitated, shock her head, and in a scornful manner continued, "all I can say is that we haven't seen not one hide nor tail of him." Grabbing a hold of Marie wrist, "Come along child, you may enjoy Mr. Alexander McKnight's company. Heaven knows ever since he's been in this ward, he has been the life of the party."

As Mrs. Riedesel and Marie walked toward the further corner of the barracks, the music became louder and louder, and then a singer started to sing a foreign sounding song, which Marie could not understand. Marie couldn't recognize the language; it sounded something like English, but Englishmen don't talk that way, she thought.

"Mr. McKnight, I'd like to introduce you to Julia Jefferson's foster daughter, Miss Marie Montgomery," said the volunteer director. "I thought that between you two, you could add some life and entertainment to help the patients feeling better, and hopefully, they will rehabilitate much faster."

"Miss Montgomery, I'm pleased to make your acquaintance, but please just call me *Sandy*," the ruddy faced, muscular man with a bagpipe strapped over his shoulder, said in his Scottish dialectic. He noticed Marie staring at his left leg, or what was left of it, "Please don't mind the absence of left leg. You see, I was on the receiving end of one of the Rebels' bloody cannon shots. Thank the Lord, that two of their bloody lot came by, and rescued me. Me left leg was so shattered, that old Dr. McDuff told me after I waked up, he'd have to cut it off or I'd be crippled all me life. But, you need not worry Miss Montgomery, what's remains of my left leg won't hurt you. Dr. McDuff has made sure that two of his surgery mates buried it so deep in the ground, that not even the wolves can find it. As far as the rest of me is concerned, as long I have me bagpipes, and Mrs. Riedesel allows me to occasionally play them, and sing along with me pipes, I'm a happy as a newborn lamb in the spring of the year." Suddenly, Sandy stopped talking just as if he had come to the end of a page of music, and changed the subject while Mrs. Riedesel enjoyed the enthusiasm in Sandy's voice and sparkle in his eyes. Sandy had almost always had a positive attitude, even when he was talking about the war between the Loyalists and Rebels. Today, he was different!

"Do you like music? Do you like to sing?" Sandy asked in his Americanized Scottish accent.

While Marie was considering Sandy's question, Mrs. Riedesel was anxiously waiting to hear her response. "Mr. Sandy, you must know that for most of my life, my brother and I've been slaves. We don't know where our parents are, who owns them, or even it they are alive. If it wasn't for Miss Julia and her sergeant husband, I don't know where my brother and I would be. Thank the Lord, the Jeffersons have taken us into their family as their foster children, and with General Philip Schuyler's help we have been emancipated. Then we'll have our freedom!" as her wide smile exhibited her pearl white teeth, "I suppose this is long way around the barn, to answer your initial question, whether I like music and to sing. There was one thing that our master and his family allowed us to do was to sing. Never with any fancy instrument like your bagpipes, but we have some homemade drums, and string instruments. But mostly, we sang spirituals in either the church choir or the congregation praised the Lord for whatever freedom we were allowed to have. If it wasn't for Sergeant and Mrs. Jefferson's son, Benjamin, my brother would probably be dead, because the Indians had scalped him, and I'd be a captive of the Indians."

"And I thought I had it *bad*!" declared Sandy as Mrs. Riedesel disappeared into the hallway.

* * *

"Julia, I'm delighted that you arrived, because I have another case just like the one we performed on Sandy McKnight," greeted a rather stout, middle aged man with a slightly bushy, brown mustache sprinkled with a few white whiskers, and a beaming smile that reached both of his eyes. He was dressed in a long gown with blood stains spattered all over, which probably was snow white he had first put the clock on. "The medics have brought in another soldier, this time he's one of our men, who had been struck with shrapnel similar to McKnight's leg. Since you helped me with that case, I told Mrs. Riedesel that I really preferred your assistance along with two of my regular surgical mates."

"I appreciate you holding the case until I arrived, but doctor, I don't know whether I can stand another one of these kind of cases," admitted Julia as she accepted a clean gown from Dr. McDuff, and followed him to the operating table where two surgical mates awaited them.

FOURTEEN

REUNION AND FREEDOM

Last Week in November, 1779
En Route to Heindrick's Farm in New Palatine

They had camped near Blood Creek, which had received its name just after the Battle of Oriskany, where Benjamin and Walter had occasionally camped overnight. Benjamin had decided not to explain to his ten-year old foster brother how, when or why the creek had received its name; he'd let him wait until he asked those questions. Their make-shift lean-to served them well during the evening. When they embarked from their sleeping bags, the ground was covered with a light coat of fresh snow. Benjamin and Samuel were not as lucky as he and Walter had been in catching fish for their evening meal. After brushing off the snow, and finding a few dry, dead branched, and leaves they were successfully started a small campfire, just large enough to warm the left-over coffee, and a batch of fatback fried and rolled in corn meal, plus their usual johnnie cake, which their mother had baked for their trip.

They were finally on their last leg of their trip to New Palatine, as the fog began to rise from the unfrozen batches of Bloody Creek creating a mystical aura over the well-trodden path. After watering their horses, they began traveling at a relatively steady gait for about an hour and a half, until they emerged from the narrow, shadowy, forest lane into bright clearing with wide open, frozen fields on both sides. The bright morning's sunshine beamed its warm rays on their backs as they slowed their pace to enjoy the pleasures of the panoramic pastoral scene, which was on display before them. To their left was a field covered with the remnants of burnt corn stalks, dissimilar to the traditional remains of a properly harvested field of corn. To their right, the road was bordered with a long row of post-and-rail fence disappearing into the far distance. This was place where Walter had one or twice proudly announced to Benjamin, "Now, my brother, this is the beginning of the settlement known as New Palatine. My hometown!"

The two Jefferson boys admired the rolling hills with a brook or two, maybe even three brooks meandering throughout them. As they rode further toward the frontier settlement, they saw a small flock of white-faced sheep grazing on dead grasses in a field slightly dusted with snow. Benjamin remembered the first time he had ridden this same route to New Palatine with his blood-brother; it had been earlier part of the year The fields were lush awaiting the farmers' harvesting. Now, things were different. Some fields showed evidence of destruction and burning. Animals were visibly fewer; perhaps others were under some form of shelter. In places, the snow helped to mask the obvious signs of devastation To Samuel the scene was totally unfamiliar to the urban environment he had been growing accustomed to while living with the Jeffersons in Albany. However, this scene was reminiscent of the Minisink he was raised in. To Benjamin, the township presented a haunting feeling; a feeling of death and destruction similar to what had seen as he traveled with Generals Sullivan and Clinton into the Indian country. He began to wonder what had happened to Walter and his family, to Helena and her mother, to the jolly Reverend Stouffer and his wife Redbird. It had been almost three months since he had received any communication from Walter. His imagination was beginning to run wild. Maybe the Heindrick's home had been burned; he quickly discounted that thought, because Walter's father was so proud that their new home was built of masonry, not like the one the *Indians* had burned down back in 1757. Maybe Helena's mother general store, which she now owned in partnership with her former assistant manager, Harvey Perry, had been ravaged. Maybe! Maybe! He'd have to wait until they arrived to the center of New Palatine.

Ten minutes later their slow canter brought them to a familiar site. It was George Raab's smithy-shop. Benjamin had been particularly interested in Herr Raab's shop and how he managed the blacksmith business had been how his father, George Jefferson, had obtained his trust and sponsorship to the livery business the Jeffersons shared with Herr Han Schuyler, General Philip Schuyler's brother, in Albany. As he and Samuel rode past the blacksmith shop, they saw a short, middle-aged muscular man pounding away on an anvil. Benjamin recognized the town's smithy, and reined in his horse.

"Good morning, Mr. Raab," Benjamin greeted this rugged man with his shirt opened exposing his dark hairy chest, and his shirt sleeves rolled up to his biceps even though the morning's temperature was hovering slightly above freezing. "Do you remember me?" asked Benjamin.

"Sure, I remember you, Benjamin," responded the smithy with his frosted breath coming from his nostrils, looking like a medieval magician, he placed the horseshoe he was working on the anvil, and quickly extended his hand to greet Benjamin. "You're Walter Heindrick's blood-brother." He stopped a moment, and began smiling exhibiting elation, "I understand that you and Walter are heroes rescuing two people from the attacking Indians at Minisink."

"I don't know about being heroes," Benjamin said modestly, "we were just doing our jobs. Right here with me is Samuel Montgomery, one of the persons we rescued. Now, Samuel is my foster brother, because his master and his entire family were killed at Minisink. Samuel and his sister, Marie, were fortunate that they were out in the fields when the Indians attacked."

STEPS TOWARD FREEDOM

"I'm pleased to meet you young man. I know you'll be in good hands with the Jeffersons. That remark you made, Benjamin, about you just doing your job, is about the same words Walter used when we asked him about the event in church a few weeks ago," acknowledged Herr Raab. "I suppose you've notice that we've had a few changes around here, especially those farms and fields just east of town. The Indians ended up their raids in Fort Dayton by attacking New Palatine," commented the hardy smithy with his belly-button nearly exposed, "but our militia beat them off before they got started our the village, and most of our farms."

He stopped an instant, wiped the perspiration from his brow, and said, "You, gentlemen, might find Walter Heindrick and his father down at Kerchner & Perry's General Store. About an hour ago, I saw both of them there. Of course, Walter was spending most of his time with Helena; they seem to be getting pretty serious."

"I guess we best get moving on down to the store," said Benjamin as he shook hands with the smithy, motions to Samuel, and they jumped astride their horses saying, "It was good seeing you again, Mr. Raab. You'll probably be seeing us on our way back to Albany."

"My pleasure, gentlemen." He waved to the departing pair, as they rode down the narrow, snow covered, and drifted main street of New Palatine.

As they approached a two-story, grey field stone building about the size of any house in Albany, they saw the weather-beaten, wooden sign, *Heidelberg Tavern,* hanging over its narrow, solidly built front door.

"That's the Heidelberg Tavern," Benjamin said as he pointed toward the familiar sign. "It's owned and operated by a lady named Martha Butler. Her husband, Jerome Butler, was New Palatine's second mayor. Eventually, he became one of the valley's key Tory informants. Martha Butler, who makes it very clear to anyone, who would listen that she was not related to that *damn Troy bastard, Colonel John Butler and his delinquent son Walter.* Her husband declared his loyalty to the King's Crown about the same time as his cousin Colonel John Butler, made his declaration. For a while, her husband spent much of his time with his cousin and Guy Johnson, while Martha devoted herself to working in the tavern, as well as helping the Tryon County Safety Committee in their quest for better representation in the Mohawk Valley. While her husband was away with Colonel John Butler's Rangers, frequently, Martha offered the militia members, who were drilling across from the tavern on the common, refreshments and *drinks on the house*. One day her husband left her to join-up with Colonel John and his Rangers, and never returned. Soon thereafter, she learned he had been killed while participating in an *Indian raid,* as they used to call them when the Tories dressed up to look like Indians.

"Over the months of war, Martha Butler, never wanted to be called Mrs. Butler; she preferred just plain *Martha*. She gained a considerable reputation throughout the valley for her overtures to those of the opposite gender, but never venturing *too far* according to her good friend Reverend Johan Stouffer. The preacher and she were pretty close friends. She was instrumental in having a church here in New Palatine. At the time, Stouffer was a Dutch Reformed circuit riding preacher; New Palatine was one of his parishes. There was no church here in New Palatine, so Martha allowed the preacher to use the Heidelberg Tavern until a church was constructed. That's the church!" Benjamin said to Samuel, as he proudly pointed across the main street and the village's common. "It took the church people nearly two years to complete the stone construction. Ever since the 1757 massacre, and the burnings of many of the settlement's wooden homes, including the Heindricks' home, people have been encouraged to use stone or some kind of masonry construction. Ever since the church has been finished, Reverend Stouffer and his wife, Red Bird, have lived in a small apartment in back of the church."

Benjamin had no sooner finished his last sentence, when he heard someone yelling his name. There in the middle of the road between the tavern and the general store, Benjamin saw Helena Kerchner come running toward him.

"Benjamin! Benjamin!, said yelled, her frosty breath flowing from her nostrils as she spoke. "After Walter had received your letter, he asked me to look for you. He thought you might arrive sometime today or tomorrow."

Benjamin reined up his horse, and jumped to the hard-packed snow main street; Samuel followed suit.

"Helena, this is my foster brother, Samuel Montgomery," Benjamin said to her as he proudly introduced him. "You've probably heard Walter tell you about the Montgomerys of Minisink."

"Yes, Benjamin." The auburn haired teen-aged beauty with few scattered freckles on her nose, and under her sky-blue eyes, smiled and said, "Walter has told me the story." She stopped, looked at Benjamin, then turned to her attention to the shorter youth standing between them, "Samuel, I'm mighty proud to make your acquaintance. I've heard many flattering stories about your bravery."

The embarrassed youth smiled, and said, "Thank you, Miss Helena, I've heard many nice things about you from Master Walter and Benjamin, too."

"My name is just plain Helena, Samuel," she said politely, yet firmly; as she led the young Jefferson men toward her mother and Mr. Perry's general store. "We'll be leaving very shortly for the Heindrick's home just as soon as I check in with my mother. I want you to meet my mother, Samuel, because she did something very brave also. Perhaps it was not quit as brave as what did, but nearly; she escaped from the Tories in Fort Niagara." Helena pushed in the front door of the store.

They were about to go through the store's front door, when a stout, rolly-polly man with a red, flushed face nearly ran into Helena,

"Helena," he said with a huge smile on his face, "I thought you had left for your home across the common."

"No, Mr. Perry," responded Helena ,she had not learned to call her mother's's partner by his first name, Harvey, "I just knew that Benjamin Jefferson was going to arrive sometime today, so I just went out front to see if he was there. You'll remember Benjamin from his last visit. This is his younger brother, Samuel."

"I'm really his foster brother, Mr. Perry," corrected Samuel. "But one day," he proudly continued, "I'm going to be his real brother."

Mr. Perry suggested that Helena and her guests come inside the store to warm up by the cast iron, pot-bellied stove. Around the stove they joined Helena's mother, Sarah, and Harvey's wife, Hazel. After a few introductions, Helena's mother offered a round of hot sweet apple cider, while Mr. Perry led the Jefferson's horses to the stalls behind the store for water and hay.

After nearly an hour of interesting conversation, Helen said with good humor, yet with a sense of urgency, "I hate to be a spoiler of good times, but if we expect to arrive at the Heindricks' before dark, we had better leave very soon."

Within less than half an hour, the three young friends had mounted their horses, and were headed westward toward the setting sun and the Heindricks.

* * *

It was a joyous reunion for the Heindricks and Benjamin, and a pleasure for the Heindrick parents to make their acquaintance with Benjamin's foster brother.

"We've heard a lot about you, Samuel," said Walter's father Karl. "Walter has told his mother, Rebecca, and I all about your encounter with the Indians at Minisink, and how you helped Sergeant Jefferson and his cadre to locate where your sister was being held captive. Then, Walter told us about how you and your sister, Marie, accompanied Generals Sullivan and Clinton on their campaign throughout the Indian country."

Good conversation along with Rebecca's special maple/hickory nut cookies and hot, sweet cider helped to create a most joyous reunion and get-acquainted occasion for Helena, the Jeffersons, and the Heindricks. As Rebecca and Helena were attentively refreshing the cups of cider and the plate of cookies, Rebecca saw Benjamin try to hide a yawn while Walter was enthusiastically talking about visiting White Tail's Aunt Mary. Rebecca noticed that Benjamin was unsuccessful in trying to cover up his weariness.

"Gentlemen and lady, I hate to be a kill-joy," the lady of the house announced, "but if I'm not mistaken all of us were up soon after sunrise this morning. For one thing, that means that us oldsters, Karl and I rather tired, and secondly, if you youngsters expect to make it to Oriska tomorrow, have time to visit with Aunt Mary, and return back here by sundown, I recommend that we all get to bed fairly shortly."

"Oh! Mother," objected Walter, "Benjamin and Samuel arrived only a short time ago."

"You'll," started Helena, hesitated to correct herself, "we'll have plenty time to catch up on all the news on our ride to Oriska. Don't forget that Aunt Mary is just as dear to me, as she is to you and Benjamin. I'm planning on leaving right after sunrise, and if you boys want to come along with me, you're invited."

"Sounds like Helena is the leader of the pack on this trip, guys," jested the sleepy-eyed father Karl, as he followed his wife to their bedroom, leaving the four young people huddled around the huge fireplace.

The last of the burning logs snapped and popped requesting its audience to throw another log on the fire to tide the house over the long, cold, wintery night. Taking heed of the low burning embers, Walter retrieved a couple of logs from the wood-box along the side of the fireplace, and carefully placed the logs so as not to send sparks up the chimney. "There, Mr. Fire," said Walter staring at the slow burning, seasoned logs, "keep us warm during the evening. Come morning, we'll give you another log or two so mother and Helena can prepare us some breakfast."

After finishing their last minute preparations for the trip to Oriska, each of the young people adjourned to their assigned sleeping quarters. Walter had decided that he was going to sleep on the big, bear rugs in front of the fireplace, and the Jefferson boys could use his bedroom. Meanwhile, Helena knew her assigned sleeping quarters was in the guest bedroom, which she frequently used, whenever Rebecca would call upon her to assist in the manufacture of her famous Mohawk Valley Limburger cheese.

Alone on the bear rugs, Walter thanked God for his wonderful extended family, and prayed that their Aunt Mary was alive and well.

* * *

After a hearty breakfast of smoked ham, steaming hot johnnie cake topped with warm maple syrup, baked apple stuffed with maple sugar and dried currents, and stout coffee, the four young friends were astride their horses, while Karl assisted his wife in cleaning up the kitchen. The quartet of friends and blood-brothers, Samuel being the only one in the group who had not participated in the Indian ritual of becoming blood-brothers, headed down the narrow lane lined with dormant maple trees, waiting for Spring to come, and leading the young friends to the renown King's Highway. At the junction of the farm lane, and the main artery leading toward Wood Creek, Oriska, Fort Stanwix and beyond, they turned right with a light dusting of snow coming from the west. They set a moderate gait, careful to avoid the deep wagon ruts, and the occasional woodchuck holes those sleeping critters had dug long before the winter had set in. Walter and Benjamin led the way exchanging few words, while Samuel and Helena riding along behind, talked about their family backgrounds.

After about two hours of riding, Walter said, "On and off here, we've been riding along Wood Creek. I suggest that we pick a good spot where we can water the horses, and sample whatever Helena and my mother have packed for us to eat. After the rest and refreshments, I think we should pick up our pace if we hope to arrive at Oriska by noon, which should give us at least two hours with Aunt Mary before we need to return. How does that sound?"

Walter spotted an inviting, open area near the creek, and pulled up his horse's reins. Obviously, Walter had made up his mind, for the others knew that he and his father had traveled this route many times. After pulling up their horses' reins, the quartet led their horses to an area in the creek which was not frozen. Sitting on two fallen logs, they examined the contents found in their knapsack, including more maple/hickory nut cookies, dried apples, johnnie cake, and as expected some of Karl's's famous Tryon County Cheddar Cheese.

"I don't see any of your mother's Limburger cheese," observed Benjamin.

"We debated whether we should place some of that cheese in the package," stated Helena. "Finally, we decided, that such a strange aroma would not be appropriate while visiting Aunt Mary," she finished smiling. "You must admit," she continued, "it has a smooth, creamy taste, The smell is just an added characteristic of the cheese to assure the gourmets they're eating the genuine cheese from the Mohawk Valley."

Walter, I've heard you mention something about a *carrying place* in the creeks," stated Samuel. "I've never heard of such a place."

"As you have probably noticed, Samuel, on our ride from Albany, there is considerable amount of river traffic, but there are no bridges crossing from either side of the river. The bateaux men polling their clumsy sharp-ended boats through the many rifts and shoals as far as Fort Hunter. When the water becomes too shallow or too rocky, and they can go no further, the bateaux men literally carry the bateaux and its goods they're transporting over the connecting strip of dry, or relatively dry land, from either the Mohawk River to Wood Creek depending upon which direction the vessel is going or coming from. This connecting strip of land is what is called the *carrying place;* these strips of land are strategically portioned along the river. These bateaux men have to be rugged individuals to be able to drag those heavy boats, and their loads over the place. Some day, I'll betcha they'll build a canal along this valley, so we can go right through from Albany to Oswego without going over these carrying places," predicted Walter.

* * *

They continued riding at a moderate gait. The meandering narrow lane bordered by hemlock trees weeping under the weight of the previous night's snow fall, helped to create a winter wonderland with towering pine and spruce trees stretching their stately arms toward the noonday sun peeking through their branches to admire nature's handiwork. Meanwhile, the mighty oak and hickory nut tree's stood stark naked waiting for their spring coming out time. Constantly, the magic of their surroundings reverently captivated the young people giving them the feeling of being in a beautiful cathedral, and completely mesmerized by their companionship and surroundings. To them, they were immersed with Mother Nature, and all of her grandeur. As they approached a deep, semi-circular ravine, thickly covered with trees and heavy underbrush, leading down into a low, swampy area, Walter broke the reverent silence.

"Don't go down that road, that's the where General Herkimer led his relief force to its ambush. We turn off here on the left." He slowed his horse to a walk, passed through a area of low bushes, which eventually opened into a narrow path leading them into the forest's deep thicket.

"Where are you leading us?" asked Benjamin.

"This trail leads us to the Oneida Indian settlement of Oriska, where Aunt Mary lives," stated Walter. "The Oneidas purposely have kept this route to their village obscure, hoping it would not attract visitors. Be careful of these low overhanging branches, or you'll receive some sudden whacks across your face. This trail was not designed for horses, just Indian runners," added Walter.

The trail led the young ventures through a howling wilderness. After they had traveled nearly two miles dodging branches and fallen trees, crossing a few small brooks, wading through some swampy land, they finally came to open fields covered with charred corn stalks, and loaded with unpicked cobs of corn which were twisted in total disarray. Scattered throughout the devastated fields were roasted and busted squash and pumpkins intermingled with the charred corn and remnants of other destroyed vegetables. The four young people were astounded to see such devastation, thus confirming what they had heard about the Seneca's attack on Oriska.

"I remember when White Tail and Aunt Mary told us that the Indians had been farming these lands long before the white man arrived," said Helena. "Just look at that orchard! All the trees are chopped down with frozen apples and pears still clinging to the branches. I remember seeing them full of blossoms during the spring and loaded with fruit in the fall."

They slid down from their saddles and walked the horses into what remained of the village. The haunting site reminded them of a graveyard without tombstones. As they walked past the remains of the Oneida's council house, Walter remembered the day when White Tail had led Helena and himself through the eight-foot long, eleven-foot wide building's six-foot common passage. It still had some of the tribe's five-foot high apartments on either side. Helena and Walter would always remember the friends they had met in the council house, but that was yesterday! Now only some of the charred remains of the building's main frame still stood void of human life with only squirrels and field rats scurrying about storing roasted corn cobs for the approaching winter. A short distance from the council house, they observed that Aunt Mary's little cabin still stood as they remembered it.

"That's amazing," said Walter, "that Aunt Mary's cabin appears untouched."

"I wonder how that happened," mused Helena.

Before anyone could respond to Helena's comment, they saw a little old lady emerge from the log cabin with both of her arms raised high above her head as she tottered toward Walter and Helena. "I knew you'd come! I just knew that you two would come, and see me after you had heard about the Seneca's attack on our village."

"Aunt Mary!" yelled Helena as she quickly handed her horse's reins to Walter, and raced toward the frail, thin lady with bronze, leathery skin. Oblivious to their surroundings, the two friends embraced, enjoying the pleasure of each other's presence and sense of love and respect for each other. After tethering their horses, Walter, Benjamin and Samuel joined the devoted pair. Startled, Aunt Mary abruptly broke her embrace with Helena, and stared inquisitively at the young, muscular ebony-skinned youth who was slightly taller than Walter, and the other young boy with a turban-like fur hat on his head walking with Walter toward her.

After giving Aunt Mary his usual bear hug, recognizing her anxiety, Walter announced, "Aunt Mary, this is my blood-brother Benjamin Jefferson of Albany with whom I served in the militia fighting General Burgoyne at Saratoga. This young man," pointing toward Samuel, "is Benjamin's foster brother, Samuel, who we rescued from attack on his home."

Sensing the weather-beaten lady's apprehension, Benjamin and Samuel offered their hands in greeting her.

She politely brushed her hand with theirs and said, "I'm pleased to meet you young men. Any friend of Helena and Walter's is a friend of mine."

"I, too, am pleased to meet you," responded Benjamin, "Helena and Walter have told me so many stories about you, that I feel I've known you for years."

Silently and appreciatively, Samuel was absorbed in seeing the obvious love and respect between Aunt Mary and his friends.

"Aunt Mary," said Helena, "Walter's mother and I packed a special food package for you. We, also, packed a picnic lunch for all five of us."

"Why don't we all come over to my cabin; there I can quickly stir up the campfire for some hot tea," suggested the *white lady* who had been captured as a young, teen-aged girl years ago during a Seneca raiding party in Pennsylvania, and eventually, traded to the Oneidas.

As the young people followed their petite hostess, Helena thought to herself how much Aunt Mary had aged since she had last seen her in the spring. The last raid on Oriska by the Senecas must have torn at the lady's heart, knowing that her surrogate son, Chief Joseph Brant, may have ordered the raid. While Helena and Aunt Mary were preparing the picnic, Walter, Benjamin, and, Samuel walked about the once thriving Indian settlement. They were totally astounded at the degree of destruction. Virtually every building, except Aunt Mary's cabin, was either completely burnt to the ground, or so devastated so they were inhabitable as the charred skeletal remains of a corn crib stood in the fields of destroyed crops, with no sign of man or livestock remaining.

As they walked back toward Aunt Mary's cabin, Walter remarked to Benjamin, "I assume that this is only one enormous result of the battle of Oriskany."

"What do you mean?" asked Benjamin, as Samuel listened intently to his friends' discussion.

"As I understand the situation, started Walter, "the Senecas were mad as hell at the Oneidas, because about 60 of them from Oriska, under the command of Thawengarakwen, known by the whites as *Honyery Doxtater,* joined Herkimer's four companies of militia for the Oriskany battle. Thawengarakwen must have been a real different kind of Indian. He had a sword hanging by his side as a symbol of his rank. His wife was also along with him, and like her husband, carried a gun. Two other prominent Oneida warriors, Blatcop and Henry Cornelius gave Herkimer's troops great service during the battle. Another Oneida volunteer was Thomas Spencer, a blacksmith, the son of an Oneida woman and Elihu Spencer, a Presbyterian missionary, served as a runner and a scout on the British and Loyalist troop movements.

"I understand that Blacksnake, another Oneida fighting against the British, later said, 'there [at Oriskany] I have seen the most Dead Bodies all.... over that I never Did see, and never will again. I thought at that time the Blood Shed [was] a Stream Running down on the Descending ground during the afternoon, and yet some living crying for help. But have no mercy.... for them'"

Walter continued his story, "Blatcop, the fierce Oneida warrior fighting for the Americans, rushed three times through the field of conflict swinging to right and left with his tomahawk. Many of his red brothers, who had enlisted for the British, felt his fury that day. Honyery Doxtater was wounded in the right wrist. In addition to putting her own weapon to good use, his wife continued to load his gun for him.

"The enormity of the Oriskany conflict between these Iroquois tribes marked the beginning of a civil war between the Confederacy. As I understand it, the British Indian allies, primarily the Senecas, were so resentful against the Oneidas, that they invaded and destroyed this settlement. Again, for some strange reason, they did not destroy Aunt Mary's cabin."

"We'll have to ask her how that happened," suggested Benjamin as they approached the campfire with its tiny, smoke-laden pot hanging over the flame.

By the time the young men returned, Aunt Mary and Helena had the picnic food lying out on top of a deerskin rug.

"Becoming over-ridden by an army of ants, is one thing we don't have to worry about this time of the year," said Walter as he tired to be funny about such a catastrophic site as, Benjamin, and Samuel had just examined.

"Aunt Mary," asked Walter as he attempted to converse more seriously about the devastated Indian settlement, "while we were walking around this entire village of Oriska, we did not see a single longhouse, shed, or any other building that was not either completely burned to the ground, or chopped up like fire wood, except your cabin. How do you explain that happening? Oh, yes!" he corrected himself, "we did see the remains of a corn crib, loaded with charred corn."

"Walter, you must know Joseph Brant as I do," responded Aunt Mary. "I've told you that he treats me as his surrogate mother, and he promised never to let any harm come to me. So far, he has kept his word, even though it was not always easy for him. I've heard him talking to many of his hot-headed warriors, who would not stop at murdering, butchering, and scalping anyone in their way, But, not Joseph," she said fondly. "I remember Joseph telling me about their attacks on Andrewston and Springfield. He had ordered two old men turned loose. After they were released, he told the men to go to their homes, and tell everyone there that German Flats was going to be their next target. As you know the Indians did burn and destroy those white settlements, but it was not until after the attacks did anyone find out that Joseph himself had saved the women and children of Springfield from captivity or death at the hands of his warriors. It was common knowledge among Joseph's Loyalists friends at Fort Niagara and in Canada, that Joseph's policy was not to harm women and children. Certainly, I fit into that grouping, but he honestly loves me, and he has always kept his promises to me."

"I've heard stories about him at Harpersfield, a small almost deserted settlement near the head water of the Delaware, or what remained of it after it was burned," said Walter. "As I understand the circumstances, a party of eleven or twelve Rebel soldiers, making maple sugar, were unexpectedly surprised and captured; three were killed and the other men captured and collected into a pig pen. The Indians debated what to do with them. One of the captive Rebels, Freegift Patchin, who had escaped, said that Brant was for saving their lives; most of the Indians and the Loyalists, on the other hand, wanted to put them to death, but Brant prevailed. The next day, the prisoners were informed that they were going to Fort Niagara, and that they would have to keep up with their captors or they would be killed. From Harpersfield, I believe Brant and his band went to a place called Vroman's Land, where they destroyed 20 houses and captured of killed 12 men, while releasing 7 women and children.

"I also heard that Colonel Guy Johnson told another story about Brant's attacks on Canajoharie and Fort Plank," continued Walter. "some of his warriors, who were over eager to take captives, scattered too soon and alarmed the settlement of Canajoharie, allowing most of its inhabitants to escape to Fort Plank. Afterwards, the attackers had to be content with burning all the houses in the vicinity, about 100 in number, two smaller forts, two mills, and the settlement's only church. From what I have heard, the church, not being an Anglican church, Joseph may have been able to reason it was not really a church, so he ordered it destroyed as well as the settlement's grain, and ran off its cattle. According to Colonel Guy Johnson, they killed 27 persons and took 40 prisoners, releasing some women and children. I also heard Joseph might have released some of the women and children, but small Indian raiding parties were all over the settlement, entirely on their own, and ended up killing whoever they pleased."

"I guess from what I heard," observed Benjamin, "that regardless of Brant's philosophy in the heat of battle, he may have not been able to control all of his warriors."

"What do you plan to do the rest of this winter, Aunt Mary?" asked Helena trying to change the subject. "You can't stay here," she declared as she surveyed the settlement's desolate condition. "My mother and I would love to have you come and stay with us."

"I truly appreciate you and your mother's offering, but Oriska has been home for so long. I know that Joseph will return to care for me, just as my first husband, Maple Leaf and White Tail's older brother. Maple Leaf was a wonderful and caring husband, and we had a happy and joyous life together. As you know, the Iroquois custom is to leave the longhouse, and to live separately until one remarries. I chose not to remarry," Aunt Mary stated emphatically. "You see, until this senseless attack upon Oriska, I had become *Aunt Mary* to all of the children of our village, including Joseph.

"As you know among the Iroquois, the taking of captives to assuage the loss of kin is an accepted reason for warfare. Our female elders decide whether the men should go to war. If a wife or mother, who had lost a son, husband, or daughter in war, can choose a captive man or woman to adopt into her family. In my case, I was a Seneca adoptee, taken to replace a male in a clan. Because I could not perform the social role of a male, I was traded to the Oneidas to perform women's task, because of a lost daughter.

"Even though I was born of white parents, the only white people I've become acquainted with are you and Walter," said Aunt Mary as she poured out her heart to Helena. Since I was about twelve, I've lived, loved, and worked with Indians of the Iroquois nation. I'm no longer a *white* person. I'm an Indian person, and I feel very much at peace with myself, even though I know that us Indians are probably doomed to extinction by the whites. I have no regards, for I have found my *freedom*! I'm at peace with our Great Spirit, because I know He and my Joseph will always watch over me. Most importantly," she continued, "I know that my Joseph will see his dream come true to establish a great Indian confederacy extending from Detroit to Montreal. He envisioned it independent, but still united in an alliance with the English. From village to village throughout the length and breadth of the Iroquois Nation, including the hostile Oneida and their village of Oriska. He was not too concerned about the Oneidas, because he possessed some influence over them through his marriage into the tribe. Joseph visualized all the Indian nation's citizens having the *freedom* to travel freely and safely from one village to another. And, in cooperation, if one village was attacked by another village, the nation's common council would arbitrate the differences. If attacked by an outside force, all of the nation's villages would consider it an attack upon the entire nation. I know that Joseph truly believed in this concept, and he excited Indians of every tribe about the idea."

She closed her eyes, turned her face to the heavens and mumbled some words the four youths did not understand. To break the solemnness of the conversation, Helena reached for the metal pot to serve the balance of the tea. Their conversation jumped from one subject to another, always directed to help Aunt Mary to weather her way through the severe upstate New York winters.

As he watched the sun begin to retreat behind the mountains to the west, Benjamin innocently asked Walter, "How long is it going to take us to return to your home?"

Aroused from her deep conversation with Aunt Mary, Helena looked up and saw the winter's sun slowing disappearing. She stood and hugged Aunt Mary, who cling to her as a young child would to its mother. After Walter, Benjamin and Samuel hugged the gallant white Indian lady, the quartet started to retrace their lonesome trail back to the Heindrick's farm, and their freedom..

They did not see the tears welling-up in Aunt Mary's light blue eyes, as she retreated to her cabin to await the arrival of *her* Joseph and their Great Spirit.

FIFTEEN

TO EACH THEIR OWN!

Last Week of November, 1779
On the King's Highway Returning from Visit at Oriska

On their return back to the Heindrick's farm, the four youths rode in a state of isolated silence and meditating about their visit with White Tail's Aunt Mary whose parting words kept ringing in their ears; creating a thoroughly different impression upon each other's mind. There was, however, one phrase which Aunt Mary had uttered, which each shared in their reflection; *I have no regrets, for I have found my freedom! I'm at peace with our Great Spirit, because I know that He and my Joseph (Brant) will always watch over me.*

The compassionate and perceptive Helena could understand, perhaps more than her male companions. Helena's father, Wilhelm, had dared to follow the lead of a different drummer, demanding that his reluctant wife, Sarah, and daughter follow him to Fort Niagara. He had chosen to join the Loyalist forces, and fight against his many neighbors who had decided to defy the British Royalty. To this end, his own faithful store manager, Harvey Perry, ended up killing him during the horrific and brutal battle at Oriskany. As sad as this entire saga was, Helena managed escaping the restrictions of her father, and the confines of the British Loyalist forces. Helena reasoned, that perhaps in his grave her father had finally found his *freedom!* Freedom from the crazies, who did not respect the monarchy, which so loved and respected. Freedom to do, and say what he believed. Freedom to die for a cause he believed in. "God bless my father's soul," said Helena to her horse as it narrowly lead her beneath a low hanging hemlock branch burdened with the previous day's heavy snow fall.

Along Helena's side, Walter had his own reflections starting from the time when he and his father, Karl, were traveling west in their buckboard wagon the King's Highway to visit one of their cousins, Herman Heindrick, who had been dispatched to Fort Stanwix with the Continental Army. They had been riding at slow trot when suddenly they heard a human voice faintly calling for help as they rode along side of the winding Wood Creek. Initially, they had decided to travel in the buckboard just in case they happened upon any signs of a buck deer. All thoughts of hunting deer were obviously interrupted with the frantic cry for help. After they had reined up their horse, they quickly searched out the source of the wail. During the late fall or winter, Wood Creek always had a reputation of being rather treacherous with its slippery rocks, and its partially frozen water, which was rushing toward its ultimate destination, the Hudson River and the Atlantic Ocean. As father and son carefully picked their way across the narrow stream, again, they heard the panic sound. This time it sounded like someone desperately to stay alive. After they had determined the direction from which the sound was coming, they cautiously made their way along the creek. Sometimes slipping in the creek, nevertheless, following the urgent cry for help.

The sound grew fainter, becoming a mire gurgle, then a faint whimper as if the individual was gasping for breath. Pushing through the brush, Karl and Walter judiciously maneuvered themselves over, around boulders, slipping, sliding, falling, and bruising themselves until Walter called to his father that he had found an Indian lad who appeared to be almost drowned. By the time, they reached the side of the Indian lad, Walter and his father were drenched with the rigid creek water. Their cold, however, did not concern them, their main objective was to remove the Indian lad from his icy prison. Walter father's told him that the Indian lad was still breathing, but his foot was caught beneath a boulder. Walter placed his hands under the lad's armpits, while his father tried to wrestle the boulder away from the youth's foot. Suddenly, the boulder moved sufficiently to allow Walter to try to pull the wounded Indian toward the shore, but his sudden move caused him to slip and fall giving himself and the Indian another dunking in the icy water. The sudden shock must have been just what the Indian needed. He opened his eyes, and stared at Walter and his father. After carrying him to small flat area along side of the creek, they laid the youth, who was about the same age as Walter, on a blanket of soft, damp moss.

Walter's father suggested that he retrieve the jug of home brew from the wagon. While Walter was busy shagging the brew, his father took time to examine and diagnosis the degree of the Indian lad's injury. "I believe that the Indian," Karl told his son as he returned with the jug of home brew, "has a clean fractured leg bone just above the ankle. If you will hustle and try to find two sticks suitable for crutches, I'll try to set his broken bone. Before you go, we'll give the lad a couple of swallows from the jug. Taking the jug from Walter, Karl tipped the jug to the Indian's lips as Walter lifted up the warrior's head. Instinctively, the lad sipped the brew, swallowed, flinched, and then relaxed in Walter's arm. After Karl and Walter finished their tasks, through the use of English language, some German, and Mohawk, they tried to explain to the youth how they found him, and why he was burdened with a splint and crutches.

"Who are you?" Walter asked. "Where do you come from?"

"We'd like to take you to your home," added Karl.

"I am White Tail, nephew of Chief Joseph Brant," the youth answered, surprising them with his capacity to speak reasonably fluent English.

As the three exchanged information about one another, Karl and Walter learned that White Tail was about the same age as Walter, and that he lived with his Uncle Joseph on Brant's property near General

Herkimer's home. With his rescuers' assistance, White Tail managed the crutches well enough to make it to the buckboard, where he placed himself on the buckboard's tailgate. Walter sat next to White Tail, while Karl reined-in the horse and headed the wagon toward the Brant property. They did not reach Brant's home until after dark. There they met one of White Tail's aunt, Susanna, who was a half-sister of Brant's first wife, Peggie. It was this time, they also met White Tail's other aunt, Mary, who eventually moved to the Oneida Indian village of Oriska through some form of tribal negotiations.

Walter was just beginning to recall how White Tail had, unknowingly, sacrificed his life for Walter; when Benjamin awaken him from his reverie, suggesting to the riders that they stop at their *usual* campsite to water the horses, and finish off any scraps of food they had left.

Benjamin, too, had been recalling his experience ever since he and his father, George Jefferson, had renewed their long overdue relationship with George's blood-brother, Karl Heindrick. Since that time, Benjamin, as well as Helena Kerchner, had become blood-brothers and sisters even though Walter and Helena lived in New Palatine, and the Jefferson's lived in Albany where George was a partner with General Philip Schuyler's brother, Hans, in a couple of smithy shops and stables. George had been recruited by General Philip Schuyler for special duty with General Benedict Arnold, which had required him to journey to Oriskany, just east of Fort Stanwix. George had arrived at the scene of the battle just as the Rebel forces were preparing to bring their wounded back toward Fort Dayton. It was then when George Jefferson first had seen his white blood-brother, Karl Heindrick, lying wounded in a make-shift stretcher. As soon as they recognized each other, thanks to Karl's wife Rebecca, their minds flashed back to when they were each about ten years old, and George's mother, Georgia Franklin, had served Karl's father, Ulrich Heindrick, as the wet-nurse for both of the baby boys, Karl and George. Ever since then the Jefferson and Heindrick families had developed into treasured relationship. While Walter had served as General Herkimer's drummer at Oriskany, he was joined by Benjamin Jefferson and his fife to serve General Arnold in the aftermath of Oriskany, and during the Saratoga campaign against Britain's military genius, Gentleman Johnnie Burgoyne. Eventually serving General Sullivan and Clinton in Washington's designed sweep of the Iroquois country. It was during this sweep, that the two blood-brothers rescued Samuel and Marie Montgomery.

"This location along the creek brings back many fond memories we've had here together," Benjamin said to Walter. I remember when we'd go skinny-dipping in the creek just cool ourselves off while we watered our horses."

"And of course, when your father asked us go after some kind of meat for our nightly meal," Walter said with a smile.

"I, especially, liked the times when we awaked in the morning totally covered with snow," added Benjamin, "and either your father or my father hassled us out of our bed-rolls to eat breakfast, and on to which ever way they chose to lead us and our horses."

"Oh! You men," started Helena, "you make yourselves sound so worldly; I'll bet you that Samuel can tell you some tall-tales himself."

Samuel blushed, and pushed up his woolen stocking hat, which matched the kinds the others were wearing, so his eyes shown like pearls in the evening. As a former slave, Samuel had many experiences which he'd rather forget. After some serious thought, Samuel said, "One of the happiest days I had ever had," he stopped quickly, and started over again. "One of the happiest days I ever had is when Walter and Benjamin rescued me from the Indians. Another time before that was the time when my master gave me a pony, all for myself. He told me to treat the pony nicely, and the will give you some of the most joyous times you may ever have." He stopped to take a deep breath, and with a smile he continued, "I loved that pony. I called her Freedom, because she was a dapple gray with many black and white spots, who loved to race with the wind. When the master had nothing special for me to do, he'd ask Freedom and me to ride along the fence lines, to make sure our farm animals were safe, and the fences were in good condition. I remember when White Tail's Aunt Mary told us today that she had found her *freedom*. I, immediately, thought of those care-free days which Freedom and

I had together. When the Indian was scalping me, I thought never again would I ever see my Freedom again."

His friends were stunned when they this ten year-old, ex-slave reminiscing about his past years, and how sincerely he had said every word. Samuel stared at his friends, and smiled, "But, guess what? Ever since Marie and I have been emancipated, and living with the Jeffersons I know I now have found a different kind of "freedom." Maybe I'll be able to find another four-legged Freedom, again."

* * *

As they trotted along the main street of New Palatine on their return trip to join Benjamin's father at Fort Dayton, Benjamin announced to Walter, Helena and his new brother, Samuel, that before leaving New Palatine, he would like to stop in and see Preacher Stouffer; a person who had captured his attention and respect on one of his many trips to visit Walter and his family. The four youths rode directly to the stanchions located in back of the stone church, and settled their horses with a light ration of hay and water. As they were about to walk toward the door of the separate apartment in church's rear entrance, they heard a hearty greeting, "My young friends, I'm delighted to see you!"

His cheerful and friendly voice helped to the youths to identify the stout body trudging through the unshoveled snow wearing a red, knitted stocking hat, and matching woolen scarf wrapped tightly around his neck allowing only peak of his closely cropped, salt-and-pepper beard to show. He was pulling a small wooden sled with curved runners appropriately pointed toward heaven. The rest of his body was concealed with a red, knitted sweater, which was covered with a doe-skin hunting jacket ornately decorated with Indian beads; a sure sign that his wife, Red Bird, had a hand in fashioning and constructing his jacket. "What is the occasion for you to be here at the church? It's not Sunday you know?" Reverend Stouffer did not give his visitors an opportunity to response to his first remark, before he continued, "I was just coming out back here to pile a few logs on this sled, then throw some of them in the fireplace, while Red Bird finishes baking her cornbread, and heating up a pot of hot, sweet cider. How does all of that sound to you cold urchins? You look as if you stand something warm and hearty."

"We accept your invitation," smiled Helena as she urged her male companions to assist the preacher in loading a few of the snow covered logs on his sled.

"Who is this young man?" asked Reverend Stouffer, as he held out his hand to Samuel.

"My name is Samuel Montgomery," proudly said the ten-year old former slave with a woolen stocking hat and scarf hiding his skinned head. His woolen mittens, however, matched the design and material worn by his friends, because they had been knitted by Walter's mother just before they had left the Heindrick farm.

"Samuel Montgomery?" said the preacher to clarify his hearing.

"Yes, Sir! Samuel Montgomery, and I'm Benjamin's foster brother," Samuel proudly announced to this strange, jovial acting person. "Yes, Sir! Me and my sister, Marie, have just been emancipated with many thanks to General Philip Schuyler and Sergeant Jefferson." Proud as a peacock strutting, Samuel added, "Yes sir, too, Sergeant Jefferson is also my sister and my stepfather."

"Reverend Stouffer," injected Walter. "It's a long story, sir, perhaps we best take the logs into your apartment, and then we can tell you and Red Bird Samuel and sister's story."

"That sounds like a great idea," said the agreeable minister, as Benjamin picked up the rope sled handle, and started toward the apartment's door. Helena had already reached the door, and was greeted by Red Bird. Both of the women had grown to cherish their friendship, especially when Helena's mother had escaped from the Loyalists after she had learned that her husband had been killed at Oriskany. Red Bird was the one, along with Walter's mother and the Perrys, who had helped Sarah adjust to losing her husband, and trying to keep the general store operating.

"My love," announced the preacher as he gave his wife a warm hug, and proceeded to remove his woolen clothing, and hanging them on the wooden pug near the fireplace, "look what I found out in our back yard!"

By this time Helena had already received a loving hug from Red Bird, while Walter waited in line to display his affection toward the preacher's charming wife and faithful partner. "I'm delighted to see the two of you, and especially to see you, Benjamin, we don't see each other often enough."

"Thank you, Mrs. Stouffer," replied Benjamin. "I'm honored to be here in New Palatine, it's such a charming village compared to Albany, and the people are so warm and friendly. I want to introduce to my new foster brother, Samuel Montgomery. General Philip Schuyler was instrumental in assisting him and his sister Marie in being emancipated from their former owner. My parents have already started negotiating for their adoption," he said so proudly.

"Samuel and Marie were rescued from their burning village of Minisink by Walter and Benjamin," revealed the preacher.

"But, not until after Samuel had been scalped by one of the Indians," added Walter. "It has been some time since then, but his scalp is beginning to heal relatively well," he continued, and rapping his arm around his younger friend.

The embarrassed youth apologetically retained his skull covering his head, and beamed when the beautiful, bronze lady dressed in a doeskin dress decorated with a design of colorful beads approached him, and gave him warm caress saying, "Samuel, the preacher and I are very pleased that you have joined our friends in their with visit us," she grasped his hand, and pulled him toward the fireplace, and asked, "How you like to help me to make some nice hot, sweet cider? Maybe, we can even scare up some of my favorite mince meat tarts." Bashfully, Samuel followed Red Bird toward the fireplace and the kitchen cupboard, while his brother and his friends circle themselves around the kitchen table trying to catch upon all the news since the last time they were together.

"As you probably already know from my mother," started Helena, "the four of us traveled west to see White Tail's Aunt Mary."

"You're absolutely correct, my young lady," chuckled the unpretentious veteran of the Dutch Reformed Church's riding circuit, "you must know by now how proud your mother is of you and your assistance in the general store. Even Mr. and Mrs. Perry have sung praises of your ideas on how to improve their store. I must admit," he leaned over and touched Helena's wrist, and confessed, "She has even confined to me that she thinks that you and Walter Heindrick, here, have something really special going on."

Helena turned her blushing face toward Walter, and said, "I'm not denying it. I only wish that General Washington and his troops would hurry up and get this war over."

"I agree, whole heartily," added the glowing youth approaching his seventeenth birthday. "My greatest regret for the stopping of the war," continued Walter, as he surveyed his stunned listeners, "is that I'm afraid that Benjamin and I will not see each as frequently as I'd like."

"You know very well, Walter," chimed in Benjamin, "that father will not miss a chance to, one way or other, visit with your father, my father's blood-brother, and vice versa."

He no sooner finished his last sentence, when Red Bird and Samuel appeared at the table. While Red Bird poured steaming apple cider into each others' large pewter drinking mugs, while Samuel politely walked around the table offering tarts to everyone. Everyone helped themselves to one tart, except Preacher Stouffer. Everyone stared at him while he placed two tarts on his plate. Sheepishly, the rather portly minister excused himself, "It takes me quite a few mince meat tarts to keep satisfy my ample figure, because I to work so hard!" He smiled and tenderly caressed Red Bird's slender, bronze fingers. "I must admit," he continued, "both of us are so pleased that you all took time to stop and visit with us. To tell the truth, I've seen Helena, her mother and your parents, Walter, almost every Sunday, but I truly miss seeing you and Benjamin there in the congregation. Now I'll be missing you Samuel, you see our church, our community need more youths to help us all develop and contribute to this growing nation."

"Talking about this growing nation," interrupted Benjamin, "It's almost noontime, and my brother and I are supposed to meet my father at Fort Dayton by sundown."

"Well, it's just about a nice four hour ride from here to Fort Dayton," assured Walter.

"That is, if we don't run into too many snowdrifts," chuckled Benjamin. "If we do, I'll let Samuel dig us out of the snow banks," beamed the proud, new step-brother.

"If we do get into a lot of snowdrifts," laughed the youngster with the smiling face, and twinkle in his eyes, "I'll ride the horses while you walk them through the drifts."

Benjamin grabbed Samuel's right wrist, "Preacher and Mrs. Stouffer, Samuel and I have really enjoyed our short visit, but we must be headed for Fort Dayton, or we'll have to account to our father. And," he added, "you know our father can be quite demanding."

After a round hugs with each and everyone, the two boys from Albany went out the back door, headed to the church's stables, astride their horses, and headed toward their father and Fort Dayton.

* * *

Walter and Helena left the Stouffers shortly after the Jeffersons mounted their horses, and headed across the village common to the community's only general store, and to her mother. From there, Walter had every intention to leave very soon to his parent's farm some five miles west toward Fort Stanwix.

In the privacy and intimacy of their home, the Reverend and his adoring wife clasped each other's hands, left the kitchen table; carrying a refilled cup of warm cider. They passionately strolled the few feet to the large black bear rug lying near the fireplace hearth.

"Very nice children!" acknowledged Red Bird. "Do you think we'll ever have any children of our own?" asked the middle-aged, former Oneida princess to her husband, who looked much older than his actual thirty-five years. They had been married Indian style for nearly ten years, and this was the very first time either of them had ever started a conversation on this subject.

"I agree with you, my love," said her admiring husband, "Everyone of those youngsters have some special attribute, which makes me want to just take them and hug them, and help them along life's pathway."

"Hopefully, that would be a new world. A world free of war. Freedom to win and lose as best as we can," commented Red Bird.

"Talking about freedom, my love, I have something that has been bothering me for some time," admitted the preacher. "I hope that this is the time. Perhaps this warm, cozy atmosphere, or the hard cider you used to make our last hot toddy, or maybe it's because the children's visit. Nevertheless, there is something I must really confess to you."

Dumb-founded, Red Bird stared deep into the eyes of her adored lover, wondering what he was going to say next. "I'll admit this atmosphere is warm and cozy, and so are you." She stopped, and then acknowledged his declaration by asking, "What do you need to confess to me about? I thought we agreed to keep no secrets from each other."

"I agree with you that we agreed to keep no secrets from each other soon after we met, but I did not learn of his secret until the day we had the grand opening of our new church," stared the embarrassed minister.

"Don't keep me in suspense, my dear," begged his bronze princess. "I can assure that our love is strong enough to endure any crisis."

"Well, that day after the ceremony, and everyone was participating in the picnic and other festivities, an Indian dressed in white man's clothes approached me, and quietly whispered in my ear that he had sometime very important to tell me. Then he turned about, and walked away from me. I must admit I was curious about what important news he had to tell me. So, I followed him until we stood together beneath one of the church's apple trees in back of the stables.

"First, he identified himself as a messenger from the Seneca leader, Segoyewatha, who the whites call Red Jacket and was born into the Wolf clan in a Seneca village."

"I have heard of Red Jacket. You must remember the Senecas were the Indians who first captured me, and then they traded me to the Oneidas. Red Jacket has been famous as a messenger of the British officers, and as the story goes, he received his namesake coat as a reward. However, his military career has been far from distinguished. His political and military opponents call him Cow Killer allegedly, calling him cowardly."

"After introducing himself as Bear Claw, he handed me this parchment with printing on it which read as follows:

> You have now become a great people, and we have scarcely a place left to spread our blankets. You have got our country now, but you are not satisfied. You want to force your religion upon us
>
> We are told you have been preaching to the white people in this place. These people are our neighbors. We will wait a little while, and see what effect your preaching has upon them. If we find it does them good, makes them honest and less disposed to cheat Indians, we will then consider again what you have said..

"Bear Claw also told me, that if I didn't discontinue my preaching to this community, that his hard-line chief, Red Jacket, would ask his Seneca Council to reclaim, really kidnap you as he claimed that I had done with you, and make you a member of their tribe. That was not all he said," the preacher continued, "Bear Claw told me that Red Jacket would inform our community that I have impregnated his principal rival, Cornplanter's, daughter with a child, and eventually attack our church and destroy it. They are threatening the reputation and possible destruction of us and our church. His parting words were, *Remember November 12, 1757.* That's the day when the *Indians* came through the valley, and killed and destroyed many of our Palatine settlements and settlers. In fact, it was during that raid that Karl Heindrick's lost his father, Ulrich; and I'm not going to attempt to tell how badly he must have been tortured, before they finally ran their spears through his chest."

"Now, my love, let's not dwell upon the past. As for the present, I know Cornplanter much better than I know Red Jacket," confined Red Bird. "Cornplanter is a bold and talented warrior, who fought beside Brant at Oriskany and elsewhere. After the battles, he urged the Senecas to turn to diplomacy, instead of waging war; quite different than Red Jacket! He believes that compromise will win more favors from the Americans than a continued show of force and opposition. As you may remember, Cornplanter represented the Seneca nation during the Fort Stanwix treaty negotiations, although he could do very little to prevent the erosion of the Seneca territory. He was reported as saying, *If we do not sell them the land, the whites will take it away.* How right he was," Red Bird concluded with a sorrowful resignation.

"What are you suggesting? asked the worried preacher.

"What I'm suggesting is that you call a special meeting of the church's board, and ask for their advise. A friend of Handsome Lake, a sachem of the Turtle clan, had a saying, which I think is quite appropriate for this occasion. It went something like this: *Our religion is not of paint and feathers; it is a thing of the heart.*"

"I agree with you about calling a meeting of the church board," said the relieved preacher, "but what about you and Cornplanter?"

"Tomorrow, you go ahead and convene the board, and I'll take our buckboard, and see Cornplanter. I know where he can usually be found."

"But, I don't want you riding through this wilderness alone," protested the concerned reverend.

"Oh, don't worry about me,"Red Bird said trying to ease her husband's concern. "I plan to ask Martha Butler to let me borrow her jack-of-all-trades, Harry Hunter."

"My God, you must be crazy to travel alone with that old rogue," protested the worried preacher.

"Now, my love, don't you worry about me traveling in these forests." Trying to quell her husband's anxiety, Red Bird continued, "You must remember that long before you came into my life, I was running through the woods with nary a care or injury." Then she asked a question she knew that her husband could not ignore: "Do you remember what I told you the night you asked me to marry you?" Before the preacher could respond, Red Bird answered her own question, "I asked you if wanted me to give up the most precious possession I have."

"I remember," her husband replied rather sheepishly.

"Well, what did I tell you was my most possession was?"

"You said, your *freedom*." Quickly, he asked, "Do you regret getting married?"

"At the time, and under the circumstances, I really did not know what to expect. But now that we've been married for nearly ten years. I have absolutely no regrets. In fact, my love, I believe that both of us have found a new and more beautiful freedom, than either one of us could have ever expected. We have found that we can have *real freedom* only when we first establish our own boundaries and goals."

"And," continued her husband, "when one has *total freedom*, one can automatically create only chaos."

"We agree, my dear!" said Red Bird as she sipped the last of her hot cider, and leaned on his shoulder, and said, "Tomorrow's our day to start our campaign to resolve this horrible issue. Just have faith, my husband. The rest of the night is ours," Red Bird chirped as she refilled their hot, hard apple cider mugs, while he threw another log in the fireplace.

SIXTEEN

SEEDS OF FREEDOM

A Late November, 1779 Afternoon
On their way to the Jefferson's Home in Albany

"I really enjoyed my visit to the hospital, Mother," Marie said hesitantly; she was still trying to comply with the Jefferson's desires to be addressed as either Mother or Father, but the first part of her statement that she enjoyed her visit to the hospital was sincere and without qualifications.

"I'm glad you enjoyed yourself," acknowledged Julia Jefferson. "I, too, believed that I helped to relieve the pain of one of our soldiers. Dr. McDuff and I accomplished one of the least desirable surgeries ever, that of amputating one of our soldier's legs. At least, he is still alive, and hopefully, Dr. McDuff can fit a wooden leg to his stub soon. As much as I like to assist caring for the wounded and sick, this type of case tears at my heart." To change the discussion, Julia asked her soon-to-be adopted daughter, "Did you do anything interesting?"

"Yes I did," Marie said without hesitation. "Before we did anything, Mrs. Riedesel and I chatted for a few minutes just to get to know each other. She gave a little history of the hospital, she especially wanted to discover what my interests in the hospital were. When I told her I had never been in a hospital before, she started asking me about what I liked to do. When told her that I liked to sing, she said she knew exactly where she was going to take me first; to the rehabilitation area. After that very pleasant conversation," Marie smiled and said, "Then Mrs. Riedesel escorted me into the rehabilitation area where she introduced me to most of the patients. As we were walking around the ward, I heard a rather weird, but rather an appealing musical sound coming from a distant corner of the ward. I asked Mrs. Riedesel what that sound was. Oh! she said, that's Mr. McKnight playing his bagpipes. Eventually, we worked our way toward where he was located, and Mrs. Riedesel introduced me to him. After he stopped playing the pipes, he told us that he didn't like to be called Mr. McKnight. Not that he wasn't a gentlemen, he laughed, but he preferred being called just plain *Sandy*. Then he asked Mrs. Riedesel why she had taken time to introduce me to him. Well, she said, she thought that we had something in common interest. He asked what was that, and she replied by spelling out the word, M U S I C!"

"Well," said Julia as they struggled through the street's unplowed snow toward the Jefferson's modest, but elegantly maintained white clapboard home surrounded by a white picket fence, which was nearly covered with drifted snow, "it sounds like you and Mr. Sandy got off to a good start."

"Yes, we did," admitted Marie with a dreamy smile in her blue eyes. "He tried to teach me a few of his Scottish songs, and I tried to teach him to play some of the spirituals we used to sing every Sunday back in our master's farm's little community church." She stopped talking as if she was embarrassed to be talking so exhilarated about some she had just met.

"I'm delighted that you have found a friend, my dear," said Julia, as she opened that picket fence gate which opened into their home's front yard covered with about a foot of snow. After wadding through the unshoveled snow, brushing off the snow from their boots, and as they entered the front door, Julia suggested, "Let's get our boots and these heavy coats off. I'll make ourselves some hot apple cider, while you scare up some of those wonderful maple and hickory-nut cookies you baked yesterday. Then we'll settle down in front of the fireplace, and you can continue telling me all about your conversation with this Mr. Sandy."

Just before Marie settled down on the bear rug spread out before the fireplace, she placed two additional logs in low embers of the fire. By that time, Julia had finished heating the apple cider, "So your Mr. Sandy found out that you liked music, and that you used to sing," started Marie's new mother, "what else did you talk about?"

"Well, he sang a few of his Scottish songs, and I tried to sing along with him, but he sang them so much better than I could," confessed Marie as if she was eager to tell her mother more.

"Did you sing any of the songs and spirituals that you used to sing?" Julia asked.

"Oh,! Yes!," Marie said as she smiled, as if she were hiding some deep dark secret she was reluctant to tell her mother. Still appearing as if she was telling something special held between her and Sandy, Marie suddenly burst out laughing. "Mother," she declared, "you should have heard Sandy singing some of our spirituals in his Scottish accent, especially, when he started singing about *pickin' cotton, totin' them bales, and liftin' that barge.* He was so embarrassed, that he stopped singing, and continued playing his bagpipes. By that time, most of the wounded soldiers in that ward had gathered all around us, and they kept clapping for us to continue. Some of the soldiers," Marie added, "even started singing with us. Then all of a sudden Mrs. Riedesel came in the ward, and we all stopped singing. She said, No! No! She urged us to keep on singing, because she said music was good therapy for all of us. Then her abundant breasts giggled like jelly, while she attempted to sing along with us. She even danced a few steps with one of the patients."

"Marie, it certainly sounds that all of you, including Mrs. Riedesel, had a very happy and joyful time," observed Julia.

"Yes, we did," agreed Marie. "In fact, Mrs. Riedesel even invited me to visit as often as I am able."

Julia appeared to be interested in Marie's experience in the hospital, then asked, "How old is this Mr. Sandy?" as she returned to the bear-rug with more hot apple cider.

"I don't know how old Sandy is," Marie quickly responded, and then asked, "Why do you ask?"

* * *

On their way to visit Cornplanter, Red Bird and her traveling companion Harry Hunter, were riding their horses, and pulling behind a horse packed with their food and hunting supplies along with a few trinkets and gifts for the Indians. The route they had selected to travel was commonly referred by the Indians as the *Forbidden Path*, which lead into the Seneca country. Although the route's name had always sounded rather prohibitive to her, Red Bird as an adventurous youth had frequently traveled the *path* with her father and brother as they traveled with Joseph Brant from Oriskany and elsewhere to visit their friend Cornplanter. It was during those times, when Red Bird learned that Cornplanter, unlike his principal hard-line rival Red Jacket, favored diplomacy instead of war. Red Bird and Harry Hunter had traveled westward along the familiar King's Highway until they nearly reached the site where the Battle of Oriskany had been fought. Instead of heading toward Oriska, Aunt Mary's village, they headed northwest. Due to the urgency of their mission, the pair sparingly took short intervals from their saddles to eat and water their horses. As the sun began to settle behind the mountains, a blinding snow storm forced them to construct a lean-to shelter. By the time morning arrived, the storm had subsided, but the horses found the traveling in the deep snow difficult. As they cautiously moved through the ravines, over frozen swamps, and cutting through occasional thick underbrush in the almost sunless woods. The missionaries were thankful that the rattlesnakes were hibernating in their dens making one less obstacle to contend with. Just before darkness settled in the next day, Harry Hunter was busy constructing another lean-to shelter, while Red Bird was hunting for some fresh meat. When she returned to the shelter with her rabbit,

Red Bird found Harry had just finished building a small campfire setting atop of a few potatoes. He quickly dressed and prepared the rabbit for the frying pan, while Red Bird heated up some coffee.

As they sat around the campfire eating their meal, Harry finished wiping the grease from around his mouth on his coat sleeve, and made a profound observation, "Miss Red Bird, this meal is just as tasty as some of those meals Miss Martha feeds me at the Heidelburg Tavern."

"I'm certain that Miss Martha is a good cook," Red Bird defended her friend, "and I'm certain that after all the rough traveling we've been doing, if I wasn't here you would probably have eaten the rabbit without cooking it."

"I'm not goin' to dispute that, mam," agreed Harry, "but I have to admit that I'm really pleased that we did take the time to cook the rabbit, but you have to admit that those potatoes I had placed beneath the fire coals really did get burned to nearly charcoal, but they, too, tasted pretty darn good."

"Yes, I must admit that the meal would have tasted better, if we hadn't burnt the potatoes as much as we did," said Red Bird as she wrapped herself into a bedroll. "We best get to sleep early tonight. If the weather is favorable tomorrow, we should be able to be in Cornplanter's village by noon, and in couple more days we should be back in New Palatine. By then, hopefully, our mission will be successfully completed." Red Bird didn't remember whether Harry had responded to her suggestion to get to sleep early; her exhausted mind and body were off in dreamland. Within what seemed just a few hours, the morning sun was peaking through the hemlock boughs on the lean-to's roof, and Harry was heating up the left-over coffee.

True to form, Red Bird was correct about the time when they would arrive at Cornplanter's settlement. The village did look like anything she remembered when she had visited before a year or two earlier. Much to disappointment, she learned from her old friend Cornplanter, that the Americans had invaded the Indian country in avenging fury "putting to death all the women and children," lamented the Seneca chief, "excepting some of the young women, whom they carried away for the use of their soldiers, and afterwards were put to death in a more shameful manner." Why, even the American General James Clinton, no friend of the Iroquois, wrote afterwards: *Bad as these savages are, they never violated the chastity of any woman.*"

Red Bird decided it best to let Cornplanter release all of his anger before she approached her problem, and so the Seneca chief continued, "It was during August of this year that Clinton and his accomplice General John Sullivan started to carry out General Washington's orders *not merely be overrun, but destroy the Indian country* with as many as 2,500 soldiers. You remember, Red Bird, the richness of our land with its neat frame houses and broad, lush cornfields?" She acknowledged his remark with a smile and a positive nod, as Cornplanter continued his diatribe, "Certainly carried out Washington's scorch earth mission by burning our towns, pillaging our longhouses, uprooting our crops, chopping down our orchards, slaughtering our livestock, and destroying our grain supplies. Some of the soldiers even plundered our grave sites and our burial goods." He took a deep breath, and continued, "Some of the soldiers even skinned the bodies of our fallen warriors to make leggings. However, we were fortunate. The Great Spirit had blessed us by forewarning us of their destructive path, and many of our warriors and their families had scattered into the forests, so we sustained fewer casualties than we could have experienced.. Many had fled to Fort Niagara where the British have furnished us with a number of squalid camps. As you know this winter is one of the coldest winters we've had in many moons. We expect many to starve, and freeze to death." Cornplanter sitting in his squat fashion, pushed his hands flat on the frozen ground of his tepee, ridgedly stretched his arms straight and leaned back to take a deep breathe, and asked his listeners, "Do you know what we Iroquois call the great American general George Washington?"

His audience of two nodded their heads negatively, "Well, I'll tell you," Cornplanter unyieldingly stated, "We, Iroquois, call him *Caunotaucarius*, the Town Destroyer. May our Great Spirit treat him accordingly!"

Red Bird expressed sympathy to her long-time friend, but it was time for her to change the subject, so she and Harry Hunter could complete their mission. Cornplanter, too, realized that he had not given his guest a chance explain the reason for her visit. The diplomatic Cornplanter apologized for his inconsiderate behavior, but he explained that he needed to shout-off to a sympathetic ear. "I needed your understanding ear, you see, my good friend, that our land has become a bitter land where brothers fight against each other. Honestly, we just don't know who we can trust. Everyone makes promises, and more promises, but our people continue to be abused, cheated and killed."

"Perhaps, my husband, the Reverend Johan Stouffer." She stopped, and asked, "you remember him? He was circuit-rider preacher who occasionally visited your communities."

"Oh! Sure I remember him," Cornplanter chuckled, "He was the jolly person with the pudgy face covered with a beard. He used to make all of us happy, because he never lied to us. Never made promises that he didn't keep."

"Well, he needs your help!" declared Red Bird. "You see, Bear Claw warned us of Red Jacket's accusation, that my husband impregnated your daughter with child, and that Red Jacket is threatening to destroy our church and my husband's reputation."

Cornplanter laughed, "How could your husband do such a thing? My only daughter has been in the Shawnee settlements of the Ohio Valley for the past two years with her Shawnee friend, Chief Black Fish. During a salt-making expedition in 1778 to Blue Licks, on the Licking River, Black Fish and his 100 Shawnee warriors took a prisoner named Daniel Boone. Boone was held in captivity for three months, and he was adopted into the tribe by Black Fish himself, who had lost his own son in the fighting. I understand that since his adoption, Boone has succeeded in escaping, and had returned to his village Boonesborough to defend it against yet another siege by Black Fish's warriors. So, my friend, you can tell your husband that Red Jacket's story sounds a little *fishy*." He chuckled, as he passed his peace pipe around to his guests. "As far as Red Jacket is concerned, I promise you that I'll attend to your trouble maker, and you can return to your husband. Make sure you tell him that your friend Cornplanter will plant some corn in Red Jacket's coat."

As the three departed from Cornplanter's tepee, the evening sun was settling down behind the snow covered mountains, "Join me at our evening meal, and yourselves a good night's sleep with us, then you and Mr. Harry can get off to a good start by the morning's early light."

SEVENTEEN

REHABILATION AND MORE

Late in the Afternoon of December 7, 1779
In the Living Room of Jefferson's Home in Albany, New York

Julia Jefferson had not spent much of any time at the military hospital since the last time she went there with Marie. She was busy trying to juggle her personal obligations and business activities besides being a faithful and devoted wife of Sergeant George Jefferson. Fortunately for her, the past three weeks and probably another week before her husband would return from his assignment at Fort Dayton with their seventeen year old son Benjamin and one of their latest family addition, Samuel Montgomery. She hoped that their sons, who had been visiting Walter Heindrick and his family in New Palatine which was about one-hundred miles east of the site of the Battle of Oriskany, were having a very pleasant experience. She knew that this was a new event for Samuel, he'd never been out of Minisink. Julia estimated that *her men* would be returning in about seven days. In the meantime, she had been spending much of her days baking Christmas pastries, including fruit cakes, mince pies, plum puddings, maple cookies shaped and decorated as Christmas trees, wreaths, and gingerbread Santa Clauses to fill the orders of her regular customers, together with a few extras for over-the-counter sales. While Julia was trying to prepare her supply of baked goods for the holidays, Marie, too, was spending approximately two days a week helping her mother baking. Sundays both would go to the Dutch Reformed Church, which was located near the village common; other days Marie would spend her time at the military hospital. She enjoyed working with Mrs. Riedesel, who had recognized Marie's adaptability to almost any kind of task she would assign to Marie. As a result, Marie was slowly becoming Mrs. Riedesel's dependable assistant sharing more and more of her responsibilities, but there something occurring which both had mixed emotions about. Frequently, in her spare time, Marie would find her way into the rehabilitation center. While there she and Sandy McKnight would encourage the ward's patient to join them in singing; even sometimes dancing. Obviously, the patients were enjoying the entertainment, but what really concerned Mrs. Riedesel was there seemed to be a uncommonly growing affection between Marie and Sandy McKnight. They certainly had music as a common interest between them, but she reasoned that Mr. McKnight, a white man and Marie was a former, black slave. Further, Mrs. Riedesel reasoned she could understand how Marie's attractive, light complexion, her shapely curves and her youthful exuberance could turn on any man. But, if they had children, she asked herself, what would they look like? Then she remembered that Sir William Johnson and his Mohawk wife, Molly Brant, had eight mixed-blood children. In fact, she recalled that the Mohawk people took Johnson into their tribe under the name of Brother Warraghiyagey (He Who Does Much Business) and moved their council fire to the grounds of his estate. Mrs. Riedesel, too, remembered that the majority of Molly and Johnson's children were physically sound individuals with clear, and rather attractive bronze complexion. She abruptly dismissed the subject as she saw a joyful Marie coming into her office beaming with confidence. The nurse rapidly dismissing her thoughts, reasoning that nothing like the Johnson affair would ever happen, because Mr. McKnight must be at least ten or fifteen years older than Marie, and Mr. McKnight was not rich like Sir William. In addition, Mr. McKnight had only a leg and one-half (as soon as he was fitted with a *peg-leg.*)

"Good afternoon, Mrs. Riedesel, what a wonderful time we had in the rehabilitation center this afternoon," exclaimed the effervescent young lady.

"What did you do?" asked Mrs. Riedesel as she was beginning to envision the cause of her excitement.

"What was so great about today?" asked Mrs. Riedesel.

"What so great, Mrs. Riedesel," responded Marie, "that a number of the patients who the doctors didn't think they would ever be able to walk or talk, were having a delightful time singing and dancing as Sandy and I were making our music. I don't have bagpipes," admitted the exuberant former slave, "but I concocted a set of drums out of an assortment of the kitchen's pots and pans. Those patients who didn't have any pot or pans happily clapped their hands to the rhythm Sandy and I created. We even had some of those patients who could not walk or dance beat out the rhythm on the pots and pans, or clapping their hands. Everyone was enjoying themselves. When Doctor McDuff looked in on us, he thought the patients were enjoying this type of therapy. Then that old, crotchety Doctor Ambrose stuck his head in the center, and told us to quite-down, and act more civilized."

"I'll admit that Dr. Ambrose is rather cantankerous, but he means well," said Mrs. Riedesel trying quell Marie's dour feelings. "You see, my dear, Dr. Ambrose was the first doctor assigned to this hospital. I remember when he first arrived; he used to strut around here like a some farm-yard rooster, as if he was the king of the barn-yard. All of that stopped, however, when Dr. McDuff arrived. Dr. Ambrose quickly recognized that McDuff totally out-classed him as far as medicine was concerned. Dr. Ambrose is pretty good at holding a patient's hand and taking his temperature, but beyond that the *code* around here is *to call Dr. McDuff.*

"Mrs. Riedesel, I have been so wrapped up in the rehab center, that I nearly forgot that my mother had asked me to come home and help her bake-off a batch of mince pies," Marie said as she wrapped her wool scarf over her head and around her neck, and put on her deerskin coat lined with rabbit fur. Admiring the enthusiastic and optimistic energy of her protegee, Mrs. Riedesel wistfully said, "Enjoy your evening with your mother. I hope to see you here tomorrow, because we have been informed to expect more wounded from the Indian country."

* * *

When Marie arrived at the Jefferson's home, the sun had disappeared nearly an hour previously, and was replaced with a full-winter moon circled by its hazy ring predicting snow for either the evening or the morrow. As she entered her new home, the aroma of freshly baked mince pies filled her nostrils, and reminded her of the first time when she and her brother had entered the Jefferson home. At that time, Julia had just finished baking her special spicy pumpkin pies. "What a welcoming smell you have created, Mother. I'm sorry that I'm late. We have been so very busy at the hospital, I'll have to tell you all about it."

"That sounds like a good idea," said her mother. "If you will throw on another log in the fireplace, I'll pour us a couple cups of hot apple cider, and maybe I can scare up a piece of hot mince pie for each of us."

"That's sounds great, mother," Marie said as the took a seasoned log from the fire-box, which was conveniently placed beside the fireplace, then settled on the bearskin rug scattered in front of the fireplace. While she was getting herself comfortable, Julia entered the warm room carrying a round serving tray, which George made from a thin slice of a maple tree log. She placed the tray on the floor beside her daughter, and settled herself comfortably on the other side of the tray. Each picked up a cup of the steaming apple cider, toasted each other's cups and sipped the contents of the cup. As Marie raised the cup toward her lips, the aroma rising from the cup warned her that her mother had spiced the cider with some of her husband's home-brew, "Now, my dear, tell me all about your day."

Marie eagerly described how she and Sandy McKnight had entertained the patients, and even informed her mother that Dr.

McDuff had suggested that he believed that the patients were having an excellent therapy session. Later, I also learned that Dr. McDuff had he stopped by Mrs. Riedesel's office suggesting to her that Sandy and I should continue this type of program; adding that he believed that the patients benefited psychologically, as well as medically."

"How do you feel about Dr. McDuff's proposal?" Julia asked. "Do you think you'd like to do that kind of entertainment or therapy for any length of time?"

"You know that I enjoy singing and making music, especially when it's before an audience," acknowledged Marie. "But I must admit, that I'm beginning to wonder if I'm enjoying this activity just because I'm doing it with Sandy. Mother, I really enjoy his company, and I think he even enjoys my companionship."

"Have you talked with Mrs. Riedesel about how you feel?" asked her not-so-shocked mother. "You see, my dear, the moment I first saw you two together, I recognized the same kind of chemistry between you two, as when George and I first met," as she finished eating her mince pie. "Would you like more hot cider?" Julia asked as she tried to change the subject.

"That sounds great, but let me get for us," Marie said as she effortlessly raised herself from the floor and headed toward the kitchen. "Mother," came Marie inquisitive voice, "do you believe in inter-racial marriage?"

"What do you mean, young lady? Explain what you call inter-racial marriage," quizzed Julia.

"I mean a marriage between a man and woman of two different races," Marie said flatly without adding any further explanation.

"Do you mean that you would marry a white man? A Scotsman at that? How could you ever think about such a thing? Do you mean that you and this Sandy person have been talking about getting married? Why, he has to be about twice your age! You have known him for only a few weeks," protested Marie's newly adopted mother. Julia stood up, and went into the kitchen, poured herself another cup of hot cider without offering Marie another portion. After she had comforted herself back on the bearskin rug, Julia said, "Now, young

STEPS TOWARD FREEDOM

lady, let's hear the whole story. How did you two ever get on this subject of interracial marriage?"

"It all started rather innocently," Marie began. "We had finished entertaining the patients, or as Dr. McDuff would say giving them their daily therapy. As we were almost finished picking up the pots and pans, and tidying-up the ward, Sandy told me that he really enjoyed entertaining the patients with me. Prior to my arriving, he told me, he was just content playing her bagpipes and keeping to himself. After I entered to picture, he saw how much the patients appreciated our music. He said, the entire atmosphere in the rehab ward had really cheered-up, since we started sharing our music with them. He reminded me that at least once of twice a day either Mrs. Riedesel or Dr. McDuff came in the ward and complimented us about the sudden change in the patients' attitude. He stopped a minute, and rubbed his fingers through his curly red hair with its few white strands scattered over his head, then he began to laugh and didn't explain to me why he was laughing."

"Did he explain to you why he was laughing?" asked Marie's curious mother.

"You wont believe what Sandy told me," smilingly Marie responded, "Well, it seems that one of these days when both Dr. McDuff and Mrs. Riedesel were talking with Sandy, separately they told him that they really appreciated the improvements they had witnessed since you and I have been entertaining the patients. Each agreed that most of the patients' health have improved tremendously; their concern was that the patients were enjoying themselves so much, that none of them want to be discharged. They shared their concern that the hospital was still admitting new patients, and we're going to have to empty some of the beds."

"I'm pleased to learn that Mrs. Riedesel and Dr. McDuff appreciate Sandy and your music, and keeping the patients happy," Julia said rather agitated, "but what's that got to about interracial marriage?"

"Well, Sandy told me that he really enjoyed playing music and entertaining the patients with me," Marie started on a very serious note. "He asked me if I enjoyed our *therapy* as much as he did, even if he was a white person; a Scotsman at that who talks rather humorously. I told him I had even given a though about such things. Then I asked him how he felt about associating with someone who looks like a Creole, is the daughter of a West Indian slave, and fathered by a while plantation owner." She a moment, and smiled saying, "I guess some people would probably call me a half-bred. Sandy didn't wait a second before he responded to my question; saying that he believe that *interracial marriages* offered the simplest solution this country, or any country's racial problems. He believes that over the period of a century or two all of God's children will have similar facial features and a color like mine. He told me that we all have to accept the fact that we're all God's children, and that God didn't place us on this earth to fight with each other. Sandy believes that God theorized that as we matured, we would learn how to reason and to arbitrate our differences with each other. By having similar skin complexion, the difference in races should disappear. Finally, he told me over in Scotland, and even in Boston and New York where he had lived before he came to the Mohawk Valley, he hadn't given a person's ethnic heritage much thought until he met me. I told him I didn't know whether I should feel flattered or embarrassed about his comment. I told him that I'm proud of being who I am, and how I look. I don't really care what other people think of me. I just know one thing that I know who I am, and I'm proud of what I am. He smiled, rapped his arms around my shoulders, gave me a kiss on my cheek, and said that he liked me just the way I was."

"I'll have you know, my sweet daughter, I also love you just as you are. George and I, as well as Benjamin, all believed that we're blessed to have you, as well as Samuel, in our family," assured Julia as she raised from the bearskin rug, and headed into the kitchen with her empty teacup and the partially filled cookie plate. As Julia left the kitchen, she met head-on a relieved Marie, and placed her arms around her engaging daughter, and whispered, "And, my dear, I not only love you, but I like you, and most importantly I trust you. I think that you and Sandy are to something."

EIGHTEEN

FREEDOM! WHAT DOES IT MEAN?

*Two Weeks before Christmas Eve, 1779 in the
Dutch Reformed Church's Parish, New Palatine, New York*

Reverend Johan Stouffer had much to be thankful for. Red Bird and Harry Hunter had safely returned from their visit with Cornplanter, the Seneca leader who was the principal rival to Red Jacket's hard-line and sometimes deceitful approach, had assured the preacher's embassaries that he would take care of Red Jacket. As he rubbed his closely cropped beard, New Palatine's only preacher wondered how Red Jacket could have made such reckless threat about him claiming that he had impregnated Cornplanter's only daughter. Red Bird informed her husband that Cornplanter had assured her that his daughter had been living in the Shawnee settlements of the Ohio Valley for the past two years with her dear friend, Chief Black Fish. As Red Bird related her tête-à-tête with Cornplanter to her preacher husband, she suddenly burst out laughing, as she sipped some hot cider from her ornate porcelain cup, one of a set which her thoughtful husband had given her for her forty-fifth birthday.

"What are you laughing about, my love?" asked her husband as he nervelessly massaged his salt and pepper colored beard; his warning light that his mind was working overtime about some problem. "This is serious business. You must remember that Red Jacket threatened to destroy our church and my reputation. This serious business," he repeated, as he paced the floor in front of his equally serious wife.

"You know, my dear, that Red Jacket has quite a reputation with his independent spirit in the Iroquois tradition decrying any attempts to treat them as subjugated people. We both remember hearing Red Jacket speaking with a riveting blend of passion, yet in many cases with a considerable amount of common sense, but," his wife added, "his strict traditionalism made him scorn any and all attempts to convert the Iroquois to white men's ways, especially their religion."

"I must agree with you that Red Jacket does have an unusual understanding of the white men's long term goals. I often think of a conference I attended when he was addressing a group of Protestant missionaries. As I remember the occasion, he said something like this:

> You have now become a great people, and we have scarcely a place to spread our blankets. You have got our country now, but you are not satisfied. You want to force your religion upon us.
>
> We are told that you have been preaching to the white people in this place. These people are our neighbors. We will wait a little while, and see what effect your preaching has upon them. If we find it does them good, makes them honest and less disposed to cheat Indians, we will than consider again what you have said. "Then with scorn, Red Jacket added:

Your forefathers crossed the great water and landed on this island. Their numbers were small. We took pity on them, and they sat down among us. We gave them corn and meat. They gave us poison in return.

"At times, my dear," the preacher continued as he stood before the fireplace, he turned and went to the wood box conveniently located near the fireplace, retrieved a seasoned log and placed it on the fire irons. "May I pour you another cup of hot cider?" said the gentle giant.

"I'd love another cup, and as long as you are in the serving mood, would you, please bring us some of Rebecca Heindrick's fruit cake?" asked Red Bird as she stretched out on the hard-back sofa which was placed in front of the fireplace. "You started to say something about *at times, my dear.* What had you intended to say to me?

The preacher returned to his wife with a tray holding two cups of steaming hot cider and a small plate of chunks of Rebecca's fruit cake. Placing the tray on the opposite end of the sofa, and sitting on the floor with his back up propped up against the sofa. Turning his head, which was endowed with a huge crop of the same salt-and-pepper hair, which adorned his face, he looked up toward his adored wife, and said, "At times, I feel like a dishonest hypocrite."

"My dear, you can't mean what you're saying," Red Bird said protesting his statement, "everyone knows how honest and sincere a person you are."

"Everyone except myself," responded her husband as he rubbed his whiskered chin. "You see, I think I know how many of the whites feel toward the Indians, and most all of our citizens recall what General George Washington ordered General John Sullivan to do before he started his campaign along with General Clinton."

"Please refresh my memory," asked Red Bird, "perhaps I have chosen to forget his orders. You must remember that forgetting is an active process, that is until one gets real old!"

"As I understand," Reverend Stouffer said as he assumed a professional standing position before his wife explaining to her his interpretation of Washington's orders to General John Sullivan, "The most important thing we must remember is that Washington was not just planning exclusively for Sullivan's campaign, rather he was in the process of developing his overall strategy geared toward America's future. His orders dated May 31, 1779 read similar to the following:

> *This expedition you are to command is to be directed against the hostile tribes of the Six Nations of Indians with their associates and adherents. The immediate objects are the destruction and devastation of their settlements and the capture of as many prisoners of every sex and age as possible. It will be essential to ruin their crops in the ground and prevent their planting more.*

"Washington's planned pincer movements were designed to be much more than a punishment of the Iroquois and the eradication of Fort Niagara's *hornet's nest*. As I understand, the ultimate purpose of Washington's orders to Sullivan was a declaration that the Fort Stanwix treaty boundary line, which had been thrashed out at the fort identified the *white men's* territory and the *redmen's* territory, that America intended to hold the Indians to those boundary lines. And as I understand, Washington added that America will settle: *where it damn well pleased—-even clear to the Mississippi River!*

"Now, my love," the preacher continued, "here's why I feel like a hypocrite. Knowing all that I know about how many of our American leaders feel toward the Indians, how can I face any of these Indians and tell them that I love them, that God loves them, and that we can peaceably live together? I could easily subscribe to Red Jacket's assertion, that after the small number of our forefathers had crossed the great ocean, the Indians took pity on them, sat down among them, and gave them corn and meat. And, in turn, the Americans gave the Indians poison in return. And now, the whites want to force our religion upon us. How I can, or any other honest white person, look at any of these people with a clear conscience, when we all know full well that the whites' ultimate purpose, American or British, is to take anything and everything these poor people possess."

"I understand, my love, how you feel," assured Red Bird. "I knew that you were that kind of gentle, yet strong, committed and compassionate person when I first met you. That's why I wanted to marry you. It wasn't because of the religion you were preaching. Rather, it was the kind of person you are. A loving, kind, and considerate person who will not tell a falsehood to anyone. Thank goodness, you do have a kind of conscience that will not let you sleep, if you ever cheat or lie to any person. That's why people respect you, and that's why Red Jacket wanted to defame you, and what you stand for. Thanks to Cornplanter, we will not have to worry about that matter. I suggest that you toss another log on the fire, while I prepare us another cup of hot spiced cider. Then, we'll give our thanks to our Great Spirit for all of the blessings He has given us."

* * *

Before the Reverend Stouffer and his wife realized, the time for the New Palatine Dutch Reformed Church's Christmas Eve service had arrived. During the two previous weeks, the Reverend and Red Bird were busily coordinating the preparations for the festivities with various members of the church's congregation Red Bird and Martha Butler, the owner of Heidelberg Tavern, divided up the evening's principle activities. Red Bird, assisted by Rebecca Heindrick, selected and groomed the cast of characters to enact the roles of Mary, Joseph, the shepherds, and the three wise men, as well as scripting and rehearsing the cast for their performance. Meanwhile, Martha Butler coordinated and assigned the numerous other activities such as preparing pastries, stringing popped corn for decorating the Christmas tree, making candy canes, painting and decorating pine cones to adorn the tree, among numerous women in New Palatine including, but not limited to, Helena and her mother Sarah Kerchner, Hilda Perry, and the smithy's wife, Mrs. George Raab, as well as the Mrs. Herman Swackhammer and all of her children. In addition, Martha and Helena Kerchner spent considerable amount of time designing and embellishing a rusty, sheet metal star, which George

GIL HERKIMER

Raab, the village smithy, had cut for them, with various sparkling sands, shells and together with a few turkey feathers, they created a colorful, attractive star to signify the star of Bethlehem to be placed atop of the Christmas tree. .

While ladies and children of the church were performing their assigned activities, Preacher Stouffer, Karl Heindrick, Harvey Perry, George Raab, Herman Swackhammer, and even Harry Hunter had busy decorating the inside and outside of the church with pine boughs and cones, and other colorful decorations which enhanced the stone church. One of the men's principle task was to select and harvest a suitable Christmas tree to be located in the front of church near the pulpit. Most importantly, they would have to construct a standard in which the tree would be placed and secured, so that the tree's decorations and childrens' presents could be placed safely on the tree.

Without anyone else's involvement, Preacher Stouffer and Harvey Perry, partner in the former Kerchner General Store, plotted a surprise for the children of the community. Initially, they had planned to enlist the services of Harry Hunter, but upon second thought they decided that the secrecy of their plan would be endangered before the desired time. Instead, Harvey suggested that Harvey's close friend George Raab, the smithy, would seal his lips as to their plot.

* * *

Christmas Eve in New Palatine was the antithesis of the first Christmas Eve in Bethlehem. Instead of wise men arriving on camels, the church's congregation was arriving in an assortment of horse-drawn sleighs and sleds guided by the clouded brilliance of a full-moon as it endeavored to cast as many of its moon beams through a steady sprinkling of snow. To the residents of upstate New York this was a *real* Christmas scene, this spectacularly beautiful winter scene was the dream of all the residents of the Mohawk Valley. On the other hand, for the ancients and those who reside in the tropical or semi-tropical hemispheres with their signature palm trees and sandy beaches this kind scenic beauty would be completely foreign.

The open field round the church was crowded with various sizes and shapes of sleds, sleighs, other vehicles with runners, as well as few pairs of skis staked into a snow bank. Some of the horses were fortunate to have arrived early with their owners in order to be stabled in the church's livery, while those less fortunate were still harnessed to their owner's snow vehicles; some may have been furnished small supply of hay, while others would have to wait for St. Nicholas.

As Preacher Stouffer entered the *standing room only* church's sanctuary with a dozen or so laminated historic lanterns similar to the ones, which hung in Boston's Old North Church casting an eerie, almost a supernatural dancing reflections along the church's walls. He was overwhelmed by its mystical appearance, and by the size of congregation. He had been praying for an excellent attendance as a sign of gratitude to those whose had worked so diligently and faithfully in preparing for this special evening. Surely, the Lord was blessing the community and its church, he thought. As he solemnly traversed the distance from the church's lobby to his favorite raised area just below the church's pulpit, he silently prayed to God to place the correct words in his mind, and to let his lips be His mouthpiece. Preacher Stouffer had never delivered his sermon or even spoke to his congregation from the pulpit, he reasoned that he felt more at ease with his flock when he was among them, not standing above them or speaking down to them. Carrying his faithful and frayed leather-bound Bible, he stepped reverently to his beloved place on the slightly raised area surrounding the pulpit, and turned toward what seemed to him to be a vast ocean of faces. But, as he smoothed his beard, he envisioned King David doing the same before reciting some of his favorite portions of his famed book of Psalms to mesmerized audience. Preacher Stouffer raised his arms toward the rough, unpolished ceiling beams, and in a joyous, baritone voice he welcomed the congregation with a hearty, yet sincere "Merry Christmas, to each and everyone."

The congregation responded with a spirited, "And a Merry Christmas to you."

"Tonight is the celebration of the very first Christmas more than 2,000 years ago," started the modest preacher as he gained confidence in himself and in the congregation. "According to St. Luke," he continued, "shepherds watching their flocks near Bethlehem *were sore afraid.* Then an angel said to them, *fear not, for I bring you good tidings of great joy, which shall be to all people.* And so began a religion whose theme is hope, not fear; whose doctrine is faith, not distrust; whose creed is peace, not war, and whose principle is love your neighbors as thy self."

The congregation, expecting to hear their preacher read the story of the first Christmas directly from the scriptures, seemingly he had caught his audience off-guard by starting on another track. He was beginning to have second thoughts about the direction he had planned, but momentarily he decided to continue. "As I interrupt the Christmas story, it is a search for *world peace, accompanied with love and respect for all of God's children.* This search for world peace is not exclusively a Christian conjecture, but also in Judaism, in Islam, and in every major religion. But, what these great religions teach us is that peace comes from within the heart of all mankind. Nor, will the peace, which we seek, come to us as a gift in a brightly wrapped package. Rather, one of the sad truths of this world is that peace is something one often has to fight for against those who build their power on war and mayhem. The world's search for peace—-and that's what's its all about—-has neither a beginning or ending. It is a never-ending process!

"As far as freedom is concerned, *Freedom*, like peace, must be found by each individual person based upon his or her own value sets and faith, for belief in other people's basic instincts for goodness. Out of this great civil war, which stages neighbors against neighbors, brothers against brothers, fathers against sons and vice-versa, can come new opportunities for us to achieve a more peaceful world, and find the freedom each of us are searching for, and striving for."

The preacher took a deep breath, placed his two hands in an upright praying fashion, raised his face looking toward the dancing shadows casted from the church's wall lanterns. He closed his eyes, rubbed his beard, and looked intently toward his parishioners, who sat in their pews as if they were trapped in a hypnotic trance. "In our search for world peace and freedom, would that all of the world's people could focus our prayers, our hopes, our determination on that promise made long ago "———on earth, peace, and good will toward all men."

He stepped down on to the main floor, raised his arms, and said "Let tonight be the beginning of our search for world peace and freedom. Now, let our children dramatize their impression of the first Christmas."

The nativity story, as scripted and choreographed by Red Bird and Helena Kerchner, was performed by the children of New Palatine. Even though the audience knew they were viewing the performance in a scared church of God, it was so well dramatized that entire congregation stood up, and sounded a boisterous applaud led by, Frank Swackhammer, the community's most prolific farmer of children, as well as cows, whose seven children all had roles in the drama. But, as the congregation was still clapping, there suddenly the sound of sleigh bells coming from outdoors, as the sound appeared to be drawing closer to the church, there came the sound of a hearty "Ho! Ho!" laugh, and as the person's laugh became louder and louder, then the voice shouted "Whoa!" "Whoa!" After a moment of silence, the voice yelled "Stop you dang jackass." penetrating through the church's stone walls. The congregation resounded with a polite snicker as the church's twin front doors burst, and rotund with a huge pot-belly, dressed in a bulky red coat and red pants trimmed with nearly white lamb's wool, and sporting a sizable pair of black boots. Over his right shoulder, he was carrying a large burlap bag loaded with something, and marching toward the Christmas tree yelling, "Ho! Ho!," and "a Merry Christmas, Merry Christmas to all." Many of the children responded with their own, "Merry Christmas, Merry Christmas." As the costumed individual plodded up the center aisle, he kept asking the children if they wanted any Christmas candy, fresh oranges, and dates. "Yes! Yes! We'll help you!" they responded.

After he had arrived at Preacher Stouffer's favored location in front of the church, he set his filled bag on the floor, and asked the children as they gathered around him, "Do you still want some candy?"

"Yes! Yes! Santa Claus. We want some candy!"

The person, dressed as Santa Claus, dipped his right hand in the bag and pulled, as the children pressed closer and closer to the bag. He stopped, looked at the children and politely informed he needed more room. They move slightly backwards, stopped, and stood in their places watching what Santa was very carefully removing from his bag. His right hand came very slowly from the bag. Then, instead of hearing the sound of wrapped paper around pieces of candy, they heard a very strange sound. It sounded like something making a chittering noise. Clung around Santa's right arm was a half-grown raccoon with his black-masked face staring about toward the children. The raccoon quickly scrambled on Santa's right shoulder, and Santa made a quick apology, "I'm sorry, my children. I came here with two bags in my sleigh, one with my little friend Midgie, and the other chucked full of candy. I must go out to my sleigh, and get that other bag."

"Let us go with you."

"We'll help you."

With Midgie still sitting on Santa's right shoulder, he selected a boy and a girl to go with him to the sleigh. When Santa and his helpers returned to Christmas tree near the front of the church, they were greeted by Preacher Stouffer, who had an appropriate physique for a Santa, but was not in a red suit. The preacher and Santa solicited help from some of the older children, some were delegated to distribute the candy, while others carried the wrapped gifts from the Christmas tree as Santa Claus and Preacher Stouffer called out the name on the wraped package. Suddenly, many of the adults, as well as the children were laughing and pointing toward the tree. Santa and the preacher thought the congregation was laughing at them. But no! The parishioners continued to laugh, and point toward the top of the tree. Santa and the preacher stared up toward the top of the tree, and there was Midgie cuddled around the tree top, and making his familiar chittering shout. Santa raised his right arm toward the raccoon, who returned to his master's shoulder, but in so doing, the tree started to topple over. Fortunately, Preacher Stouffer was there to catch the tree before it had completely fell to the floor. With the help of some of Santa's elves, the tree regained its balance. After the near disaster, Santa Claus, with Midgie still on his right shoulder, announced to the church's congregation, "We have many homes and churches to visit tonight before we can return to the North Pole. So, Midgie and I wish you and yours a very Merry Christmas," as the two rushed through the church's front door. There was the loud sound of sleigh bells, and then a "Ho! Ho!, and a Merry Christmas to all."

Preacher Stouffer returned to his favored location in front of pulpit, as the children and adults returned to their respective pews, he announced, "This has been the very first Christmas Eve we have celebrated in our new church. As we have discussed earlier, in our quest for world peace and freedom, let this night be our own beginning. And," he stopped, rubbed his beard, and chuckling he continued, "as far as Midgie is concerned, just remember that along our way to freedom and world peace, there will always be surprises for us. As far as the result of our own quest is concerned, it will all depend upon the kind of attitude we saddle ourselves with.... a cheerful and positive attitude will take us all a long ways."

EPILOGUE

This book and humankind's search for *freedom* will never have an ending, ending. This kind of search will always be a constant and an evolving process for humankind. In a play upon the words of Margaret Wolfe Hungerford, *Freedom is [only]* in the eyes of the beholder.*

*The word "Only" was added by the author.

Over the ages, human beings and I assume, even neo-human beings as well, were constantly in the quest for what they may have called *freedom*. Freedom from oppression, from tyranny, from servitude, from want (what ever that happened to be). Webster's Third College Edition of New World Dictionary of American English states that freedom is the broadest scope of these words, implies the absence of hinderance, restraint, confinement, or repression. According to Webster, *liberty* is often interchangeable with *freedom*.

Paul Roland, in his book *Drie Hundert Jahre Pfalzer,* states that traditionally, historians give the following six reasons for the mass exodus of the Palatines from Germany in 1709 to the Netherlands, England, and eventually to America:

* religious persecution
* the predatory wars of the French king, Louis XIV
* bad harvests
* weather disasters
* the influence of clever advertising by Newlanders
* letters from emigrants to relatives and friends in the Fatherland.

Nancy Wagoner Dixon, in her book *Palatine Roots,* writes that people like to assign a single reason or motive to a man's actions, but she says that men are far too complex to dance to a single melody. There is substantial evidence that ever increasing taxes helped to create massive debts upon the average Palatine; no one was immune to these ever increasing debts perpetrated upon the masses as the German princes strove to keep up with the ostentatious splendor of France's Sun King, Louis XIV, as he drained the German coffers dry, time and time again with raids and his demands.

Jan De Vries in his book, *Economy of Europe in an Age of Crisis,* tries to describe the general European system of taxes, uses France to illustrate where the *lord of the manor,* or as the French refer to the position, the *seigneur* was responsible for:

> First of all…an annual recognition payment, which served to recognize the rights of the holder of the seigneurial authority in the area. When the land passed into the hands of another peasant through inheritance, exchange, or sale, the seigneur [or the lord of the manor] would collect the fees…
>
> The seigneuralos enjoyed…the right to levy tolls; to require villagers to use seigneurial mills, wine presses, or ovens; to monopolize the sale of the wine produced in the seigneurie; to monopolize the keeping of pigeons and rabbits, to hunt and fish within the jurisdiction of the seigneurie.

In addition to seigneurial dues and rent, land was subject to tithe payments. Protestant and Catholic countries alike preserved this obligation....The tithe holders, incidently, were rarely the local parish priests. By the seventh century the recipients were not even always ecclesiastical.

Finally, were the royal taxes. In nearly every state some type of land tax yielded the bulk of government revenue.

To summarize, all these taxes formed a pyramid, with the poorest, those least able to afford them, bearing the whole load on their shoulders: the peasants on the land. One must remember that most of the European economy was based upon an agrarian society.

As if their frustrations came from governmental laws and policies, Mother Nature was not very kind to the Europeans as a whole; the last gasp of the ice age in 1709 came with its portent of yet another famine. The winter of 1708-1709 was one of the coldest recorded to date in Europe. Henry Jones quotes this church book notation found at Berstadt near Bufdingen, some sixty miles from Dachsenhausen:

> 1709: There has been a horrible, terrible cold, the likes of which is not remembered by the oldest parishioners who are over eighty years old. As one reads in the newspapers, it spreads not only through the entire country, but also through France, Italy, Spain, England, Holland, Saxony, and Denmark, where many people and cattle have frozen to death. The mills in almost all the villages around here are also frozen in, so that the people must suffer from hunger…

At Runkel, only sixteen miles away, another pastor wrote:

> 1709: Right after the New Year, such a cold wave came that the oldest people here could not remember a worse one. Almost all mills have been brought to a standstill, and the lack of bread was great everywhere. Many cattle and humans, yes—- even the birds and the wild animals in the woods froze. The Lahn [River] froze over three times, one after the other.

That year another pastor living north of Dachsenhausen wrote:

> .... that humans had been reduced to cattle fodder. The violence of the cold was such that the...most spirituous liquors broke their bottles in cupboards of rooms with fires in them. There were no walnut trees, no olive trees, no apple trees, no vines left. The other trees died in great numbers, the gardens perished and all the grain in the earth. It is impossible to imagine the desolation of this general ruin.

One must remember that the grain mills were water-powered, and once the ice slowed or stopped the water flow, the mill had no power; no grain could be ground for the folks who could not store a winter's supply of flour or meal, and depended on going to the mill regularly to collect their supply of food for their table, as well as, for their livestock.

So, we can only surmise which of the above reasons most influenced the Palatines on their first *Steps toward Freedom* as English indentured servants toward their quest for *freedom* set their feet in America, and eventually in the Mohawk Valley of New York State. In all probability, most of the Palatines still in their homeland who were on the lower rung of the economic ladder believed that there was no escape for them, until they started receiving attractive advertisements from the colonial proprietors, such as Ulrich Simmendinger talking about the *golden promises* of Queen Anne.

When some of the Palatines decided to *escape* their misery and began from the Palatine on their three week journey down the Rhine and its Neckar and Main tributaries to Holland. There they met an ambitious British official, and resident of the Hague named James Dayolle. He was determined to route these *strong and laborious people* to England. More than half of the first four emigrant, proud and desperate groups to arrive were farmers and vinedressers, while the occupations of the others were some thirty-five other trades, the next highest number of occupations being carpenters and textile workers plus a few schoolmasters and surgeons.

Dayrolle proposed that transports bringing troops from England to the Low Countries to fight against the French in the War of the Succession be returned to England with the Palatines. After Dayrolle had related his idea to England's Secretary of State Boyle, he went immediately to Queen Anne and obtained her approval to dispatch transport ships to Rotterdam, and return to England with the *poor Palatines,* most of them had only the clothes on their backs and whatever they could stuff into their flimsy, threadbare carpetbags. Dayrolle reported to the Duke of Marlborough that a large presence of Roman Catholics *were mix'd among them,* and recommended that *none to come over but such as are Protestants.* The Duke of Marlborough replied, "There is no great inconvenience, to let them go with the rest," adding that "the difficulty in discriminating would be too great. Anyway, the Catholic Palatines were a problem for London authorities to handle." Soon the Palatines learned that they had learned to be promises given in Queen Anne's name. In their deplorable condition, they "ate their bread in tears." City officials were anxious to "rid their city of the Palatines." The queen, in turn, decided to save only "poor German Protestants." The Roman Catholic Palatines in London and in Rotterdam awaiting transportation were given the choice of becoming "poor Protestants" to be saved by the queen, or returning to their homes along the Rhine. Many of the Palatines were devout Roman Catholics, yet some found it necessary to change their religion, while the others were ordered to return to Germany.

On April 7, 1710, finally ten ships were ready to sail with the Palatines from Portsmouth, England for New York City; they pulled anchor on April 10. By the time, they reached their destination, the Palatines had been on the ships for nearly six long months. The sufferings they experienced were severe, to say the least. People were packed into cramped quarters; some who were below the main deck could get neither fresh air nor sunlight. The lack of good, healthy food was another problem. This coupled with being cramped into foul, stinking quarters, which were creeping with infected fleas and body lice, made the Palatines' lives almost unbearable. Disease decimated them. Their sickness was called by the doctors of that day as the "Palatine fever." Now it is referred as *typhus*. Under such miserable traveling conditions, the younger children were the first to die; they died in great numbers. The last letters before the journey from Portsmouth in April reported eighty deaths on one ship and one hundred sick on another. Thomas Benson, a surgeon, reported that on his ship alone, 330 persons had been sick at one time. The *Lyon* entered New York harbor on June 13, 1710. One ship, the *Herbert,* was wrecked on the east end of Long Island on July 7th, while the last ship of the convoy did not land in New York until August 2, 1710.

Thus ends, or begins the Palatines' first series of *steps toward freedom!* For another series of *steps toward freedom,* we will next examine the situation with the Iroquois.

* * *

The ancestral homeland of the five tribes of the Iroquois Confederacy stretched from Lake Nipissing in the present Province of Ontario southward to the Susquehanna River region of Pennsylvania ranging west from New York's Adirondack Mountains, along the Mohawk River to the shores of Lake Erie completely encircling the Algonquian tribe. From east to west, the Five Nations were the Mohawks, Oneidas, Onondagas, Cayugas, and Senecas; gradually from the south the Tuscaroras drifted northward, and were adopted as the sixth nation of the Iroquois Confederacy. On March 12, 1772, the area of white habitation west of Albany County was organized as Tryon County, named in honor of the royal governor of the

Province of New York. Unfortunately for the Iroquois, this white advancement westward had also enveloped the land of the Mohawk tribe, who lived along the Mohawk River. It was along this tract of land that the Palatine immigrant settlers first sought out after being released by the English from their disastrous naval supply experiment in the present-day Catskill area. Once these energetic and industrious Palatines purchased section of this rich, fertile land, they started cleared the of trees, bushes, and undergrowth for farming. Eventually, these Palatine settlements became the area's of densest white settlement in Tryon county with its numerous farms, rich grain fields, and thriving communities, eventually, becoming one America's most productive breadbasket in the whole Province of New York. As a result, this intrusion of the *whites* into the original home of the Mohawks was fast becoming taken over by the white settlers and their large farms. These "whites", not only acquired much of the Mohawks' land, introduced *white man's politics*. It was no longer white against red, but gradually the whites were being segmented into two political parties, the Tories or Loyalists and the Whigs or the Rebels; thus adding another dimension and confusion for the Indians; determining which "whites" do they join with?

Initially, the Iroquois lived in stockaded villages located usually in easily defensible high places, and preferably near a supply of water. The log palisades were from fifteen to twenty or more feet in height surrounded by a deep ditch with the dirt being thrown up to form an embankment next to the palisade. After 1600, when the power of the Iroquois Confederacy was at its apex, and particularly after 1700, with the end of the Iroquois wars, fewer of the inner villages of the Five Nations were palisaded. A mere modest type enclosure was all that was needed to keep the forest animals from scavenging in the village. Toward the end of the 1700's, the Iroquois began to build the same type of log houses used by the white frontier settlers, this type of dwellings survived to some extend well into the nineteenth century, but gradually gave way to the sturdier dwellings copied from the whites. For example, on October 8, 1778 when Colonel John Butler and a small party entered Unadilla, an Indian castle near the Susquehanna River, Butler described Unadilla as *finest Indian town I ever saw; on both sides of the river. There were about 40 good houses, square logs, shingles & stone chimneys, good floors, glass windows, & etc.*

The Iroquois community was basically a matriarchal society. The practice of matrilineal descent gave women a unique position. Each clan was entitled to a certain number of chiefs, and the matrons of the clans could appoint, and depose the chiefs. The white wampum belts, which indicated the hereditary names of the chiefs, were kept by the women. When a chief died, he did not pass his title on to his son, for titles were hereditary only in the clan; the son belonged to his mother's, not his father's clan. The chief's title would be inherited by one of his brothers, or one of his sister's sons, or another male member of his clan matron's lineage. The women had significant influence with the warriors, and could frequently make or break a war party either by their support or disapproval of the warriors' mission. It was the women, who provided the warriors with moccasins and charred corn pounded into meal and sweetened with maple sugar, for their journey. The women also had the power to veto a war declaration by withholding supplies.

Hunting and the waging of war were the primary responsibilities of the men, while agriculture was the women's business; in addition to numerous other tasks. The men did, however, cooperate with the women in clearing the fields of trees, stumps and rocks, taking most of the heavy work upon themselves, but the responsibility for planting and harvesting fell entirely upon the women. The women and girls also gathered many wild berries, fruits, nuts, roots, fungi, and other edible woodland products. Maple sugar and syrup were used as sweeteners, and sunflowers were raised to obtain the oil from the seeds to be used as a hair dressing, mixing in pigments for tattooing, and cooking. Tobacco was also grown extensively and much prized, not only for smoking but for use as incense to ward off evil in the religious rites; believing that the plant had communication with the spirit world.

Indian warfare was, as a rule, very individualistic. In this respect, it contrasted sharply with the pattern of the whites, where soldiers recognized obedience to superior officers and accepted the necessity of taking orders from those superiors. The highest white military officers, in turn, took orders from the rulers of the state. In the white society, there was therefore a hierarchy of command. The Iroquois chief, in contrast, ruled by persuasion, if at all. No better example of the rule of independent judgement on the warpath can be identified in the behavior of the warriors in altering the defenses and tactics of their leaders just prior to the Battle of Newtown in 1779, when Butler and Joseph Brant labored unsuccessfully with the Indians to make them see the wisdom of withdrawing from a site of a probable disastrous defeat, and seeking a safer, and *a more advantageous situation.* Butler understood the gravity of the Indians' defeat at Newtown, however, it was the place they had chosen to make their stand. The Iroquois were unable to repulse the invader at the Newtown doorway to their country, as a result those families, whose villages and crops had been destroyed by General John Sullivan's American troops, began flocking into Niagara. According to British General Frederick Haldimand any relief was going to be *too little and too late.*

Not only did the Indian and white cultures collide, but their long-range goals also clashed. The whites, whether Dutch, French, British or American wanted more land, even if it was initially Iroquois territory. By either hook or crook, the whites, especially the Americans, were bound and determined to stretch the land claims to the west coast. Washington's initial goal was the Mississippi River, but as was confirmed by the Lewis and Clarke expedition the Pacific coast was the ultimate American goal. Comparing these American goals to those of the Iroquois, who maintain their freedom and culture they had become accustomed to since the dawn of time, the Master of Life had commanded all people to live in love and harmony. According to most versions of the story, his spokesman was a Huron holy man, Deganawidah— the Peacemaker, who set out across Lake Ontario in a stone canoe. Landing on the southern shore, the holy man came upon Hiawatha, a clan leader of the Mohawk descent, who had lost all his daughters to tribal strife. The holy man offered condolence that lifted Hiawatha's grief and dried his tears; the same consoling words would later be repeated at Iroquois council meetings to promote good feelings and open minds. Then the prophet described the great *Tree of Peace* under whose branches the tribes would meet to resolve their differences. He enunciated principles of justice and equality; bloodshed would yield to a new sense of brotherhood among the people. One Mohawk chief, Thayendanegea, known by his English name Joseph Brant, who dedicated himself to these principles, and was determined to lead the Iroquois nation to greatness. Brant was the brother of Molly (Mary) Brant, Sir William Johnson's Mohawk wife, who bore them eight mixed-blood children. As America's first civil war proceeded, initially, the Iroquois people tried to remain neutral, but as the war dragged on, the Oneida and Tuscarora generally supported the Americans, while the Mohawk, Cayuga, Onondaga, and Seneca sided with the English. This was probably due to Brant's influence. As a teenager, Brant fought under his sister's husband's side during the French and Indian War; also served as Sir William's interpreter. Johnson also saw to it that Brant was well educated in a Connecticut school, where he acquired a first-rate mission school education, and translated the Christian Gospels into Mohawk. Along the way, Brant became an eloquent speaker at the Mohawk councils. It is not surprising, that when the British started courting the Iroquois, they turned to Chief Joseph Brant to orchestrate the four tribes to joining the British cause.

As in any civil war there are always two sides. Unfortunately, Brant chose the losing side, but not because he did not give his full measure This author believes that not only Brant and his Iroquois were misled by the British with their trinkets, liquor, promises, etc., but the Americans, too, took advantage of their Indian allies. In short, the American government and the wave of European fur traders, colonists, soldiers, land speculators, Christian missionaries succeeded in "short changing" (robbing) this nation's native people of their birthright.

At this time, I think some of Chief Joseph Brant's thoughts, as reported in Isabel Thompson Kelsay's superb book, *Joseph Brant: 1743-1807.* Kelsay states two of Joseph Brant's friendly neighbors, Augustus and Asahel Bates made a formal statement that they believed Joseph Brant lived and died in the faith of the Christian religion; adding that sick or well, Brant was always the same man. His lifetime random and feverish thoughts always appeared to take command of his brain and actions, and not go away. It is this author's opinion that Brant's thoughts and reflections mirror the aspirations and frustrations of not only the Mohawk chief, his women and children, but also those of the present day. During Brant's day, the Native Americans began to sense the overwhelming tide of *whites;* reluctantly, some accepted their destined *doom,* while others like Brant, chose to fight to the bitter end or seek their *freedom* in other locals, such as Canada. Most never lost their faith believing that their *steps toward freedom* would finally bring them to a *dead-end trail,* if they did not stage a desperate struggle against the raising tide of the *white invaders.* In their *steps toward freedom,* the Iroquois, as well as the other Native Americans, were caught in the proverbial *rock and a hard-place,* a "no-win" situation, as the American Whigs and Tories, waged their first *civil war.* In so doing, the Indians lost their paths toward freedom as Chief Joseph Brant laments:

> *my wish ever was for Peace....we are an independent People....it was the British that prevented the Treaty...The establishment and enlargement of civilization and Christianity among the natives must be most earnestly desired...born of Indian parents... ever supposing us to be faithless, what could be apprehended of dangerous consequence from us, considering the smallness of our numbers and our situation?...Those you call savages.*

> *... the English might have last all America had it not been for the friendship & Assistance of the Indians...at the peace they [the Indians] were left in the lurch to fight alone...Stinking Rum...An unfortunate accident....Every man of us thought, that by fighting for the King, we should ensure to*

ourselves and children a good inheritance... my beloved Wife Catherine.

...justice is all I wish for the Indians with an aching heart, and never to rest 'til they have planned them out of them...the Interests of the Indians has ever and I hope Ever shall be my greatest aim...and remain free people...God willing.

...the Gates were shut against them..without being united we are nothing...should we be deprived of making the most of our Landed Property, many must starve, many must go Naked...many of our Nations perfect strangers to Farming...we came to a proper understanding...we want nothing more than what we enjoyed before the American War, the land we then lived on was our own and we would do what we pleased with it...I am totally dispirited...Then we shall begin to know what is to befall us the People of the Long House.

On November 24, 1807, as John Norton, Brant's secretary and confidant, watched Brant on his English death bed, in an English room, covered with fine English blankets, and in full view his dagger and the pipe-tomahawk gift he had received from his wife Catharine, his third and last wife whom he had married when he was thirty-six years old, and she only twenty years of age. Norton heard Brant's last words requesting him to *"have pity on the poor Indians, if you can get any influence with the great, endeavor to do them all the good you can."*

From that moment to the present there have been few dissenting voices, either in Canada or the United States, in regard to the essentially noble character of Joseph Brant. *"Brant,"* says one historian, *"combined the role of a British gentleman-officer and an Iroquois warrior diplomat."* Others declared, *"the acts of a noble, generous man...a loyal subject, and a man of noble action...He was a son to be proud of...if greatness consists of courage, sagacity and honesty, then he is the most distinguished Amerind in American history.* Finally, another stated *"Brant carried the sword in one hand and the prayer book [his own Mohawk Episcopal translation] in the other hand;" "he had few rivals for daring leadership;" "he was as near to the ideal of the noble red man as we are ever likely to see." "Brant was the most civilized savage of his time."*

On November 24, 1837, thirty years to the day after her beloved husband died, his wife, Catharine Adonwentishon Brant, died, still wearing the gold wedding band engraved *Thayendanegea to Catharine,* and having lived over fifty-seven years as Mrs. Joseph Brant, first woman of the Mohawks.

* * *

Although the above remarks have been virtually copied from the author's third book, *Roads to Niagara,* in his trilogy saga about the settlement and defense of New York's Mohawk Valley during the 1700's, he believes that Brant's thoughts, reflections and frustrations will serve well as an appropriate summation this book. Each group of characters were in the process of finding their *freedom.*

First, the Palatines succeeded escaping the tortures they were experiencing in Germany, only to find themselves as indentured servants of the British. Eventually, they were successful in overthrowing their yokes, settling themselves along the Mohawk River, and obtaining their *freedom* from the English monarchy. Eventually, ridding themselves not only of the British, but also their lands' of American's Native settlers. One could say that Wilhelm Kerchner may have found the freedom he was searching for through his tragic death he suffered during the Battle of Oriskany, in all probability his wife and daughter,too, had gained a share of the freedom they desired.

Secondly, the Native Americans had found themselves in the middle of America's first civil war. They had initially believed that it was just going to be a *white man's war*, and they chose to remain neutral as long as possible. Like a young puppy following his master as he hands the puppy small portions of food; many of the Native Americans performed similarly following along with their benefactors, who bribed them with many gaudy trinkets, blankets, guns, ammunition, and other trivial bribes, but always there was an abundant supply of rum (or some other form of alcohol) to the point their *white guardian* would have them securely on the master's lease, and losing the *freedom* they so cherished.

After brother-to-brother conversation with his brother, General Nicholas, Johan Jost Jr. joined forces with the Loyalist army commanded by Colonel John Butler; leaving his wife Maria and children in their Mohawk Valley home. By the end of 1779, they were reunited at Fort Niagara; eventually, finding their *freedom* in Kingston, Canada.

The ex-circuit rider Palatine preacher, Reverend Johan Stouffer and his Mohawk princess wife Red Bird had found their *freedom,* even though Johan was a first generation Palatine immigrant, and Red Bird was a Native American, they found their freedom when they learned each shared similar interests, value sets, and common beliefs in human respect and dignity. After Red Bird's meeting with Cornplanter assuring her that the reverend was completely innocent of the accusations and threats of Red Jacket enabling them to continue their service to New Palatine's church and to its community.

During their early acquaintance, Maria Montgomery and Alexander "Sandy" McKnight spend much time exploring their views on racial differences spurred by the differences in their respective backgrounds. The seventeen year old mulatto, Maria, had spend almost her entire life as a master farmer's slave to eventually become a foster child of the black family of George and Julia Jefferson; Maria had received her *initial phase of her freedom.* On the other hand, Sandy McKnight, a disillusioned New Englander, who left his Rebel sympathizing wife and family in Boston to travel to New York, and join the Loyalist forces to fight for the England royalty, had one of his legs amputated, and became enamored with this attractive former slave girl. Through their mutual interest in caring for the hospital's sick, and the entertainment of them through his bagpipe playing and Maria's singing and dancing, they were able to find meaning and self-assurance for themselves and their patient audience. During their endless conversations, they believed that perhaps the solution to racial differences might be the encouragement of inter-racial marriages, which could eventually lead to a blend of skin colors. Though Sandy and Maria had marked differences in their ancestry their common interests, and willingness to explore and debate important issues; they, too, had found their *freedom.*

As to the *steps toward freedom,* which the remaining characters in this saga took, I will leave it to the reader's imagination. *Freedom* must be defined by each individual, in order to know when, and where he/she has found that evasive state of mind and environment.

SOURCES AND REFERENCES

For those who may be interested in reading more about the Palatine settlement of New York's Mohawk Valley, and Burgoyne's campaign to capture it, the following books and readings have serve me well as reference sources.

Anderson, Fred, *Crucible of War: The Seven Years' War and the Fate of Empire in British North America, 1754-1766,* New York, New York: Alfred A. Knopf, 2000.

Berlin, Ira, *Many Thousands Gone: The First Two Centuries of Slavery in North America,* Cambridge, Massachusetts: The Belknap Press of Harvard University Press, 1998.

Boyla, Brian Richard, *Benedict Arnold: The Dark Eagle,* New York, New York: W. W. Norton & Comapny, 1973.

Brayman, James O.,*Daring Deeds of American Heroes,* New York, New York: Miller, Orton & Mulligan, 1857.

Coffin. Charles Carleton, *The Boys of '76; A History* of the Battles of the Revolution, New York, New York; Harper and Brothers, Publishers, 1876.

Cruikshank, E., *Butler's Rangers: The Revolutionary Period, (Third Reprint Edition,* Niagara Falls, Ontario: Renown Printing Company, 1988.

Dixon, Nancy Wagoner, *Palatine Roots: The 1710 German Settlement in New York as Experienced by Johann Peter Wagner,* Camden, Maine: Piction Press, 1994.

Ellis, Davis, *The Saratoga Campaign,* New York, New York; McGraw-Hill Book Company, 1969.

Friedman, Thomas, *Lesson Plan for 9/11,* New York, New York; New York Times, and Corpus Christi, Caller Times,Texas, September 6, 2002.

Fry, Plantagenet Somerset, *The Kings and Queens of England and Scotland,* London, England: Doring Kindersley Limited, 1990.

Furneaux, Rupert, *The Battle of Saratoga,* New York, New York: Stein and Day, Publishers, 1971.

Gray, William, *Soldiers of the King,* The Boston Mills Press; Erin, Ontario, 1995.

Graymont, Barbara, *The Iroquois in the the American Revolution,*Syracuse, New York: Syracuse University Press, 1972.

Hamilton, Edward P., *Fort Itconderoga: Key to a Continent,* Boston, Massachusetts: Little, Brown and Company, 1964.

Herkimer, Gil, *Roads to Niagara,* Corpus Christi, Texas: Alfa Publishers, 2000.

Hislop, Codman, *The Mohawk; Rivers of America,*New York, New York: Rinehart & Comapny, Inc., 1948.

Klein, Melvyn, *Each of Us Carries a 9/11 Burden,* Corpus Christi, Texas: Corpus Christi Caller-Times, September 21, 2002.

Lewis, Paul, *The Man Who Lost America: A Biography of Gentleman Johnny Biurgoyne,* New York, New Yuork: The Dial Press, 1973.

Lunt, James, *John Burgoyne of Saratoga,* New York, New York: Harcourt Brace Jovanovich, 1975.

Morgan, Kenneth O., *The Oxford History of Britain,* New York, New York: Oxford University Press, 1988.

Moore, Christopher, *The Loyalists: Reveolution, Exile, Settlement,* McClelland & Syewart, Inc., Toronto, Canada, 1994.

Morison, Samuel Eliot, *The Oxford History of the American People; Volume One, Prehistory to 1789,* New York: New American Library, 1972.

Nelles, Charles Macklem, *From Stone Arabia; Volume One,* Victoria, British Columbia: Pandora Publishing, Ltd., 1995.

New York State Division of Archives and History, *The American Revoution in New York: Its Political, Social and Econmic Significance,* Albany, New York: the University of the State of New York, 1926.

Old Fort Niagara, Youngtown, New York; 300 Years of History Guardhouse of the Great Lakes- The British (1759-1796); http://www.oldfortniagara.org/britishhisory.htm; Old Fort Niagara Association, P.O. Box 169, Youngstown,New York, 14174-0169.

Patrick, Hazel, Spellman, Jane, and Watkins, Willaim, *The Mohawk Valley Herkimers and Allied Families,* Herkimer, New York: Herkimer County Historical Society, 1989.

Randall, Willard Sterne, *Benedict Arnold: Patriot or Traitor,* New York, New York: Willaim Morrow and Company, Inc., 1990.

Strobeck, Katherine M., *The Fort in the Wilderness,* North Country Books, Inc.: Utica, New York, 1978.

Taylor, Alan, *American Colonies: The Penguin History of the United States,* New York, New York: Viking Penguin, Eric Foner, Editor, 2001.

Taylor, Allan, *Morgan's Long Rifles,* New York, New York: G. P. Putnam's Sons, 1965.

Watkins, William, *Slavery in Herkimer County: African-Americans Were Here inthe Valley from the Beginning,* Herkimer, New York: Herkimer County Historical Society, LEGACY, Issue No. 3, 1990.

Wilbur, C. Keith, *The Revolutionary Soldier, 1775- 1783,* Old Saybrook, Connecticut: The Globe Pequot Press, 1993.

ABOUT THE AUTHOR

Born and reared near New York's Mohawk Valley, Gil Herkimer (Allen G. Herkimer, Jr.) traveled extensively throughout the United States and overseas as a corporate executive, management consultant, university professor, and textbook author.

Upon retirement as professor emeritus, he returned to his first loves---traveling, beach combing, promoting jazz, and studying history. He proudly declares himself a native New Yorker, who lived in Southern California for nearly twenty years. He presently resides over looking beautiful Corpus Christi Bay in Texas.

Herkimer's first novel, *Roads to Oriskany*, is the first book of his *Roads* trilogy, which includes *Roads to Saratoga* and *Roads to Niagara*.

Printed in the United States
54348LVS00003B/148-198